MW00323754

MAPS

FOREWORD

Ross C. "Rocky" Anderson, Salt Lake City Mayor

When I learned about Bill Kerig's *Utah Underground*, I was excited and intrigued. Utah, and particularly Salt Lake City, is a spectacular place to live, work, and play; however, many people outside the state seem to view Utah through the distorted lens of erroneous stereotypes. *Utah Underground* will help dispel those misperceptions through its descriptions of the richness and variety of our places, our events, and our people.

Salt Lake City is the world headquarters of The Church of Jesus Christ of Latter-day Saints, and much of the history and heritage of Utah involves that church and its early pioneers. But there is nothing one-dimensional about Utah or its people. Utah is an amazing, beautiful, vibrant place, with a richness and diversity of many cultures, faiths, and ethnic origins that add strength to our communities. Visitors to Salt Lake City quickly understand why the most recent edition of *Places Rated Almanac* named Salt Lake City the best place to live in North America—and why *Money* magazine ranked Salt Lake City the "best in the West."

Throughout Utah, people share many common community values, and this concern has resulted in clean air and water, low crime rates, and high levels of educational attainment. The capital, Salt Lake City, is a thriving, diverse metropolitan area that offers unparalleled access to big-city cultural events and institutions, such as Utah Opera, the Utah Symphony, Ballet West, Repertoire Dance Theatre, and Salt Lake Acting Company, while being within minutes of hiking in designated wilderness areas, skiing at world-class resorts, mountain biking on the Shoreline Trail surrounding much of the Salt Lake Valley, and running up beautiful City Creek Canyon.

No other place offers such easy access to so many cultural, arts, and recreational opportunities. On one Saturday, I went scuba diving in a volcanic crater, bobsled racing on the Olympic track at the Utah Winter Sports Park, skiing, rock climbing, horseback riding, and golfing, then finished the day with a set of tennis and a workout at Salt Lake City's fantastic new Sports Complex. Whatever recreational pursuit you seek is within minutes of downtown Salt Lake City.

Our nightlife is just as varied. Outside of Utah, Salt Lake City is often perceived as being a bit staid and boring. Nothing could be further from the truth. We have clubs ($5 for a temporary membership, or you can just get someone to "sponsor" you for admission) that offer live jazz, blues, and virtually every other kind of music any night of the week. And we also have dozens of excellent restaurants and nightclubs.

Perhaps the best indicators of the vitality of Salt Lake City are the fabulous community gatherings we host. At the Gallivan Center Plaza, thousands of people attend free concerts every Wednesday and Thursday evenings during the summer.

The Salt Lake City and County Building is a place where Mayor Rocky Anderson loves coming to work.

The plaza is filled with music and people spread out on picnic blankets, dancing children and adults, laughter and conversation. In July 2001 we hosted the first annual Salt Lake City International Jazz Festival. It was a huge success, with jazz lovers filling Washington Square at the City and County Building as they listened on three balmy summer evenings to some of the world's best jazz musicians.

Salt Lake City is home to people of many faiths and is extremely diverse in its ethnic population. We have large Hispanic and Pacific Islander populations, and we are a major resettlement city, with strong Tibetan, Somali, Bosnian, and Croatian communities. Events in Salt Lake City often resemble a United Nations gathering.

Our city also has a strong and open gay community. This year's Gay Pride Parade (in which I was honored to participate as grand marshal) was a huge success, with thousands of people from throughout the community joining in support. The Gay and Lesbian Center is a welcoming place, and there are several successful gay and lesbian clubs that offer a variety of musical and entertainment options. One of my first executive orders included a prohibition to end discrimination against gays and lesbians in city hiring.

I could fill many pages about how Utah is often misperceived and underappreciated, but fortunately I don't have to, because Bill Kerig has written this book. Use it as a starting point to learn about all this great state has to offer. You'll be amazed. Enjoy!

PREFACE

hope this guide is different from any you've ever picked up because, in general, I don't like guidebooks. Though I've bought plenty, and I admire the thoughtful and thorough work contained between their covers, I've always abandoned them a few days into the trip. They just seemed to have been written for someone not very much like me.

I suppose that segues into a bit about my predilections. All right, then, I'm a guy who prefers a good coffee shop to a gallery, a diner over a museum. I'd rather ski than look at monuments, and I like bartenders who linger over patrons, customers who tip on every drink. I prefer vintage clothes to The Gap, old homes to new, and I have a lot of memories mixed into the flavors of my favorite meals. I like movies with messages, books that aren't full of their own importance, and I don't trust people who call me "sir." I live, write, and recreate in the best place in the world: Utah.

Since we're talking about Utah and not, for instance, Illinois, let's get the answer to The "M" Question (see page 5) out of the way. I am not a member of The Church of Jesus Christ of Latter-day Saints and hold no prejudice toward anyone who is. Which means this guide will neither condemn nor condone anyone's religious beliefs. There are plenty of bigots and zealots out there who can take care of all that.

Is this book for you? If you're someone who likes to drive to the scenic vistas of life, take a snapshot, and move on, then the answer is no. Close it now, put it back on the shelf, and select one of the fine guides sitting beside mine.

If, however, you are someone who likes to venture beyond the scenic vista, who likes to get in and mix it up, who prefers to experience the picture rather than check it off a list, then buy the book; we'll have some fun together.

This book was born of the nutty notion that the world thinks Utah is weird. I want to clarify something here and now: It is weird. Yet not in the way you think. The weird thing about Utah is that it *isn't* the most popular destination in the country. It should be.

Many of you will scoff at this suggestion. I know what you think of Utah—it's only Saints and skiers, you can't get a drink here, and other than the great skiing it's just a boring place. I know that's what you think because that's what I once thought too. Then I moved here. The first time was in 1984. Back then those preconceived notions seemed, to a Boston-bred twenty-two-year-old, to be pretty much true; I left after a year. A decade later I returned to write and produce a feature film in Utah. During the two years I spent here, I found things had changed significantly. Utah was a damn fun place with a burgeoning high-tech economy, plenty of jobs, and an affordable cost of living. Still, I thought there must be a better place out there somewhere. You don't know what you got 'til it's gone, right? After two more years of sprinting on the treadmill in California (I ran a dot.com there, didn't everybody?), I realized I was wrong and moved back to the Beehive State. This time I bought a hundred-year-old home, with a mortgage that's less than the rent of a Santa Monica studio, and dug in. I was so sold on Utah that I harangued the good folks at Mountain Sports Press into letting me write this book.

I let fun, an open mind, and spontaneity guide my research. Much of it I did from atop a pair of skis, a mountain bike, a bar stool, or a motorcycle. I found people who were so excited to turn me on to their favorite secret spots that, taken together, they formed an ad hoc underground network of real fun. Hence the title of this guide. I let one bar lead me to the next. A coffee shop led me to a spa. The spa led me to a paragliding school, where an instructor told me about a wild backcountry chute to ski. And so on. I love Utah more today than I did when I started this book. I love the recreation, the natural beauty, and all the contradictions. The state is a clean, upstanding place founded by people who were passionate about a specific version of organized spirituality. For this it's been given a bum rap. But think about it, is it such a bad thing for a place to be founded on the basis of passionate belief rather than, say, greed?

With this book I've tried to capture the excitement of all the wonderful people who've shown me their side of this misunderstood state. I've endeavored to shine a light on the Utah that is fun, funky, and filled with strange paradoxes and weird dichotomies. I had a blast writing this book, and I hope you will have as much fun with Utah as I have. Please let me know how I've done by writing to me at bk@billkerig.com.

ACKNOWLEDGMENTS

To the all the people who made researching and writing this book a fun and fascinating trip, I offer my most heartfelt gratitude. Special thanks to:

Governor Mike Leavitt, for taking the time to share his vision.

Salt Lake City Mayor Rocky Anderson, for his chutzpah, energy, and for penning the eloquent Foreword on the same week he quit coffee.

Nathalie Gochnor, for her thorough and professional help in ushering me through the Utah corridors of power.

Deborah Lindner, for getting it and helping others to.

Kimball Thompson, for his *Digital IQ* and many Wasatch connections.

Kip Pitou and Natan Rafferty at Ski Utah, for their rock-steady assistance.

The gals at the Hell's Backbone, for the hula hoops and hugs.

Gwendolyn Zeta, for the birds and sanctuary of the Boulder Mountain Lodge.

Sally Elliot and Karen Kesler, for the sunset at the Sky Ridge B&B in Torrey.

Dave Fields and Fred Rawlins at Snowbird, for the escape of the Tram and the deliverance of the Upper Cirque.

Chip Carey at The Canyons, for nights at the Grand Summit and tree-skiing days with Captain Jack.

Alta's Connie Marshall, for the powder.

Shawn Stinson, for his Park City perspective.

Christa Graff at Deer Valley, for all the skiing during Sundance.

Nikki Lowry at the Sundance Institute for the facts on the fest.

Bob "Sully" Sullivan, for giggin'.

Brian Wimmer, for his friendship, the cabin, and the good sense to have a brother who can comp a dinner at the Tree Room.

John Morgan, for his street and Saint smarts.

Beth, Carson, and Jensen Moon for the rad family side of Park City.

Rebecca Cecil at the Grand America, for letting the gypsies into the palace.

Brian Jensen, for the rainbow tour.

George Severseon and Reagan Leadbetter, for getting, and airing, it early.

The Stingers' Joe Buzas, for the dogs, the kraut, and the best ballpark in America.

Xeteva Garden's Daniel Pettigrew, for the underground beta on St. George.

Tony Weller of Sam Weller's Books, for the literate lunch and historic look at Salt Lake.

Moab's Lee Bridger, for his inspiring audacity.

Jose Knighton at Moab's Back of Beyond Books, for his coyote's eye-view on Moab history.

Bill Ferguson, for the serenity of Los Vados.

Debra Evans and Daniel Brown at the Red Mountain Adventure Spa, for their hospitality, the hammock, and a healthier look at life.

Steve Mayer at Cloud Nine, for sharing the sky.

Solitude's Martha Olson, for skiing and talking fast.

The Happy Sumo's Rulen, for turning raw fish into laughter.

The Avenue Arts and Wellness Center's Emily Cannon, for providing respite in hot rocks.

The Breathe Day Spa's Jennifer and Dean Tutor, for the two-hour vacation.

Mary Nickle at Time Out Associates, for sharing the peace and the process.

Jackie Pratt and Stephen Paul at Golden Braid Books, for the oasis and the Oasis.

Eric Boyer at Evolution Outfitters, for the edges and base welds.

The Café Eclipse, for opening just when and where a glass of wine and patio were needed.

Betsy Burton at the King's English, for keeping the castle doors open.

Lee Cohen, a victor among victims.

Kristen Ulmer, a diva among derelicts.

Gordy Peifer, for skiing fast and staying in focus.

Theresa van Zante, for managing with unfailing humor in the dark trenches.

Ida May Norton, for saving me from myself.

Scott Kronberg, for making the inside look good.

Michelle Schrantz, for cover art instead of just a cover.

Erin Johnson, for going with the flow.

Pauline Brown and Kate Hoffine for putting us on the map.

Amy Sorrells, for fitting together the puzzle.

Alan Stark, for selling the vision.

And to Mountain Sports Press's Bill Grout, for starting the boulder rolling.

HOW TO USE THIS BOOK

This book won't answer all your questions about Utah, and I sincerely hope it won't take all the mystery out of visiting or moving to the state. Come to think of it, no book could do that; Utah is a weird and wonderful place that's as fascinating as it is complex. I don't pretend that this guide is a comprehensive listing of all the cool places and things in the state. My hope is that it's a good starting point and something of a Utah primer. I've tried to organize and write this book as if it were a long email that friends could print out and use to get started here. I hope this is a book you might read on the plane on your way in, and refer back to at night in your new house or hotel room.

Once you're in Salt Lake City, I suggest you pick up copies of *The Catalyst, City Weekly, The Event*, or *SLUGG* (the latter only if you're into a more underground scene). All are free and available at coffee shops, bookstores, and places like that (see page 28 for information on these publications). These publications, all filled with an independent spirit and admirable verve, will give you timely information that the book format just can't. You should also check out City Search (http://utah.citysearch.com), the official travel site of the State of Utah (www.utah.com), Ski Utah (www.skiutah.com) or tune your rental-car dial to 88.3 KCPW (the Salt Lake National Public Radio station), 90.9 KRCL (Radio Free Utah), 90.1 KUED (the University of Utah station), or 107.5 (The End) for timely info. For more websites that deal with Utah see page 25.

Since I think it's best to explore what's under your nose before what's across the county, I arranged this book by location. I've broken the state into six regions and in some cases broken those regions down into neighborhoods. The best way to use the book is (1) figure out where you are or want to be, (2) choose what you want to do there, (3) use one of my suggestions as a starting point. Once you get in the loop, you'll find that Utah really does offer an "underground" of fun and cool places that the people here (relentlessly friendly and helpful) will continue to turn you on to. Oh, yeah. There's a fourth step: Have fun.

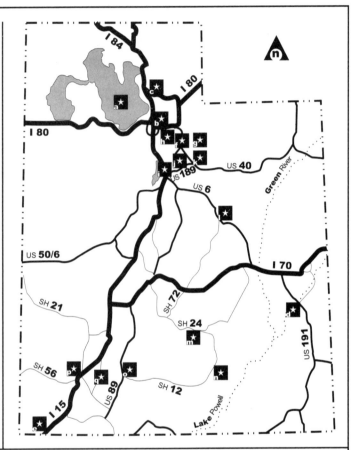

STATE OF UTAH

a.	Great Salt Lake	j.	Sundance Resort
b.	Salt Lake City	k.	Heber City
c.	Ogden	l.	Price
d.	Moab	m.	Torrey
e.	St. George	n.	Boulder
f.	Park City	o.	Panguitch
g.	Deer Valley	p.	Cedar City
h.	The Canyons	q.	Brian Head
i.	Provo		

THE BUZZ
ON THE BEEHIVE STATE

Webster's New Universal Unabridged Dictionary defines context as "the set of circumstances or facts that surround a particular event or situation." Your visit to Utah (extended or otherwise) is the event for which I offer the following contextual whirl.

UTAH HISTORY

The first residents of this state of Saints and skiers were big, unkempt, and unruly. Between 230 million and 65 million years ago (during the Mesozoic era), Utah was a major stomping ground for dinosaurs of all kinds. Their fossilized remains are still being unearthed in the southern and eastern parts of the state. For a long time after the dinosaurs checked out, a vacancy sign hung high over the entire area.

About 2,000 years ago, the Anasazi and Fremont people checked in. They apparently lived well; they had enough leisure time to draw pictures on cliff and cave walls all over southern Utah. These drawings, for all we know, may have been the equivalent of today's subway graffiti, but now they're called petroglyphs and given official sanction in protected and remote areas in many canyonlands locations.

After the ancient wall painters, came the Ute and Navajo tribes. Although they didn't leave much in the way of wall paintings, they did leave pottery and arrowheads (which can still be found on benches near rivers where the early Utahans may have camped).

As was to be the hallmark for Utah, the first white men who ventured into this land were religious pioneers. They were not Latter-day Saints, however, but Catholics—Franciscan priests. Father Francisco Atanasio Dominguez and Father Silvestre Valez de Escalante were looking for an overland route between Santa Fe, New Mexico, and Alta, California. They came as far north as Utah Lake (about 40 miles south of today's Salt Lake City) and turned around.

After the padres came a less pious lot who were interested primarily in hunting beaver. Back then it was some sort of fashion statement for men to wear beaver pelts on their heads. They paid good money for the privilege. Therefore, intrepid trappers would journey out from what is now Denver, make large loops through Utah, and, like orbiting comets, swing back to Colorado's Front Range to sell their pelts. One of these mountain-men trappers, Jim Bridger, was credited with being the first European to see the Great Salt Lake. When the fashion of the day shifted to silk, however, the fur trappers stopped venturing into Utah, and furry little critters all over the West breathed a sigh of relief.

Heber C. Kimball, Brigham Young, and Wilford Woodruff are memorialized atop the This is the Place monument at the mouth of Emigration Canyon.

Back East, however, something was afoot that was to change everything. In upstate New York, on September 21, 1823, as the Book of Mormon recounts, an angel named Moroni appeared to Joseph Smith. The angel told Smith "there was a book deposited, written on gold plates." On these plates was contained "the fullness of the everlasting gospel."

Smith was directed to the plates, translated them into what became known as the *Book of Mormon*, and began The Church of Jesus Christ of Latter-day Saints. Although many flocked to the burgeoning religion, many others (the U.S. government included) saw early Mormonism as something to be stamped out.

The early Latter-day Saints tried Ohio and then Missouri but were persecuted in both places. The LDS church established its headquarters in Nauvoo, Illinois, and from 1830 until 1845 membership in the early church grew rapidly (about 11,000 members were recorded in that small town), as did suspicion and hostility.

The early church pushed the three big buttons: money, sex, and power. Partially because of the LDS practice of members tithing 10 percent of their income to the church, its coffers swelled impressively. Polygamy was also practiced. The idea of one man having several wives scared the bejazus out of all sorts of other denominations of Christians. And finally there was power. Not only did Mormons tend toward large families, which quickly could become large unified voting blocks (particularly vexing in a young democracy), but the early Mormon Church also openly mixed church and state.

Fear and alarm over this fast-growing new church led to intolerance and in Carthage, Illinois, Joseph Smith and his brother were jailed. Then, on June 27, 1844, while still in jail, both men were murdered by an angry and self-righteous mob.

Smith's successor, Brigham Young, decided it was time to get out and so the first party of pioneers (148 people, 72 wagons, 93 horses, 66 oxen, 52 mules, 19 cows, 17 dogs, and a handful of chickens) headed west along the trail of the Donner party. After many hardships they arrived in the Great Salt Lake Basin on

July 21, 22, and 23, 1847. The next day, July 24, Young, who had been delayed by illness, made his entrance into the Great Salt Lake Valley. Despite the fact that the area must have looked about as inviting as the Mojave Desert, Young proclaimed, "This is the right place."

July 24 is still celebrated statewide as Pioneer Day, and the spot upon which Brigham Young uttered his famous declaration is remembered as This Is the Place Heritage Park at the mouth of Emigration Canyon. The story goes that there was but one tree in all of the Salt Lake Valley, and one can't help but wonder what Young was thinking when he decided that this barren desert was to be their new Zion. Nonetheless, the man had vision and the follow-through to bring it to fruition. And so, inspired by their leader's proclamation, the early settlers planted trees, established streets, and laid plans to erect a temple at the center of it all.

GOLD OR GOD

Just a year later, gold was discovered at Sutter's Mill, California, and almost overnight Salt Lake City became a vital stopover for gold rushers. Although the thousands of gold-hungry loonies tromping through this growing promised land must have tweaked Brigham Young, he decided to make the best of it. The church opened trading posts to provision the gold rushers, and from these roots later founded the Zion Mercantile Cooperative Institution (ZCMI) in 1868. It was the nation's first department store.

Brigham Young made his theocracy formal in 1849 with a petition to the U.S. government for official statehood for the state of "Deseret." No one can deny Young's chutzpah: He not only asked for what is present-day Utah but also for big chunks of Nevada, California, Idaho, Oregon, and Wyoming. In all, he petitioned for dominion over 480,000 square miles of land and its inhabitants. The feds said no.

In 1850, however, the U.S. Congress did create the Territory of Utah (which was taken from a Spanish word that refers to the Ute Indians). Then Washington turned its back on Utah and the LDS church. From Washington, Utah might as well have been Mars. Easterners didn't much care what some far-flung religious group was doing out there on the barren banks of a dead inland sea. All that was to change, however.

In 1852 polygamy was officially adopted as a tenet of the LDS church, and Washington officials pricked up their ears. Maybe they were making a mistake letting the Latter-day Saints do as they pleased out there in the desert. By then some 70,000 Mormon pioneers had migrated to Salt Lake City, the gold rush had fueled an economic boom, and the theocratic government suddenly seemed to have some serious momentum.

So in 1857, President James Buchanan sent Alfred Cummings to Utah to take over the reins of government from Young. Cummings didn't come alone, however; he brought 2,500 troops with him. He was not welcomed. Young declared martial law and waged a mostly casualty-free war against the federal troops. After a year-long standoff, however, Young finally gave in. He'd let Cummings run the state, but he would still run the church. Since the vast majority of the state's population was LDS, it's hard to imagine that Cummings found much success. Early pioneers must have regarded Cummings as just what he was: a pitiful puppet sent from an uninformed Washington.

Thus began an uneasy relationship between the federal government and Utah. Although the fruits of these seeds of discontent can still be felt in small pockets of rural Utah, the Salt Lake Valley has ironically become one of the most flag-waving, patriotic places in the nation. In Utah it is most definitely God and country—in that order, of course. It's also interesting, given the history, to note the federal government's strong tendency to recruit FBI and CIA members from Utah's universities. But I'm getting ahead of myself.

SPIKE THE PUNCH
Back in 1859, the relationship between Utah and the feds was still divisive. Ironically, it was just ten years later that Utah brought the nation together. Forty miles north of Salt Lake City, the golden spike was driven at Promontory in 1869, and the nation had its first transcontinental railroad. That same year, silver was discovered in Park City, and the stampede was on. Although the pioneers were well poised to get in on the action, Brigham Young thoroughly opposed mining. "There is no happiness in gold," he said. So early Latter-day Saints left the mining riches to the Irish, Italians, and Scandinavians who flooded into the area.

By 1878, Park City was a thriving and wild, non-Mormon settlement that had telegraph and rail connection with the outside world, dozens of saloons and houses of ill-repute, as well as a Catholic church in the center of town. As rail access made mining a more lucrative activity, other mining towns sprang up. Alta, for example, had 1,800 people and 26 roaring saloons. It was the beginning of the end for a solely LDS-controlled Utah.

With the outsiders came, of course, evil influences and the seeds of the culture clash that still exists (but to a far lesser extent) between Mormon and non-Mormon. The outsiders also brought hard cash into the state, which was good for everyone. Yet when it became obvious that there was serious money involved, it wasn't long before the federal government took a more active interest in this once-ignored state. On top of a growing yen for tax revenues, word of polygamy had spread to the outside. One of Young's disgruntled wives had written a scathing tome entitled *Wife No. 19: The Story of a Life in Bondage*.

Faced with growing national outrage at the practice, and sensing a weakness in the LDS church precipitated by the death of Brigham Young, the federal government passed the Morrill Act in 1879. A one-two punch to Mormonism, the Morrill Act prohibited polygamy and also cut the value of property it would allow the Mormon Church to own to a mere $50,000. (This would be roughly akin to the Italian government telling the Vatican to turn over everything except its birdbaths.) When LDS Church leadership found ways to avoid these measures, the government enacted the Edmunds Act of 1882 that made polygamy a felony. Hundreds of polygamists were rounded up and jailed.

This tactic proved effective for the feds; it drove many prominent Mormons underground and changed the habits of others. In 1890, Wilford Woodruff, the third president of the LDS church, declared that the practice of polygamy should be discontinued. Ever since then, The Church of Jesus Christ of Latter-day Saints has prohibited polygamy and any church members who do enter into plural marriage face disciplinary action (including excommunication).

In the 1890s, however, this was the victory the federal government needed; in 1896 it finally admitted the state of Utah into the Union as the 45th state. For LDS church members, this was a mixed blessing. With official statehood came separation of church and state and thus the end of Brigham Young's inspired theocracy. Throughout the 20th century, Utah's population continued a trend toward cultural diversity. The church still exerted considerable influence, but the steady stream of immigrants lessened it considerably

In the 1970s, Utah's mainstay economy moved from mines and agriculture into the far more lucrative world of tourism. Today the largest influx of "outsiders" is coming here to mine minds, not metal. The combination of Utah's large and inordinately young and well-educated workforce, a low cost of living, and intangibles such as world-class recreation and wholesome family environment has led to a high-tech boom from Provo to Ogden.

The awarding of the 2002 Olympic Winter games has not only provided federal money to improve the Salt Lake corridor infrastructure but also has proved to be a catalyst for a growth and building spurt unequaled in the history of Utah. Will the Olympics turn Utah into a major, world-class destination? Will Salt Lake ascend to become a true first-tier city? All that remains to be seen. What can be safely predicted, however, is that the level of excitement and fun to be had in this state is on a serious upswing.

THE "M" QUESTION

Let's be honest here. The first thing you wonder when you meet someone from Utah is whether they're a member of The Church of Jesus Christ of Latter-day Saints, or to put it more commonly, whether they're "Mormon." Right? So let's talk about how to approach the subject. First, there's nothing wrong with the question. The LDS church is not some secret coven; its members will not have to kill you if they tell you about it. Asking people if they're LDS is more like asking an Irishman if he's Catholic than if he's in the IRA. Though even with the plucky Irish you'd step with caution when entering the realm of religion, for some reason this doesn't seem to hold true for Latter-day Saints. Many times I've heard it asked this way: "Oh, you're from Utah. Are you Mormon?"

This is pretty much a bull-in-a-China-shop way to handle The Question. It will probably elicit a response, but it may also rankle as it does. After this question had been repeated ad nauseum to an especially spunky Utahan, she replied: "Why yes I am. And you're from New York. Are you a Jew?" Needless to say, turning this conversation onto a positive track was like trying to U-turn an aircraft carrier. It can be done; it just takes a lot of effort and space.

If you're a proponent of the direct approach, try "Are you LDS?" This, of course, stands for "Latter-day Saints" and is roughly akin to saying "Are you Jewish?" which is smoother than asking "Are you a Jew?" This tack also implies that you know at least a tiny bit about the church and are considerate enough to be polite.

Here are some bullet points from the official LDS website that will help you with The Question. You can find these tips and many more at www.lds.org.

• The official name of the church is The Church of Jesus Christ of Latter-day Saints. This full name was given by revelation from God to Joseph Smith in 1838.

• Although the term "Mormon Church" has long been publicly applied to the church as a nickname, it is not an authorized title, and the church discourages its use.

• The term "Mormon" is correctly used when applied to the *Book of Mormon: Another Testament of Jesus Christ*, which is named for a prophet of ancient America who compiled that record. "Mormon" is also acceptable when used in a title such as "Mormon Tabernacle Choir" or "Mormon Trail" or as an adjective in such terms as "Mormon pioneers."

• The term "Mormon" is not objectionable when used to refer to a member of The Church of Jesus Christ of Latter-day Saints, though "Latter-day Saint" is preferred.

A more socially delicate way to handle The Question is to let the person tell you gradually, in his or her own way. If you just listen, the answer will become clear pretty quickly. In general, Mormons will probably not swear much, and you can be sure they won't use Jesus Christ's name in vain. Even "Jack Mormons" (slang for those who don't practice strict observance of all the church's rules) will probably not take their Lord's name in vain.

As most people know, LDS members generally do not drink alcohol or caffeine, and stay away from tobacco products. This is in keeping with the "Word of Wisdom" that, in Mormon doctrine, was given through the prophet Joseph Smith in 1833. It is something of a health code that Smith passed along to his followers. The admonition is in the *Doctrine and Covenants of The Church of Jesus Christ of Latter-day Saints* and reads: "Use of wine, strong drinks, tobacco and hot drinks is proscribed." Drinking a Coke or a coffee won't send anyone to hell (actually there isn't much of a hell in LDS doctrine, at least not in comparison with my boyhood Catholic version), but most Mormons won't drink either.

Another facet to The "M" Question is that you wonder what Mormonism is all about. You probably won't ask the question, since you're most likely in a hurry and just want a quick answer.

The truth is, you probably can get away with asking this one without running much risk of having someone try to convert you; though Mormons are interested in spreading their gospel, methods of conversion tend toward leading by example rather than pushing the hard sell.

In case you don't want to ask the question but would still like a brief explanation, I'll give it a whirl. Understand that this is based on my own oversimplified understanding and that I am not LDS and have not received any education from the church. With that disclaimer, here's my primer: The word "Mormon" comes from the *Book of Mormon*, which in LDS doctrine is "a volume of Holy Scripture comparable to the Bible." It's one of the four books upon which the LDS faith is based. Others are *The Holy Bible, The Pearl of Great Price,* and the *Doctrine and Covenants of The Church of Jesus Christ of Latter-day Saints.*

The *Book of Mormon* was "written by many ancient prophets by the spirit of prophecy and revelation," reads the introduction. "Their words, written on gold

INTERVIEW WITH A CURMUDGEON

*S*alt *Lake-based writer and National Public Radio producer Scott Carrier grew up non-LDS in Utah. This may or may not account for his sharp analysis and honest, though sometimes scathing, social commentary. Or maybe he was born to be the disarming curmudgeon he has become. Whatever the case, his opinions are unbridled and straight from the hip.*

B.K.: *You grew up here. How was that?*

S.C.: *Growing up around Mormons did me no harm. I didn't care in the least that they tried to convert me. The church makes clear the boundary between the status quo and non-status quo. You were either in the norm, which was Mormon, or out of the norm, which was non-Mormon.*

B.K.: *Do you think Salt Lake is changing?*

S.C.: *Yes, because the world outside is changing. It used to be that when I was traveling around the country and I said I lived in Salt Lake, people would ask me how I could stand to live here. I didn't care that they thought it was a weird place; I preferred that. It kept them out, and living here was much easier. Less traffic. Shorter lines at the grocery store. Then, five years ago, it started to be that when I would say Salt Lake, they'd say, "Oh I hear that's a nice place."*

B.K.: *Why the change?*

S.C.: *The Mormon Church began to be seen as a more middle-of-the-road religion, the recreation companies got their word out, and at the same time, other cities were deteriorating. Next to the ugly stuff going on in other places, Salt Lake looked great.*

B.K.: *You cited the election of Salt Lake's liberal mayor, Rocky Anderson, as a major turning point. And now, for the first time in Salt Lake's history, there are more non-Mormons in Salt Lake City than Mormons. What do you think of this trend?*

S.C.: *I like it and I don't like it. I like the way things are opening up, but I don't want more people here. In addition to our increasing birthrate, now the younger, fun-seeking people are moving here; (Carrier heaves a sigh) people just aren't afraid of the Mormons anymore.* **U**

Author's note: Scott Carrier's book, Running After Antelope *(Counterpoint Press, 2001), which is a collection of his NPR radio pieces, as well as stories written for Harpers and Esquire, is a great read that includes witty, humorous and poignant insights into Utah and the West.*

plates, were quoted and abridged by the prophet-historian named Mormon." The plates were buried on a large hill in upstate New York. In 1823, Joseph Smith, a 14-year-old boy, was visited by an angel named Moroni who told him to retrieve the plates and translate them. He did so and started The Church of Jesus Christ of Latter-day Saints.

As their name implies, members of The Church of Jesus Christ of Latter-day Saints are Christians who see Jesus Christ as their savior (his atonement made possible everlasting life for humankind). Mormons also believe in a living prophet (the church's president) and a 12-apostle system. They tend to be a very family-oriented people. For a more thorough description of the LDS church and its teachings, call 801-240-1000; visit Temple Square in downtown Salt Lake City; click to www.lds.org; or write to Church of Jesus Christ of Latter-day Saints, 50 East North Temple Street, Salt Lake City, Utah 84150.

WHAT'S UP WITH THE WEIRD ADDRESSES?

I know, I know, the street addresses are confusing and obtuse, but that's only when you first confront them. After a while, addresses such as 363 East 1779 South roll off the tongue with all the poetry of a Rubik's Cube. Tripping the light fantastic of metaphoric and musical possibility, you can almost hear the song lyric: "They say the neon lights are bright on 2102 South 400 East." Hit is written all over it.

The Utah grid system will never be poetry, never the stuff of pop song or urban legend. It's clunky as a square bicycle wheel, but it is very functional if you understand the underlying logic. Things clear up when you realize why the early Mormon pioneers numbered every street and address as they did. The numbers provided coordinates that always told you how far from the Temple you were. Since the Temple was the center of their lives, it made good sense to keep in mind how far one had strayed (geographically or figuratively) from that center. In Salt Lake City, that center is located at the corner of Main Street and South Temple, which is the southeast corner of Temple Square. From that point, all street numbers get larger as they run off into the four quadrants (east, west, north, south). Main Street, which runs north and south, provides the "zero" line between the east and west quadrants, and South Temple, which runs east and west, forms the other axis, or "zero" line, between the north and south quadrants.

East and West streets run north and south, and North and South streets run east and west. Okay, that sounds confusing, but remember the number of the street indicates how far it is from the Temple. Thus 100 East is 100 units from the Temple, with a unit being a potential street address. Each block is made up of 100 units.

When writing a street address (in Utah or anywhere else), you always write the number of the street first and the name of the street second. We write 501 Broadway, not Broadway 501. The rub in Utah is that the street name is often a number and an adjective describing which quadrant of the grid it's in. So in the address 955 East 300 South, 955 East describes where it is on a street that's called 300 South. Together, the two expressions (955 East and 300 South) describe exactly how many units that address is from the center of the grid.

Got that? Okay then, here are a few more curves. Utahans don't say 1200 East; they say 12th East. Yet they know they aren't talking about 12th Avenue. When you hear people say 9th and 9th, they're talking about the neighborhood at the corner of 900 East and 900 South.

Just when you think you've got the logic down, you run into streets that are known by name and not number. Harvard Avenue, for example, is actually 1110 South until you get to 1700 East, at which point it becomes 1175 South. Thus it is just called Harvard Avenue.

If you're ever given a Salt Lake address that has a street name instead of the coordinates, the best thing to do is to translate it back into numbers. There's a listing of all the numbers that correspond to the street names in the Community Pages section at the front of the Yellow Pages phone directory.

I hope that clarifies it for you. I must confess, it's taken years to understand and be able to drive around the grid. Even today, I have to translate (the way someone who's not yet fluent in French has to translate to English before understanding the meaning of each word) from the grid into an interior landmark system. It works this way: I hear 1113 East 2100 South and have to think, okay that's Sugarhouse, near the big Barnes and Noble. Only then can I start to comprehend where someone is talking about. My Utah-born wife, on the other hand, can hear the numbers and know which way to go without associating landmarks to get her there.

You'll find the same grid system in many other Utah towns as well. The globe has its poles for navigation, and Mormon-settled towns have their numbered streets. This is how you can always tell whether a Utah town was settled by Mormons or miners. The miners laid out their towns haphazardly and named streets after rich people. They reserved the centers of their towns for markets and bars and stuck their churches off to the side.

As the late writer and teacher Joseph Campbell pointed out, you can tell a lot about what people value by what they put at the center of their town and which buildings reach highest into the sky. At one time, the tallest building in Salt Lake was the Temple, then it was supplanted by the State House; now the tallest building is the one used to run the business affairs of the worldwide LDS church. Infer from that what you will. I'm more interested in what Campbell's standards for evaluation would reveal about the American trend of building villages around Wal-Marts. Another subject for another time.

WHAT'S UP WITH THE LIQUOR LAWS?

"You can't drink there, right?" I wish I had a buck for every time someone asked me that about Utah. That's definitely the perception. Here's the reality: In 2000, nearly four million gallons of wine, whiskey, and spirits were consumed in Utah. That's not including the ocean of beer that was swilled.

"Anyone who says you can't get a drink in Utah doesn't know what he's talking about," said 78-year-old Twilite Lounge owner Bob Cairo. "You can walk into a hundred restaurants and drink any damn thing you want. If you want to come to a club like mine, you can also drink anything you like. It's just gonna cost you a few bucks. If you can't afford a few bucks, maybe you shouldn't be spending money on booze."

If you just said
"Oh my heck"
it's probably not for you.

ST. PROVO GIRL FROM SQUATTERS. ONLY IN UTAH.

(Reagan)

Although a nuisance at worst, the Utah liquor laws have come to symbolize the difference between conservative and liberal cultures in Utah. This billboard for Squatters Brewery's St. Provo Girl beer, which appeared next to Interstate 80 in Salt Lake City, made the division simple.

Mr. Cairo may be a bit bombastic (his sixty years in the saloon trade have given him the right to be), but he is quite right in his assertions.

Utah, like the rest of the country, decided prohibition wasn't working almost 80 years ago. In 1933, the Twenty-first Amendment to the U.S. Constitution ended national prohibition and gave individual states the right to choose their own system of controlling and distributing alcoholic beverages. At that time, Utah's population consisted overwhelmingly of non-drinking Mormons, so it should be no surprise that the laws enacted reflected a disdain for alcohol. The state made the decision, as did 18 other states, to control the sale of alcohol itself and not merely issue licenses and let private enterprise and the market set their own standards.

Utah opted for state control of liquor for two reasons. The first was to discourage alcohol consumption (the official line is "promote moderation"). The introductory sentences on the State of Utah's website read: "Utah's liquor laws are based on the general philosophy of making alcoholic beverages available in a manner that reasonably satisfies the public demand." It continues: "As a control state, Utah believes that moderation can best be achieved by neither promoting nor encouraging the consumption of alcohol, but rather by controlling it." The state cites studies that show "per capita consumption of alcohol beverages is significantly lower in control states than in the open states." Officials claim consumption is 25 percent lower and that this is evidence of a safer and more productive state.

The second reason Utah decided to become a control state was to make money. It worked. In fiscal year 2000, the Utah Department of Alcoholic Beverage Control took in $138 million in total sales of alcohol and showed a gross profit of $64 million. This money goes into school lunch programs, to cities and towns, and also into the general fund. So you can feel better when ponying up for a cold one because a slice of that booze money is earmarked for fish sticks for second graders.

Before I get into the particulars of how to navigate the labyrinth of Utah's liquor laws, here are some tips that will make it easier. First, in matters of liquor, treat Utah as you would a foreign country. I know it's part of the United States, but if you'll put that out of your mind for a moment and regard the laws and customs of Utah as you would those of, say, Japan, you'll be able to look upon them as quaint and harmless, which in effect they are.

Next, I advise becoming a wine drinker while you're here. The wine selection that's available at Utah state liquor stores is good and inexpensive. Good imported beer, on the other hand, will cost you a mint. Hard liquor is also pricey.

LEGAL DRINKING AGE
It's 21 in Utah, just as it is everywhere else in the country.

BEER
Utah is known for its beer—its bad beer, that is. The misconception about Utah beer is that it's much the same as what we used to call "near beer," which had about as much alcohol as orange juice. Not only is this patently wrong, but as with Utah's other liquor laws, there's much confusion over the issue.

There are two ways to measure the amount of alcohol in beer: by weight or by volume. Most of the world measures the amount of alcohol in beer by volume. In Utah, however, breweries are required to measure by weight. This may or may not be due to the fact that measuring by weight gives the impression that there is less alcohol in the beer.

A "6-point beer (hard beer)," which is 6 percent alcohol by volume (and a hardy beer that you'd find in the rest of the country), becomes 4.8 percent when measured by weight (or by Utah rules). Or, in reverse, Utah's 3.2 percent beer would become 4.0 percent when measured by "normal" standards. This means you have to drink only two to four more ounces of Utah beer to equal a regular beer; drinking a six-pack of Utah beer would equal roughly five beers from another state.

In Utah, beer is sold in taverns, restaurants, private clubs, and airport lounges. Approximately 500 businesses sell beer for consumption on the premises. Half of them are located in the Salt Lake City and Park City areas. Beer can be sold from 10:00 A.M. to 1:00 A.M. seven days a week. Beer may be purchased without ordering food and is sold on draft and in bottles and cans.

Beer of the 3.2 type is also available at supermarkets and grocery and convenience stores. Full-strength beer can be bought at state liquor stores but at a hefty price. You're better off drinking the locally brewed suds, which taste great. Kegs of beer are not available for purchase by nonretailers.

WINE

You can buy wine in state liquor stores or in restaurants that have full liquor licenses. You can also bring bottles of your own wine to restaurants and have them open them for you. For this the establishment will charge you a "corkage" fee. Any bottle you bring is also, by law, required to have a State of Utah sticker on it. This proves the wine was bought, and taxes paid on it, in Utah. If it doesn't have the sticker, the restaurant is supposed to refuse to open it for you. Most will.

The three best state liquor stores for wine are at 255 South 300 East, 1863 East 7000 South (both in Salt Lake City), and 1901 Sidewinder Drive in Park City.

LIQUOR

Full liquor service is available in licensed restaurants, airport lounges, and private clubs. I'll get to those definitions presently.

TYPES OF WATERING HOLES

For most people in the rest of the country, a "bar" is a place where you consume alcohol. It may be in a restaurant or not. It may also be a place where beer is brewed or not. In Utah, the distinctions are more important.

Three types of liquor licenses exist for purveyors of alcoholic beverages: a tavern license (which means only 3.2 beer is served); a restaurant license (which means a full complement of both heavy and 3.2 beer, wine, and liquor is served but cannot be displayed); and a private-club license (which means a full slate of heavy and 3.2 beer, wine, and liquor is offered and displayed). Each designation comes with a handful of quirks.

RESTAURANT LIQUOR LICENSES

Restaurants are allowed to sell liquor, wine, or heavy beer from noon to midnight and 3.2 beer from 10:00 A.M. to 1:00 A.M. You must be dining in the restaurant or (as many restaurateurs have told me) have the "intent to dine" to be served an alcoholic beverage. It's legal to be served at your table or in the waiting area. Unlike in the rest of the country, your host will not routinely hand you a wine list when you're seated. You'll also notice that there aren't liquor bottles on display in a back bar.

You must request a wine list or alcoholic beverage menu. Although you must be 21 to drink in an establishment with a restaurant liquor license, anyone under 21 is allowed in the restaurant. There are approximately 500 fully licensed restaurants in Utah. Most are located in the Salt Lake City, Park City, Ogden, and Provo areas.

PRIVATE CLUBS

The designation of private clubs is essentially an arcane, lame, and harmless institution. What would normally be considered a bar in much of the rest of the country is called a private club in Utah. Private clubs can admit and serve only "members" and their "guests." Becoming a member means paying for an annual membership (anywhere from $15 to $24) or buying a two-week temporary membership (usually $5). This temporary membership allows you to bring five guests in with you.

Or you can get into a private club by becoming a guest, which means going to

When the King of Beers is written in the same neon as the Olympic flame and rings, you know the Olympics are going to shine a large light on Utah's liquor laws.

the door and asking to be sponsored by anyone who happens to be entering the place. Although this approach might appear overly forward, no one who goes to private clubs will be in the least bit offended. Everyone does it. Sponsoring just means saying "He's with me." It can be a good way to make new friends.

Each member is permitted five guests, if anyone happens to be counting. I've seen doormen tell patrons who their sponsor is. ("Welcome to Joe's. Your sponsor tonight is Sally. Have a good time.") This rigmarole is often no more than a silly game played with a shrug and smirk by all those involved.

Once you're inside a private club, it looks pretty much like any bar anywhere. Private clubs display and sell liquor, wine, heavy beer, and 3.2 beer from 10:00 A.M. to 1:00 A.M. Monday through Saturday and from noon to midnight Sundays and holidays. They can sell you a drink with or without food, and patrons may be served at a bar or table. They can't sell you a double, but they can sell you a single with a "sidecar" that is the other half of a double in a separate glass. Everyone just dumps the two together as soon as the bartender steps away.

Utah law also requires "restaurants, private clubs, and airport lounges to use a metered dispensing system that is calibrated to 1 ounce for dispensing the primary liquor in a mixed drink. Secondary alcoholic flavorings may then be added to a mixed drink as the recipe requires." This means you can have all the multishot drinks (such as a Long Island iced tea or a mudslide) you like; the second, third, and fourth shots are considered "flavorings."

There are approximately 300 private clubs in Utah; most are located in the Salt Lake City, Park City, Ogden, and Provo areas.

TAVERNS

Establishments with "tavern" liquor licenses sell 3.2 beer, and the liquor laws qualify these as places where "the revenue from the sale of beer exceeds the revenue of the sale of food." No one under 21 is allowed and there is no wine, heavy beer, or hard liquor available. Taverns are open from 10:00 A.M. to 1:00 A.M. Monday through Saturday and from noon to midnight Sundays and holidays.

AIRPORT LOUNGES

These places in the Salt Lake International Airport are basically all-bets-are-off watering holes where liquor, wine, heavy beer, and beer are served from 8:00 A.M. until 12 midnight to anyone who's 21 and older. It doesn't matter whether you have the "intent to eat." Alcoholic beverages may be sold with or without food, and patrons may be served at a bar or table.

STATE LIQUOR STORES

Utah has 37 full-service state liquor stores. There are also 97 "package agencies" throughout the state that offer slimmer selections. In both types of places, you can buy packaged liquor (with the Utah State tax sticker), wine, and imported beer.

PUTTING ON A RAVE?

You don't need booze to throw a rave, but if you did, here's what you'd have to do. From the state's website: "Single event permits are available from the Utah Alcoholic Beverage Control Commission for groups that want to sell liquor, wine and heavy beer at temporary (three-day) events. These are available to corporations, incorporated associations, political and religious organizations conducting civic or community enterprises or conventions. The permit allows for the *sale* of alcoholic beverages to the general public, or to the organization's own invited guests for the duration of the event. The permit allows for cash bars and the sale of alcohol for fundraising purposes. Permits are issued by the commission once a month. Application must be made by the 10th of each month and the fee is $100."

PRIVATE PARTIES

Just in case you're worried that your Super Bowl party is going to land you in the clink, here's the rule: "Individuals and organizations hosting private social, business, or recreational events or functions are not required to obtain a permit from the state if the event is not open to the general public, and alcohol is provided to invited guests without cost."

Now that you've plowed through these Utah liquor regs, you probably need a drink but don't want to go to all the trouble. The truth is, all these laws and rules seem much worse than they are. For more information, contact the Department of Alcoholic Beverage Commission at 801-977-6800, or http://www.le.state.ut.us.

ECONOMY AND BUSINESS

Perhaps the most underground aspect of Utah is its high-tech economy. Scattered information about the high-tech sector has leaked out—*Money* magazine named Salt Lake City the West's most livable city in December 2000; Dun and Bradstreet ranked Salt Lake City the third best "High-Tech Hot Spot" in the nation in November 2000; *Inc.* magazine in December 2000 ranked Salt Lake City as the second-best large metropolitan area in the country for entrepreneurial businesses; and in 1999 the Western Blue Chip Economic Forecast, which was based on a study by Dun and Bradstreet (and published on December 21, 2000) ranked Utah second

Not many Harley riders work at the Utah State Capitol. There aren't many bikes or scooters or mopeds either. In fact, as I pulled up to the building on my motorcycle, the leader of the school group that was taking a tour eyed me with great suspicion. I kickstanded the bike and, under the watchful eye of the scowling chaperone, hurried up the wide front steps of the Capitol.

As I pulled open heavy brass doors, I entered the massive and airy rotunda that's created by the Capitol dome. Measuring 165 feet high at its center, with a 95-foot chain that holds a 6,000-pound chandelier, the Utah Capitol has the feel of serious power and grandeur that you'd expect to find in Washington, D.C. The high ceilings and marble walls give the air a hushed and echoey quality, as if you're in a library or a morgue. Riding a Fat Boy through here would be deafening.

COURTESY GOVERNOR'S OFFICE

Utah Governor
Mike Leavitt

The beehive motif is in great use in the Capitol. It's engraved in the glass doors and suggested in cone-shaped lamps and fixtures. As you enter Republican Governor Mike Leavitt's office, you notice small gold beehives on the door handles.

At six-feet-something, Governor Leavitt looked, on the first day of August 2001, like a man who had been working in the hive. He wore no jacket, no tie, and had his cuffs rolled back as if he were fixing a car engine. He folded himself into a leather chair at the head of an oval conference table in his plush office, and we got right to it.

Bill Kerig: *We all know the history of Utah, but what is Utah today?*

Governor Mike Leavitt: *Utah is surprisingly cosmopolitan. We're the sixth most urban state in America and have the fourth fastest-growing ethnic minority population in the country. We have a growing workforce. That is a highly significant demographic for us, both culturally and economically. We're a well-educated, tech-savvy state with an affordable cost of living, remarkable beauty, and lots of recreation.*

B.K.: *How has it changed since you took office in 1992?*

G.L.: *When I became governor, 8 percent of our population was in an ethnic minority group. That number is 13 percent today, and by the time I finish this term, that number will be 17 percent. By 2010, one in five Utahans will be from a minority group. When I became governor, the state had 1.7 million people, and we're now in excess of 2.1 million. Those are big shifts.*

(continued on page 16)

(continued from page 15)

The nature of the jobs is changing too. One in every four jobs in the state today was created in the past eight years. We've gone from a state that was heavily oriented to agriculture and defense to a state that's rapidly becoming a high-tech center. Our high-tech community is growing at three times the national average, and there have been periods in the past ten years when we've added 50,000 jobs a year. That's an entire city.

B.K.: Well, since you're going that way, what's the Utah Silicon Valley Alliance?

G.L.: Silicon Valley, which has always been the heartland of high tech, is an hour and ten minutes [by plane] from where we sit. There are many days when you can get from here to downtown San Jose faster than you can get from Berkeley to Stanford.

You can buy a home in Utah for $170,000 that will cost you $700,000 there. They've had a hard time recruiting into Silicon Valley because of the combination of all of the things that have happened as a result of their vibrancy. We see Silicon Valley as a partner for us, so we're reaching out to say, "You have something that we want, and we have some things that you need."

B.K.: And those are?

G.L.: Utah's one overriding comparative advantage is its workforce; it's growing at twice the national average. One-third of the people in this state are under the age of 18.

If you're in industry and you're asking how you can position yourself to have a workforce that is well-educated and tech-savvy, you'd first say, where are the numbers? The numbers are in Utah. Once you identify where the numbers are, then you have to say, what kind of workforce will that be?

This is a state where it's almost part of a family ethic to be online. In Utah we have more computers per household than any state in America. It exceeds Silicon Valley, and it exceeds the Boston area. We have more URL addresses registered per capita than any place else. We have more patents per hundred dollars of research money than anywhere. We have a couple thousand high-tech companies here already. You'll find places with more Ph.D.'s, but you won't find places with people who, on average, have more education than in Utah.

Our primary economic objective is to make Utah a capital for high-tech employment and investment. So the Utah Silicon Valley Alliance is recognition of our proximity, and all the pieces we have here that make us a natural partner for Silicon Valley companies. We've been working to make sure that venture capitalists, entrepreneurs, and tech executives know about Utah and the growth opportunity that's here.

B.K.: And how's that going?

G.L.: We're still growing in high tech during a difficult time. Not all of it is coming out of Silicon Valley—a lot of it is being developed here—but we are making progress in forming that alliance.

B.K.: Silicon Valley has Stanford and Berkeley; Route 128 has Harvard, MIT, BC, BU, and on and on. What does Utah have?

G.L.: Utah State, University of Utah, BYU, and a first-rate medical school. We've identified a series of what we refer to as "economic ecosystems." In science, an ecosystem has all the things needed to sustain life. In an economic ecosystem, some of the things required to sustain life include research, workforce, successful companies, and management. And there are many areas where we have unique economic ecosystems. One of those is biotech. We have the Huntsman Cancer Institute. We have medical devices; we have areas of artificial limbs and organs. We also have a substantial presence in the electronic-games business and graphics. When people come here to ski, we hand them a map of all the ski resorts. When investors come here, we have a map of our economic ecosystems. We're happy to take people by the hand and introduce them to all the right people.

B.K.: The buzz on you is that you get high tech. You're obviously into it. What's your personal relationship to high tech?

G.L.: I've always been intrigued by technology and its potential. I bought the first Radio Shack P.C. It had a 128-kilobyte memory. You have ten times more on your watch than that machine had. And in the early 1980s, I began building what was kind of a forerunner of an intranet. In the business I was operating, I had 30-something offices operating in the western states. I concluded that we really ought to connect and centralize and eliminate much of the paper and much of the communication. I caught that vision fairly early. To build it, however, was much more difficult than it is today. We had telephone bills that were $18,000 a month. But over time that created a leadership position for us. I never forgot that.

When I began working in state government, I thought I'd do the same thing as far as getting government online. We're now to the point that you can renew your driver's license, buy a fishing license, and access a lot of other state government functions online. My aspiration is that every service in state government will be available 24/7 on the Internet.

B.K.: That's good.

G.L.: Then I began to see its potential in education. I came to understand what a powerful tool technology is in the hands of a master teacher. I concluded we should make heavy investments in that area, and we have. We were one of the first states in the country to have every school wired to the Internet. In a speech I gave in 1993, I described a 3-speed bike and said we must learn to make it a 21-speed and know how to ride it. I challenged our people to put the equivalent of a community college in every high school, and we accomplished

(continued on page 18)

(continued from page 17)
that. I challenged them to create full-degree offerings that could be issued over the Internet by 1996. We didn't make it by 1996, but we did by 1998.

Then I also formed, along with some other western governors, Western Governors University. It's now five years old, and we've been through a long and interesting experience in trying to organize a university that is both virtual and offers degrees on the basis of demonstrated competency. It's a much different kind of university. We're focused on teacher training in the area of technology. We have 250 degree-seeking students and 1,400 students overall. It's fully accredited. We've even granted five master's degrees.

B.K.: You're involved in something called eUtah. What is that?

G.L.: Part of it is having every service that we offer in state government available 24/7, as I previously mentioned. Another piece of it is the website www.finditinutah.com. The idea is to create online localized directories and search capacity. So if you want to buy something on the Internet, you'll be able to search within the community and support local businesses instead of ones all over the world. We'll end up with every business having an online presence.

B.K.: Is this the first state to do that?

G.L.: To my knowledge we are.

B.K.: The bulk of the culture here is still traditional and family-based. The Internet culture, the dot-com culture, is nontraditional, frenetic, and not known for its high ideals, standards, or lasting values. Do you think a high-tech Utah represents a merging of two cultures?

G.L.: It is a merging of traditional values with high-tech know-how. I suspect if people want New Orleans, they'll live in New Orleans. If they want San Francisco, they'll live in downtown San Francisco. But if they're looking for a place that's open, with lots of recreation that's beyond anything anywhere else, that's a place where you want to raise a family, Utah's a good choice. That's not a bad niche; it's one we're certainly willing to accept.

B.K.: So Utah will be the family values version of Silicon Valley?

G.L.: It's an interesting dynamic. There was a time during the dot-com boom when high tech was basically, as someone defined it to me, "a bunch of 26-year-olds in tight clothes running fast," and there is that culture here. There are a lot of people in that category, but there's also a large mature community that is interested in families. If you live in Utah and you have those instincts and you want to be at your kid's soccer games, sometimes you're not inclined to work 19 or 20 hours a day and sleep on a cot at the office. But there's a balance that's created, and people will tell you repeatedly that, in the long run, that's better and that this is a great workforce because people have lives.

B.K.: Which might even be a rudder in the water for a runaway high-tech culture.

G.L.: We want to be who we are and to do it well. We think it's working.

Utah aspires to be a capital of high-tech employment and investment. We want to be in the top tier, and we're approaching that. We're not there yet, but we're close.

B.K.: *How are the Olympics going to help you out?*

G.L.: *Three ways. It will demonstrate our competence as a community—a demonstrated competence that 3.6 billion people will see. That's a branding opportunity you can't buy with advertising.*

Second, it puts us on the world map. I believe when the Olympics are over, and all those visitors leave, they'll have the snow-packed peaks of the Wasatch Mountains and the red rock country in their minds, and they'll have a warm glow in their hearts because of the hospitality of our people.

Third, a project this big stretches every part of a community, and that makes everything better. The service has to get better in a restaurant. The caterers have to work to perform at a different level. The facilities have to be brought up to world-class level. People have to dust off languages they learned years ago because now they have a chance to reuse them. That stretching unites a community. Everything has to get better and, as a result, you end up stronger.

B.K.: *And prouder?*

G.L.: *When the Olympic torch enters Rice Eccles Stadium, the hearts of this state will be beating in unison with a sense of satisfaction and pride that we have received the world graciously. There are very few moments in a state's history when hearts beat together in anticipation of the same thing.*

It was that way on the day we got the Olympic games. No matter where you were, people were listening. People were pulled over at the sides of the road with their radios on. There were people huddled around televisions at workplaces. Mothers had their children in the family rooms; we were all watching Juan Antonio Samaranch open an envelope. And as he said the words "the city of Salt Lake City," there was an explosion of excitement at the City and County Building where there were 130,000 people. I was in Hungary at the ceremony, and there was an explosion there. People were standing in their living rooms cheering. Everyone, even the critics, in that moment when the envelope was opened, felt their hearts race. There's something about a moment like that—it allows all Utahans to watch the television, listen to the radio, and have their hearts accelerate at the same moment. That's the power of the Games, and it will happen again when the flame comes here.

I don't know the number, but there will be well into the hundreds of thousands of people who at some time will be volunteering to host the world. That's just a great cultural exercise; there's nothing like it that I know of. It's just amazing.

B.K.: *You were just in Aspen, which always wins surveys as having the best*

(continued on page 20)

(continued from page 19)
nightlife among ski towns. Could Salt Lake City be competitive in that realm? As a ski town?

G.L.: *We haven't done a good job branding ourselves, and that's one of the opportunities the Olympics provide. A lot of people are going to see the state and understand it and experience it. I hope that we can show people just who we are. We don't want to pretend to be something we're not. I'd be satisfied if people understood who we are and didn't have a lot of misconceptions that may have come from years and years of stereotyping.*

People talk a lot about our liquor laws, and they are unique to this state, but the truth is, when people come here for the Olympics, there will be twice as many places to get a drink than there were in Nagano and Lillehammer combined.

B.K.: *You've described your environmental policy with a new term:* en libra. *What is* en libra?

G.L.: *I can best explain* en libra *by telling you about two bumper stickers I saw in Salt Lake on the same day. The first one said, "Earth first. We'll mine the other planets later." The second one said "Save the earth. Kill yourself." I'm thinking that somewhere between those two stickers is where the vast majority of the American people are. They want good stewardship, and they want balance when it comes to management of land and resources. We have repeatedly fought environmental battles at the extremes.*

En libra *is a philosophy of environmental management based on a series of principles that have emerged from dealing with major environmental legislation and have proved themselves. For example, many environmental disputes*

in the nation for new information technology jobs. Nevertheless, much of Utah's thriving new-economy business environment has remained cloaked by the same misconceptions that have kept the rest of the state in shadow.

Shining a light on the Beehive State reveals that Salt Lake City and the rest of Utah are stealing the lion's share of business expansion from all the other Western states. So what's going on? First, the state wants growth. A marketing campaign that compares the Salt Lake Valley with Silicon Valley has convinced a lot of people, but the key to the marketing is the truth behind it. The state has a high quality of life, is eminently affordable, and has the nation's youngest and most educated workforce.

The state's 10 universities awarded 24,000 bachelor and associate degrees in 1999 and more than 4,000 postgraduate degrees. Unlike in many other places, the bulk of Utah's college grads seek to stay in Utah, near family and the recreation they've come to expect. This is a wired group as well. According to Scarborough Research, 73 percent of Salt Lake City households own at least one computer, which makes it the number-one computer-savvy city in America. For this reason, are about whether the national government ought to run the environment, or whether the local governments ought to run it. En libra *says we need national standards, but you must have a neighborhood strategy. If you take away the capacity of the local community to solve a problem, you can't possibly, in ten thousand pages, consider every local circumstance. So one of the tenets of en libra is national standard, neighborhood strategies.*

Another is markets before mandates. Many disputes are about whether we ought to compel people to do things or whether we ought to sway them. This is a philosophy that says whenever possible, use incentives. There are times when you have to use mandates, but you should always try the market before the mandate. There are eight of those principles, and en libra *is a term that embodies that philosophy of balance and stewardship that Governor [John] Kitzhaber, [a Democrat] from Oregon, and I made up.*

B.K.: *And it means?*

G.L.: *It's a Latin term that means "toward balance." It's a philosophy I have followed in my administration and am exporting as well.*

B.K.: *With a state full of such great recreational opportunities, which ones do you do?*

G.L.: *I ski; I play golf. We're going on a river trip at the end of the week. I hike a couple days a week.*

B.K.: *So you get out and get to experience it?*

G.L.: *Being governor means you get to do a lot of interesting things in the state, but at the same time, I don't get as much time to do them as I'd like.*

That seemed to be my cue to turn off the tape recorder and let the man get back to work. **U**

in July 2000 *Wired* magazine named Salt Lake City one of the 46 "Hot Spots" that matter most in the new global high-tech network.

If the virtual world is in good shape, what about the real world? Real estate, both commercial and residential, remains very reasonable, and downtown Salt Lake City is still filled with the kind of old warehouses and hundred-year-old brick buildings that are particularly attractive for refurbished start-up businesses. There's also an ample supply of cool old buildings where you can install a T1 line and have an international business concern going in a month. In how many places can you go skiing on your lunch break or have an afternoon power meeting while fly-fishing?

Those are some of the reasons eBay chose Utah for its first services support center in 1999. Another factor was the state's high percentage of multilingual workers. Multilingual in Utah? you ask. Why? Three reasons: Utah is a large resettlement community for Tibetans, Somalis, and other displaced peoples. It's also home to a worldwide church, which means Mormon families from all over the world move to Utah to be closer to their spiritual roots. Perhaps most responsible for the diversity of languages spoken here is the Mormon missionary program. At 19-21 years old, many Mormon kids spend two years in a foreign country on a mission. Part of this service often requires learning another language. When they return from their missions they're fluent. So international companies such as eBay that deal with customers who speak many different languages find Utah ideal. They're able to hire affordable, work-oriented, multilingual employees who tend to raise families early in life.

The same factors about Utah that eBay found appealing have attracted other companies. DLJ Direct Inc., a leading online brokerage firm headquartered in New Jersey, plans to open a 140,000-square-foot investor services facility in Sandy. Novell, PowerQuest, and Net Documents are all headquartered in Utah, and Intel has just built a new 300,000-square-foot research and development facility in Riverton. The Intel campus could employ as many as 8,000 people. When the company first announced its plans, however, many of its employees, citing the popular Utah misconceptions, balked. Management offered affected employees a three-day, expense-paid preview trip to help them decide if they would relocate to Salt Lake City. After the trips, Intel had no more problems.

Another feature companies find attractive is the simple matter of Utah's geographic location. The flights to Silicon Valley and L.A. are each less than an hour and a half, which is less than many execs' normal commute. Since Salt Lake is a Delta hub, air transportation in and out is excellent, and flights are plentiful. Utah is two hours behind New York time and an hour ahead of West Coast time, which makes doing business with anyone in the country convenient.

The one thing Utah doesn't have is a bundle of lucrative tax incentives for businesses. Yet with all the other attractive aspects, it doesn't much need them.

The new economy meets old-world values in Utah.

POPULATION AND PEOPLE

Utah's population is growing—and fast. In 1999 it surpassed 2.12 million and is expected to exceed 3 million by 2030. With a 29.6 percent growth rate from 1990 to 2000, Utah is the fourth fastest-growing state in the country. The neighboring states of Nevada (which posted a 66.3 percent increase in the same period), Arizona (up 40 percent), Colorado (up 30.6 percent), and Idaho (28.5 percent) make up the other five fastest-growing states.

The reasons for Utah's continued growth are simple. First, at 21.7 births per 1,000 population per year, Utah has the highest birthrate in the country. It also has the second-lowest death rate (5.6 per 1,000 per year) in the nation. In short, people here have more kids and live longer than in most other places in the United States.

The other reason for growth is migration. People are moving to Utah at the rate of more than 40,000 per year, in line with a national trend toward moving to the West. Add in the plentiful recreation opportunities and the low cost of real estate (a single-family home in a nice neighborhood can still be had for less than $150,000), and you have the ingredients for a population boom. That's just what Utah has experienced in the past decade.

The fastest-growing area is Summit County (at 6 percent annually), which has within its borders Park City, Deer Valley, and The Canyons. Note, however, that statistics for growth in resort areas do not reflect the massive explosion in ownership of second homes.

More than 75 percent of Utah's population lives in Salt Lake, Davis, Utah, and Weber Counties, which together comprise the Wasatch Corridor that extends from Provo through Salt Lake City to Ogden. Although this area has more than its fair share of urban sprawl, it also contains metropolitan centers that are fast becom-

HOMECOMING OF THE ELDERS

You may witness a scene at the Salt Lake International Airport that leaves you puzzled. A huge cluster of people, anywhere from 50 to 100, gathers, all carrying signs, flowers, and balloons. Many of the women are crying; the men are biting their lips. There's a lot of hugging going on. This is either a homecoming or a farewell for a young Mormon missionary.

Many, but not all, LDS 19- to 21-year-old men and women leave home and go on two-year missions for their church. This is a major rite of passage for the teen and an emotional experience for the family. After the farewell, the family will not see the same youngster again, because when missionaries come back, they are no longer the insulated, naive high schoolers who went out. They are changed, moved along down the road toward maturity.

Both the exit and the re-entrance are wonderfully emotional affairs. I'm thrilled when a single person meets me at any gate—never mind flowers, balloons, and signs. I get warm fuzzies knowing that some kid's family cares enough about him or her to put on all of that hullabaloo. **U**

OLYMPIC VENUES

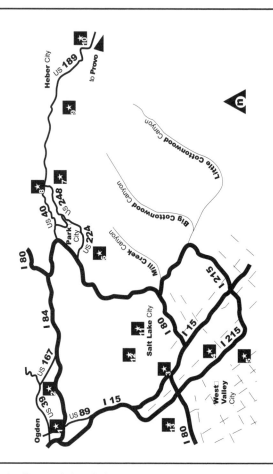

1. The Ice Sheet at Ogden (Curling)
2. Snow Basin Ski Area (Downhill, Combined Downhill, Super G)
3. Salt Lake Ice Center (Figure Skating, Short Track Speed Skating)
4. E Center (Ice Hockey)
5. Utah Olympic Oval (Speed Skating)
6. Utah Olympic Park (Bobsleigh, Luge, Skeleton, Ski Jumping, Nordic Combined)
7. Park City Mountain Resort (Giant Slalom, Snowboarding—Racing and Halfpipe)
8. Deer Valley Resort (Slalom, Freestyle Aerials, Freestyle Moguls)
9. Soldier Hollow (Biathlon, Cross-Country Skiing, Nordic Combined)
10. The Peaks Ice Arena (Ice Hockey)
11. Rice-Eccles Olympic Stadium
12. Olympic Medals Plaza
13. Salt Lake International Airport

The 2002 Olympic Winter Games will be held in Utah February 8-24. The games be centered around Utah's capital, Salt Lake City, but the venues will be spread throughout the Wasatch Front. Events are listed in parenthesis. For more information visit www.saltlake2002.com.

ing vibrant centers of urban life. The median age in Utah is 26.7 years, a statistic that makes it the youngest state in the country.

With this many people, you'd expect an unemployment problem, but the reverse is true; the state has one of the lowest unemployment rates in the country. Utah is, however, a place where the average wage is only 84 percent of the national average. According to the Utah Department of Workforce Services, an elementary school teacher in Utah makes an average wage of $22.10 an hour. On average, a technical writer earns $21.90 an hour, restaurant cooks $8.80, dental assistants $9.70, a cashier $7.20, and a sheriff's patrol officer $16.10. These are not high wages, and the median household income is only about $35,000, but people still live fairly comfortably in Utah.

The people who do really well here are those who work virtually and are able to earn L.A., New York, or Boston rates for their high-tech skills while living in Utah. Any doubt that there are quite a few such people is permanently dispelled by a trip to the airport on Monday morning. Thousands of Utahans take advantage of the inexpensive flights to commute to Los Angeles, San Francisco, and San Diego. I've heard it said that Park City is the fastest-growing suburb of Los Angeles.

For more information on Utah people and population, as well as most other Utah facts, log onto www.dced.state.ut.us/factbook.

WEBSITES

Throughout this book, I've offered as many links to specific websites as I could find. Yet niche-specific sites that give no context can sometimes leave you feeling as if you've been dropped behind enemy lines in a dark and foreign country. For a 10,000-foot view, try this handful of broad-based sites that will give you context for more specific consideration.

GENERAL UTAH SITES

• www.maps.utah.gov is a portal to all sorts of free maps pertaining to Utah. Click your way through to maps that show climate patterns, topography, population, recreational opportunities, wildlife habitats (which sits right next to hunting maps on the site), highways, utilities, and all sorts of other things you probably don't need but are cool to look at. Some of the maps are static; others are dynamic and allow you to zoom in and out. All of the maps can be printed out.

• www.saltlakeinfo.org is a good starting point for any exploration of Utah. Although its URL is misleading—the site covers much more than Salt Lake City—this site functions as a portal to all the official (chamber of commerce type) websites that deal with Utah tourism.

• www.southernutah.com is a central resource that has a huge database of recreation, entertainment, and business opportunities in southern Utah.

• www.utah.com is the official travel site of the State of Utah and the best place for a primer on it. The site is government-sponsored, and some of it tends to be a bit staid, but a few minutes on this site will get you ready for the Beehive State. The "Where's Jeff?" column is a fun take and worth a few minutes. In it, a Utah hound named Jeff takes weekly forays into charted and uncharted Utah.

- **www.utah.gov** is the official site of Utah government, yet it's not as square as you'd expect. This is a fat site with lots of useful info—free concert listings, state park info, highway updates—as well as messages from the governor, a slick Real video promo on Utah (*The State of Things to Come*), and vehicle registration renewal online.

RECREATION
- **www.skiutah.com** is the official site of the Utah Ski and Snowboard Association. Functioning as a one-click portal to all mountain resorts in Utah, this site offers hot deals, lodging guides, and a comprehensive snow report. A well-organized, slick site that can usher you to each resort's site, skiutah.com should be the top bookmark for all Utah skiers and riders.
- **www.utahoutdoors.com** is the online counterpart to *Utah Outdoors* magazine. Featuring detailed information on boating, fishing, golf, and other outdoor activities, as well as streaming and downloadable video clips of Utah adventures, utahoutdoors.com is a good starting point for organizing your plans in the great outdoors. Click on the Utah link on the top left-hand corner of the site to get to an extensive database of outdoor recreation activities and information.

RELIGION
- **www.episcopal-ut.org** is the Episcopal Church's Utah website. On it you'll find diocesan information, a church locator, and information on Episcopalian doctrine.
- **www.firstbaptist-slc.org** is the website for the First Baptist Church of Salt Lake City. On it you'll find a listings of the pastors, office hours, services, and Sunday school.
- **www.geocities.com/Athens/Rhodes/6110/uparc** is the ungainly URL for the website of the Utah Pagan and Alternative Religious Community (UPARC). This is an organization dedicated to supporting, strengthening, and sustaining pagan and alternative religious communities in Utah.
- **www.lds.org** is the official site of The Church of Jesus Christ of Latter-day Saints. On it is everything you want to know about the Church—its history, its gospel, its current-day missions—as well as a cool Internet genealogy service where anyone (Mormon or non-Mormon) can search for his or her family history for free.
- **www.saltlakejcc.com** is the website for the James L. White Jewish Community Center. At press time, it was still under construction.
- **www.slbuddhist.org** is the website of the Salt Lake City Buddhist Temple. Home to a Buddhist sect called Jodo Shinshu Honganji Ha, commonly known as Nishi Honganji, the Salt Lake Buddhist Temple is affiliated with the Buddhist Churches of America and teaches Jodo Shinshu Buddhism. The site explains the methodology and functions of the temple and contains a brief summary of Buddhist history and beliefs.
- **www.utahcatholicdiocese.org** is the central site for the Catholic Church in Utah. On it you'll find Catholic news and events and links to schools, services, and other Catholic organizations.
- **www.zencenterutah.org** is the website for the Utah Kanzeon Zen Center. The

site contains info on training, courses, membership, and an innovative meditative course called "Big Mind." The center is run by Genpo Roshi, one of the foremost Zen masters in the country.

ENTERTAINMENT

• **www.digitalcity.com/saltlakecity** is a good place to begin your search for Salt Lake City happenings. With categories such as entertainment, shopping and services, news and sports, this is a site to get you up to speed on the minute-by-minute of SLC. There's also a chat section where you can get real-time info about SLC, and a local-expert section where you can read descriptions of people who have signed up to be unpaid "local experts," then drop them a line and ask questions. This site is the best bet for AOL users.

• **www.krcl.org** is the online component of Utah's listener-supported "Radio-Free Utah" community radio station. Listen to KRCL online (or on the FM dial at 90.9 in Salt Lake, 96.5 in Park City, and 89.7 and 106.1 in Moab) for a good peek into the diverse and open-minded Utah.

• **www.kuer.org** is the online version of KUER FM 90. This local station is affiliated with the two major public radio networks in the country, National Public Radio (NPR) and Public Radio International (PRI). The site has local news and headlines as well as good talk. Listen to it live on the web.

• **www.1075.com** is the website for KENZ FM 107.5 The End alternative rock radio station. On it you'll find contests, giveaways, singles connections, and the general gestalt of the Utah alternative rock scene.

• **www.utah.citysearch.com** is very similar to digital city.com, but this site is owned by Ticket Master, so it's a touch slicker than the AOL site. Like its competition, citysearch gives you all the movie listings and recommendations for hot takes on current events. The site's restaurant reviews are quite good and well written.

BUSINESS-ORIENTED SITES

• **www.finditinutah.com** is a comprehensive listing of all the businesses in Utah. This site is somewhat like a Yellow Pages online for Utah, only better. Finditinutah.com offers Utah businesses the ability to build their own websites for free and then links them all together in a Utah intranet that anyone on the Internet can use. Sponsored by the state and created by Intel, this is a slick site that can save a lot of searching.

• **www.utah.org** is the state's site for the Department of Community and Economic Development. Business travelers will want to check here.

• **www.utahbusiness.com** is the online component of *Utah Business* magazine. Featuring a live stock ticker that tracks the stock price of Utah companies as well as giving Utah business news, this is a good place to get your finger on the pulse of the dollars-and-cents side of the Beehive State.

MEDIA

The media tell you a lot about a culture. They report, refine, describe, and define the things people think are important, funny, fun, and fascinating. As I've mentioned elsewhere in this book, Utah is a culturally fractured place—all the various subcultures here have been galvanized by the dominant and conservative culture—and the media reflect the plurality and diversity of voices within the Beehive State. Most of the media are clustered around the state's capital, Salt Lake City. As for regional media outlets, I have included them in their specific sections.

MAINSTREAM NEWSPAPERS

Salt Lake City has two main daily newspapers: *The Salt Lake Tribune* and the *Deseret News*. Both are run under a joint operating agreement by the Newspaper Agency Corporation (www.nacorp.com, 801-237-2800). Under the arrangement, the two papers share advertising, printing, circulation, and business functions, but their editorial positions are independent and mostly opposed.

The Salt Lake Tribune (801-257-8742, www.sltrib.com) comes out in the morning and serves the city's liberal population, and the LDS church-affiliated *Deseret News* (801-237-2100, www.deseretnews.com) comes out in the afternoon and covers the issues from a more politically conservative standpoint. Both are top-quality newspapers that stand with the nation's best. (Incidentally, the name "Deseret" stems from the days before Utah gained statehood. Back then, the huge chunk of land that today encompasses parts of modern California, Nevada, Arizona, New Mexico, Colorado, Idaho, and Oregon was known as the territory of Deseret.)

ALTERNATIVE NEWSPAPERS

Catalyst (801-363-1505) is an excellent alternative monthly that deals with community, arts, the environment, and health. With an open-minded, intelligent, and gentle tone—think *Outside* magazine meets *Tricycle* (the Buddhist publication)—the *Catalyst* is the best publication for alternative health, mind-body awareness, and environmental concerns. It also has the best horoscopes in Utah.

City Weekly (801-575-7003, www.slweekly.com) follows in the liberal tradition of the *L.A. Weekly* or the *Boston Phoenix* by usually running a head-turning cover story that confronts and sometimes confounds hot-button issues. For example, *City Weekly* seems to have had more fun with polygamy than anyone since 1890. Not afraid of any sacred cows, the paper is noted for its aggressive reporting that cuts to the heart of politics, society, and religion even as it turns a critical eye on arts, entertainment, and movies. A tough-talking paper that calls things as it sees them, *City Weekly* lives up to its billing as "Utah's independent newspaper."

The Event (801-487-4556,www.eventnewsweekly.com) is a newsweekly published every Thursday. For 20 years, this spirited publication has been covering arts, news, and entertainment in Utah. *Event* is less punk than *SLUG* and more counterculture than *City Weekly*; if the three papers were classic alternative bands, *SLUG* would be Black Flag, *Event* would be the Clash, and *City Weekly* would be U2.

The Pillar (801-265-0066, www.pillarmag.com) bills itself as Utah's "true alternative newspaper," and it's not wrong. Serving the gay, lesbian, bisexual, and transgendered community, *Pillar* reports on news, issues, events, and entertainment of particular interest to its readers. With professional and responsible reporting, the paper brings a fresh and intelligent perspective to local gay issues and supplies the region with national news from GayNet News Service.

SLUG (801-487-9221, slugmag.com) is a raw, ultra-alternative monthly published on newsprint. *SLUG* stands for Salt Lake Underground, and it is. This mag is long on passion, short on fancy design, and the perfect complement to a cup at the Coffee Garden. It's also the best source to tap for the real energy of the local music scene; what snow is to Alta, *SLUG* is to Salt Lake music.

The Web (801-328-4758, www.usee.org) is a quarterly newspaper printed by the Utah Society for Environmental Education. This is a serious little paper dedicated to educating people about the environment. It is not some slick glossy that purports to care deeply about the environment while it runs double-page spreads of Ford Excursions. This is the real deal.

Wild Utah (435-615-9609, www.wildutah.net) is a nascent biweekly that takes a no-holds-barred but fun look at Utah. Published every other Wednesday by a group that calls itself Transcending Mundane Inc., in Park City, this is a small newspaper with funny comics and unique features such as the "Phat Tats" item that has photos of cool tattoos.

MAGAZINES

I-15 Magazine (801-257-9645, www.i-15magazine.com) is a glossy lifestyle mag named for that wide strip of asphalt that links Salt Lake City to Vegas and L.A. Using Interstate 15 as a metaphor, this new magazine takes a "life accelerated" approach to movie stars, sports, fashion, design, and all things hip.

Salt Lake Magazine (801-485-5100, www.saltlakemagazine.com) is a bimonthly publication that caters to an affluent and active readership. The magazine features profiles of people from around the state, outdoor activities and attractions, and historical aspects of Utah. The "Datebook" section offers a good directory for fundraisers, art openings, plays, readings, concerts, dance, and other performances. The "Dining Guide" section is comprehensive, and the "Utah Scene" section features collages from social gatherings and events in Salt Lake City and the intermountain West.

Sports Guide (801-467-9516, www.sportsguidemag.com) is a monthly newsprint magazine that covers outdoor recreation, fitness, and travel in the West. From instructionals to travel features, *Sports Guide* offers a comprehensive and timely look at running, riding, skiing, and a host of other fun activities in the great outdoors.

Utah Business (801-568-0114, www.utahbusiness.com) bills itself as "a magazine for decision makers," and that's exactly what it reads like. Every issue of this magazine is a Who's Who of the successful and established Utah business community.

The front section, "Players," gives a rundown of executive-level hirings and promotions, and the "Around Utah" section has blurbs on local business happenings.

Wasatch Digital IQ (801-363-1200, www.wasatchconnect.com) is the best Utah publication for reporting on the burgeoning high-tech economy. This glossy monthly is headed up by the gregarious and knowledgeable Kimball Thompson and features in-depth coverage of high-tech issues and companies along the Wasatch Front.

TELEVISION
Although we all claim that we "don't watch much TV," just in case you do choose to flip on the idiot box, here are the eight main television channels that serve the Utah market.

- KUTV 2 CBS
- KTVX 4 ABC
- KSL 5 NBC
- KUED 7 PBS
- KULC 9 PBS
- KBYU 11 PBS
- KSTU 13 FOX
- KJZZ-TV, UPN 14

RADIO STATIONS
If you don't cotton to AM country, the drive into Utah is a pilgrimage across great expanses of radio wasteland. Once in Zion, however, you can take heart, because salvation flows from your radio dial. Here are a few of the refreshing stations:

KCPW 88.3 and **105.1 FM** (801-359-5279) is an all-talk station that not only has the best of National Public Radio, Public Radio International, and the BBC, but also has a savvy and smart local-affairs hour every day from 9 A.M. until 10 A.M. Tune here to hear NPR's *Talk of the Nation, Fresh Air, All Things Considered,* and *Marketplace.* On the weekends, KCPW has *This American Life, Savvy Traveler,* and my favorite, *Car Talk.*

KUER FM 90.1 (801-581-6625, www.kuer.org) is the University of Utah's public radio station. Affiliated with National Public Radio and Public Radio International, KUER broadcasts news and talk all day and jazz at night.

The FM station KRCL 90.9 in Salt Lake, 96.5 in Park City, and 89.7 and 106.1 in Moab (801-363-1818, www.krcl.org) is "Radio-Free Utah." The tag line for this community radio station used to be "The Lion of Zion, operating from behind the Zion Curtain." They've since dropped that great catchphrase, but not to worry, they've maintained the vibe. With shows such as *La Voz de la Hente* (the voice of the people), *Concerning Gay and Lesbians, Pacific Islander, Evolving Male,* as well as soulful reggae programs (*Smile Jamaica, Conscious Reggae, Lions Den*), KRCL is the most fun and raw radio station in Utah.

KENZ 107.5 The End (801-485-6700, www.1075.com) is Utah's "rock alternative." A Citadel Broadcasting station, The End has audacious morning deejays and a playlist that's similar to KBCO's in Boulder, Colorado; it introduces the best of the new music and spins echoes of the hip old stuff (by old I mean 1980s, not 1950s).

UTAH IN THE MOVIES

Salt Lake City is a long way from Hollywood. Or is it? Well, you take Sunset to the 101, the 101 to the 10, and the 10 to the 15. As you go up and over the San Gabriel Mountains, you stop saying "the 15" and start saying "I-15," and a dozen hours later you're in Zion. One day's drive takes you from the Sunset Strip to South Temple, so it's really not that far.

Ah, but that's geographically; in terms of cultural connection, you might think L.A. and Salt Lake have about as much in common as a Ferrari and a butter churn. Hang on; you might be surprised.

Utah, not California, is home to the biggest festival of film in North America. Every year, a massive flock of Los Angelistos (as many as 20,000) fly out of the City of Angels and into the City of Saints to be a part of it. Like migratory geese, they come for the annual Sundance Film Festival in Park City and Salt Lake City.

Okay, well film festivals are all well and fine, but the actual movies are made in L.A. with no Utah connection whatsoever. Right? Well, here again, you'd be surprised. Just for fun, I matched films shot in Utah against the alphabet and found a film for every letter except K, Q, U, and X. Here's the list, but it is by no means complete:

Across the Great Divide, Back to the Future 3, Cujo, Death Valley Days, Easy Rider, Forrest Gump, The Grinch Who Stole Christmas, How the West Was Won, Indiana Jones and the Last Crusade, Jeremiah Johnson, The Last of the Mohicans, Maverick, Nurse Betty, The Outlaw Josey Wales, Planet of the Apes (both versions), *Romancing the Stone, Seven Brides for Seven Brothers, Thelma and Louise, Vanishing Point, Waiting to Exhale, Year of the Dragon,* and *Zack and Reba.*

What the Hollywood sign is to L.A., this sign is to Salt Lake City.

Left The United Methodist Church in downtown Salt Lake City, founded in 1870, today is flanked by the spires of the new, high-tech economy. *Right* The altar at the Kanzeon Zen Center in downtown Salt Lake City.

The complete list is five times this size. One reason so many films have been shot here is the state's large cadre of both in-front-of- and behind-the-camera talent. The fact that Utah is a right-to-work, nonunion state also means it's much cheaper to shoot here than in, say, California. But the state's natural beauty is the primary reason so many miles of film have been exposed out here. Utah has the red rock desert, the white-capped mountains, and just about every other backdrop you could want for a film. For *Net Worth,* which I wrote and produced, we shot the Great Salt Lake for the Pacific Ocean, and it worked fine. For more information about Utah's celluloid side, contact the Utah Film Commission (801-741-4540, www.film.utah.org).

RELIGION AND SPIRITUALITY

Utah can freak some people out because of the way religion and spirituality aren't cloistered away until Sunday morning. The LDS emphasis on day-to-day spirituality—being Mormon is as much about lifestyle and community as it is about church and Sunday—seems to have seeped into non-Mormon culture.

This influence forces people to give some thought to their own spiritual path. It's as if the mere presence of the LDS church makes you ready yourself to state your own membership or nonmembership when you arrive here. Even as you're wondering whether this or that person is Mormon, you can't help but wonder what you are. Subliminally, you can almost hear "Welcome to Utah. Now state your beliefs." Though this is purely subtextual communication it's nonetheless powerful.

This can make people—particularly those raised in places where religion was encountered on Sunday mornings, holidays, weddings, and funerals—a bit uneasy. That's probably not such a bad thing, but it tends to stir up both inner and outer conflict. Every day some reference to the battle over ideals is on the front page of either the *Deseret News* or the *Salt Lake Tribune*. Though this tension makes for great reading, it also makes for a place where it's difficult to be either blissfully ignorant or close-minded about your own spirituality.

The misconception is that the LDS church seeks to put spiritual blinders on everyone. I've found this to be mostly untrue. In fact, I've found this to be a culture that gives one great license to be fervent. Perhaps because Utah was founded by religious pilgrims seeking a safe place to practice their faith, there still exists an air of tolerance toward all things spiritual.

"It's about balance and counterbalance," said Mary Nickle, who operates Time Out Associates, a meditation and healing arts center in downtown Salt Lake City. "For every up there's a down; for every right there's a left. Here in Utah the extremely conservative conventional society opens the door and even attracts a more open group of people, especially where spirituality is concerned. There are many people who don't fit the [more mainstream] spiritual forms and they come here to actively and avidly seek a forum for their own spiritual expression."

Alexandra Fericke, a student-in-training at the Kanzeon Zen Center Utah, echoes similar notions: "Salt Lake's strong Mormon presence creates the need for a spiritual counterweight," she said. "There's also a sweetness to the people here that leads to more openness. Over the last few years we've had more and more people coming to our center as Zen has been widely recognized and accepted here."

Not only is Zen accepted in Utah but so is every other spiritual or religious practice you can think of. Indeed, Salt Lake City's first-rate *Catalyst* magazine, which bills itself as "Utah's Progressive Monthly," has page upon page of stories, listings, and advertisements relating to alternative spirituality and mind-body programs.

There are centers for Judaism and Muslim faiths, and there's even the Pagan Alternative Resource Center that's dedicated to supporting the more earth-based practices. Yep, although it may come as some surprise that all this spiritual stuff exists in Utah, it really shouldn't freak anybody out. After all, we're all human beings first, members of organized religions or spiritual seekers, a far distant second.

COLLEGES AND UNIVERSITIES

Utah puts heavy emphasis on higher education. It also puts its money where its mouth is; in 2000, Utah ranked first in the nation for higher-education spending. Importance of education is part of the culture in Utah, and it starts in secondary schools. Utah is ranked fourth in the country in the number of residents who have high school diplomas (91 percent) and ninth in residents who have attained bachelor degrees (27.9 percent).

Utah has seven public, four-year, degree-granting universities and colleges, as well as three private higher-learning institutions. The University of Utah, Utah State University, and Brigham Young University are the largest institutions in the state in terms of enrollment, number of degrees conferred, and research and development expenditures. Total student enrollment in Utah public and private four-year, degree-granting universities and colleges in fall 2000 was 141,844.

Here is a brief rundown of Utah's colleges and universities. For more information, visit their individual websites.

PUBLIC INSTITUTIONS

College of Eastern Utah (451 East 400 North, Price, Utah 84501, 435-637-2120, www.ceu.edu), located about 120 miles southeast of Salt Lake City, is a two-year, small, open-access, comprehensive community college that provides general and liberal education as well as applied-technology programs leading to associate of arts, science, or applied science degrees. Certificates are awarded for short-term and applied-technology programs.

Dixie College (225 South 700 East, St. George, Utah 84770, 888-GO-2-DIXIE, www.dixie.edu) is located 300 miles south of Salt Lake City in St. George, the heart of Utah's "Dixie." This comprehensive community college offers two- and four-year degrees. The degree work in computer and information technology is a popular curriculum that combines programming, multimedia, and web design.

Salt Lake Community College (4600 South Redwood Road, Salt Lake City, Utah 84130-0808, 801-957-4111, www.slcc.edu) is a two-year, multicampus college that offers vocational and technical studies, adult and continuing education, as well as developmental education designed to support students making the transition to college life. SLCC provides more technical and vocational training than any other college, university, proprietary school, advanced-technology center, or high school district in the state. In an average year, the fifty-three-year-old college serves more than 55,000 students through credit and noncredit courses. The college is in partnership with about 500 local businesses and school districts to provide training for specific jobs. Its partnership with Union Pacific Railroad recently was selected from more than 7,000 partnerships statewide to receive the Outstanding Partnership Award in Customized Training and Workshops.

Snow College (150 East College Avenue, Ephraim, Utah 84627, 800-848-3399 www.snow.edu), founded in 1888, is a small, two-year, state-run liberal arts college with campuses in Ephraim and Richfield. This school prides itself on its small class size and its inexpensive tuition. Snow is also an "open admissions" institution, which means students can be admitted if they graduate from high school and take the ACT or SAT. The college's rural setting gives students a chance to focus on getting their associate degree either as a stepping-stone to a bachelor's at another college, or as their ticket to enter the workforce. Snow offers 64 areas of study ranging from accounting to zoology.

Southern Utah University (351 West Center Street, Cedar City, Utah 84720, 435-586-7700, www.suu.edu), founded in 1897, has evolved from a teacher-training school into its current role as a comprehensive, regional university. Located 250 miles southwest of Salt Lake City, SUU has a total enrollment of about 6,000 and serves the southern region of Utah with undergraduate and graduate programs and applied-technology training.

University of Utah (240 South University Street, Salt Lake City, Utah, 84112, 801-581-7200, www.utah.edu), located on 1,500 acres of verdant hillside in the city, has an enrollment of more than 26,000 students and offers 75 undergraduate degree programs, 50 teaching majors and minors, and 96 graduate majors. A major research park is located on 320 acres adjacent to the campus. The park has 34 buildings housing 44 companies and portions of 37 university departments, employs an estimated 6,100 people, and contributes approximately $600 million annually to Utah's economy. Various companies conduct joint research with university departments, use faculty as consultants, and/or employ students. Research park companies have added more than 4,700 jobs to the state's economy. The university has three main libraries—the J. Willard Marriott, Eccles Health Sciences, and S. J. Quinney Law—that are open to the general public 100 hours per week when classes are in session. It also has the Alice Sheets

The University of Utah's campus sits on a verdant hill above downtown Salt Lake City.

Marriott Center for Dance, the 15,000-seat Jon M. Huntsman Center, the George S. Eccles Sports Center, the 2,000-seat Kingsbury Hall, the Pioneer Memorial Theater, the Gardner Concert Hall, and the 46,500-seat Rice Eccles Stadium, which is the site of the opening ceremony for the 2002 Winter Olympics. The university is also home to an excellent public radio station, KUER, at FM 90.

Utah State University (Logan, Utah, 84322-1600, 435-797-1000, www.usu.edu), about 80 miles north of Salt Lake City, is a four-year state university founded in 1888. Sitting on 400 acres of hillside overlooking the town of Logan, USU is home to more than 20,000 students, 45 departments in eight academic colleges (agriculture, business, education, engineering, family life, humanities, arts and social sciences, natural resources, and science) as well as an extensive school of graduate studies. USU also offers a broad online curriculum at www.online.usu.edu.

Utah Valley State College (800 West University Parkway, Orem, Utah 84058-5999, 801-222-8000, www.uvsc.edu) is a two- and four-year college located in Orem, 45 miles south of Salt Lake City. The campus is adjacent to Interstate 15 and has beautiful Mount Timpanogos as a backdrop. Originally formed to provide training to support the industrial needs of World War II, the college has evolved from a trade school to a state college offering everything from short-term vocational programs to four-year degrees in a wide range of majors. The college now enrolls nearly 22,000 students, 90 percent of them residents of Utah. UVSC is home to the David O. McKay Events Center, a multipurpose arena built in partnership with the county. The McKay Center not only hosts the college's athletic programs but also is the site for many major concerts.

Weber State University (3750 Harrison Boulevard, Ogden, Utah 84408, 801-626-6000, www.weber.edu) is located about 35 miles north of Salt Lake City in Ogden. With a total of 16,000 students, Weber State is a university that excels in aerospace research and development, and offers two- and four-year degrees. Students at Weber recently built and launched a satellite into orbit.

PRIVATE INSTITUTIONS
Brigham Young University (Provo, Utah 84602, 801-378-4511, www.byu.edu), located 45 miles south of Salt Lake City in Provo, is a four-year well-respected private university sponsored by The Church of Jesus Christ of Latter-day Saints. Dedicated to the integration of academics and the LDS gospel, BYU has had a strong tradition of excellence in academics and athletics since 1875.

LDS Business College (411 East South Temple, Salt Lake City Utah 84111-1392, 800-999-5767, www.ldsbc.edu), founded 115 years ago by The Church of Jesus Christ of Latter-day Saints, is a two-year college that is part of the worldwide LDS church education system. The campus is centered in the Enos A. Wall mansion in downtown Salt Lake City. This majestic Renaissance-style villa was designed by Richard K. A. Kletting, who also designed the Utah State Capitol. Classes average about 18 students, and the college offers associate degrees in accounting, business, computers, health services, interior design, and office management. Students also may earn an associate degree in general education and then transfer to a four-year university.

Westminster College (1840 South 1300 East, Salt Lake City, Utah, 84105, 801-484-7651, www.wcslc.edu), located in the Sugarhouse section of Salt Lake City, is a small, four-year only, nondenominational liberal arts college that has about 2,200 students. With an average class size of 17, Westminster offers "Ivy League tradition in the spirit of the West" through 27 bachelor of arts or science undergraduate degrees, as well as many graduate and postbaccalaureate certificates.

MY PICKS
What do the gowned and tuxedoed presenters always say before they present the Oscars? "Every one of these worthy nominees deserves this award." It's always something like that, right? Well, as I sit here typing my picks for the best this and the most fun that, I can assure you that not only am I sans tux but also that every business or activity included in this book is an award winner of sorts. These are the places I tell my friends about. The one's I've listed here are just the places

that I'd mention first in each category. There are undoubtedly places I've missed, those of you who will feel snubbed, and to you I extend an invitation to send your suggestions (to bk@billkerig.com) for other categories and future nominees. Here then, without further ado, are my Utah picks:

ACTIVITIES
Best entertainment value: Stingers baseball games, Salt Lake City
Best place to get away and recharge: Boulder Mountain Lodge, Boulder
Best romantic getaway: A cabin at Sundance Resort
Best place to watch a film: Brewvies, Salt Lake City
Best motorcycle road: Highway 12, southern Utah
Best mountain-bike ride: Wasatch Crest Trail, Mill Creek Canyon, Salt Lake City
Best change-your-life experience: Attending Boulder Outdoor Survival School
Best day spa: Avenues Arts and Wellness Center, Salt Lake City
Best event: Sundance Film Festival, Park City and Salt Lake City
Best golf course: Entrada, St. George

LODGING
Best hotel: Grand America, Salt Lake City

NIGHTLIFE
Best beer bar: Shooting Star Saloon, Huntsville
Best jazz: Mother Urban's Ratskellar, Park City
Best nightclub: Harry O's, Park City
Most un-Utah nightclub: Club Axis, Salt Lake City
Best live-music dive bar: Burt's Tiki Lounge, Salt Lake City
Best neighborhood bar: Twilite Lounge, Salt Lake City

RESTAURANTS (AND FOOD)
Best burger (for over-21-year-olds): Shooting Star Burger, Shooting Star Saloon, Huntsville
Best burger for anyone: Hire's Big H, downtown Salt Lake City
Best Mexican food: Red Iguana, Salt Lake City
Best sushi: Ichiban Sushi, Salt Lake City
Most fun sushi bar: Happy Sumo, Park City
Best diner: Mom's Café, Salina
Best connoisseur's dinner: Bistro Toujours, Deer Valley
Most romantic dinner (urban): Martine, Salt Lake City
Most romantic dinner (rustic): The Tree Room, Sundance
Best organic dinner: Hell's Backbone Grill, Boulder
Best steak: Prime Steak House, Park City
Best coffee shop: Cup of Joe's, Salt Lake City

SHOPS
Best thrift store: Deseret Industries, downtown Salt Lake City

Best vintage furniture: Green Ant, Salt Lake City
Best large bookstore: Sam Weller's, Salt Lake City
Best small bookstore: The King's English, Salt Lake City

RESORTS

Best nightlife in a ski town: Park City
Best family-destination resort: The Canyons
Best place to learn to snowboard with your kids: Brian Head
Best expert skiing: Snowbird-Alta (on the combination ski pass)
Best place to ski the day after the storm: Snow Basin
Best tree skiing: Deer Valley
Best spot for secret powder stashes: Solitude
Best area for snowboarding: Brighton

SALT LAKE CITY

S alt Lake City has had a remarkable history, and one gets the impression that it's just begun. Founded in 1847 as the hub of the fledgling and persecuted Church of Jesus Christ of Latter-day Saints, Salt Lake quickly found itself at the crossroads of conflicting ideas, cultures, and desires. First came the gold rushers headed for California. They brought their money, lust, and liquor to the Valley of the Saints. Because they were a transient bunch, however, Latter-day Saint leader Brigham Young and his early minions had no trouble selling them supplies and spiriting them on their way. With the discovery of silver and gold in Utah, however, these wild mining men, their saloons, and ladies of ill repute were tougher to shake. When the Golden Spike, which united the nation's first transcontinental railroad, was driven in Promontory, Utah, in 1869, it gave Salt Lake a serious economic injection but also wounded the Mormon theocracy. From the railroad came the outside, and from the outside came major federal interest.

Not surprisingly, this era brought colorful conflict to Salt Lake, the reverberations of which continue to shape the city. At the end of the nineteenth century, polygamy was abandoned, and Utah gained statehood. The next twenty years brought a surge in growth as Mormon and non-Mormon alike prospered. Both mining and agriculture boomed through World War I, and Salt Lake became a Wild West town with one hand on the earth and the other on the wallet. The depression brought a temporary hiatus to development in Salt Lake, but Roosevelt's New Deal provided resurrection. World War II saw an ascendant Salt Lake economy, and the city celebrated its centennial in 1947 with all the promise and idealism of golden youth.

Just when the city needed to mature, however, things began to go awry. Suburbanization leached its core energy, and later the shopping malls signaled a self-destructive bent that could well have nailed shut the city's coffin.

At the same time, agriculture and mining were replaced by tourism as the state's mainstay. Resorts such as Park City burgeoned, but at the end of the twentieth century, Salt Lake City's center offered only boarded-up buildings, empty streets, and weeds growing in the sidewalks. Then, just as the city's midlife crisis threatened to approach irreversible decline, Salt Lake found a new reason to live: the Olympics. The awarding of the 2002 Olympic Winter Games not only signaled a new direction for Salt Lake, but also may prove to be the elaborate life-giving ritual that will usher this city into its long-overdue maturity.

With the aid of federal and regional tax money, a concerted effort has been made to restore downtown Salt Lake. For the past four years, Salt Lake has had only one season: construction season. Morning, noon, and night, the staccato drill

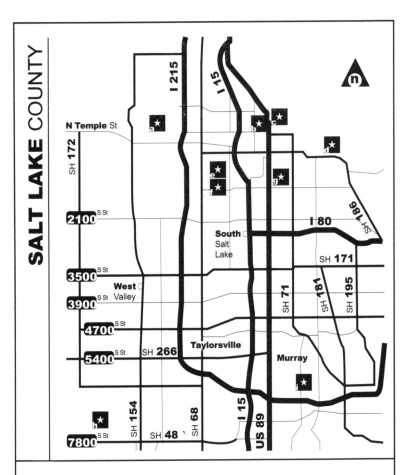

SALT LAKE COUNTY

a. Salt Lake City International
b. Temple Square
c. State Capitol
d. University of Utah
e. Jordan River State Park
f. International Peace Gardens
g. Liberty Park
h. Salt Lake City Municipal Airport
i. Wheeler Historic Farm

of jackhammers and the beep, beep, beep of dump trucks backing up have been to Salt Lake what Muzak is to an elevator.

Roads have been repaved and widened, the city infrastructure has been relaid, parks have been built, and the boards are coming off the downtown buildings. Once again trolleys are plying the city streets. As I write this, all over Salt Lake, crews are working around-the-clock to finish everything by the Olympics. Stand in the penthouse of the central Grand America Hotel (still under construction) and you can see a city coming back to life. Everywhere there are cranes and commotion. Walk the town at night and hear the city's pulse. There is excitement in the air here, a sense of expectation that is palpable, and it's not only about the Olympics; it's about coming of age.

For those who have spent any time in Denver in the past ten years, the cycle will be familiar. All over Salt Lake, new businesses (including saloons) are opening, and the heady fever of optimism is in the air. On the west side of downtown, a huge development, called Gateway, is all cranes, bulldozers, and 24-hour work crews. By the time of the Olympics, the developers say, Gateway will be a completed area of stores, condos, and upscale eateries the likes of which Salt Lake has never seen. Today, Salt Lake County has nearly 900,000 residents and an average growth rate that puts it among the fastest in the United States. Still, in downtown a few boarded-up buildings and vacancy signs leave the slightest hint of doubt about whether Salt Lake will boom again in the near future. Yet if I were a betting man (and I am), I'd lay my money (which I have in a sense by owning a home here) on Salt Lake charging headlong into becoming a prime-of-life, world-class city.

Because all cities are essentially a collection of neighborhoods, I've divided Salt Lake City into a half dozen main boroughs: Downtown, the Avenues, Foothill and University, Sugarhouse, 9th and 9th, and 15th and 15th.

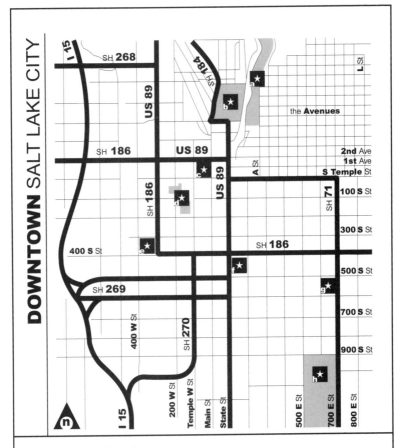

DOWNTOWN SALT LAKE CITY

a. Memory Grove Park
b. Utah State Capitol
c. Temple Square
d. Salt Palace
e. Pioneer Park
f. City and County Building
g. Trolley Square
h. Liberty Park

1 . Downtown

RESTAURANTS

3rd West Bistro (300 West 300 South, 801-328-3463, www.3rdwestbistro.com) is a terrific French bistro located in an old tire store. An eclectic and ambitious place, 3rd West offers exceptional French food served by a white-aproned staff. The decor is a minimalist version of 1920s deco style, which works surprisingly well in this formerly industrial setting. Large parties of connoisseurs will want to try the Chef's Table. A prix fixe of $65 (not including wine) per person buys a seven-course meal of off-the-menu specialties. Hours: Monday-Friday lunch 11 A.M.-2 P.M., dinner 5 P.M.-9:30 P.M. (later on weekends), Sunday brunch 10 A.M.-2 P.M., dinner 5 P.M.-8 P.M.

Absolute (52 West 200 South, 801-359-0899), run by husband-wife team Staffan and Kim Eklund, serves up the best Swedish food in the state. If your idea of Swedish food is something you saw on *The Muppet Show*, you owe it to yourself to check out this place. An upscale, Euro-feeling bistro right next door to Capitol Theater, Absolute offers excellent seafood and Scandinavian specialties. Try the toast smogen and the matje herring. Hours: Monday-Friday lunch 11:30A.M.-4 P.M., and dinner 5 P.M.-9:30 P.M. Saturday dinner only 5 P.M.-10 P.M. Open Sunday on occasion.

Al Forno's (239 South 500 East, 801-359-6040) is the type of place that everybody likes. The food isn't cheap, but this simple eatery with its minimalist Milano style draws people from every walk. At lunch you'll find a lot of suits here, and at dinner they'll be joined by the U of U crowd. Owner James Batestas has created a place with white linen, butcher paper on the tables (don't you just love to draw on it with crayons?), and a staff that's brisk but excited about the food. Try the fettuccine picante with chicken breast and Asiago sauce. Vitello cotomata is the choice for veal lovers. And the extensive wine list of Mediterranean vintages is well picked and well priced. Come early—this place is popular. Hours: Monday-Friday lunch 11:30 A.M.-2:30 P.M., Monday-Thursday dinner 5:30 P.M.-9:30 P.M., Friday and Saturday dinner 5 P.M.-10 P.M.

Anchors Aweigh (64 West 400 South, 801-521-2072) is a 24-hour food and coffee joint that does a major after-midnight business caring for revelers from Port O' Call and the other neighboring watering holes. Open all the time.

Atlantic Café and Market (325 South Main Street, 801-524-9900) is a sidewalk café where you can get a good Café Lavazza, a fine and inexpensive slab of lasagna, or a cold beer, all while pretending you're in Prague or a rundown section of Paris. Owned and operated by Miroslav Bako, a Croatian, the Atlantic not only serves good food and beer until midnight on the weekends but also sells magazines and imported foods (such as the ever-popular canned tripe) from the

Balkans. This explains why the majority of the clientele is speaking a language you can't even recognize, much less understand. Hours: Monday-Thursday 9 A.M.-11:30 P.M., Friday and Saturday 9 A.M.-1 A.M., Sunday 9 A.M.-11 P.M.

Bambara (202 South Main Street, 801-363-5454) is the hottest table in town. This chic eatery, located in the Hotel Monaco, features purple velvet booths and glossy marble floors and walls (one wall was the teller's counter in the bank that used to occupy the space). It also offers the best eclectic menu in the city. Drawn from Italian, Native American, French, and Asian influences, the food is elegant, and the service makes you feel like a touring rock star. When executive chef Scott Blackerby couldn't find the herbs he needed for his dishes, he started his own garden—on the roof. The fruits of his labors now grace every dish. Try the grilled prawn salad or the tea-cured duck. Hours: Monday-Friday breakfast 7 A.M.-9:30 A.M., Saturday and Sunday 8 A.M.-1 P.M.; Monday-Friday lunch 11:30 A.M.-2:30 P.M.; Monday-Thursday dinner 5:30 P.M.-10 P.M., Friday and Saturday 5:30 P.M.-11 P.M., Sunday 5:30 P.M.-9 P.M.

Big City Soup (235 South 400 West, 801-333-7687, bigcitysoup.com) is a great lunch spot with, you guessed it, killer soup. Hours: Monday-Friday 11 A.M.-3 P.M. Closed Sunday.

The Blue Iguana Expresso is the place for a hot burrito and a Jones soda at 3 A.M.

Blue Iguana (165 South West Temple, 801-533-8900) is an upscale Mexican eatery nestled into a brick nook just off the west wing of the Capitol Theater. If you find yourself craving a tamale during the finale of the ballet, this is your place. And you won't feel overdressed supping here in your Saville Row. The food is downtown-fine, and the atmosphere is south-of-the-border elegant. Hours: Monday-Thursday 11:30 A.M.-9 P.M., Friday and Saturday 11:30 A.M.-10 P.M., Sunday 4 P.M.-10 P.M.

Blue Iguana Expresso (165 South West Temple, 801-322-4796) is the 24-hour Mexican eatery that's owned by the same folks who own the Dead Goat Saloon and the much nicer Blue Iguana restaurant. If you need a hot burrito and a Jones soda at 3:00 A.M., venture here. Sandwiched between DV8 and the Downtown Underground Safari

INTERVIEW WITH MAYOR ROCKY ANDERSON

*S*alt Lake City Mayor Rocky Anderson is a progressive liberal in a state not normally known for its open-mindedness. He is a maverick, a risk taker, and a fun, if busy guy.

When I called to ask for an interview, I was surprised by his quick response; we sat down the following week.

The Salt Lake City and County building is a spired, turreted, granite-blocked old building with gargoyles leering down from the eaves and a wide stairway leading up to Mayor Anderson's office. The floors gleam, the ceilings are twenty-plus feet, and the hallways are wide enough for indoor soccer.

Mayor Anderson's assistant, Christy Cordwell, served me coffee and, with a wink, told me to take it when the mayor came for me. Shortly afterward, the mayor bounded out of his office and wrung my hand. A natty dresser, he moved with a runner's determined step. We sat down across a long conference table in his large office. He looked for a long moment at my cup of coffee. Was he insulted? Had I committed a faux pas? Then he focused on me.

Rocky Anderson is a man who looks you in the eye and listens well to questions. Unlike other politicians I've interviewed, he answered my questions (most politicos give their rehearsed speeches that often have nothing to do with your questions). Rocky Anderson personifies change in Utah. He is a whirling dervish for progressive policy who is not always popular, but who knows, loves, and cares about Utah. I've included part of our Q&A here.

Bill Kerig: We all know the history of Salt Lake City, but I wonder, exactly what is Salt Lake City today?

Mayor Rocky Anderson: Salt Lake City is a thriving, diverse metropolitan area that has unparalleled access to everything that can improve quality of life for residents and visitors. There's no place in the world that I know of with the kind of ready access we have to so many things. I don't know of another city where two blocks away from the State Capitol, you can be in an incredible canyon that's beautiful for a good run, hike, or dog walk.

B.K.: What about nightlife? You know the rap—you just can't get a drink here.

M.A.: Because of a few oddities in our liquor

Salt Lake City Mayor Rocky Anderson

laws, we're perceived as being something very different from what we really are. People think we're a dry state, which simply isn't true. You can walk into any good restaurant in Salt Lake City and get a drink just as you can anywhere else, as long as you're going to be eating. You won't even notice the difference—unless, of course, you order a double and the sec-

(continued on page 47)

Bel Morgan Kerig

Caffé Molise, in downtown Salt Lake City, is the sweetest little café you can imagine.

Club, this is the place for a down-and-dirty late-night bite. The food is good—considering the cooks have to stay up all night—and the service is fast; the staff remains incredibly cool even during the crazy 1 A.M.-3 A.M. rush of clubbers and night owls. Open all the time.

Caffé Molise (55 West 100 South, 801-364-8833) is just about the sweetest little Italian café you're going to find. Hours: Monday-Friday lunch 11:30 A.M.-2 P.M., dinner 5:30 P.M.-9 P.M., Friday and Saturday until 10 P.M.

Cannella's (204 East 500 South, 801-355-8518) is a family-run joint that serves big ole red-sauce Italian meals that Tony Soprano would fully appreciate. The food is simple and "to die for" (read with appropriate Jersey accent—emphasis on the "d"). Cannella's is jam-packed at lunch, less so for dinners. Patrons know the staffers, who work like a well-oiled machine. The atmosphere is distinctly down-home friendly and fast. Hours: Monday-Friday 9 A.M.-3 P.M., Thursday-Saturday dinner 5:30 P.M.-10 P.M.

The Cedars of Lebanon (152 East 200 South, 801-364-4096, http://cedarsoflebanon.uswestdex.com) offers good, solid Lebanese, Armenian, Moroccan, and Israeli food, and the decor is simple and authentic. The back room has the obligatory pillows and low stools and tables where you'll want to take a nap after your

(continued from page 45)

ond shot comes in what they call a sidecar. But those are fairly minor inconveniences, and there are certainly places in this country that have more restrictive liquor laws than we have.

We have a Saint Patrick's Day parade after which we all go to the Gallivan Center for dancing and an Irish coffee with real Irish whiskey. It's the same with the Wednesday After Five Come Alive Concert Series. There's good rock 'n' roll, and you can buy a beer and walk around. We also have an annual jazz festival with world-class talent—Jack Jones, Nancy Wilson, Yellow Jackets, Pete Frick, the Four Freshmen—and a beer garden there too.

On any night you can go out for great theater, concerts, dining, you name it. At Club Axis, you can have fifteen hundred to two thousand people just having a wild time. Some nights are gay nights; others are straight nights. I've been in there when they had a drag show going on.

We have clubs for eighteen- and twenty-year-olds where they can come to dance. We have one of the first brew-pubs anywhere in the West.

B.K.: *You really know your way around nightlife.*

M.A.: *I think our nightlife is important for everybody. Whether people choose to imbibe or not, there's great entertainment in a lot of places, and we need to let visitors know these places exist.*

B.K.: *What about the future of the liquor laws?*

M.A.: *They'll change. There's been an evolution over the years from brown-bag laws to mini-bottle laws to what we have now. At least we're opening up the dialogue, which displeases a lot of people—the alcoholic beverage commission opined in some publication recently that I ought to keep my mouth shut and people wouldn't get upset about it. I thought it was a rude way for them to put it, but it also showed the arrogance of these people toward anybody or any movement wanting reasonable change in the liquor laws. These folks love to have as much control as possible. And I think that's not a good thing for any of us, whether we consume or don't consume alcoholic beverages. It's a bad thing for the state as a whole to have some of these ridiculous oddities like the club membership requirements.*

B.K.: *So there will be a change?*

M.A.: *There's been tremendous change already, and there's no doubt that we'll see a continuing evolution toward more rationality in our liquor laws.*

B.K.: *Will the Olympics be, as the* Irish Times *claimed, the most boring Games in history?*

M.A.: *Whoever wrote that has never been to Salt Lake City. That 17 days is going to be a great party.*

B.K.: *What will the Olympics do for Utah?*

M.A.: *First, it's certainly bringing a lot of good economic development to Utah and to Salt Lake City in particular. Second, as people see what we*

(continued on page 49)

meal. Belly dancers Friday and Saturday nights. Hours: Monday-Friday 11:30 A.M.-2:30 P.M. and 5 P.M.-10 P.M., Saturday 5 P.M.-11 P.M. Closed Sunday.

David Chase Café (278 East 900 South, 801-363-7182) is a charming and chic little café that seems somewhat lost in a never-never-land between downtown and 9th and 9th. The strange location, however, makes parking a breeze. This place is worth the short drive from wherever you are. Expect healthy, creative Mediterranean food, homemade bread and cheesecake, and decor that's unpretentious and classy. Get a superb lunch for about twelve bucks. Hours: Monday-Friday 11 A.M.-3 P.M. Closed Saturday and Sunday.

Ginza (209 West 200 South, 801-322-2224) is a perfect sushi bar tucked in a small brick building that seems somehow abandoned and forgotten. Once inside, however, you'll see that no one has forgotten this joint—certainly not the trendy, well-heeled clientele who chow raw fish off white linen. One caveat: It's a hassle to park and eat there on nights the Jazz play in the neighboring Delta Center. Try the mikomi udon or the katsu-don. Both lunch and dinner are good and popular. Hours Monday-Thursday 11:30 A.M.-10 P.M., Friday 11:30 A.M.-10:30 P.M., Saturday 5:30 P.M.-10:30 P.M. Closed Sunday.

Ichiban Sushi (336 South 400 East, 801-532-7522) isn't one of those restaurants where pronunciation is half the point and the staff's arrogant attitude is exceeded only by the size of the bill. No, Ichiban Sushi is a fun, irreverent place to get some raw fish and a rare meal. I mean, how many sushi restaurants will you find in a hundred-year-old former Lutheran church? Ever been to a sushi bar with stained-glass windows, a high belfry that stretches toward the heavens, and test tubes for vases on the table? Neither have I. Ichiban is owned and operated by the husband-wife team of Clint and Peggy Whiting. She is the Japanese-trained sushi chef (one of the few Caucasian women ever to train for this in Japan); he is the host, manager, and self-professed "window washer, light bulb screwer, and all-around gofer." They started the restaurant in Park City but eventually tired of the long shoulder seasons (running a restaurant in Park City means making your year's income in six months) and moved to Salt Lake a couple of years ago. "We have geared our menu so that it's not all just hard-core sushi," said Clint. "There are a lot of easy, nonthreatening starter rolls." Even the menu is nonthreatening; Ichiban uses the ski-trail rating system (green circles, blue squares, black diamonds) to designate beginner, intermediate, advanced. On the wall facing you as you enter the former church is a large mural of happy-looking tumbling sumo wrestlers. Sit where the altar used to be and revel in the joy of heavenly sushi combinations such as the house favorite Mars roll. Save room for the wasabi ice cream, one of the few taste treats you'll ever have that simultaneously burns your mouth, makes your eyes water, and cools you off. Large groups will want to call ahead and book the balcony (where the organ would be). Reservations are a good idea. On busy nights expect to wait as much as an hour for the sushi bar. Hours: 4 P.M.-10 P.M. seven nights a week.

(continued from page 47)

have in terms of quality of life, it will debunk those erroneous stereotypes that make people think this is a one-dimensional place controlled by one religion that has restrictive alcohol laws. People will see this is an amazingly beautiful and vibrant place where people have a great time, the economy's strong, and there are shared community values in terms of keeping crime down and keeping the air and our water and our streets clean.

B.K.: *Is it in your best interest to combat the notion that it's no fun here?*

M.A.: *Oh, absolutely. As Stein Eriksen said, we lose a lot of skiers to Vail, Colorado, because of this perception regarding our liquor laws.*

B.K.: *I lived in Vail for a decade, and I can tell you the skiing is much better here.*

M.A.: *Yeah. And the fact is you can go out in Salt Lake City and have a great time. It's truly a great ski town. For some reason, people think about skiing in Utah as just going to the resorts, but the best resort area is Salt Lake City. To be able to stay in the wonderful elegance of the Grand America Hotel and then drive twenty or twenty-five minutes to the best skiing anywhere in this country is incredible.*

B.K.: *Are you a skier?*

M.A.: *I am.*

B.K.: *Good skier?*

M.A.: *Yeah, I'm a pretty fair skier. I don't get out as much as I'd like to.*

B.K.: *What do you think of the Alta-Snowbird one-pass?*

M.A.: *I've skied since I was in sixth grade, and I like the rustic separate environment of Alta. I like the fact that Alta keeps snowboards out. Not that I have anything against snowboards or snowboarders, but it's just nice to find a refuge now and again. And I also love Snowbird. I have a time-share up there. So I guess I like the separate identities. But maybe it's just a case of getting attached to the old ways.*

B.K.: *I'm really excited about it. I mean, 4,700 acres of skiable terrain!*

M.A.: *It adds a lot of variety to a ski day, but you wonder, how much can you ski in a day? There are days when I don't even stop for lunch, and I still can't cover everything I want.*

B.K.: *That's true. I'll probably end up just skiing the tram anyway. So you're a Little Cottonwood skier?*

M.A.: *I mix it up. I go all over, but I guess I don't get up to Deer Valley much.*

B.K.: *You don't like the cruisers?*

M.A.: *I don't like the prices.*

B.K.: *You pay for lift tickets?*

M.A.: *I don't take gifts.*

B.K.: *Should tourists and transplants be leery of the Mormon influence?*

M.A.: *I live here and it doesn't really impact my life one way or the*

(continued on page 51)

Incantations (159 South Main Street, 801-533-2722) serves up notable Peruvian food in a plain and simple atmosphere. If you're wondering what Peruvian food is, think Mexican with a little more soul. Try the tamales or the seviche. Hours: Monday-Thursday 11 A.M.-9:30 P.M., Friday and Saturday 11 A.M.-11 P.M.

The **Judge Café** (8 East Broadway, corner of 300 South and Main Street, 801-531-0917) was a well-known speakeasy during prohibition but today it's a place where you can breathe easy. The Judge is familiar and friendly in an old-world San Francisco sort of way. The building was constructed in 1911 and still has many of the painstakingly crafted details that made it classy back then. The hand-laid tile floor (it looks like a zillion black and white Chiclets) grounds a classically black and white retro café where you not only can get one of the best breakfasts in Salt Lake but also can view the basketball shoes of yesteryear. Owner Carole Couch has collected hundreds of the sneakers of those tall guys who play that game in their granny bloomers. She used to make players an offer they seldom refused: "Give us your old sneakers, and we'll give you a free meal." Accusations of foot fetishism notwithstanding, Couch collected more than 500 shoes, the most notable of which were from Michael Jordan and Dr. J, as well as the rookie shoe of Jazz star John Stockton. If great breakfasts and retro-cool barge-sized footwear aren't enough, consider that the Judge also has a long, low-slung espresso bar where you can get your caffeine fix and get a jump on this sleepy, largely decaf town. Serves breakfast and lunch. Hours: Monday-Friday 7 A.M.-2 P.M.

BEL MORGAN KERIG

A little bit Fifties, a little bit Samuri, Kenji offers healthy fast food with a dash of soy sauce. Downtown Salt Lake City.

Kenji's Japanese Grill (45 East 200 South, 801-519-2378) offers sit-down or drive-through service that's fast and polite. As the menu will tell you "There's no MSG, and no deep frying." This is "high-octane fuel for the body, healthy, inexpensive, and highly addictive." Whether it's takeout sushi or Kenji's teriyaki steak, the food here is stellar, priced right, and won't expand that spare tire around your middle. There's a small patio where you can chopstick your chow while you try not to feel dwarfed by the tall buildings looming over you. Kenji's is also across the street from the Gallivan Center, which is a fine place to take your lunch on a sunny day. Hours: Monday-Friday 11 A.M.-8 P.M., Saturday and Sunday 11 A.M.-9 P.M.

Koko Kitchen (702 South 300 East, 801-364-4888) is a small family-owned

(continued from page 49)

other. As you would anywhere else, you find the activities you like to do and the places you like to go, and ninety percent of the time you don't know somebody's religious affiliation. When these divisions arise, it's usually in the context of the liquor laws or some of the other silly things our legislature might do every once in a while. But go to where there's nightlife, go eat at one of our many fine outdoor restaurants, go shopping anywhere on Main Street, and you'll see there's nothing Mormon or non-Mormon about it. Salt Lake is a far more diverse community than most people think.

B.K.: What place does the gay community have in Utah?

M.A.: The gay community is incredibly strong, open, and supportive in this community. Yesterday I attended a commitment ceremony for two women. There was a big crowd with both of their families and friends. It was very touching.

B.K.: I know Salt Lake is opening up, but that doesn't lose you votes?

M.A.: Probably, but that's really not my standard. There are also several gay and lesbian clubs here that do very well.

B.K.: So the gay community does have a place in Utah and Salt Lake City?

M.A.: Yes, it's huge.

B.K.: And they're welcome?

M.A.: Yes. Absolutely. In fact, one of my first executive orders was to sign a nondiscrimination ordinance that was primarily to extend to gays and lesbians employment protections in city hiring.

B.K.: What about your favorite places? Favorite coffee shops?

We both eye my cup of coffee.

B.K.: Do you drink coffee?

M.A.: I just quit two weeks ago. I was drinking it all through the day. Now that I'm off it, I sleep better, but I'm afraid I don't have any vices anymore. It's going to be very boring.

B.K.: So where did you drink it?

M.A.: I really like the privately owned places. I like the Salt Lake Roasting Company and Cup of Joe. Those are my two favorite places.

B.K.: How about other types of joints?

M.A.: Okay, for seafood, it's the Market Street Grill. For Mexican, Red Iguana and La Frontera ... I'm going to make some enemies by doing this.

B.K.: Good.

M.A.: Okay, Sunday morning breakfast. The Park Café, Ruth's, and now the Orbit Café all have really good breakfasts. For steak you can't beat Corleone's at the Manhattan Club.

B.K.: Do you drink?

M.A. (smiling): Occasionally.

(continued on page 52)

Japanese eatery with a counter where you order and pick up great soba noodles, sushi, and rice bowls. Eat at the small tables inside, where you'll feel you're in the kitchen with the cooks, or better yet, try the sunny, grassy patio out back, where you'll dine with the birdies splashing frivolously in their fountain. Try the tofu pot stickers or the ebi udon. Many vegetarian dishes, some vegan entrées as well. Hours: Monday-Friday 11 A.M.-8 P.M., Saturday 11:30 A.M.-8 P.M. Closed Sunday.

Lamb's Grill Café (169 South Main Street, 801-364-7166) is just the ticket for a Boston boy who's homesick for some old-school East Coast flavor. A place with history, Lamb's has the feel of a Beacon Hill powerbroker's place. And well it should. For more than 60 years, the Main Street eatery has been a favorite lunch spot for bankers, politicos, and pooh-bahs of all stripes. Originally established in Logan in 1919 by Greek immigrant George P. Lamb, the restaurant moved to downtown Salt Lake City in 1939. Since then, not much has changed. You'll still be greeted by the low black marble counter with its high-backed red leather chairs. The wainscoting and the deco detailing behind the counter have that fine low-key elegance that beckons memories of a time most know only from movies like *The Sting*. Even the

(continued from page 51)

B.K.: *How about your favorite bars? Start with dive bars. Have you ever been to Burt's Tiki Lounge or the Twilite?*

M.A.: *I used to bartend at the Twilite Lounge.*

B.K.: *The mayor of Salt Lake used to be a bartender at one of the best dive bars in the city?*

M.A.: *Yeah. They had a help-wanted sign, so I went to Bob Cairo and said, "I'm here to apply for the job." I had a beard at the time and he said, "I don't hire people with beards." So I walked down to the beauty college and had them shave it off. Then I returned to the bar and said to him, "I'm back to apply for the job again." He said, "What do you mean, you're back?" I said, "I was the guy with the beard." So of course he hired me ... Boy, when you get into great night places, there are so many. Manhattan, Port O' Call, Bricks ... the problem I have with picking favorites is there are so many great places.*

B.K.: *Okay, last question: You have your fun-loving cousin coming in from New York. What's the one thing you tell him not to miss?*

M.A.: *Mmmm. It would either be a hike up Big Cottonwood Canyon ...*

B.K.: *Which one?*

M.A.: *The hike to Dog Lake, or straight up the face of Brighton. I used to train for skiing up there. Or a run up City Creek Canyon. It's mind-blowing even for people who live here that they can get that only a few blocks from the Capitol.*

At this point Mayor Anderson jumped from his chair and bolted into the outer office.

water glasses, thick and scratched by countless washings, are authentic. The table-cloths are white linen, and the baked potatoes are served in charred aluminum foil with pats of gold-wrapped butter. This is a place where single-malt Glenfiddich is drunk neat, and espresso comes in tiny, thick cups. The breakfast menu is also terrific, surprisingly inexpensive, and must be the only one in the state that features finnan haddie. Lunches are the big meal; expect suits and men of a certain bearing. Dinners attract a more diverse clientele than one would expect. The T-shirts that half the diners wear seem horribly out of place, even disrespectful, but that's common dining-out attire today. For dinner, order the lamb chops (what else?). Served up juicy with jiggly green mint jelly, they're a treat Teddy Roosevelt might have loved, and even might have had at Lamb's. Jazz or classical musicians provide the atmosphere on weekend nights. Hours: Monday-Friday 7 A.M.-9 P.M., Saturday 8 A.M.-9 P.M. Closed Sunday and holidays.

Martine (22 East 100 South, 801-363-9328) is located in a historic Utah brown-stone (made of red rock) and has high mahogany booths, large deco-style hanging lights, and an old bank vault that serves as the wine cellar. This cosmopolitan

---

M.A.: Come here. I want to show you something I put together. I reviewed the promotional materials we had just before I went to Sydney for the summer Olympic games. And they were very boring, staid, and didn't convey anything exciting about us. So I got together with the graphics guy who worked on my campaign, and in one day we whipped out this brochure.

He handed me a slick, very colorful brochure filled with lots of high-action and nightlife photographs.

M.A.: I wrote the copy for it. The main thrust of it was access. It's what makes Salt Lake City the amazing, unique place it is. No place else can claim this kind of access to so many great things within minutes of wherever you are in Salt Lake City.

B.K.: I had no idea of the extent to which we're singing the same tune. Everything you've been saying is what I've been trying to tell people.

M.A.: That's great. We need it. How do you get people to realize this really is a resort city? How do you let them know they can get to the world's best skiing in twenty minutes from great nightlife, great dining, great culture, the arts ...

B.K.: You tell them to read my book.

M.A.: Great. I'm glad you're doing it.

At which point I drank the last of my coffee and shook his hand. As I left, I fished in my pocket for some mints. That mayor was a hell of a nice guy, and a potent force for change, but his coffee sure was awful. No wonder he quit drinking the stuff. **U**

The Oasis Café and Golden Braid bookstore provide a calming island in a sea of tumult.

eatery has the elegance of candlelight, a single gold rose at each intimate booth, and a savory tapas menu. But what do you call a place like this? The folks at Martine call it a "retro Euro café serving modern Mediterranean entrées and new-world tapas." I'd call it the best romantic dinner spot in the city. It's also a place where, if you order off the tapas menu, you can savor many delightful dishes and get out for far less than you'd spend at a more traditional restaurant. Hours: Monday-Friday lunch 11:30 A.M.-2 P.M., Tuesday-Saturday dinner 5 P.M.-10 P.M.

Metropolitan (173 West Broadway, 801-364-3472) is the most L.A.-style, upmarket restaurant in Salt Lake City. It nails every detail and turns a night of dining into a vacation rather than merely a meal. The industrial cement walls in the foyer are hung heavily with awards and plaques. The food is terrific, and the service is professional and quite urban-hip. The design of the restaurant, with its sweeping banquettes and smooth shapes crafted from a blunt industrial building, is impressive. Many call the Metropolitan the best restaurant in Salt Lake. Although I recognize its brilliance, it reminds me too much of a bad year I spent living in L.A. Hours: Tuesday-Thursday 5:30 P.M.-10 P.M., Friday and Saturday 5:30 P.M.-11 P.M.

Oasis (151 South 500 East, 801-322-0404) is one of the most aptly named places you'll find. To ascend the steps leading from the sidewalk up into the fountain-centered courtyard is to enter a bastion of calm, counterculture tranquillity. Serving healthy and imaginative foods in an easy and open atmosphere, Oasis is not especially inexpensive, but it's worth the price to have a glass of wine and a simple but excellent vegetarian meal. Oasis also has a café area where you can sip a coffee and admire the high-quality artwork shown there. The restaurant shares the same chilled-out space with the spiritual Golden Braid Books, which in my mind makes it the perfect place to feed your face and your soul. Menus change with the seasons. Hours: Monday-Friday 7 A.M.-9:30 P.M., Saturday 8 A.M.-10 P.M., Sunday 8 A.M.-9:30 P.M.

The Other Place (4693 Broadway, 801-521-6567) has a history as a place where downtown businessmen used to meet. Serving breakfast, lunch, and dinner, it's a place where you might get a gut-bomb breakfast (pancake sandwiches) or a fat Greek salad or see the restaurant's most regular regulars, "Trolley" Wally Wright, who created Trolley Square. Hours: Monday-Saturday 11 A.M. -7 P.M., Sunday 8 A.M.-10 P.M.

Park Café (604 East 1300 South, 801-487-1670) is a light, bright, black-and-white-linoleum-floor type of place. You can dine healthy (egg-white-and-chicken scrambler) or heavy-duty (biscuits and gravy). Fortunately, Liberty Park is right across the street, so you can walk off the calories. The patio is the best spot, as the inside gets loud when the place fills up. The service is not lightning fast, and the espresso machine is eternally broken, so don't bother with that. Hours: 7 A.M.-2:30 P.M. seven days a week, Tuesday-Saturday 5 P.M.-9 P.M. Closed Sunday and Monday night. Breakfast only weekend days.

Red Iguana (736 West North Temple, 801-322-1489) is a kitschy, old-school Mexican restaurant that serves the best smothered burrito in town. The huevos rancheros also rule. This place is popular with the Hispanic and downtown yuppie communities alike. Plus, you can get a cold beer with your lunch. Since it's also on the way to the airport, it's the best place to mow down before you get on the big silver bird. Hours: Monday-Thursday 11 A.M.-9 P.M., Friday and Saturday noon-10 P.M., Sunday noon-9 P.M.

Rio Grande Café (270 South Rio Grande Street, 801-364-3302) serves great Mexican food in a raucous, fun atmosphere inside the old train station. From the margaritas to the massive "biggest enchilada" to the carnitas, it's hard to get off on the wrong track here. Hours: Monday-Thursday lunch 11 A.M.-2:30 P.M., Friday and Saturday lunch 11:30 A.M.-2:30 P.M.; Monday-Thursday dinner 5 P.M.-9:30 P.M., Sunday dinner 4 P.M.-9 P.M.

Sage's Café (473 East 300 South, 801-322-3790, www.sagescafe.com) is an old house turned into a hip little 100 percent vegan restaurant. Wednesday is vegan pizza night, and Thursday is Taste of the World night. Scott Evans, who works there as a waiter, also publishes the *Wasatch Front Vegetarian Dining Guide* (www.vegetarianvoice.com). Sage's serves good beer, espresso, and some wine, but don't ask for cream in your coffee. The woman at the table next to ours did and was rankled by the soy-only alternative. Hours: Wednesday-Thursday 11 A.M.-10 P.M., Friday 11 A.M.-11 P.M., Saturday 9 A.M.-11 P.M., Sunday 9 A.M.-10 P.M. Closed Monday and Tuesday.

Urban Bistro (216 East 500 South, 801-322-4101) is one long room with cement floors, pastel walls hung with surrealistic art, and simple yellow pine chairs. The style is straightforward: You'll come in with the lunch crowd, line up, order, and then take a seat. Open for a half dozen years, the Urban Bistro is worker-chic, which means the place might be playing Leonard Cohen on the stereo, serving angel hair and salmon, and filled with young button-downs but probably not with suits. Hours: Monday-Friday 11 A.M.-3 P.M. Closed Saturday and Sunday.

COFFEEHOUSES AND CAFÉS

Beans and Brews (906 South 500 East, 801-521-5221) is a well-established purveyor of beans and bean juice that has lately attracted a hipster-looking early-20s crowd. The many stools and chairs assembled in the parking lot are the favored perches, but I prefer the green velvet couch in the cave under the big faux red rock arch. Hours: Monday-Thursday 5:30 A.M.-10 P.M., Friday 5:30 A.M.-11 P.M., Saturday 6:30 A.M.-11 P.M., Sunday 6:30 A.M.-10 P.M.

Cup of Joe (353 West 200 South, 801-363-8322) was the leader in the refurbishment of this downtown warehouse district, and owner Joe Pitti said it wasn't an easy go. "I grew up in Brooklyn and I've lived in Hell's Kitchen, so I wasn't afraid of anything Salt Lake City had," he recalled. "But the stuff I saw here was a whole 'nother program ... you certainly wouldn't believe you were in Salt Lake."

Now, six years later, his patrons say the same thing: These days, "you wouldn't believe you're in Salt Lake" is used as the highest praise. What was once a rubber factory, then a junkie and heroin-dealer haven, is now a sprawling café with constellations of antique coffee pots hanging from the ceiling. Pitti, a short, hyperkinetic man with a shaved head and a fast wit, not only roasts all the beans and runs the shop but also tours nationwide in a one-man show called *Psychic Driveby*. He is also one of a couple dozen local actors who appear regularly in plays at the Salt Lake Acting Company and at Pioneer Theater. Pitti's artistic bent has also led to having live music three or four nights a week and a poetry slam on the third Saturday of each month. The slam has been known to attract upward

Cup of Joe offers a casual and cool place to get a cup.

of 200 people. Hours: Monday-Friday 7 A.M.-midnight, Saturday 8 A.M.-midnight, Sunday 9 A.M.-8 P.M.

Salt Lake Roasting Co. (320 East 400 South, 801-363-7572) is the kind of big, airy place where you feel comfortable flipping open your laptop and tapping away (even plugging in is okay). Filling a large two-story brick building, the Roasting Company roasts its own beans, serves good quiches, salads, and sandwiches, and is run in the efficient manner of a place that's been around long enough to work out the kinks. Its tall windows face north, which keeps the interior dim, cool, and just the way a coffee shop should be. Long before Starbucks and the other purveyors of bean-water moved in, the Roasting Company became, and still is, the hub for Salt Lake coffee achievers. Hours: Monday-Saturday 6:45 A.M.-midnight. Closed Sunday.

Undergrounds Coffee (344 South State Street, 801-322-0769) serves Café Lavazza coffee, vegan and vegetarian food, and savory soups to a serious hip-hop beat. Attached to the Uprok skateboard shop, Undergrounds is not just a coffee shop; it's an ongoing celebration of street. From the poetry slams on the last Thursday of every month to the open-mike freestyle event every Friday, Undergrounds is a vortex for rare vinyl and all things hip-hop, skate, and street in Salt Lake. Hours: Monday-Friday 7 A.M.-11 A.M., Saturday 10 A.M.-1 A.M., Sunday 1 P.M.-7 P.M. ("sometimes").

CAFFEINE, STRAIGHT UP
Java Jo's (corner of E Street and 1st Avenue, 801-532-2899) offers up drive-through coffee with a chocolate-covered espresso bean on the lid. Chomp, then slurp for max effect. Hours: Monday-Friday 5:30 A.M.-7 P.M., Saturday 7 A.M.-5 P.M., Sunday 8 A.M.-4 P.M.

HOTELS

When I was 23, I enjoyed sleeping in youth hostels or motels where you had to bring your own soap (and Lysol). As long as it was cheap, I liked it. In those days, I'd skimp on accommodations and splurge on meals and drinks. Since then I've reprioritized my funds somewhat, and the novelty of cockroaches and hearing other people snore through paper-thin walls has pretty much dissipated. Today, I prefer to spend a few more bucks for a comfortable place to sleep and fewer on drinks. Dinners I still will throw down for. So, the two hotels that I'll recommend for downtown Salt Lake City are not the cheapest by any means, but rather the ones that I feel give real value for your money and provide a memorable experience. For a comprehensive list, call 1-800-847-5810 or go to www.visitsaltlake.com.

The **Grand America Hotel** (555 South Main Street, 800-621-4505, www.grandamerica.com) has grandeur on such an extreme scale that it rivals Las Vegas' Bellagio Hotel. Who can resist such magnificence? Not I. As the days ticked off to the 2002 Olympic Opening Ceremonies, platoons of workers lugged and craned massive chunks of marble and granite to all corners of the new Grand America Hotel.

Nonetheless, the hotel was opened and teeming with activity. We checked in and walked through its massive lobby, only half of which was done. The other half, which was slated to be a café, had wheelbarrows and ladders parked in it. Checking in behind us were the Dallas Mavericks pro basketball team. Although these men were giants, you can be sure not one of them had to duck once in their stay at the Grand. This place is built in a style that is not only grand but authentic. Our suite was so soundproofed that we couldn't even hear a jack hammer clattering away seven floors below our window. The reason for the last-minute scramble and inaudible workers is that zillionaire owner Earl Holding is building a 100 percent top-drawer hotel (the night we visited, he told me with pride that all the carpeting in the hotel is hand-sewn and made of English wool). All the bathrooms are done up in Italian marble. The walls of the hotel are draped with massive, rich tapestries. From the ceilings hang 51 hand-blown glass chandeliers suitable for the palace at Versailles. Every room has two 30-inch televisions and data ports for high-speed Internet access, French doors leading to the bedroom, sumptuous linens, plush robes, two-line phones, personal safes, and ironing amenities. Room service is 24 hours. With rates that range from $249 to $4,500 (for the Presidential Suite), this is definitely the place that will slim the fat wallet, but it's worth it.

Hotel Monaco (15 West 200 South, 801-595-0000, www.monaco-saltlakecity.com) is a boutique hotel that was created out of an old bank. This is a place where marble floors meet stuffed velvet, where art deco and Victorian share the same bedroom. The design has so many different elements—from art deco to classical to Victorian to film noir to mod—that it constitutes a visual stew that is perhaps unlike anything you'll ever see. Its overblown style is at once elegant, ironic, and edgy. Don't get me wrong, it's pleasing and fun, perhaps because it seems to break every design rule in the book with absolute élan. For all its verve in design, however, the Hotel Monaco is perhaps the most accommodating hotel you'll ever stay in. For one thing, it's pet friendly, which means Fido can share your suite. And if you don't have a pet? The Hotel Monaco will provide one for you in the form of a live goldfish in every room. This is a nice touch. "It's part of our guppy love program," said sales manager Kelly Spence. We got attached to our goldfish, named him Lucca Brazzi because he "slept with the fishes," and got separation anxiety when we had to leave him. If it's not Bowzer you need but rather doors that don't require you to bow down to walk through, the Hotel Monaco also has rooms for you. With an entire floor of tall rooms that feature tall doors, vanities, and extra-long beds, the Monaco has become another favorite of visiting NBA teams. The concierge can arrange something for you called the Xtreme program that includes mountain biking, hiking, rock climbing, and other mountain adventures. Every room has a Sony TV, fax, high-speed Internet access, a Sony dream machine instead of a clock radio, a stereo, and a minibar that comes complete with Oreos and Pringles. The turn-down service doesn't leave stale mints on your pillow; the staffers leave Snickers bars. Now that's my kind of hotel. Rates range from $99 to $325.

SHOPPING
BOOKS

Golden Braid Books (151 South 500 East, 801-322-1162) is a softly lit New Age and spiritual bookstore where you can sit and read amid the gurgle and hush of fountains and chime music. From the Kama Sutra to Christian mystics to the Dalai Lama, Golden Braid offers a terrific selection of spiritual and self-help books that always make me feel better just looking at them (simply knowing there's so much help out there buoys my spirits). You can also rent yoga or massage videos, buy a Buddha or a fountain, or listen to meditation music on the listening station. Golden Braid shares the building with the Oasis Café. Together, the two make for the kind of wonderfully serene and calm atmosphere that's rare. Hours: Monday-Saturday 10 A.M.-9 P.M., Sunday 10 A.M.-6 P.M.

Sam Weller's Bookstore: New, Used, and Rare Books (254 South Main Street, 801-328-2586 or 800-333-SAMW, www.samwellers.com) is a huge independent bookstore in the tradition of New York's Shakespeare and Company or Denver's Tattered Cover. The store was born in the early 1920s when German immigrant Gustav Weller, who was at the time running a used-furniture store, encountered someone with a large collection of used Mormon books. He made an offer that wasn't refused, and shortly thereafter, his small furniture shop became Zion's Bookstore. The bookstore opened August 11, 1929, mere weeks before the big stock market crash and the onset of the Great Depression. With the whole family pitching in to keep the business going, the store scraped its way through the depression and World War II by selling a collection of predominantly Mormon books.

After serving in the war, Sam Weller came home and took over the store in January 1946. Like his father before him, he ran it as a family business. His wife Lila did the bookkeeping and much of the organization of an ever-growing inventory. In 1961, Zion's Bookstore was moved to its current location at 254 South Main Street, and a year later son Tony was born. Named for a character in Dickens's *Pickwick Papers*, young Tony grew up between the shelves. As times changed, so did Sam Weller's Bookstore; it gradually evolved into a general-interest bookstore with a strong inventory of Mormon tomes.

Although the bookstore today is known simply as Sam Weller's Books, old-timers still call it Zion's Bookstore. As Tony grew up, so did the selection of books. In 1988 he took over the management, and like his father and grandfather before him, he soon married and brought his wife to work in the store. To meet him today is to meet a man who is well-read and effusive in expressing his fiercely independent views. The result? Sam Weller's now carries what may be the most diverse range of books of any bookseller in the country. Where else would you find an extensive and rare Mormon collection mere feet from a large gay and lesbian section and an even larger occultist collection?

The store has more than a million books in its inventory, six miles of shelf space, and offers a slick on-line reference and rare-book-buying service. The place is not the most orderly of bookstores, but don't be dismayed—it's staffed by 35 book lovers, 10 of whom have more than a decade of bookselling experience. My favorite haunts are the rare-book rooms upstairs that lie temptingly behind an iron safe door and a steel-barred jail-like gate. Ask the staff to be let in; it's worth it. Inhale the fusty aroma of the ancient wisdom of old books, be enveloped by the hushed calm of the vault, or buy a first edition *Wizard of Oz*. Open Monday-Saturday 10 A.M.-8 P.M. Closed Sunday.

MARKETS AND PROVISIONERS

Rico Mexican Market (779 South 500 East, 801-533-9923) is housed in a recently refurbished little brick building across the street from Artesian Well Park. Rico makes its own brand of tortillas, tamales, rellenos, burritos, seviche, and enchiladas. If you're a Mexican food aficionado but have tired of going out every time you need a fix, Rico is your place. Pick up excellent and fresh Mexican and take it home to eat or freeze. Rico also has all sorts of Mexican ingredients and provisions that you won't find this side of Tijuana. Hours: Monday-Saturday 10 A.M.-7:30 A.M. Closed Sunday.

Salt Lake City's proximity to recreation is unrivaled. Here Jim Conway rides singletrack near Sugarhouse.

SPORTS SHOPS

Wasatch Touring (702 East 100 South, 801-359-9361) is owned by brothers Charlie and Dwight Butler, who have run this great neighborhood multisports store for 29 years. From climbing gear to camping, from backcountry ski gear to mountain bikes, from kayaks to kiddie bike strollers, this is a place to buy or rent top-line gear from guys who know what they're doing. The store has a wide selection of telemark gear and Utah outdoor guidebooks. And last on the list but first in your heart, Lou Lodefink, one of the most colorful characters in Salt Lake, wrenches on bikes, boards, and boats there. Hours: Monday-Saturday 9 A.M.-7 P.M., open Sunday 10 A.M.-6 P.M. December through March. Closed Sundays in summer.

UNIQUE BOUTIQUES/VINTAGE CLOTHING AND FURNITURE

There are, of course, many, many stores and shops in downtown Salt Lake City, but I've picked out a few that will make you say "I didn't expect to find this in Utah."

Grunts and Postures (779 East 300 South, 801-521-3202) is a vintage clothing and import store that has Jell-O molds screwed to the facade of the building. Then it gets weirder and more eclectic: a lot of hand-carved Indonesian art, hip retro clothes (both new and used), and fun selections of hats and shoes that'll have you stepping out in style. "Thank goodness there's a store like this in Utah," one woman shopper told me. "I found this place six years ago, and I wouldn't have survived here without it." As for the name, I tried to get to the bottom of it but got only some half-baked story about how it was really describing rock 'n' roll. Doesn't matter a damn bit; the place is cool, cheap, and a must-shop. Hours: Monday-Saturday 10 A.M.-7 P.M., Sunday noon-6 P.M.

Heavy Metal Shop (63 Exchange Place, 801-467-7071) delivers just what its name promises: lots of heavy metal music. The store not only sells the music and T-shirts but also has hosted signings with such bands as Alice in Chains, Primus, and Slayer (the latter even featured the shop on the cover of its *Divine Intervention* album). Established in 1987, Heavy Metal has all the black T-shirts and rebel discs you could want, but it also carries a surprisingly complete selection of punk (from Black Flag on up). "A lot of people have the wrong idea about my shop," said owner Kevin Kirk. "They think my customers are drug addicts, but they're not. They spend all their money on music; there's nothing left for drugs." Kirk, who has a wife and two children and neither drinks, does drugs, nor smokes, said he was ushered out of the Sugarhouse area as part of an effort to sterilize the neighborhood. Perhaps it was the music, but more likely it was T-shirts that read "Too drunk to f***." Whatever the case, the Heavy Metal Shop is not a place you'd ever drift into from the mall. Hours: Monday-Saturday 11 A.M.-7 P.M.

Manhattan Loft (2233 South 700 East, 801-466-5577, www.manhattanloft.com) is the hippest place to buy the kind of cool furniture for urban- and suburban-style living that you see in movie versions of East Village lofts or in the pages of *Surface*, *Metropolis*, *W*, or *Totem* magazines. From Chameleon furniture to Malibu (hip retro storage furniture made in Sweden) to Corbusier-designed pieces to more than 10,000 pieces of artwork, Manhattan Loft has what you need to look as if you're living in a hipper style than found on the *Friends* set. Hours: Monday-Friday 11 A.M.-7 P.M., Saturday 10 A.M.-6 P.M., Sunday noon-4 P.M.

Mischievous Cards & Gifts (559 South 300 West, 801-530-3100) offers ribald and raunchy cards, gifts, and all those naughty adult gizmos and gadgets you'd never expect to find in a Utah boutique. Hours: Monday-Saturday 10 A.M.-7 P.M. Closed Sunday.

Nativo (353 West 200 South, 801-531-8555), which is next door to Cup of Joe in the Artspace Rubber Company building, is an artful store that my wife assures me is " a seriously cool woman's store." The clothes, the shoes, and even the eclectic mix of housewares are hipper and more "designer-ly" than you'd expect to find this side of New York's fashion district. Where else are you going to find a persimmon tea set and, in the same joint, a gown to wear to a black-tie affair? Hours: Monday-Saturday 11:30 A.M.-7 P.M. Closed Sunday.

THE FREE AND THE FREAKY

Artesian Well Park (500 East 800 South) is an oasis that beckons the thirsty traveler, or at least a cool spot to get free mineral water. World cultures known for their longevity all have one thing in common: high mineral content in their water. Coincidence? I think not. So every chance I get, I fill some jugs at the Artesian Well Park. Not really much of a park, rather more of a nicely bricked corner, this isn't a place you go to chuck the disc for your Frisbee dog. Rather, it's the place to get free water out of three spigots from which flows perhaps the sweetest, most highly mineralized water you'll find anywhere. Will it make you live longer? Who knows?

MASSAGE AND MEDITATION

Back in 1989, Mary Nickle's Time Out Associates was the first business to request a Yellow Pages listing under the heading "meditation instruction." Today there are five such listings and the same number under massage schools. The Yellow Pages also has two and a half pages devoted to therapeutic massage. I use the term "therapeutic massage" because in Utah, unlike in some other states, the term "massage" is not used interchangeably with "escort service" or any sort of potential sex-for-hire arrangement (there are 34 listings in the Yellow Pages under "escort services" for those interested in researching that sort of thing). No, in Utah, massage is licensed, therapeutic, up-and-up, and widespread. Here are just a few of the many massage and meditation centers in Salt Lake City. For more info on this sort of thing, pick up a copy of the *Catalyst* magazine (801-363-1505).

Healing Mountain Massage School (455 South 300 East, 801-573-2230) teaches everything from hot-stone massage to magnet therapy. It also gives its students hands-on training, which means inexpensive day spa services (such as oriental hot-rock therapy, salt glo scrubs, and herbal body wraps) and massages for you and me. Rates run from $15 to $30 depending on the treatment and are by appointment, seven days a week.

Kanzeon Zen Center Utah (1274 East South Temple, 801-328-8414, www.zencenterutah.org) teaches ongoing meditation classes, Zen painting, and tai chi to all levels. The center is run by Genpo Merzel Roshi, one of the foremost Zen masters in the country. He's also the spiritual leader of the White Plum Asanga, which is the largest Zen lineage in the United States. Roshi has developed a teaching system called the Big Mind process that is more readily understood by Westerners than traditional Zen teaching systems. Hours: 8 A.M.-7 P.M. seven days a week.

The **Meditation Center** (1268 South Temple, 801-364-1224) has daily meditations Monday-Friday at 7 A.M. and 7:30 A.M. and an introduction to meditation class Tuesday evenings at 7:30 P.M. Call for information on classes and workshops.

Red Lotus School and Urgyen Samten Ling Meditation Center (345 West Pierpont Avenue, 801-355-6375, www.redlotusschool.com) teaches meditation, qi gong, and butoh as well as tai chi and kung fu. Call for information about classes.

Sacred Sweat Lodge Ceremonies (1324 East 5985 South, 801-272-4372) is run by Reverend Anne Clock and holds ancient Native American ceremonies at the Womb of the Earth sweat lodge. Open 7 P.M. on full moon nights.

Soma Yoga Studio (625 South State Street, 801-461-0083, www.somastudio.com) teaches ongoing classes in Ashtanga-style yoga, which combines deep breathing and alignment awareness into a meditative unfolding process. Open seven days a week. Call for class times.

Time Out Associates (440 South 700 East, Suite 102, 801-530-0633) is run by Mary Nickle, a Reiki master, graduate of IntraScope Center for Energy Studies, and 25-year veteran of studying and teaching meditation techniques that focus on the spirit's integration with the physical body. In addition to meditation classes and instruction in the arts of energy healing and clairvoyance, Time Out offers first-rate massage therapy, aura readings, and energy balancing in a surprisingly simple, non-woo-woo atmosphere. It's set in a comfortable, neutral-feeling place where you don't have to wear crystals or patchouli to feel at home. Time Out is in the basement of an office building that's shared by architects, dentists, and lawyers. Call for appointments or class schedules.

MOVIE THEATERS

Brewvies Cinema Pub (677 South 200 West, 801-355-5500) won't get the new movie releases quickly, but it may be worth waiting to see them here. Where else can you chill on a couch, drain a Guinness, and eat a burrito all while watching the big screen? Salt Lake's only movie bar is one of my favorite places in town. Go before the show and shoot some pool, or just chill and unwind. Another unexpected bonus: since you must

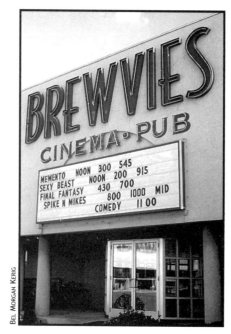

Brewvies Cinema Pub is the best place to watch a flick. Where else can you wash down your popcorn with a pint of Guinness?

be 21 to get in, you won't have teenagers playing grab-ass while you're trying to watch the film. Brewvies has three screens and tends to cater to real film buffs. Recently I watched *A Clockwork Orange* and was treated to an after-show talk by lead actor Malcolm MacDowell. Hours: Doors open at 11 A.M. seven days a week. Closing after the last show.

THEATER

You might not think that Salt Lake City, the capital of wide ties and sensible shoes, would have much of a theater scene. You can search the downtown crowd and never see a beret or a black mock turtleneck. Yet costumes deceive. There is a thriving theater community in Salt Lake, with a surprising depth of offerings.

Kilby Court (741 South 330 West, 801-320-9887) is as underground as you're going to get in Utah. Situated on a dead-end cul-de-sac in a rundown warehouse section of town, Kilby Court encompasses two old automotive garage buildings and a courtyard surrounded by chain-link and slat fence. Run by Mike Snider and Phil Sherburne, Kilby Court hosts a true garage band and avant-garde art scene. But don't expect some swank, refurbished Greenwich Village loft. This is a full-on garage. Sit around the barrel fire and tiki torches in the courtyard and you'll feel you're in the nightclub that Sanford and Son would've opened. Don't let the humble surroundings fool you, however, because these guys are passionate about their mission. "We're not here to make money," said Snider. "We're here to give small bands and small artists exposure." And indeed, some of the bands that play between the cinderblock walls here are pretty damn good (albeit raw). Expect to see bands such as Nogin Toboggin, the B-Movie Rats, and Dashboard Confessional. Cover charge is usually $5, and no liquor is allowed. The place sells Cokes and bottled water. Most shows are all ages. Call the hot line for a recording. Open year-round.

Off Broadway Theater (272 Main Street, 801-355-4OBT) features parodies, comedies, and improvs in a century-old theater in the middle of downtown. The improv troupe is called Laughing Stock, and the members are wonderfully funny and quick-witted. Although this is Utah, don't expect the shows to be tame, but by the same token, don't expect humor in the style of Andrew Dice Clay. If the productions were movies, they'd be rated PG-13. Don't worry about sitting in the front; they won't pick on you unless, of course, you ask for it. Shows are Thursday night 7:30 P.M., Friday 7:30 P.M. and 10 P.M., Saturday 7 P.M., 9 P.M., and 11 P.M. Tickets are $10, $8, and $6; all tickets are $5 on Thursday.

Rose Wagner Performing Arts Center (138 West Broadway, 801-355-ARTS, toll-free ticketing 888-451-2787, www.arttix.org) has two theaters, including the Jeanné Wagner Theater. This new theater hosts *The Vagina Monologues* if that gives you any idea of its fare. Days and hours vary depending on which shows are playing.

The **Salt Lake Acting Company** (168 West 500 North, 801-363-0526, www.salt-lakeactingcompany.org) is a 30-year-old independent theater company devoted to producing unconventional, highly charged new plays. It is the best, most adventurous, alternative theater this side of SoHo. I'm not kidding. This theater has some serious *cojones*. Based in an old Mormon ward house built in 1890, SLAC not only is as far away from conservative doctrine as it could get; it also has no fear of lampooning sacred cows. Every year the company puts on a show called *Saturday's Voyeur* that began as a send-up of a play called *Saturday's Warrior*, which was sort of a Mormon *Godspell* (some thirty years ago). Though today's *Voyeur* has nothing to do with *Warrior*, it has kept the original *Voyeur* name and tone. In the play, everything Utah is fair game for serious and sidesplitting satire. This annual attraction has become something of a comedic almanac of life in Utah and is SLAC's annual fundraiser. The most interesting of SLAC's theater, however, may be its New Play Sounding Series. Four times a year, the Sounding Series stages readings of unfinished works before a live audience. After the reading, the playwright takes the stage and discusses the play with the audience. The Sounding Series not only gives a rare and intimate glimpse into the creative process but also provides valuable input to the creative team putting on the plays. And the price is right; it's free.

The finished works you'll see at SLAC are also far from conventional. Expect to be rocked by the acting, writing, and overall verve of SLAC productions. I have been particularly impressed by the hard-hitting *White People* and *Freedomland*, two plays that take off the gloves and come right at you. Other plays SLAC has staged are *Angels in America, Three Tall Women,* and *All in the Timing*.

For the 2002 Olympics, SLAC commissioned more than a dozen Utah writers to explore, confirm, and celebrate their connections to Utah and the West. In an evening designed to reflect the inherent but largely ignored cultural diversity within Utah, SLAC will weave together a series of quirky monologues and thoughtful reflections on life in the West.

The building houses three theaters, a 50-seat hall downstairs, a 100-seat chapel theater, and the 200-seat main stage. Open year-round. Call for show times.

SPORTS

When you think Utah and sports, you probably will come up with the Utah Jazz, which of course plays high-level hoops in the NBA. If your opinion of Utahans is that they are a quiet, conservative lot, just attend a Jazz game. The Delta Center is rated the loudest stadium in the NBA, so bring your earplugs and throat lozenges. There are, however, a handful of other, lesser-known sports teams in Salt Lake City that deliver even more bang for the buck than the mighty Jazz.

The **Stingers** (77 West 1300 South, 801-485-3800, www.stingersbaseball.com) are the Northern Division champion farm team for major-league baseball's Anaheim Angels. This surprisingly talented AAA team plays in what may be the most beautiful ballpark you'll ever see. From behind home plate, you look out over the crisp and bright green grass of the field to the towering beauty of the Wasatch Front mountain range as the setting sun turns the sky purple and the peaks rose. Without the blown-up salaries and egos found in the majors, Stingers baseball is real baseball, American baseball, *Field of Dreams* baseball. There's an amazing purity and unhurried grace to a Stingers game. Here are players who hit, run, and field not for big bucks but for the love of the game—and for you. Baseball played this way is American poetry. Stingers 84-year-old owner Joe Buzas, who has worked in baseball for 61 years, says "it's the best entertainment value in the world." With the most expensive ticket at $8 (seniors and students pay $5, and kids get in for $4), he may be right. Buzas started his baseball career as a shortstop for the 1945 New York Yankees and has "been making his living from his hobby ever since." You can feel the love that both he and his daughter, who now helps him run the team, have for the game in virtually every nook of the park. From the kid's playland behind the center-field wall to the between-inning special attractions to the seventh-inning stretch, during which you might listen to a local politician or local grade schoolers sing "Take Me Out to the Ball Game," there's a consistently genuine tone that permeates every aspect of a night at the park. Perhaps that's because Joe never misses a game. Look for him in the right corner of his box, behind home plate. All in all, I'd agree with Joe; a Stingers game on a warm summer night is the best entertainment value in Salt Lake. The season runs from April until September, and home stands tend to be a week at a time with games every night.

The **Utah Grizzlies** (3200 South Decker Lake Drive, West Valley City, 801-988-8000 or 801-988-PUCK, www.utahgrizz.com) are the International Hockey League farm team of the NHL's Dallas Stars. Playing games in the E Center, the Grizzlies were the Denver Grizzlies until 1995 when the squad moved to Salt Lake City. Expect to see a talented team of up-and-comers play a crisp, fast-paced style of hockey. Most of these players are hoping to move up to the NHL or to earn their way back up to the bigs. They dig hard and they hit. Although you'd expect to see lots of fights as guys try to earn their stripes, Grizz games are surprisingly clean affairs. Beer is available. The box office is open Monday-Friday 10 A.M.-6 P.M. and Saturday 10 A.M.-4 P.M. Tickets are also available at all Smith's Tix locations. Game times: Monday-Thursday 7 P.M., Friday and Saturday 7:30 P.M., Sunday 5 P.M.

The **Utah Starzz** (301 West South Temple, 801-325-STAR, www.wnba.com/starzz) are the state's WNBA professional women's basketball team. Here's a chance to see good hoop without all the trash talking and poor sportsmanship of the NBA. The women play at the Delta Center from May through August and tickets are always available on game day.

NIGHTLIFE
BREWERIES AND BREW PUBS

Red Rock Brewing Company (254 South 200 West, 801-521-7446, www.redrock-brewingcompany.com) is the best place to go before a Jazz game or any night after work. This nonintimidating tavern is a good place to socialize, watch a game, or eat a surprisingly good meal (the food is better than you'll find at most suds shops). Perhaps that's why in October 2000 it was named National Brewpub of the Year by the National Brewpub Association. It's one of the few spots that has both a tavern and restaurant liquor license. Because the section of the restaurant next to the bar has a tavern license, you can sit at the bar and drink beer without ordering food. The rest of the restaurant operates under a restaurant liquor license, so as long as you have the "intent to eat," you can order wine, beer, or liquor. Red Rock brews not only beer but also root beer, orange soda, and cream soda; kids groove on this. Seating 270 people, the place is large and always busy but low-key. Open seven days a week from 11 A.M. Sunday–Thursday it serves food until 11 P.M. and closes at midnight. Friday and Saturday food until midnight, closes 1 A.M.

Squatters (147 West Broadway, 801-363-2739) is a brass-and-fern-type of brew pub that serves good sandwiches, pastas, and a solid Sunday brunch. The patio out back is a great spot to sip a cool one on a summer night. It's right across the street from the Rose Wagner Performing Arts Center, which makes it a fine place for a pre- or postshow pint. Hours: Monday–Friday 11:30 A.M.–1 A.M., Saturday 10:30 A.M.–1 A.M., Sunday 10:30 A.M.–midnight.

Uinta Brewery (389 West 1700 South, 801-467-0909) will give tours that end with free sampling and the chance to buy beer by the half gallon (called a growler) or six-pack, or T-shirts, hats, and such stuff. Uinta offers the state's top-selling craft-brewed beer: Cutthroat (Utah's state fish) Pale Ale. Both the Cutthroat and King's Peak Porter recently won gold medals at the Great American Beer Festival in Denver. Tap Room hours: Monday–Friday 9 A.M.–5:30 P.M., Saturday noon-5 P.M. Tours of the brewery are by appointment. Saturday is the best day for a tour.

SPORTS BARS

Iggy's Sports Grill (677 South 200 West, 801-532-9999) has three satellite dishes that serve 12 TVs and a big screen, 21 beers on tap, and a full restaurant liquor license. Whether you didn't get tickets to the Jazz or you want to see your home team play hockey or World Cup soccer, the boys at Iggy's will find it for you. Decked out nicely in cherry wood, brass, and a lot of green, Iggy's has the clean, well-lit feel of a bank with bat-and-ball memorabilia. The food is sports-bar good, and the clientele is passionate about living *la vita sporto*. Don't bother trying to watch anything but college football on Saturdays during the season, and don't be surprised to find a couple dozen fans all wearing team jerseys and hats to the bar. Hours: Monday–Thursday 11:30 A.M.–10:30 P.M., Friday and Saturday 11:30 A.M.–11 P.M., Sunday 11:30 A.M.–9 P.M.

Red Rock Brewing Company (254 South 200 West, 801-521-7446, www.redrock-brewingcompany.com). See entry in the Breweries section.

MARTINIS AND MANHATTANS

Club Bambara (202 South Main Street, 801-363-5454) is an upscale nook located in the chic Hotel Monaco. Have a merlot or a martini in a romantic vibe that's perfect for after the theater. One caveat: The place is small and smoking is allowed, so you'll have to wash or dry-clean that favorite sweater or blouse the next day. Private club. Hours: 5 P.M.–1 A.M. seven days a week.

Kristauf's Social Club (16 West Market Street, 801-366-9490) is a small martini bar and professionals' party place. A mix of suits and students, this place packs 'em in on Friday and Saturday nights. Private club. Hours: Monday-Saturday 4:30 P.M.-2 A.M. Closed Sunday.

DIVES

There are times—and we've all known them—when you're just damn sick of being good. This is especially true in this city of sunshine and Saints. What to do when you're feeling like this? Find a good dive and grab a cold one. It's cheaper than Prozac, and if you pick the right place, you'll soon realize your life ain't so bad after all. Salt Lake has many such haunts. All of them have either very small windows or none at all, so you won't have to worry about being seen, except by all those other beer guzzlers who are just as down as you are. Here are a few classic dives:

Bar-X Inn (155 East 200 South, 801-532-9114) isn't pretty, but it is a dark place to escape from the brightness of Salt Lake. Eat a knockwurst sandwich, hunch over your beer, and wait for the world to change. Staff members answer the phone "the legendary Bar X." So what's "legendary" about the place? "Well, they didn't start letting women in until the mid-1970s," said manager Linda Anderson. "We didn't even get a ladies rest room until 1984." Does that make it a gay bar? "No, just the opposite," said Anderson. "This is a men's bar with the accent on men." Which means you can be sensitive somewhere else. During the day, the crowd is what Anderson called "colorful." I'd call it a rough crowd of blue-collar beer drinkers who don't speak the King's English but will welcome a geek reporter into their midst like a long-lost brother. Drunks can be that way sometimes. The nighttime crowd is a different story, as the daytime drinkers run out of gas and make room for a more collegiate crowd. On the whole, said Anderson, "it's a bouillabaisse of humanity." I couldn't have said it better myself. Hours: 10 A.M.-1 A.M. seven days a week.

Deseret Lounge (323 South Main Street, 801-595-7003) is a good place to have a humble beer. There's not a damn thing special about this place, which in itself makes it special. It's not freighted with any self-conscious atmosphere; it's a simple beer joint with a long bar in the front and pool tables out back. Although it's in downtown Salt Lake, it seems to attract a disproportionate number of down-and-out cowboys. Go figure. Hours variable: "Open every day, from morning until close."

Junior's Tavern (202 East 500 South, 801-322-0318) has a sign in the front window that reads "Jazz, blues, and beer," but don't expect to find a quartet dropping beats in the back of Junior's. No, that type of action is for younger places, places that have something to prove. Junior's doesn't. After 26 years on the block, it's an institution. Jazz and blues are still played here, but "I can't remember the last time we had a live band," said the bartender. Nonetheless, this is still a place where you can, as Sheryl Crow once suggested, "listen to Coltrane and derail your own train." The bar top is lacquered-over sheet music, and one of the two long walls that form this one-room bar is stacked with antique beer cans. In the back, a pool table squats under a bright, hanging light. Junior's spends half its life as a neighborhood tavern for older men, and half as a hangout for young beer drinkers of both sexes. Both crowds are friendly. The bartender claims he pours the cheapest pint of Guinness in the state. If you don't mind eating in the smoke, you can have a great meal by ordering a big sloppy red-sauce Italian meal from Cannella's next door and having it served to you at Junior's. Hours: Noon-2 A.M. seven days a week.

Twilite Lounge (347 East 200 South, 801-532-9400) is listed under dives because I didn't have Comfortable-Neighborhood-Bars-Where-Nice-People-Hang-Out as a category. Even if I did, that wouldn't be quite right either. The truth is, the Twilite Lounge defies categorization. An old bar run by an old man, the Twilite attracts an eclectic mix of young grad students, teachers, and gray-haired barroom intellectuals (no, the two terms aren't necessarily oxymoronic, just usually). Seventy-eight-year-old proprietor Bob Cairo started working at the Twilite Lounge when it was part of his father's Busy Bee restaurant, which opened in 1919. "When I was 12, he told me to start washing dishes and not to stop until he said so," said Cairo. "I'm still at it." Cairo, who works the bar daily, has definite ideas about how a joint should be run. "I won't sell a membership to anyone under 23," he said. "They just don't know how to handle liquor yet." So if you're 21 or 22, don't bother with the Twilite. This is also not a place where pugilists or big mouths want to wander; the police station is next door. The decor, which Cairo still speaks about as "the remodel," dates from 1961 and reflects the straight-ahead solid-color tone of the prehippie early 1960s. Jet-black hand-carved chess pieces are mounted to a deep red wall (was it a law back then to paint the inside of every bar red?), and you can still get a game of chess on two boards in the back room. Ask for the pieces at the bar. The jukebox, which has everything from Miles Davis to Black Sabbath, provides the tunes, and the clientele shifts with the clock. At about 10:30 P.M., the Twilite fills with just-off-work waiters and waitresses, grad students, and professorial types. Private club. Hours: Monday-Friday 11:30 A.M.-1 A.M., Saturdays 6 P.M.-1 A.M. Closed Sundays.

DANCE/LIVE MUSIC

Salt Lake is not typically known for its nightclubbing, but you will probably be surprised at what's available. This city can still be an uptight place, so when people go out, they tend to go off.

Bricks Club (579 West 200 South, 801-328-0255) is a sprawling nightclub in an old warehouse. It has many large brick rooms, each with its own feel and vibe, a pool-table room, an area for 18-and-older dancers (with its own entrance), and the best rooftop lounge in the city. The club no longer has a specified gay night but rather bills itself as a "club of alternative lifestyles." Which means "gay people are welcomed on every night," according to the doorman. Cover charge nightly. Hours: 9 P.M.-4 A.M. seven nights a week.

Burt's Tiki Lounge (726 South State Street, 801-521-0572) is Salt Lake City's best and most kitschy live-music dive bar. The ceilings are draped with dried-out and

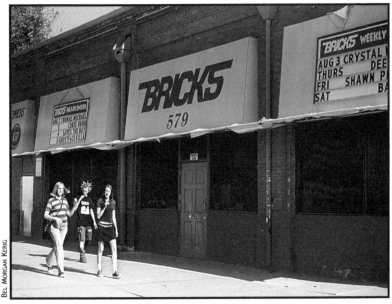

BEL MORGAN KERIG

Bricks is a sprawling nightclub with the best rooftop lounge in the city.

brittle palm fronds. The walls are hung heavily with postcards and posters that provide a hint of the kind of bands that Burt's books. Front and center are posters of Elvis and John F. Kennedy; hanging right above them, in his rightful place, is the king of independent movie soundtracks and underground gestalt: Tom Waits. Any joint that can do Tom Waits and little umbrellas in the drinks gets my enthusiastic vote. Stop here for a cold one or to see any of the local bands that get inspired when they plug in at Burt's. It's a private club, but a year-round membership is only $12. Hours: Tuesday-Saturday 2:30 P.M.-2 A.M., Sunday and Monday 5 P.M.-2 A.M. (hard alcohol is not served Sunday after midnight in accordance with Utah law).

Club Axis (108 South 500 West, 801-519-2947, www.clubaxis.com) is the most un-Utah nightclub in Utah. Check into this place and you'll swear you're in LA, New York, or San Francisco. Every night is something different here (see entry in Gay Scene for more thorough description). Open seven nights a week.

Club DV8 (115 South West Temple, 801-539-8400) is a private club with a cool name that's open only on Friday nights and when it has concerts. Every Friday, join a deejay for Flashback Friday, which offers the best of the 1970s, 1980s, and early 1990s. Call the hot line to find out about shows.

Club Manhattan (5 East 400 South, 801-364-7651) feels like a real grown-up nightclub in this land of so many timid and pale pretenders. Descending the stairs and entering the old-school swanky doors of Manhattan means a mandatory I.D. check by a behemoth bouncer. Don't bother with fake I.D.s or try to ply him with chat. He's heard it all before; he's been there 15 years and regularly confiscates as many as 15 fake I.D.s a night. Then you'll step to the register and pay a cover (anywhere from $7 to $15). Though Club Manhattan is technically a private club, you won't hear any prattle about memberships; pay the cover and come in. Don't and you can stay out; there's no shortage of patrons here. Next you're frisked. That's right, frisked. There is a serious vibe to this place, and it works. The style is pure old-school lounge—semicircular banquettes line the walls, cigarette girls circulate with trays of butts and stogies (seems a lot of women here favor cigars), the lighting is subdued and feels tired, and a well-waxed dance floor divides the gawkers. People dress to come to Manhattan, and the style varies according to theme. On Monday, bust out the polyester for funk and disco. Thursdays see a lot of skin; the theme is billed as a combination college night and ladies night. On Fridays, the posse of deejays and deejay wanna-bes sport billowy Fubu shirts, bandannas, and silky sweats—welcome to hip-hop night. Saturday, it's 1970s, 1980s, and top-40 dance with Robert Stroud. Club Manhattan is also one of the best places to see live jazz bands, but the schedule varies. Manhattan also offers food from Corleone's Italian restaurant, which is inside the nightclub. Full dinners are served from 6 P.M. until 10 P.M. nightly, and a late night menu is available until 1 A.M.. Club Manhattan is open Monday-Saturday and occasional Sundays for special events. Doors open at 7 P.M.

Dead Goat Saloon (165 South West Temple, 801-328-4628) is a basement bar that's best on Blue Goat night. Owner John Paul Brophy is the kind of iconoclastic Salt Lake character that no downtown should be without. As the name implies, the Goat is a nothing-fancy nightclub with dingy, indomitable soul. "This place used to attract a biker crowd but now brings in a wide mix of people from 21 to 65 in what may be the most eclectic mix of people of any Salt Lake nightclub," said general manager Amber Stacey. There is live music seven nights a week: Monday nights are Blue Goat nights with live blues bands, and local radio station KRCL broadcasts blues from this bastion of un-Utahdom on the last Monday night of the month. Sundays are acoustic open-mike nights, Tuesdays are for blues jam sessions, and the rest of the nights are for local and national bands (Los Lobos played here not long ago). The menu has expanded but still lists that burning jalapeño burger. Private club. Hours: Monday-Friday 11:30 A.M.-1:30 A.M., Saturday and Sunday 6 P.M.-1:30 A.M.

Liquid Joe's (1249 East 3300 South, 801-467-JOES) bills itself as "the intermountain good-vibe zone." Here you can catch the best of the local bands, such as Chola, the Disco Drippers, and The Given. Private Club. Hours: 4:30 P.M.-1 A.M. seven nights a week.

The **Zephyr Club** (301 South West Temple, 801-355-CLUB (2582), www.zephyr-club.com) gets the coolest mix of live music in the state. From the wide balcony you will see a curious cross section of Salt Lakers; the bands the Zephyr books (like Dick Dale, king of surf guitar) tend to appeal to the young crowd as well as a fair share of gray-haired hipsters. You might see jazz, funk, punk, or anything else here. The feel is fairly upscale and respectable, but that doesn't mean it doesn't go off. It does. As with most private clubs, a year-long membership is $20; a temporary one is $5. Show tickets vary. Doors open at 8 P.M. and close at 1 A.M. seven days a week.

SINGLES SCENE

Utah's single scene is the same as anywhere else. You can pick up almost any one of the papers and look in the personal section, take a class at the U of U, or look for your soul mate on the chairlift. Or you can shop for your mate online. Click to www.utahsingles.com to get in touch with a database of thousands, or if you're a single member of the LDS church you may also want to check out www.ldssingles.com. Billed as "the premiere meeting place for single adult members of The Church of Jesus Christ of Latter-day Saints," this site claims thousands of members and offers Mormon singles a way to meet others in Utah or around the world. If those options don't work, you can always do it the old-fashioned way: go to a singles bar. Here are the best:

Murphy's Bar and Grill (160 South Main Street, 801-359-7271) is a "step down in social clubs." That's what owner Rob Eddington lists on his business card, anyway. Murphy's is, literally, a step down from Main Street. Inside, Murphy's extends far underground in a long low room with a bar down the right-hand wall, and the appropriate quantity of Irish-beverage signage down the left. Awash in all the smoke-darkened Kelly green you could want, Murphy's is just what it promises: an Irish bar where you can get a shot of Jameson's, a bottle of Harp, or some drink-inspired b.s. "We're a downtown neighborhood bar," said Eddington with the sort of matter-of-fact delivery you might expect of an Irish barkeep. What you might not expect is an impressive beer selection that includes Chimay, an ale bottled and brewed by Trappist monks that sells for $12 a bottle. Rob and his son Lance run the place and love what they do. It shows. Private club. Hours: Monday-Friday 11 A.M.-1 A.M., Saturday and Sunday noon-1 A.M.

O'Shucks Bar & Grill (22 East 100 South, 801-596-8600) is a place that Fred Flintstone would groove on. Duck under the red rock arch and enter the cool darkness of this cave. Belly up and have a drink with Barney Rubble. Like ole Barney, O'Shucks is all lunch-pail and nothing fancy. Get your beer here, and once in a while see a good band take to the tiny stage, but search elsewhere for your cosmopolitans and feng shui. Owned by the same folks who own O'Shucks in Park City, this place is a beer and pool-table bar in a basement. Hours: Monday-Friday 11:30 A.M.-1:30 A.M., Saturday 5 P.M.-1:30 A.M. Serving food until 10 P.M. on weekdays and Saturdays. Closed Sundays.

Port O' Call Social Club (78 West 400 South, 801-521-0589) is known around town as the best singles' spot, which for me isn't necessarily a good thing at all. Visions dance to mind of mid-50s men in toupees leering after smiling sorority sisters. You know the kind of place—it's the sort of joint that makes you yearn for a shower

Salt Lake City's Port O' Call is one of the best singles spots in town.

fifteen minutes after you've sat down. Well, Port O' Call is not that place. In fact, Port O' Call is not any one place. It's really about five different places on three levels under one roof. It has an open-air rooftop lounge (which in 1998 was named one of the Best Beer Gardens in America by *Playboy* magazine); a shiny, waxed dance floor; a brass-and-fern-style bar; a sportsman's cellar (seven pool tables, air hockey, foosball, and such); and a wide restaurant in the back. Scattered throughout are 42 televisions airing virtually any sport you can think of (Port O' Call has 18 satellite and cable receivers). Port O' Call is Salt Lake's biggest and best beer, booze, and brass bar. Whether it's the number-one pickup spot I don't know. I do know that on any given night there will be 800 people in Port O' Call, most happily buzzed under kindly lighting in an upscale *Cheers* type of atmosphere. Private club. Hours: 11 A.M.–1 A.M. seven nights a week, 365 days a year.

GAY SCENE

It should come as no surprise that a large slice of Utah's population views homosexuality as immoral. That said, however, it may come as something of a surprise to find a large gay community alive and thriving in Utah. If that seems to be an anomaly, history offers explanation.

Minority groups (whether distinguished by religion, gender, race, or creed) have time and again proved that persecution merely serves to galvanize, strengthen, and ensure the longevity, organization, and isolation of the oppressed. Such is the situation in Salt Lake City. Because of an atmosphere that until recently was vehemently anti-homosexual, the Utah gay and lesbian community has become entrenched and purposeful in its dedication to alternative lifestyles. As a result, the past few years seem to have brought about a more laissez-faire attitude toward the gay community. This is not to say it's a comfortable coexistence: Anger lies just beneath the surface, and a mere five-minute conversation (with either gay or antigay factions) can erupt in accusations of immorality from both sides.

Although party lines remain drawn in passionate opposition, it's limited to inflamed rhetoric. The two groups have managed to find a way to peacefully coexist in downtown Salt Lake City. Zipperz, one of Salt Lake's half dozen gay bars, is only three and a half blocks from the Mormon Temple and only a few more from the capitol building, but I know of no confrontations. Is that testimony to human toleration in spite of religious or cultural dogma? I'd like to think so.

Anyway, despite or perhaps because of strong antigay rhetoric, the gay community is well established in Salt Lake City. The city has a gay and lesbian community center in downtown (361 North 300 West), a gay and lesbian student union at the University of Utah, a gay swim club (the Queer Utah Aquatic Club-QUAC), a gay men's choir, a gay bowling league, a gay rodeo (www.ugra.net), as well as a half dozen gay bars and a burgeoning gay-friendly neighborhood.

For a more thorough exploration of Utah's gay culture, pick up a copy of *The Little Lavender Book* (a lesbian and gay community directory), which is free and available at many gay-friendly businesses or at 801-323-0727, www.lavender-book.com, or www.4gayutah.com. Here's a rundown of Salt Lake's gay bars and clubs. Most are on the west side of downtown.

Club Axis (108 South 500 West, 801-519-2947, www.clubaxis.com) has many wild nights, but the wildest is its Friday gay night. Billed as "Club Revolution; Pure Pride Rebellion" this club goes off as none other in the state. The front room is a large, brick-walled space that's been given over to TV monitors, multilevels, and Mylar balloons, but the back room is where it really gets nuts. Relentless techno drives a madly gyrating, mostly shirtless dance floor teeming with Utah's young, sweaty, and wild. Then the drag queens take the stage and do their thing. Friday night normally attracts a predominantly gay male clientele, but many women also hit the dance floor. It should be noted that straight men and women are also welcome on Friday night, but I wouldn't recommend it for any but the most gay-friendly straight males. Cover charge varies. Full bar. There is an 18-and-older area in the back with its own entrance, dance floor, and nonalcoholic bar. Private club. Call for hours and show times.

Club Blue (60 East 800 South, 801-517-4074) is Salt Lake's sole men-only gay bar. Catering to a Levi's and leather crowd, this is a bar for men who like men. Boys who like boys will do better at other joints. "We don't pull any punches here. No drag queens are allowed, no cologne, no perfume, no wild hair, no club wear, nothing feminine is allowed in this club," said the club's owner. "By law we cannot discriminate against women, so they can come in, but this is a gay men's bar, for gay men. Why do women need to be in here?" Tuesday nights a deejay spins trance music, Thursday it's underwear night ("and it just goes off"), and Friday nights are for leather or uniforms. Private club. Hours: Monday-Saturday 8 P.M.-1 A.M., Sunday 5 P.M.-midnight.

The Deerhunter (636 South 300 West, 801-363-1802) doesn't have a sign out front, but it doesn't seem to need one. "The people who come here know what they're here for," said a patron knowingly. I didn't have to wait long for an explanation. "Attention Patrons: It's Open Season at The Deerhunter," read the sign over the doorman's head. "Bucks and Does Permitted. Happy Hunting." A more explicit sign for a pickup joint I can't remember. If I still didn't know what this place was all about, the ultradim (dark, actually) lighting and the cowboys who were coupled in the corners told me. The crowd is older than at Club Axis; some are into playing pool or darts, while others are most definitely on the hunt. Private club. Hours: noon-2 A.M. seven nights a week.

Paper Moon (3424 South State Street, 801-466-8517) is Salt Lake's exclusively women's nightclub. A private club for lesbians that has deejay-spun dancing, and karaoke on Sunday and Tuesday. Hours: Monday–Saturday 3 P.M.–1 A.M. Closed Sunday.

Radio City (147 South State Street, 801-532-9327) claims to be the oldest gay bar west of the Mississippi. Since I have no way to check this, I'll take their word for it. A small, not pretty gay bar in downtown. Private club. Hours: 10 A.M.–1 A.M. seven days a week.

The Trapp (102 South 600 West, 801-531-8727) is a country-western gay bar that serves beer in big jars and seems to attract more than its share of drag queens. Private club. Hours: 11 A.M.–1:30 A.M. seven days a week. Sunday BBQ at 4 P.M.

Zipperz (155 West 200 South, 801-521-8300) doesn't have a sign that says Zipperz, but it does have a small neon tube in the front window that reads "Pride." The front room has tall windows that open to the street, high bookshelves lining the walls, and overstuffed chairs. The carpet sports a floral print, and the entrance looks more bookish than bar-ish. As you walk to the rear, however, the complexion of the place changes. Photographs of naked and seminaked men adorn the walls near the bar. Down the stairs is a long, low-ceilinged room where smokers and dancers clog the dance floor. Once a month, a dueling piano and comedy show takes the stage upstairs. The doorman told me Zipperz will soon open a rooftop patio. This is a place where straight men or women can feel reasonably comfortable. Private club. Hours: Monday–Saturday 4 P.M.–2 A.M.

GOTH SCENE

Just as the yin-yang symbol must have both its light and dark side to be complete, so too does Salt Lake's nighttime scene require a bit of the black to compensate for all the light. Although you'd expect the Goth scene to be tiny and fragile as a spiderweb, you need only look to the World Wide Web to see how widespread and organized it is. Visit www.utahgoth.net and you'll see that the dark side of Salt Lake (in clothing, anyway) is alive and thriving. On the site you'll find an extensive and detailed list of Utah Goths as well as a calendar of events and some fun pictures of past events. Here are the two main Goth clubs:

Area 51 (451 South 400 West, 801-534-0819) has parking right next to a big sign that reads "Jesus Saves." It may have been posted just for the Area 51 clientele. For what better group to reach out and save than a bunch of black-clad Goth clubbers? It's not solely a Goth club, but as its name implies, Area 51 tries to stay within a dark side/*X Files* motif. With the exception of its lighter techno/trance offerings on Sunday nights, the club puts it together for the Skinny Puppy crowd. There are two levels of dance floors, with an 18-and-older section for the youngsters. Two patios let you escape the smoke. Wednesday is ladies night, when women get in free. Bands such as Disease, Hate Dept., Kevorkian Death Cycle, and the Switchblade Symphony have played here. For some reason, no hats are allowed in Area 51, so leave the lids at home. Private club. Hours: Tuesday–Sunday 9 P.M.–2 A.M. Closed Monday.

Club @ (740 South 300 West, no phone number) is not what you'd call a name, and @ is not exactly what you'd call an ordinary nightclub. Open Friday and Saturday nights, Club @ is the host of the Third Communion Dark Arts Festival (in June), which is quite an interesting use of this former Mormon Church. The club operates on two levels. Upstairs is a dark, Goth dance club (black light, fog machine, and such) where Marilyn Manson would feel at home. The music is Gothic, ethereal, darkwave, and electroindustrial. Downstairs there is also room to dance, but it tends to be used for sitting and smoking. The air is thick, the lights are low, and the patrons miss no details in their Gothic black wardrobes. Lounging here will make you feel that you've slipped into a postapocalyptic black-and-white Fellini film, or Dante nightmare. Wear black, go Goth, and pound to Nine Inch Nails. Currently Club @ has no liquor license. Sodas and Sobes are served. Cover is usually $5. Hours: Friday and Sunday 9 P.M.–1 A.M.

STRIP CLUBS

Most of Utah was founded on and makes every effort to maintain a high moral code, but there is no escaping a different law. This tenet was set forth not by the Mormon prophet Joseph Smith, but rather by Scottish philosopher and economist Adam Smith (*Wealth of Nations*). The great and golden rule is the law of supply and demand. In Salt Lake City, as almost anywhere else on the globe, men will pay money to watch women take off their clothes. In Salt Lake, as in other major metropolitan cities, there is no shortage of establishments to satisfy that demand.

There are two different types of "gentlemen's clubs" in Salt Lake. The first kind serves alcohol and has a private-club license. In these establishments, the dancers disrobe only down to pasties (stick-on nipple covers) and thongs (those little T-shaped pieces of material that pass for bathing suits in Brazil). There are no private dances or lap dances, and no touching is allowed between patron and performer. All dancers are licensed by the State of Utah, and the relationships between the state and these establishments are understandably tense and under constant review.

The second type of strip club are the "juice clubs." So called because they don't serve alcohol, in these clubs, dancers disrobe completely, and private dances are allowed. The minimum age for admission is 18 instead of 21. These all-nude dance clubs are the least popular with the powers that be in Salt Lake. "They've been trying to shut us down since day one," said Paradise club owner Jerry Nielsen. "It's been fourteen years and we're still here."

Now, however, South Salt Lake has passed an ordinance that bans nude dancing completely. Nielsen is fighting it, and the case has gone to the federal level. The effect of this crackdown has been to make all the strip clubs get persnickety about following every law to the letter. "We do our absolute best to comply with all the laws," one club manager told me, "and they do their absolute best to catch us breaking them." Which means strip clubs are the biggest sticklers as far as

upholding the laws. "Strip clubs are definitely not the kind of place where you want to be loud, disorderly, or picking fights," another hostess said. "You'd be better off getting in a fight at a biker bar than at one of Salt Lake's strip clubs."
Listed here are a few establishments of the two different types. For more information on Salt Lake City's adult scene, visit www.zexmag.com. (*Utah's Adult Entertainment Guide*).

JUICE-CLUB STRIP JOINTS

American Bush (2630 South 300 West, 801-467-0700). Hours: Monday-Friday noon-midnight, Saturday 6 P.M.-midnight.

Leather and Lace (2700 South 377 West, 801-487-9419). Hours: Monday-Friday noon-midnight, Saturday 6 P.M.-midnight.

Paradise Adult Entertainment (2285 South Main Street, 801-485-8708). Hours: Monday-Friday noon-midnight, Saturday 6 P.M.-midnight.

PRIVATE-CLUB STRIP JOINTS

Golden Fleece (2750 South 300 West, 801-467-4600). Hours: Monday-Friday 11:30 A.M.-1 A.M., Saturday 7 P.M.-1 A.M. Closed Sunday.

Golden Trails (921 South 300 West, 801-363-2872). Hours: Monday-Friday 11:30 A.M.-1 A.M., Saturday 7 P.M.-1 A.M. Closed Sunday.

Million Dollar Saloon (3420 South State Street, 801-486-0100, wwwmilliondollarsaloonslc.com). Hours: Monday-Saturday 11 A.M.-1 A.M., Sunday 11 A.M.-midnight.

Northern X-posure Show Club (1737 North Beck Street, 801-355-1488) is three miles north of downtown (take 300 West, which turns into Beck Street). Hours: Monday-Saturday-11 A.M.-1 A.M., Sunday 3 P.M.-1 A.M.

Rascals (3900 South 832 East, 801-269-8383) is the only strip club in town that has a ladies night. That means women can come to see the Men of Crush every Tuesday night. Hours: Monday-Friday 11:30 A.M.-1 A.M., Saturday 7 P.M.-1 A.M. Closed Sunday.

Southern X-posure Cabaret (5142 South State Street, 801-288-1488). Hours: Monday-Friday 11:30 A.M.-1 A.M., Saturday 7 P.M.-1 A.M. Closed Sunday.

State Street Sociables (3055 South State Street, 801-484-4846). Hours: Monday-Friday 11:30 A.M.-1 A.M., Saturday 7 P.M.-1 A.M. Closed Sunday.

2. The Avenues

S alt Lake City, or "Great Salt Lake City" as it was known until 1868, had no
plans of becoming a center for commerce. That simply happened. In 1849 the
first store was opened in downtown, and by 1854 there were so many saloons
on Main Street that it became unofficially known as "Whiskey Street."

The launching of more and more successful commercial enterprises in downtown Salt Lake City brought the need for an urban residential district. The business owners needed a place to live. So the North Bench of downtown was platted
to include lots that were half the size of those in the rest of the city (these people were merchants, not farmers, so had little need for large plots of land). The
streets of a sloping section just to the east of Capitol Hill were laid out in the same
grid style as the rest of Salt Lake City, except that these thoroughfares were nar-
rower and the sidewalks tiny ribbons or nonexistent.

The Avenues were also given a different system of street names; beginning on the
north side of South Temple Street, the roads that ran north and south were named

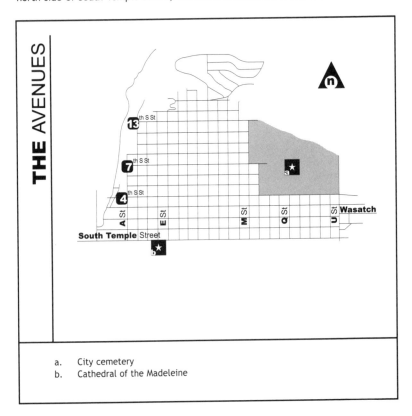

a.   City cemetery
b.   Cathedral of the Madeleine

for the letters of the alphabet, while those that ran east-west were numbered 1st Avenue, 2nd Avenue, 3rd Avenue, and so on. Because the street signs in the Avenues section did not give coordinates based upon one's relation to the Temple, the early pioneers must have concluded that the folks who would live in this area would most likely not be Mormon, and most weren't. Indeed, the immense and beautiful Cathedral of the Madeleine Catholic Church was built at the base of this section.

Even though the Avenues area is less than a mile from the Temple, this area was Salt Lake City's first bedroom community. The people who lived there—artisans, merchants, and railroad workers—commuted (mostly by foot) to their jobs in downtown.

Now, 150 years later, the Avenues area still stands just a bit left of mainstream Salt Lake City. The old homes have a distinctive East Coast feel reminiscent of Boston's Beacon Hill area (scenes in movies such as *Dumb and Dumber* that depict Boston were shot in the Avenues). The population that seems to favor this section of Salt Lake tends toward grad students, professors, and white-collar professionals. With its great old architecture and shady trees, the area is a desirable place to live but not a wildly exciting place to visit. Still, a few places are worth mentioning here.

RESTAURANTS

Café Shambala (382 4th Avenue, 801-364-8558) takes its name from a mythical Tibetan kingdom of pristine beauty where peace and love flourished. This café is not quite that ethereal, but it is nonetheless a great place to fill your belly with healthy food. The mythical Shambala could be reached only by the worthy, whereas anyone with five bucks can get a good breakfast, lunch, or dinner at Café Shambala. Pilgrims who reached the mythical Shambala were said to achieve eternal bliss; once at Café Shambala, expect to achieve at least a sigh of relief. This is not an elegant place—it's bare and simple—but the Tibetan people who work here are kind and hardworking, and the food is good and plentiful. Hours: Monday-Saturday 11:30 A.M.-9:30 P.M.

Einstein's Bagels (481 South Temple at E street, 801-322-0803) offers 16 types of bagels, soups and sandwiches, and good coffee in a cafeteria-style atmosphere. Try a mango bagel for something different. Hours: Monday-Friday 5:30 A.M.-6 P.M., Saturday 7 A.M.-4 P.M., Sunday 7 A.M.-3 P.M.

Guru's (481 South Temple, 801-355-4878) is essentially the same as the Guru's in 9th and 9th (see page 108 for more details) but a bit smaller. A great place to get healthy food at a reasonable price. Hours: Monday-Thursday 11 A.M.-10 P.M. Friday and Saturday 11 A.M.-11 P.M.

Pagoda (26 E Street, 801-355-8155) is the kind of old-school restaurant that was called "Oriental" when it opened. That explains why the menu is a mixture of Chinese and Japanese. Opened 54 years ago, the restaurant has a facade straight out of those 1950s movies that depicted "Orientals" and their abodes. From the outside, it looks like a replica of a Japanese pagoda. Inside it's pure 1950s kitsch. Yet this is not a place that has freighted its dated buildings with the sort of irony

The classic, 54-year-old "Oriental" Pagoda restaurant has the kitsch décor and good simple food of a classic Asian restaurant.

that passes for hip these days. From the rice-paper dividers to the hanging lanterns to the black vinyl chairs, this restaurant knows what it is and sticks to it. It's a place of simple, undeniable charm where nothing seems to have changed (not even the staff) since the 1950s. And the food? Well, it's not chic nor subtle—standard chicken and sukiyaki, tempura and sweet and sour—but it's good and simple, and the portions are large. The hours are long, and the people are great. Takeout is also available. Hours: Tuesday-Thursday 5 P.M.-11 P.M., Friday and Saturday 5 P.M.-12 A.M., Sunday 3 P.M.-10 P.M.

Ruby's Café (564 East 3rd Avenue, 801-532-7829) is a quiet little nook where you can get a cup of good coffee, some quiche or a sandwich, and enjoy yourself in peace. Ruby's is essentially a catering business, with the café serving as a showcase for the fine foods it offers, but you can linger over a paper here and not be bothered. Hours: Tuesday-Friday 10:30 A.M.-5:30 P.M., Saturday 8:30 A.M.-5:30 P.M.

COFFEEHOUSES AND CAFÉS

Einstein's Bagels (481 South Temple at E street, 801-322-0803). See entry under the Restaurants section.

79 (401 East 1st Avenue, 801-532-2899) is a drive-through coffee shop that offers a great cup fast. You also get a couple of little chocolate-covered beans for good measure. Hours: Monday-Friday 5:30 A.M.-7 P.M., Saturday 7 A.M.-5 P.M., Sunday 8 A.M.-4 P.M.

Ruby's Café (564 East 3rd Avenue, 801-532-7829). See entry under the Restaurants section.

SHOPPING
GALLERIES

Q Street Fine Crafts (88 Q Street, 801-359-1899) is a clean, well-lit space of the type you'd picture as a perfect gallery in a two-story brick building. Showcasing unique handmade jewelry, ceramics, and the coolest cheese graters you'll ever see, this shop offers a lot of stuff that looks as if it came from MOMA (the Museum of Modern Art) or the Guggenheim Gift Shop. Hours: Tuesday-Saturday 10 A.M.-6 P.M.

GORDY PEIFER

Pouch Gauthier rides the meadows just uphill from the Avenues in Salt Lake City.

SPORTS SHOPS

Wild Rose Mountain Sports (702 3rd Avenue, 801-533-8671) is a neighborhood bike store that says it has "bikes for dirt, bikes for pavement, clues for both." Located in an old brick building, the store is comfortable hang out where you can talk about all things bike. In the winter, Wild Rose specializes in high-end telemark and skate skis. This place also proudly sells Iams dog food, and it's the only place in the state that sells Montana Coffee Traders Coffee. Hours: Monday-Thursday 9:30 A.M.-7 P.M., Friday and Saturday 9:30 A.M.-6:30 P.M.

MASSAGE

Avenues Arts and Wellness Center (1136 3rd Avenue at T Street, 801-521-2787, www.avenuescenter.com) is run by Emily Cannon, a multifaceted, hugely energetic being who in 1997 decided to take a run-down beauty parlor and make it into something special. She accomplished her mission in a way that only someone with experience in film, psychology, art, alternative health, education, and community service could. The Arts and Wellness Center reflects Cannon's passions. The architecture is pure, open, and inspired. You walk into a large open foyer that connects the gallery and day spa with a great room that is often used for weddings. Stepping into this place instantly gives you a sense of relaxation. You stroll around, gazing at the exceptional paintings and sculptures as the low-pitched call of a flute drifts in and mixes with the gurgling sounds of small fountains. The smell of burning sage is in the air. This exceptional space is the site for classes in art, yoga, tai chi, and pilates. Down the hall and down the stairs are treatment

Bel Morgan Kerig

The Avenue Arts and Wellness Center has a gallery, a day spa, a space where tai chi and yoga are taught. A calm and refreshing place just up the hill from downtown Salt Lake City.

rooms where clients receive all manner of massage, wraps, and herbal therapies. I had a hot-rocks massage that was terrific and oddly energizing (due, I'm told, to the clearing of chakras). Just up the hill from bustling Salt Lake City, the Avenues Arts and Wellness Center is open Monday and Wednesday-Saturday 10 A.M.-6 P.M., Sunday noon-6 P.M. Closed Tuesdays.

Utah College of Massage Therapy (25 South 300 East, 801-521-3330, www.ucmt.com) teaches courses in acupressure, cranial sacral therapy, Russian sports massage, structural bodywork, deep tissue, and just about every other type of massage you can name. The school also offers inexpensive massages to the public ($25 for an hour) so that its students can get hands-on experience. The student massages are available on weekends 8 A.M.-5:30 P.M., but this great bargain is hardly a secret in Salt Lake. Go early, or wait in line.

3. University and Foothill

When you think of the area surrounding a major university, you probably imagine lots of music stores, cafés, bars and restaurants, bookstores, and theaters. Often it's the most fun and vibrant part of town. Well, you can scale down those expectations a bit for Salt Lake's university area. The streets leading up to the University of Utah have some such spots, but don't expect Berkeley, Boulder, or Harvard Square. Because the U of U is largely a commuter school, there is little campus spillover to create the kind of energetic atmosphere you might hope for. The area does, however, have some classic little haunts and good outdoor recreation close to downtown.

The University of Utah sits high on a hill overlooking downtown Salt Lake. The houses here are large, and the lawns well kept. It's an elevated, verdant section of town; the last stand of buildings as you pass east from downtown.

Foothill Drive, which starts in downtown as 400 South, climbs the hill toward the U of U, and then veers to the south toward Interstate 80, forms another section of town known simply as Foothill. For the purposes of this book, I've combined it with University.

RESTAURANTS

Bangkok Thai (1400 Foothill Drive, 801-582-THAI) won't remind you of Kosa Mui or the famed Phuket. It won't bring to mind Leonardo DiCaprio in *The Beach* or a sparkling blue lagoon either. Bangkok Thai is in a shopping center, almost on top of Dan's Foods, but has the best Thai food in town. If you're looking for exotic atmosphere, you'll want to explore elsewhere, but if it's good panag curry or phad Thai you're Jonesin' for then step right up. The best night for the money is meatless Monday, when all vegetarian entrées are $7.99. Chow down, have a beer, and walk out for about the price of a movie ticket and a bucket of popcorn. Hours: Monday-Friday lunch 11:30 A.M.-2:30 P.M., Monday-Thursday dinner 5 P.M.-9:30 P.M., Saturday lunch noon-4:30 P.M., Friday and Saturday dinner 5 P.M.-10 P.M., Sunday dinner 5 P.M.-9 P.M.

Bombay House (1615 South Foothill Drive, 801-581-0222) is another of those places where the exterior belies a world-away interior filled with the smells of curries, and where the gurgle from the aquarium soothes the jangle of the outside world. The billowing fabric motif gives you a feeling that it's okay to loosen your belt and hunker down. Booths are good for couples. Vegetarians will find plenty to savor, as will carnivores. All the curries are wonderful. A word of caution, however: Unless you've desensitized your tongue with gallons of too-hot tea, don't ask for your food on the upper end of the spicy register. If you do and need a supreme coolant, try a mango lassi or a rose milk. Hours: Monday-Saturday 4 P.M.-10:30 P.M.

Brumby's (224 South 1300 East, 801-581-0888) used to be a coffee and pastry shop. Recently its owners, Paul and Karen Gladstone, upgraded its bean-juice fare

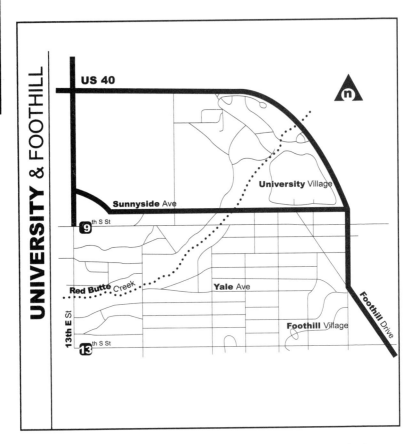

US 40

University Village

Sunnyside Ave

9th S St

Red Butte Creek

Yale Ave

13th E St

13th S St

Foothill Village

Foothill Drive

n

for a broader selection, but they kept its cozy, read-a-paper-and-kick-back atmosphere (as well as its coffee). The patio is the place for a summer lunch, and the chocolate-dipped macaroons are the antidote to a tough tax return or a bad morning at the office. The patio at Brumby's is a perfect place to buy and read the *New York Sunday Times* and let the world slide by. Hours: Monday-Tuesday 7 A.M.-2 P.M., Wednesday-Saturday 7 A.M.-10 P.M., Sunday 10 A.M.-9 P.M.

Gepetto's (230 South 1300 East, 801-583-1013) is a pizza place that serves up live music nightly. The patio is a nice place to spend a warm summer evening, although the savory smells from Brumby's next door may have you wishing you'd gone there instead. Gepetto's is a casual joint that serves pizza, pasta, and salads in a laid-back atmosphere. Hours: Monday-Thursday 11 A.M.-10 P.M., Friday-Saturday 11 A.M.-11 P.M. Closed Sunday.

The Pie Pizzeria (1320 East 200 South, 801-582-0193) is a place you drop into, both literally and figuratively. As you descend the stairs into the cool of the shady

With a secret club feel, graffiti-covered brick walls, low arched doorways, and vinyl chairs, The Pie has the coolest pizza joint vibe in town.

brick-walled interior, you feel as if you're entering some secret club that you imagined when you were a teen—some sort of Dead Poet's Society meeting place. This place has a presence greater than its brick walls, low arched doorways, and vinyl chairs. You feel you're part of something when you come in here—and maybe you are. There, painted and penned on every brick in the place, are the names of the thousands who've come before you. The initials and graffiti are layered and thick, like the pizzas that come whipping out of the oven. Although it's only 21 years old, there is a sense of tradition here—you can almost hear a U of U alumni anxiously asking, "Is the Pie still there?"—that belies its years. This cool, dark place springs to life nearly every night. Early in the evening, families come for pizza—a beer for the adults and the pepperoni for peewee. Then college students descend into The Pie and things pick up. The music swells, and the crowd presses in. This is when it's the most fun, 9:30 P.M. until 3 A.M. on Friday and Saturday nights. To see the tide of revelers at The Pie before you come, click your way to www.thepie.com. The website features a live, streaming video web cam. Since The Pie operates under a restaurant liquor license, you'll either have to eat, or tell them you're about to, if you want a beer. Hours: Monday-Thursday 11 A.M.-1 A.M., Friday and Saturday 11 A.M.-3 A.M., Sunday noon-midnight.

Piñon Market and Cafe (1300 South 2095 East, 801-582-4539) is a great place to stop on your way to a picnic up Mill Creek Canyon. This place has a large deli case where you can pick up a picnic or just ogle the art of the salads. Order any of the wonderful sandwiches, and be sure to get a homemade cookie. Piñon Market has a small air-conditioned café where you can eat, and there's a patio outside. The coffee is good and the staff is friendly; all have that chipper buoyancy found in people who like their jobs. Hours: Monday-Saturday 7 A.M.-7 P.M. Closed Sunday.

Ruth's Diner (2100 Emigration Canyon Road, 801-582-5807) challenges the conventional wisdom about how, in the restaurant business, only three things matter: location, location, and location. Or was that the real estate business? No matter, Ruth proves the tired tenet wrong. This is the kind of up-the-canyon diner that used to be favored by Harley riders and the eclectic Salt Lakers who knew old Ruth and the great meals served up there. Located a few miles up Emigration Canyon Road from Foothill Drive, Ruth's has been worth driving a few minutes more for since 1930 (it's the second-oldest restaurant in Utah). Ruth was a cabaret singer in Salt Lake's early days, and the restaurant she opened was across the street from "a small house of ill-repute." Today the fare at Ruth's is as much nostalgia as it is food, and the takers are many. When my parents come to visit, a trip to Ruth's is always in the plans. The food and service are excellent, and the patio out back is breezy, sun-dappled, and splendid. Ruth's is no longer any sort of secret in Salt Lake, however, and lines are more the norm than the exception. Hours: 8 A.M.-10 P.M. seven days a week.

Santa Fe (2100 Emigration Canyon Road, 801-582-5888, www.cuiscenery.com) is owned by the same folks who own Ruth's, with which it shares the parking lot. One of the owners, Curtis Oberhansly, is also the coauthor with his wife, Dianne Nelson Oberhansly, of *Downwinders: An Atomic Tale*. A well-written legal and historical thriller, it is the number-one selling book in Utah (outselling even the *e-Book of Mormon* and *The Life of Joseph Smith*). You'd expect people with such a finger on the pulse to operate a fittingly hip restaurant. And that's what Santa Fe is, finally. Although Ruth's has a bombproof reputation and a rock-steady business, Santa Fe next door struggled for a time. Not anymore. The service is solid and professional, the wine list is large and impressive, and the menu (thankfully devoid of hackneyed southwestern yelping—or yuppie—coyotes) is an original and varied blend of new southwest meats, fishes, pastas, and chickens. Go for Santa Fe's signature double-cut grilled pork chop with an applejack glaze and sweet potato home fries. The baby back ribs, served with a sticky mango-chipotle barbecue sauce, are also terrific. The upstairs dining room is high-ceilinged, with vaulted angles and a floor-to-ceiling stained glass wall. It's canyon classy. Outside the doors to the patio is perhaps the best part of the Santa Fe. The multitiered deck, with the hushing gurgle of the creek flowing below, is a perfect place to spend a warm summer night (it's considerably cooler up the hill at the Santa Fe than it is downtown). Although it was short-sleeve weather when we left the valley, one of our party was chilled on the deck. Not to worry, the waitress brought her a warm blanket—southwestern, of course. Downstairs from the restaurant is the Canyon Club, a private club with a full bar and a deck only an olive spit from a babbling stream where ducks entertain. Hours: Monday-Saturday 5 P.M.-10:30 P.M., Sunday brunch 10 A.M.-2:30 P.M., Sunday dinner 4:30 P.M.-9 P.M.

COFFEEHOUSES AND CAFÉS

Brumby's (224 South 1300 East, 801-581-0888). See entry in the Restaurants section.

Einstein Bagel (240 South 1300 East, 801-583-1757) is a chain bagel store, but its coffee is good, it's open early, and there's a fine patio out front where you can nosh or sip. Hours: Monday-Friday 5:30 A.M.-5 P.M., Saturday 6 A.M.-4 P.M., Sunday 7 A.M.-3 P.M.

Starbucks (1400 South Foothill Drive, 801-583-2208) is exactly what you expect. Reliably good coffee in a cool nook under Red Butte Café and Blockbuster Video. Hours: Sunday-Thursday 6 A.M.-9 P.M., Friday-Saturday 6 A.M.-9:30 P.M.

BEER

Big Ed's (210 South University Street, 801-582-9045) has you wondering who Big Ed is as soon as you walk into this old and small tavern/restaurant. So I inquired. "I am," said a small Taiwanese woman. "You're Big Ed?" I asked. She was about five feet nothing. "Yes, me am him." Okay then. Short for Edna perhaps? "Actually I buy the place from Big Ed twenty-five years ago," said owner Linda Ling, who moved from Taipei to Salt Lake City in the 1970s. "I keep name because it good for business." Big Ed, alias Linda Ling, is a small woman with a big presence in this funky and somewhat cramped University Street institution. Big Ed's has a short bar with a half dozen old stools lining the right side of the place; a dozen or so tables and low booths run along the other side. A murky fish tank glows from the corner. The signs are hand-written in long-faded magic marker. Big Ed's is the only place

The only place in town where you can get a beer with breakfast, Big Ed's is an institution.

in Salt Lake (that I know of) where you can get a cold beer with your breakfast (as long as you wait until 10 A.M. to eat your eggs). It has 46 seats, and you'll know more people when you leave than you did when you walked through the old wooden door. The tables are close together, and acoustic baffles are nonexistent; you hear every syllable from the conversation at the table across the room. In most cases, this would bug me so bad I'd never come again, but in this place, where the barmaid reads Tom Robbins's *Still Life with Woodpecker* through her dreadlocks, the strange conversations add flavor to the beer and toast. Big Ed's is a magnet for characters and kooks. From the crazy professors to the self-professed crazed, Big Ed's draws them in. The best dish

GORDY PEIFER

Things can get pretty rowdy just off the Shoreline Trail in Salt Lake City. Kris Baughman drops in.

on the strange menu (from eggs to hot dogs) is the gawd awful. Built atop a brick of hashbrowns and chili and topped with fried eggs, the gawd awful is the perfect, if unlikely, complement to a cold draft of "Not Official 2002 Olympic Ale." The combination can be either a cure for a hangover or a guarantee of one. Hours: Monday-Friday 7 A.M.-9 P.M., Saturday 8 A.M.-3 P.M. Closed Sunday.

HIKING AND MOUNTAIN BIKING

Most Salt Lake City mountain bikers throw their bikes in their trucks and drive 15 or 20 minutes out of town, but the area University/Foothill has a network of trails that provide scenic, almost in-town riding.

The Bonneville Shoreline Trail begins on Sunnyside Avenue, about a mile up from Foothill Drive. From there, at the mouth of Emigration Canyon (the trailhead is across the street from Hoogle Zoo), the trail stretches 10 miles to the north and west to City Creek Canyon. The first climb is a bear—straight up—but short. Once you get above the skirts of these foothills, you can go either farther up the canyon or out and around the corner to the north. Both ways offer single-track riding that rules. I like to head north and ride the roller coaster of up-downs that the trail offers as it heads across numerous gullies. Take this trail behind the university and the hospital and across Dry Gulch to City Creek. Along the way, you'll see numerous spurs that bear exploring. The trail is not too technical, usually quite dry, and close enough to town so that you'll pass two water taps along the way. Not a backcountry adventure, but a fun in-town track.

Red Butte Gardens (300 Wakara Way or 2250 East, 801-581-IRIS, www.utah.edu/redbutte) has 100 acres of trails and gardens—from desert plants to wildflowers to aquatic gardens—and forms as fine a summer concert venue as you'll ever find. The hiking here is tame—it's more of a stroll—but the plants and flowers aren't the kind you'd want to rush past anyway. Admission is $4 for adults and $2 for kids. As for the concerts, this isn't the place you're going to go see Slayer; it's more of an Indigo Girls or Lyle Lovett venue. Open 9 A.M. until dusk seven days a week. Call for concert info.

MUSIC

The Gray Whale CD Exchange (248 South 1300 East, 801-583-9626, www.graywhalecd.com) is a hip little CD store where you can listen to good new music, buy it cheap on used discs, and check out the new-release board that will give you the date to get the latest from your greatest. The board gave the dates for upcoming releases from Brian Eno, Radiohead, Nusrat Fateh Ali Kahn (haven't you just been counting the days, waiting for the new Nusrat?), and many more. This board is an example of the wide range of tastes collected in the belly of the Gray Whale, and this comprehensive store is filled with fun music and an unpretentious staff. The same folks also own Gray Whale stores in Cedar City, Draper, Layton, Logan, Ogden, and at 1763 West 4700 South, as well as the Gray Whale Games and Movies across the street. Hours: Monday-Saturday 9 A.M.-11 P.M.

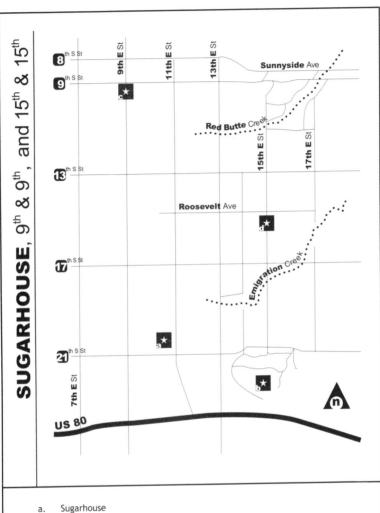

SUGARHOUSE, 9th & 9th, and 15th & 15th

8th S St
9th S St
13th S St
17th S St
21th S St

9th E St
11th E St
13th E St

Sunnyside Ave

Red Butte Creek

15th E St
17th E St

Roosevelt Ave

Emigration Creek

7th E St

US 80

a.   Sugarhouse
b.   Sugarhouse Park
c.   9th & 9th
d.   15th & 15th

4. Sugarhouse

Sugarhouse was born with the shining hope that it would one day manufacture pure, sweet, white sugar, yet like the biblical seed of a saint, it has lurched down a wandering path between the light and the dark, between the sweet and the spicy, for more than 150 years. Now, like the prodigal son, it is once again coming back to serve its community.

Stretching from 1300 to 3300 South and 500 to 2300 East, Sugarhouse is home to wide, tree-lined streets, hundred-year-old brick bungalows, and an autumn-spring mix of senior citizens and first-home-owning couples. It is a place where 1972 Lincolns park next to shiny new Audis with Thule roof racks that carry all the toys than any double-income-no-kids (DINK) could ask for.

Sugarhouse has become popular with so many urban professionals (many of whom work in the burgeoning high-tech sector of Salt Lake's economy) because of the low price of real estate (a century-old bungalow can be had for $150,000), proximity to Interstate 80 (10 minutes from downtown, 15 minutes from the base of the canyons), and a quirky and conflicted town square at 21st South and 11th East.

At the center of Sugarhouse is a tall monument erected to honor the early industrial spirit of Brigham Young and his minions. Back in 1853, Young spied the lowly beet and had an idea: He'd convert its crimson sweetness to pure white granulated sugar. Sugar-mill machinery was shipped in from Liverpool, England, and deposited in the then-outlying region of Salt Lake.

Dipping into Parley's Creek (which flows down Parley's Canyon beside the interstate), the mill found its power, and the early pioneers began the first effort to manufacture beet sugar in the western United States. What came of the effort, however, was not sugar. No, the flaming beet was not ready for conversion to granulated white. A thick, brown molasses was the best the mill could do (one wonders how close the workers may have come to making moonshine), and Brigham Young shut down the mill in 1855.

BEL MORGAN KERIG

Erected to honor the early industrial spirit of Brigham Young and his minions, this monument today forms the axis from which Sugarhouse spins.

After it had been converted to a paper mill (to make the sheets the *Deseret News* was printed on), then to a bucket factory, and finally to a machine shop for the Utah Central Railroad, the mill was torn down in 1928. The monument was constructed a year later, and the moniker of the neighborhood was cemented. Although a plaque on the monument remembers Young and the early industrial efforts, the spire is crowned on two sides with an image of an Indian chief. Why this memorial to early industrialism bears the image of a decidedly nonindustrial Native American instead of Brigham Young is a mystery to me and indeed to everyone I queried. It may or may not be significant that the Indian is closest to the light at the top of the spire. If you know more, email me.

At about the time the early settlers were gearing up to convert the beet, Young also commissioned the construction of a darker yet perhaps more essential institution of society: a prison. Spanning an area of 180 acres between 1500 South and 1700 East and 2100 South to 2400 East, the prison was the first penitentiary in the state. Just as the early pioneers worked in earnest to convert the raw beet into table sugar, so too the early wardens and social workers must have labored to rehabilitate the fallen souls.

One hopes the prison found more success than the mill. If longevity is the measure, then sinners proved a better harvest than beets. It wasn't until 1951 that the prison was moved from Sugarhouse to its present location at the Point of the Mountain.

Today Sugarhouse continues waxing and waning from the dark to the light, from witchcraft to Wonderbread. Now there's a park where the prison once stood. In the wide town square, the Bingham Gallery, which sells landscape paintings of does and pheasants, has supplanted the gypsy fortune-teller's shop as well as the Heavy Metal and Hip Hop stores. Yet just next door is the Blue Boutique lingerie, sex toy, and head shop.

Many people I talked to insisted that the outlaw- and artist-oriented Sugarhouse is losing an ongoing war with insidious mallification. Though I can see their point, it seems to me that the current mix of sole proprietorships and corporate businesses pretty well fits what the population of swelling urban professionals would ask for. It is a hamlet with a feel of a small, 1940s, East Coast town center that has been surrounded by large chain-store retailers.

This is an area with good and interesting boutiques, antique and vintage furniture stores, upscale markets, restaurants, galleries, gyms, sports shops, and cafés. At the top end of the square is a massive Barnes and Noble Booksellers store and café. Although this B&N is pretty much the same as any other B&N—two levels, a fine selection of books, magazines, music, and a Starbucks espresso bar—I for one would rather see the square anchored by a bookstore than, for example, a Wal-Mart. It's also hard to knock a place that lets you read its books for free, serves good coffee, and holds poetry readings.

Next door to B&N is the library. Beside that is the Blindside Skate and Snowboard Shop, and just over from that is the Wild Oats health-food market. Behind B&N is a group of forgettable and ubiquitous stores such as Old Navy, Bed Bath and Beyond, and the like. The positive contributions these stores make to the hamlet are their wide parking lots. Leave the car here and walk downhill into Sugarhouse. Have a beer, eat a vegan grilled cheese, buy a book or a bong, get a tattoo or a snowboard, or maybe have your fortune told by a tarot-card reader. This is a funky section of town with a wide mix of people—from Goth kids to grandmas—so go with an open mind and a little time on your hands. If you're at home in Boulder, Colorado, or Burlington, Vermont, or Bend, Oregon, you'll be at home in Sugarhouse.

RESTAURANTS

The **Blue Plate Diner** (2041 South 2100 East, 801-463-1151) is just as you might expect, an old-school diner. From the *Leave-It-to-Beaver*-era Schwinn bikes that are chained to the railing of the patio, to the yellow Formica soda-fountain counter, to the velvet painting of Elvis over the register, the Blue Plate is all about

From the Leave-it-To-Beaver era Schwinn bikes chained to the railing, to the yellow formica soda fountain counter, to the velvet painting of Elvis over the register, the Blue Plate Diner is an old-school eatery with follow-through.

follow-through. The 1950s theme is present everywhere but not overdone into a plastic Disneyland motif. Yes, the Blue Plate is pretty much right on the money. The crowds are testament to that. Opened in November 2000, this diner has had a crowd since day one. And why not? The breakfasts are big and can be washed down with espresso, and the lunches and dinners are straight-down-the-middle Yankee fare: meat loaf, spaghetti and meatballs, chicken-fried steak. Two points of caution, however: One, no booze is served; two, if you've had too much booze the night before, this is no place for you. The usually crowded single room has a linoleum floor, loud waitresses, and usually more than enough yammering kids to push you into the headache zone. Perhaps that's why there's an old-fashioned pain-relief vending machine that offers Excedrin. Hours: 7 A.M.-10 P.M. (breakfast until 2. P.M.) seven days a week.

Bubba's (4291 South 900 East, 801-268-3374), with its Southern-style good food, has been open and popular on the south side of Salt Lake for nine years. Owned and run by Marco Schlentz, who's from Louisiana, Bubba's is a funky, simple restaurant filled with mismatched furniture and butcher-paper signs. Check out the shrimp étouffée, the jambalaya, or, of course, the ribs. All the meat is hickory smoked, and Bubba's bottles its own killer brand of "Bubba-Q Sauce." Featuring a full liquor license and takeout, Bubba's is a fine place to load up on BBQ. Hours: 11:30 A.M.-9 P.M. Closed Sunday.

Fiddler's Elbow (1063 East 2100 South, 801-463-9393), down the alley just west of the First Security Bank, has a sign that reads "An American Roadhouse," but the manager insists Fiddler's is a "tavern." She also didn't like the term "sports bar," but that's essentially what the place is. There's nothing here to love but a lot to like. The room is large and airy (capacity 135), and the food, served in large portions, is solid and good. Don't expect haute cuisine and you'll be fine. There are 32 kinds of beer on tap (all 3.2), including Guinness, three dart boards, two pool tables, and nine TVs, including a 6-by-10-feet high-definition screen. Fiddler's is a wide-open, functional, moderate environment (suits to jeans) where you can watch a game and enjoy a roasted turkey dinner. It has a patio that's open from April until October. Lunch and dinner daily. No kids allowed. Hours: Monday-Thursday 11 A.M.-11 P.M., Friday and Saturday 11 A.M.-midnight, Sunday 9 A.M.-10 P.M.

The **Formosa Grill** (2115 East 2100 South, 801-461-0661) is nothing like it sounds—that is, if you didn't know that Formosa is the name the early British colonialists gave to Taiwan. If you knew that, you might know that the island of Taiwan is a melting pot of many cultures. In which case you might expect a classic American-Chinese menu (moo goo gai pan, kung pao this, and moo shu that), as well as Japanese items (tempura and teriyaki), Cantonese-style lobster, and Szechuan-style tofu. But would you expect tatami rooms from the Land of the Rising Sun? Well, this place has them, complete with the low tables, rice-paper walls, and the take-your-shoes-off-at-the-door Japanese customs. The name suggests you can get grilled items, but don't hold your breath. There's only one menu entrée for grilled chicken. Go figure. Yet in a strange way, the contradictions give this place a cool retro charm right down to the koi pond wishing well. All in all, this is good and predictable Oriental fare in a fun, old-style atmosphere. At press time, the Formosa had applied for a liquor license. I hope it's granted, because this is a place that begs for a fuchsia-colored drink topped with a tiny umbrella. Hours: Monday-Thursday 11:30 A.M.-9:30 P.M., Friday and Saturday 11:30 A.M.-10:30 P.M. Closed Sunday.

Hunan Garden (2121 East 2100 South, 801-486-8088) is every bit as old-school as neighboring Formosa Grill. When I think of "going for Chinese" as a kid, I think pu-pu platters (a name that pleased us kids immensely because it sounded so very naughty). I am still a big pu-pu fan, and I'm here to tell you the Hunan delivers, right down to the crackling little blue flame in the middle of the platter. The Hunan got new management a year ago, but don't expect anything nouveau. "Everyone liking our spicy food," the hostess told me. Indeed she was right. If the kung pao shrimp sets your tonsils on fire, you can quell the blaze with a beer but not with any sort of mixed drink. Hours: Monday-Thursday 11:30 A.M.-9:30 P.M.; Friday and Saturday 11:30 A.M.-10:30 P.M.

Michelangelo (2156 South Highland Drive, 801-466-0961) is exactly the type of spot I wanted to tell people about when I set out to write this guide: a small, hidden enclave overflowing with charm, character, and tremendous food but unknown to most people. Set in an odd mini-strip mall behind ASI Tattoo in Sugarhouse, Michelangelo's from the street looks like some sort of manicure shop for gray-haired ladies. Descend its stairway, however, and you're in a different world. You're greeted by the rich smells, the resonant multilingual chatter, and the simple Tuscan ambience that have made this spot an underground (literally) favorite of the Sugarhouse and U of U crowds for five years. Owner and chef Marco Gabrielli said he tried to create an atmosphere and food that were "like a home, à la mama." He succeeded. Every one of the all-male wait staff is required to speak Italian; Marco said it was because he doesn't speak English very well, but it may have as much to do with atmosphere as communication. Our waiter was Croatian, could speak a half dozen languages, and charmingly carried off lines that would have been unbearably corny without the accent. The portions are large, the prices medium, and the food is simple and wonderful. They use only cheese that "runs more than gold by the ounce," and their fish is flown in daily on Delta. Try the "pappa" peasant-style pomodoro soup (tomato soup mixed with bread and a slice of parmigiana with a drop of truffle oil). Come early, as your choices will shrink as the night wears on (so much of the food is flown in that when it's out, it's out). This is a secret spot where you might find anyone, including Salt Lake's former mayor Deedee Coradini. Hours: Tuesday-Saturday 5:45 P.M.-9:30 P.M.

Pizza d'Carlo (2021 South 840 East, 801-485-1400) bakes up excellent gourmet pizza in New York, Chicago, and Sicilian styles. If that sounds like an unusually wide span, consider this: Owner and pizza baker Carlo is perhaps the only Ecuadoran Sicilian New Yorker Utahan you may ever meet. The tag line on Carlo's menu ("When was the last time you felt passionate about your pizza?") tells you that this guy makes outrageous pies with a vengeance that his Sicilian ancestors would be proud of. Carnivores will groove on Carlo's Anti-Veggie (pepperoni, Italian sausage, Philly steak, hamburger, salami, Canadian bacon, and ham), while the Pissal-Adiere (anchovies, garlic, black olives, capers, tomato, and parsley) will intrigue and satisfy the less meat-hungry. Yes, the pies here rule, but perhaps the best feature of Pizza d'Carlo is the 24-hour delivery. Any time, day or night, you can get a hot pie in your hotel room or brought to your couch. Now that's a tasty idea. Hours: 11 A.M.-10 P.M. seven days a week, dining and pickup. Delivery 24/7.

Rasputin (2148 South 900 East, 801-486-4952, www.restaurant.com/rasputinslc) has spare decor—babushkas tacked to the wall—and the Russian music comes from an old boom box. But if it's good, simple Russian food you're looking for, this is the place. The pierogis (meat-filled pies) and galuptsi (cabbage rolls in vegetable sauce) are plain, filling, and delicious. The borscht is excellent. Oleg will be your host, probably your server, and he may be your cook and dishwasher too. He is a charming, hardworking man who speaks passable English and keeps a copy of the *Communist Manifesto* on the bookshelf at the front. Rasputin serves beer, soda, coffee, and tea. Hours: Monday-Saturday 11:30 A.M.-3 P.M., 5 P.M.-9 P.M. Closed Sunday.

Salt Lake Pizza and Pasta (1063 East 2100 South, 801-484-1804) is owned by the same people who own Fiddler's Elbow. The two restaurants are next door to each other and share the same kitchen. Just as Fiddler's Elbow offers solid tavern food, Pizza and Pasta offers solid Italian food. Again, it's not outstanding, but it's good, and the place has a full liquor license and serves some passable red wines. Children welcome. Hours: Monday-Saturday 11 A.M.-11 P.M., Sunday 11 A.M.-10 P.M.

COFFEEHOUSES AND CAFÉS

Blue Kats Coffee and Junk Food (2106 South 1100 East, 801-466-7007) is a coffeehouse bistro that specializes in vegan and vegetarian food and spicy entertainment. Wednesday nights feature a fashion show of lingerie and club clothes starring the Naughty Nurses from the Blue Boutique next door (Blue Kats is owned by Tony and Laura Martinez, who also own the racy Blue Boutique and Gift Emporium). Thursdays are open-mike nights. You can get a grilled cheese sandwich made with soy cheese, a chai, or a meatless burger. Unlike the Coffee Garden, perhaps its closest competition, Blue Kats is decorated in bright colors and has, you guessed it, lots of paintings of blue cats. It lacks the aggressive vibe and black-clad clientele and staff found at so many "hipster" coffeehouses. "We get everybody in here," said a manager, "from porn stars to missionaries." Hours: Monday-Saturday 7 A.M.-3 A.M., Sunday 10 A.M.-3 A.M.

Dragonfly Café (1698 South 500 East, 801-474-2241) is a gas station turned into a café. This place is done up artistically, has a great patio, good sandwiches, and features live music on weekends. Hours: Monday-Friday 7 A.M.-10 P.M., Saturday 8 A.M.-10 P.M., Sunday 8 A.M.-5 P.M.

Mill Creek Coffee and Bagel Company (1045 East 2100 South, 801-485-3333) is short on ambience but serves up good coffee, fast, and has a bagel bar to boot. Hours: Monday-Saturday 6:30 A.M.-5 P.M., Sunday 8 A.M.-3 P.M.

Scandia Kaffe House (1693 South 900 East, 801-467-0051) looks like a gift store, which is partially right. What it doesn't look like is a troll's living room, but if owner Erna Neergaard was telling me the truth, that's what the sign ("troll stua") inside over the Norwegian sweaters says it is. This place is part café, part Scandinavian-themed gift store, and part Nordic market. You can eat a vinerbrod pastry or a marzipankaker (ask Erna), buy a jar of pickled herring or my favorite Rokt Kaviar (which my Swedish ski buddies translate as "fish in a tube"—it's better than it sounds), or find out about the next Sons of Norway meeting. This is the sort of place where the mailman stops for lunch. Hours: Monday-Saturday 8 A.M.-5 P.M. Closed Sunday.

CAFFEINE, STRAIGHT UP

Sure, you can get a cup at Blue Kats or the Starbucks in Barnes and Noble or Scandia or a handful of other places, but if you're in need of a quick, stiff jolt of joe, not atmosphere, here are a few places in Sugarhouse.

21 21 Coffee (2105 East 2100 South, 801-466-6656) is owned by the same people who own the Blue Plate Diner next door. The facade is every bit as cool as the Blue Plate's, but the follow-through is not. "We're not really a hangout type of place," said the gal working the drive-through. "We're more of a drive-through for people coming to work downtown." Still, the espresso is Italian and served with a choco-late-covered bean on the lid—a perfect pep pill to accompany go-juice on the go. Hours: Monday-Friday 6 A.M.-7 P.M., Saturday 7 A.M.-4 P.M., Sunday 8 A.M.-4 P.M.

Caffe Expresso (902 South 1100 East, 801-322-2077, and 3815 South Highland Drive, 801-424-0272) is a drive-through espresso bar that also serves pastries. Good Italian espresso with speedy, smiling servers. The outlet on South Highland also serves good wraps and sandwiches. Hours: Monday-Friday 5 A.M.-7 P.M., Saturday 6 A.M.-7 P.M., Sunday 7 A.M.-6 P.M. (until 5 P.M. at South Highland).

S H O P P I N G
ADULT AND ALTERNATIVE

ASI Tattoo (2166 South Highland Drive, 801-484-8700) is not the place for people who want their tattoo parlors grungy. Very well lit and quite clean, this is the place to get a tattoo without getting the heebie-jeebies. Hours: Monday-Saturday noon-10 P.M., Sunday noon-6 P.M.

Black Light Store (1400 South 1100 East, 801-486-3654) is a new endeavor taken on by the usually black-hatted proprietor Richard Faldino. "It was always my dream to open a shop like this," he said. When I asked him to sum up what his store was all about, he said, "It's a kind of fantasy, alternative, Goth, hippie thing." Which means tarot cards and black-light posters of mythic goddesses and metal stars in an atmosphere redolent with burning incense. Hours: Tuesday-Friday 2 P.M.-8 P.M., Saturday noon-8 P.M.

Blue Boutique (1080 East 2100 South, 801-485-2072) is not your grandmother's bou-tique. Although a wide range of club clothes (BC Ethic shirts, Sha Sha shoes with the secret "g-spot" hiding place, pornstar clothing, go-go boots, fur cowboy hats, and platform shoes) make up the bulk of the inventory, there are plenty of edible undies, flavored condoms, emotion lotion, and cherry-flavored body paints. A doorway at the back of the shop cautions "adults only." Through this portal lies an inspired collec-tion of naughty sexual goodies as well as less imaginative porn videos and smut mags. The back wall offers a wide selection of bongs (no one here minded that I called them "bongs"—see the Wizards and Dreams entry in this section), pipes, and other smok-ing paraphernalia. In yet another nook off the main boutique is a piercing and tattoo parlor. A serious bit of Utahan irony is represented by the plaque on the front of the

The Cosmic Penguin is not the type of shop you'd expect to find across the street from a Barnes and Noble, but that's Salt Lake for you.

building. It reads: "Official outlet of ZCMI, America's First Department Store. This building served as a Zion Cooperative Mercantile Institution. The Granite Mart was the last branch to close of the 150 ZCMI outlets throughout the Intermountain West." The ZCMI stores were owned and operated by The Church of Jesus Christ of Latter-day Saints. Hours: Monday-Saturday 10 A.M.-10 P.M., Sunday 1 P.M.-7 P.M.

The Cosmic Penguin (2144 South Highland Drive, 801-486-1212) is owned by Matt Platt, a man who doesn't mince words. "We're pretty much a head shop," he said. In addition to the T-shirts, pipes, rolling papers, dugouts, and water pipes (don't say "bong"—see the Wizards and Dreams entry in this section), Platt also sells "a lot of Bob Marley stuff." Hours: Monday-Saturday 11 A.M.-7 P.M., Sunday noon-5 P.M.

Psycho Active (1057 East 2100 South, 801-466-8002) is the tattoo and piercing salon that's downstairs, through the black-light room, from Wizards and Dreams. Although I didn't research by submitting to the needle, the place looked clean and professional, even if it preferred head-banging music to the smooth sounds of the Dead upstairs. Hours: 11 A.M.-7 P.M. Closed Sundays.

Wizards and Dreams, the Counter Culture Connection (1057 East 2100 South, 801-486-2505, www.wizardsanddreams.com) is one of those businesses that you get the feeling wouldn't exist without the sturdy backdrop of conservative culture to rebel against. A Grateful Dead-themed store that features tie-dye, incense, beads, and bootleg concert videotapes up front and smoking paraphernalia in the back, Wizards is keeping the 1960s—and Jerry Garcia—alive. The handblown glass pipes in the back are impressive for their artwork, if not necessarily for their nobility of purpose. A word of caution, however: Don't call the water pipes "bongs." "Bong is an illegal word," explained the sales clerk. "They are water pipes." "Hookah," on the other hand, is a legal word, so I'm safe in telling you that that Wizards and Dreams also sells some handsome Indian hookahs as well as the water pipes. Hours: Monday-Saturday 11 A.M.-8 P.M., Sunday 11 A.M.-6 P.M.

BARGAINS

The **Sundance Outlet Store** (2201 South Highland Drive, 801-487-3400) is the bargain-basement version of the expensive and rustic/luxury catalog from Robert Redford's Sundance resort and institute. Here they sell overstocked and discounted items, such as leather sofas, dining room sets, as well as clothing and jewelry, at around 30 percent off retail. Hours: Monday-Friday 10 A.M.-7 P.M., Saturday 10 A.M.-6 P.M., Sunday noon-5 P.M.

BOOKS

Barnes and Noble (1104 East 2100 South, 801-463-2610), a nationwide chain, is probably not a store you expected to find listed in this book, right? Truth be told, I didn't expect to put B&N in here either. Then I had to admit something to myself: I like the place and spend a lot of time there, drinking coffee, reading books that I never buy. Okay, revelation time: Not all big corporations are bad. Whew, now that I've got that off my chest, I can tell you that the Sugarhouse B&N superstore is big and airy and has a large café where the manager told me you are free to sit as long as you like. He'd prefer you bought something but won't show you the door if you're inclined just to hang and read. Opened in fall 1998, this B&N also has large music and kids sections upstairs (there's a story hour for kids every Saturday at 1 P.M.). Poetry readings on one Friday night every month. You can order any book and get the dot-com price, and if it's shipped to the store, you won't pay taxes either. Very much worth it on expensive books. Hours 9 A.M.-10 P.M. seven days a week.

Central Book Exchange (2017 South 1100 East, 801-485-3913) has an estimated 100,000 used paperbacks in high stacks and homemade racks. You can pay cash for a book or trade in your books. CBE will give you half your purchase price in credit for more books. The store has been there 28 years and has just about every once-popular paperback you can think of. Hours: Monday-Saturday 10 A.M.-7 P.M.

Experienced Books owner Keith Clawson knows his tomes.

Experienced Books (2150 South Highland Drive, 801-467-0258) is the place for you if you like to get lost in bookstores. The dusty, fusty smell of old books greets you as you enter this charmingly cluttered warren. A beautiful white cat with white eyes will check you out as you browse. A poetic, handwritten note on an old easy chair in the back lets you know where this feline stands: "Please do not sit in this chair, unless you want cat hair on your derriere." Owner Keith Clawson has created a downstairs bunker that allows for complete retreat into the world of words. The unpainted particle-board shelves stretch from floor to ceiling. Forget feng shui; this is a bookworm's labyrinth. Hours: Monday–Friday noon-8 P.M., Saturday noon-6 P.M. Closed Sundays.

GALLERIES

Retro (1064 East 2100 South. 801-485-6020) belies the popular notion that Utahans aren't art lovers. "For an artist to open a gallery in Utah to sell his own work borders on insanity," said painter Darryl Erdmann of his Retro Gallery and furniture store. "And I wouldn't have done it a few years ago, but now the demographics have changed and it's viable." Erdmann paints large-canvas vibrant acrylics and oils in his studio in the back. He offers these original works and reupholstered retro furniture along with selections from the 28 other small artist studios that rent the rest of the building. Hours: Monday-Saturday 11 A.M.-6 P.M. Closed Sunday.

MARKETS AND PROVISIONERS

Artichokes & Company (1790 South 1100 East, 801-474-2784, www.artichokesandcompany.com) is primarily a mail-order catalog store where unusual and fine provisions are packaged into wooden crates and shipped all over the world. The postal availability of these fine products, however, does not diminish from the pleasure of browsing the store. From Jones Soda to Dubliner cheese, the proprietor told me, the aim of this store is to have "high class for everybody." Hours: Monday-Friday 9 A.M.-7 P.M., Saturday 10 A.M.-6 P.M.

Liberty Heights Fresh (1242 South 1100 East, 801-467-2434, www.libertyheightsfresh.com) is the kind of small market you'd find in Manhattan's Upper East Side. Opened eight years ago, Liberty Heights offers an incredible selection of imported olive oils, fresh baked bread, cheeses and chocolates from around the world, cured meats, stunningly bright fresh flowers, lots of fresh produce, and my favorite: a half dozen different kinds of olives. Floating in porcelain urns the size of water-cooler bottles are green olives marinated in cardamom, black olives in garlic, and on and on. This market will fill your soul at the same time it stuffs your stomach. Okay, so it empties your wallet too, but hey, some of the good things in life do cost money. Hours: Monday-Saturday 8 A.M.-8 P.M., Sunday 9 A.M.-7 P.M.

Orchard Street Market (2030 South 900 East, 801-463-1499) anchors a spot down toward the bottom of Sugarhouse where a block of automotive garages has been supplanted by much more user-friendly businesses. Torque wrenches have given way to tortillas, pizza ovens now yawn where pistons once screamed, and chi has displaced gasoline as the divine energy. Also home to Hip and Humble and the Feng Shui Shop, this enclave revolves around the Orchard Street Market. An upscale gro-

With an incredible selection of imported olive oils, fresh baked bread, cheeses and chocolates from around the world, as well as a dozens of different kinds of olives, Liberty Heights Fresh is a market that will fill your soul at the same time it stuffs your stomach.

cery that specializes in local produce, it also offers good beers (hefeweizen, Moose Juice Stout, Eddie McStiff's, and Captain Bastard's), fine cheeses and sausages, and blood oranges. Hours: 8 A.M.-8 P.M. seven days a week.

Wild Oats (1131 East Wilmington Avenue, 801-359-7913) is, like Barnes and Noble, one outlet in a large chain. Yet here again, this is a corporation that seems to have its heart in the right place. One day a month, it donates 5 percent of all proceeds to local charities. As of press time, this store had donated some $34,000 to local "grassroots organizations that fight for the preservation and conservation and the fair and loving treatment and education of all humans, animals, and living things." Only pesticide- and growth-hormone-free organic produce is sold here. There's also a good selection of all the other things you'd expect to find in a health-food market, but perhaps the best feature of Wild Oats is the free samples that are generally offered 11 A.M.-3 P.M. and 4 P.M.-7 P.M. Graze while you shop, and you don't even have to sneak! Hours: Monday-Saturday 8 A.M.-10 P.M., Sunday 10 A.M.-6 P.M.

MUSIC

The **Record Collector** (1115 East 2100 South, 801-484-6495) is not the kind of store featured in the movie *High Fidelity* in which the record-store clerks berate and humiliate customers whose taste in music is less versed and hip than their own. Owner David Hansen, who has been selling "collectible vinyl" for the past 14 years, holds strong opinions about his music, but he keeps them to himself. "Since I quit drinking, I rarely give people shit," he said. "Now I'm much more into taking people as they are and selling them whatever they think is cool." Which means a selection of rare vinyl that ranges from the Surfaris to Bobby Darin to Tchaikovsky. Yes, Hansen is much more egalitarian than he used to be. Now he'll laugh at you after you leave. Hours: Monday-Saturday "about 11 A.M. until around 6 P.M." Closed Sunday.

NEW AGE/SPIRITUAL

Fertile Ground (2124 South Highland Drive, 801-463-4891, www.fertileground.com) provides "things for people engaged in alternative religions and healing practices," said owner Marian Reinholtz. "We are creating a community centered around earth-based and pagan practices." In existence for 14 years, Fertile Ground offers Claymore Scottish swords (as in *Highlander*), knives, tarot cards, Wiccan and witchcraft books, crystals, incense, smudge kits, as well as classes in tarot-card reading, Reiki, beginning witchcraft, and shamanic drumming. "I've had my share of people who come in and tell me I'm evil and unholy," said Reinholtz, "but by and large I've found people are quite accepting here in Utah. We hold rituals in public parks, and no one says a word." So does her group discriminate? "We don't exclude Christians," Reinholtz said. "If they want to come in and experience another path, they're more than welcome." Nice to know it works both ways. Hours: Monday-Friday 11 A.M.-7 P.M., Saturday 11 A.M.-6 P.M. Closed Sunday.

SPORTS SHOPS

Blindside Skate and Snowboard Shop (2121 South Highland Drive, 801-412-9200) is the largest specialty skate and snowboard shop in Utah. With three locations, its orders are large enough for the shop to pass some of the economies of scale down to the consumer. But that's not the reason to go. The real reason is the largest Volcom stone in the world that revolves in the front window. Just as the Irish make pilgrimages to the Blarney stone, so too can singleplankers make their trek to the Volcom stone. There's also an in-store plywood half-pipe for skating, and a large collection of snow and skate vids to watch while you hang. Not every vid is available, however, just the ones rated PG. "We always want to keep it mommy-friendly," said manager Thomas Lee. Hours: Monday-Saturday 10 A.M.-9 P.M., Sunday noon-6 P.M.

Evolution Outfitters (2146 South Highland Drive, 801-983-8001), with boot fitting, service, retail, rental, and repair, is the best full-service ski shop in Salt Lake City. In addition to Evolution brand skis, which are manufactured in downtown Salt Lake City, the shop also sells and rents Head, Atomic, and Volant skis, Nordica, Salomon, Atomic, and Head boots, and Napapijri, Rip Curl, Lafuna, and Moonstone clothing. Evolution's try-before-you-buy program allows you to take

Evolution Outfitters is Sugarhouse's best ski shop.

the price of the demos off your purchase price on any new skis. Whether you've got a core shot in your new Monster Crosses, or you just want to go faster in the spring snow, ski tuner Eric Boller is the man to see. Winter hours: Monday-Saturday 8 A.M.-8 P.M., Sunday 8 A.M.-6 P.M. Summer hours: Tuesday-Saturday 9 A.M.-6 P.M. Closed Sunday and Monday.

UNIQUE BOUTIQUES

Dancing Crane Imports (673 East 2240 South, which is also Simpson Avenue, 801-486-1129) is billed as an "emporium of world culture." And that it is. From the moment you step into the warehouse-sized space, you realize you're onto a cool store. The first thing you see is a granite ball that spins as water shoots up from beneath it. Just behind the spinning sphere is the 27-by-17-feet *Eye of the Zodiac* mural painted by Arthur Roberg on the floor. This place sells every Eastern, New Age, African, Australian, Balinese, Native American, rain-forest, local-artist, Mexican, Buddhist, and Tibetan art or artifact that you could ask for. Not only does it sell belly-dance clothing, but also staffers will teach you the proper way to use it. They also teach Reiki and yoga. They sell rugs and tapestries, singing bowls and native drums, Native American fetishes and Irish faeries. The cluttered community board is a who's who of woo woo for Salt Lake, and in the café I guarantee you'll feel you're far, far from Salt Lake. Hours: Monday-Saturday 10 A.M.-7 P.M., Sunday noon-5 P.M.

The **Feng Shui Shop** (2030 South 900 East, 801-531-1357) has front windows with the words "balance, joy, peace, and harmony" painted on them. The words are low on the window, at calf height, and, like the concepts they represent, underlie all that is found within this marvelous little shop. The gurgling sound of fountains and an air redolent with the sweet smell of candle wax and incense greet you. The offerings are many and varied—from Japanese wedding chests to Now and Zen chiming alarm clocks (I had to buy one and am happy I did)—but it is the overall feel of this shop that is perhaps the best reason to visit. There is, as promised by the name and those words on the window, an aura of peaceful harmony here. The ancient eastern art of feng shui (pronounced *feng shway*), which teaches a way to design and decorate that encourages the movement of divine energy (chi) through your home or business, guides not only the selection of what to include in your life space but also where and how. Feng shui workshops, consultations, and group presentations are offered along with the many and varied treasures in the shop. Hours: Monday-Saturday 10:30 A.M.-6:30 P.M.

The **Lotus Gallery and Persimmon Tree** (1019 East 2100 South, 801-467-6662) offers Japanese antiques, gifts, and fine furnishings. It is a peaceful and beautiful space where staff members wear kimonos and serve you free green tea and ginger cookies as you shop. Koi swim lazily in a pond, and the sound of running water spreads a hush over the cool, dimly lit store. The Japanese antiques are museum quality (and priced accordingly), and the owners, James and Sandra Crowley, have written a book entitled *Wabi Sabi Style* that explains the concepts and philosophies of Japanese garden and home decor. Although the Buddha collection is fabulous just to see, you can buy each icon as well as samurai and emperor dolls. This is a store where you can purchase a $7 leaf box or a $7,000 dragon. Out the back door is a Japanese garden center with imported bamboo, fountains, and marble meditation benches. The Crowleys also offer shodo calligraphy classes, ikebana flower-arranging classes, traditional tea ceremonies, as well as consultations on design and wedding-gift registry. Winter hours: Monday-Saturday 10 A.M.-7 P.M. (extended hours during holidays). Summer hours: Monday-Saturday 10 A.M.-6 P.M.

VINTAGE CLOTHING

PIB's X-Change (2144 South Highland Drive, 801-484-7996) is the kind of second-hand-clothing store that plays Bjork's *Dancer in the Dark* soundtrack CD and sells the ironically hip clothes that were cutting edge when we saw them on *Good Times* starring J. J. "Dynomite" Walker, or *Welcome Back Kotter* starring a little-known actor named John Travolta. Hours: Monday-Friday 11 A.M.-9 P.M., Saturday 11 A.M.-8 P.M., Sunday 1 P.M.-5 P.M.

Sulisha Creations (2144 South Highland Drive, 801-485-3668) is the place for you whether you want silky Egyptian fashions or belly-dancing classes. Hours: Monday-Friday noon-6 P.M., Saturday 11:30 A.M.-5 P.M. Closed Sunday.

VINTAGE FURNITURE

Sugarhouse has become a hotbed for vintage furniture and decor. Whether you're looking for a purple velvet couch that would fit perfectly in a Nevada bordello, a lime-green vinyl loveseat, or a set of chrome martini shakers, one of the following places will have it and much more.

The **Green Ant** (2011 South 1100 East, 801-595-1818) is a treasure trove of 1950s-1970s furniture and decor. "Sugarhouse is the vintage furniture Mecca of Salt Lake," said owner Ron Green. And his store fits right in. Crammed with lime-green sofas and turquoise-blue coffee tables as well as the latest issues of *Wallpaper, Dwell,* and *Surface* (hip new designing magazines), this is the place to come if you seek that fine, ironic *Leave It to Beaver* cum *Brady Bunch* aesthetic. Hours: Monday-Saturday 11 A.M.-6 P.M. Closed Sunday.

Hip and Humble (2030 South 900 East, 801-467-3130) is a name that begs the question "Well, is it either?" It's akin to calling a play "brilliant and mesmerizing." You're just handing a loaded gun to the critics. So it was with a cynic's eye that I wandered into this cluttered home store. The candle and soap scent whisked me back to my grandmother's house, and the combination of new and vintage cottage-style furnishings summoned memories of Nantucket Island—both happy and humble memories for me. And although I didn't spy anything that I'd describe as "hip" (Grandma never wore a beret, and Nantucket wasn't long on black mock turtlenecks), this is a nice little store. Hours: Monday-Friday 10 A.M.-7 P.M., Saturday 10 A.M.-6 P.M., Sunday noon-5 P.M.

Home Again (1994 South 1100 East, 801-487-4668) is a furniture consignment store that blends the traditional with the funky. Some prices seem quite high, but good shoppers will keep coming back because merchandise moves through here quickly; the longer an item stays in the building, the lower the price will be. Feel free to make offers; there is some wiggle room built into the prices. Hours: Monday-Friday 10 A.M.-6 P.M., Saturday 11 A.M.-6 P.M.

Timeline (2132 South Highland Drive, 801-486-3665) has reconditioned retro furniture and a great collection of vintage martini shakers and spritzers. There's also a great old chrome whirlpool that has been converted into a fish tank. Ivan's the man to see here. Hours: Monday-Saturday 11 A.M.-6 P.M. Closed Sunday.

FITNESS

24-Hour Fitness (1121 Ashton Avenue, 801-466-2030) is a new sprawling gym where you won't feel you're on top of your hulking neighbor. With its rows of cardio equipment and racks of free weights and machines, you wouldn't think the place would ever get crowded. Nonetheless, it does, but only at peak hours (5:30 P.M.-8 P.M., especially on Mondays and Tuesdays). The place is open around-the-clock, so work out at an off-peak time. Features include a four-lane lap pool, co-ed Jacuzzi, sauna and steam rooms, as well as spinning, aerobics, and kick-boxing classes. The nursery also offers two hours of babysitting for $2 per child. Nonmembers pay $15 per visit, but anyone interested in joining may be able to use the club for free. Open all the time, seven days a week.

Lifestyles 2000 Fitness Center (1033 East 2100 South, 801-484-8786) has all the cardio, free weights, aerobics, and machines that you'd expect from a fitness center. With its low ceiling and tight quarters, you'll never feel lonely in this place. Proximity to other sweating, heaving bodies notwithstanding, however, Lifestyles is a good place to get a basic workout. Women will also enjoy a female-only workout area upstairs, away from all those grunting sweaty men. Guest fee is $15, but if you tell them you want to join, you may be able to test-drive for free. Hours: Monday-Thursday 5:30 A.M.-11 P.M., Friday 5:30 A.M.-9 P.M., Saturday 7 A.M.-7 P.M., Sunday 9 A.M.-4 P.M.

Streamline Body Works (1948 South 1100 East, 801-474-1156) is a neighborhood pilates studio upstairs and a Body Works facility (massage and skin care) downstairs. Run by a husband-wife team (she teaches pilates, he runs Body Works), Streamline offers beginning, intermediate, and advanced pilates classes. This alternative-health business is situated in one of Sugarhouse's old brick bungalows, but the place has been refurbished into a clean, sleek, well-lit, and inviting space. The porch is a perfect place to chill after class or a massage. Pilates instructors were all trained in Boulder, Colorado, and seem affable. Hours vary depending on class and massage schedule.

MOVIES

Cinemark Movies 10—Salt Lake City (1300 East at Interstate 80, 801-466-3797, www.cinemark.com) is not hip or cool, but it is a cheap way to see all those movies you missed the first time around. Tickets go for a whopping $1 before 6 P.M., and $1.50 after. Tuesdays it's a buck all day. At this price, even *Hudson Hawk* might seem like a good movie. Or maybe not. Open seven days a week.

NIGHT LIFE

BEER

Although you can get a cold one at a number of places, there are only a few spots where beer outstrips food as the main offering. Here are the best two in Sugarhouse:

Fats Grill (2182 South Highland Drive, 801-484-9467) is right next door to the Tap Room but a mile away in ambience. A clean, airy, well-lit place with 14 pool tables and a comedy club downstairs, Fats is as much about food and pool as it is about beer. The food is reasonably priced and better than most pub fare; the tables are new and in great condition. All the cues still have the tips on them. Hours: Monday-Thursday 11 A.M.-1 A.M., Friday 11 A.M.-1:30 A.M., Saturday noon-1:30 A.M. Closed Sunday.

The **Tap Room** (2148 Highland Drive) is a small chalet-styled building wedged into a narrow alley. "Welcome to the church of hops" was the greeting I received when I stepped inside. Within minutes, I was adopted into a fraternity of old drunks, construction workers, and snowboarders. Not that it was any feat. The small smoky bar is so tight that it is virtually impossible not to talk to the patrons. If Cheers were a tenth the size, the extras not so pretty, and Coach an old woman, it would be the Tap Room. Hours: 11 A.M.-1 A.M. every day.

NIGHTCLUBS

Caribbean Nights (1051 East 2100 South, 801-474-9590) is a wide-open dance-hall nightclub that looks and feels as if it should be in downtown Puerto Vallarta. It has an authentic Latin style that's just a little worn, just a little beat-up, and you get the feeling that if the stuccoed walls could talk, you'd want to listen. The deejay sits up on a high altar and leads worshiping throngs through seismic shifts of passion. Tuesday night is house music, Wednesday it's hip-hop, Thursday sees the dreadlocks and rasta of reggae, Friday is Latin alternative, and Saturday is for salsa and merengue. The best nights are Wednesdays and Saturdays. Hours: Monday-Saturday 6 P.M.-1:30 A.M. Closed Sunday.

5. 9th and 9th

O n the corner of 900 East and 900 South, known simply as 9th and 9th, is a
small cluster of businesses that together form an enclave for nontraditional
Salt Lakers. The corner is anchored by the Coffee Garden café. Lounging at
the tables out front is a latte-drinking, cigarette-smoking crowd with hair that runs
the gamut from professorial gray to punk purple. Next door to the Coffee Garden is
a boutique where you can buy a blouse with a Buddha on it, and beside that are a
burrito bar and takeout sushi counter. Across the street from the Coffee Garden is
the 75-year-old Tower Theatre (which shows art, independent, and foreign films), a
fiercely noncorporate CD store, and an adult- and gay-themed gift and card store.

Interestingly, all these businesses are on the west side of the intersection. On
the east side are the cleaned-up and corporate new-economy-style Starbucks,
Guru's, and Great Harvest Bakery. Though fractionalized, 9th and 9th is one of the
best alternative nooks in Salt Lake City.

RESTAURANTS

Barbacoa (859 East 900 South, 801-524-0853) offers huge, killer burritos in a no-
nonsense cafeteria-style atmosphere. A solid eatery with clean tables, a well-lit
dining area, and a great patio out front, this place is affordable, fast, and professional. Though the burritos might make you long for a cold one, alas only soda
is served. Hours: Monday-Thursday 11 A.M.-9 P.M., Friday and Saturday 11 A.M.-10
P.M., Sunday noon-8 P.M.

BEL MORGAN KERIG

The 9th and 9th Center offers coffee shops, restaurants, and an independent, art-house theater.

Café Eclipse (680 South 900 East, 801-359-1122) is a block north of 9th and 9th but has an intelligent iconoclastic vibe that marches in step with the hipster crossroads, philosophically if not geographically. The chic minimalist decor may make you feel that you're eating inside an Ikea catalog, but the food is bistro-style and tasty. The wine list features affordable and bankable favorites and the patio at Café Eclipse is wonderful for an early evening dinner or a sunny lunch. Brunch offered Saturday and Sunday. Hours: Monday-Friday 11 A.M.-10 P.M., Saturday 10:30 A.M.-10 P.M., Sunday 10:30 A.M.-8:00 P.M.

Great Harvest Bakery (905 East 900 South, 801-328-2323) offers perhaps the best value in town. Buy a cup of coffee or a drink and they'll give you a fat slice of fresh-baked (still hot) bread with butter or honey for free. The patio out front is sunny and comfortable. You'll try to just eat the freebie, but the bread is so good you'll go back in and buy a loaf. Hours: Monday-Friday 6 A.M.-6:30 P.M., Saturday 6 A.M.-6 P.M. Closed Sunday.

Guru's (912 East 900 South, 801-355-4878) has a sign on the outside of the building that reads "Give and Take Out," which refers to Guru's strong bent toward community service and self-improvement. Once you're inside, get on the curling path of inlaid stones known as the "path to enlightenment." That would make the counter the altar and the food the offering. Don't expect to smell patchouli as soon as you walk in, however. The brainchild of a former Einstein Bagels owner and a corporate executive at Franklin Quest (the company that makes Day Planners), Guru's is a little like a health-food version of Starbucks. Everything is well thought out and centered around a theme of self-improvement through meditation and service. The food is healthy, cheap, and fast. Although you order your food at the counter, the staffers who serve it are courteous and efficient. Not only does every meal have a message (written on the bottom of the plate or bowl), such as "The sole meaning of life is to serve humanity," but also every Guru's employee is required to perform community service while on the clock. Now that's a business that cares. Hours: Monday-Thursday 11 A.M.-10 P.M., Friday and Saturday 11 A.M.-11 P.M. Closed Sunday.

Wasabi Sushi (865 East 900 South, 801-328-FISH or 3474, www.wasabitogo.com) is a little takeout sushi joint that has a full line of raw, rice, and rainbow rolls. Oh yeah, they have one other "r"—bottles of the original Red Bull from Thailand. It tastes the same as the cans, but the bottles don't have carbonation, and they're a buck cheaper. There are a half dozen stools at the counter where you can eat your meal, but it's like eating in the kitchen. No fancy knife play and guys yelling out things in Japanese, just good sushi and a reasonable price. Monday-Saturday 3 P.M.-10 P.M. Closed Sunday.

COFFEEHOUSES AND CAFÉS

The **Coffee Garden** (898 South 900 East, 801-355-3425) is a coffeehouse you either love or hate. The ratty couches and cool 1950s linoleum tables; the laissez-faire

Coffee Garden at 9th and 9th is one of Salt Lake's hippest coffee shops.

counter staff; the kick-back clientele, and the thoroughly mellow atmosphere compose a definite coffeehouse gestalt. For many people, this place is just a little too edgy, a little too conscious of what they see as a hackneyed rebellious pose. For others, it's just the antidote needed to make it through the day in white-bread Salt Lake. It's coffee served with a side of "get-over-yourself" attitude. If that's an attitude you groove on, you're going to be glad you found the Garden. The tables outside are the spot for lingering over a beverage or a smoke. If you like things a little more sterile, there's always Starbucks (across the street). I take my friends from Boulder, Colorado, to the Coffee Garden but my dad to Starbucks (he was dissed at the Garden for ordering decaf). Hours: Monday-Thursday 6 A.M.-11 P.M., Friday and Saturday 6 A.M.-midnight, Sunday 7 A.M.-11 P.M.

Starbucks (902 East 900 South, 801-530-0484) sits right behind a hand-painted mural attesting to the ascendant and cosmic powers of coffee. If the clerks or patrons at the Coffee Garden aren't to your liking, this is a bankable spot with a less "diverse" crowd. Its front window also offers an anonymous view of the confluence of 9th and 9th that's perfect for caffeinated voyeurs. Hours: Monday-Thursday 6 A.M.-10 P.M., Friday 6 A.M.-10:30 P.M., Saturday 7 A.M.-10:30 P.M., Sunday 7 A.M.-10 P.M.

S H O P P I N G
GIFT SHOPS
Cahoots (878 East 900 South, 801-538-0606) is an eclectic card store with candles, lotions, and potions. The farther you walk to the rear of this store, the more gay- and adult-oriented it becomes. There are jokes and gag gifts that made my mom blush (and leave the store). Hours: Monday-Friday 10 A.M.-8 P.M., Saturday 10 A.M.-7 P.M., Sunday noon-5 P.M.

Floribunda (920 East 900 South, 801-359-4013) is a space where women can be women. Whether you're looking for fine wrapping papers or the perfect gift, this store has a grace that's present from the help to the hemp. Hours: Monday-Saturday 10 A.M.-6 P.M. Closed Sunday.

The **Southwest Shop** (914 East 900 South, 801-531-8523) is not filled with cheesy earth tones and orange prints that decorate at least half the chiropractors' offices in the West. No, the Southwest Shop is much more real, much more low key. From berets to Mexican blankets, tribal masks to Navajo pottery, this is a shop with an authentic vibe and nice people working there. Hours: Tuesday-Saturday 10 A.M.-6 P.M. Closed Sunday and Monday.

MUSIC

Salt City CDs (878 East 900 South, 801-596-9300) has a sign next to its listening section that reads "We guarantee our picks are 100% free of soulless corporate influence, bio-engineered music, and animal testing. Music so pure it floats." That pretty much describes the place. Kick back on one of the old couches, throw a pair of headphones on, and listen to any one of a dozen sampler discs that spin daily. A hip store with good tunes. Hours: Monday-Saturday 10 A.M.-8 P.M., Sunday noon-5 P.M.

SPORTS SHOPS

Contender Bicycles (878 South 900 East, 801-364-0344) is a new, high-end bike shop where you can buy road or mountain bikes. Hours: Monday-Saturday 9 A.M.-6 P.M.

The Tower Theatre is Salt Lake City's home to independent, art-house, and foreign film.

MOVIE THEATERS

The **Tower Theatre** (876 East 900 South, 801-412-1824) is a 75-year-old venue that's spelled the cool English way: theatre. Wherever you see that spelling, you're not going to see blockbusters. And so it is with the Tower. For art, foreign, and independent films, this is the best place in Salt Lake City. The Tower also hosts great midnight movie faves such as *The Rocky Horror Picture Show* and *Spinal Tap*. This is also the best place in the valley to get independent and obscure video titles (arranged by director, if that gives you a hint). Although the Tower has recently gone through some wobbly times, the new management is slowly but steadily renovating the room, upgrading the equipment, and generally making it a better place to see quirky and interesting films. The one drag about seeing a film at the Tower is its utter lack of parking. You're relegated to street parking, which can fill fast with the Coffee Garden crowd.

6 . 15th and 15th

Located slightly up the hill from the bottom of the Salt Lake Basin, this area is filled with moderately successful professionals and young families. Most of the homes were built in the 1920s or earlier and have been well refurbished. If Sugarhouse is a great place for starter homes, this is where those people move next. This corner has a warm, cottage feel to it that's just to the left of staid, just to the right of hip. If 9th and 9th were Martha's Vineyard, 15th and 15th would be Nantucket.

RESTAURANTS

Einstein Brothers Bagels (1520 South 1500 East, 801-466-8669) ain't H&H bagels (for those loyal to the killer roundies you get in NYC), but it is a place where you can chose from a couple dozen types of bagels, good coffee, sandwiches, or other breakfast and lunch foods. It's part of a chain, but it's still solid and good. Hours: Monday-Friday 6 A.M.-5 P.M., Saturday 6:30 A.M.-4 P.M., Sunday 7 A.M.-3 P.M.

Fresco Italian Café (1513 South 1500 East, 801-486-1300) is a very fine, small, white-tablecloth café. On a warm summer night the patio is cool and very much in demand. Reservations are a must. Leave time to linger in The King's English bookstore, either before or after your meal. Full wine list. Open 5 P.M. nightly, last seating 9:30 P.M.

Fresco Café is a fine Italian café where the shady patio offers a romantic and sublime spot for a summer dinner.

Mazza (1515 South 1500 East, 801-484-9259) is owned and operated by Ali Sabbah, from Tyre, Lebanon, which means he probably knows what he's talking about when he lets you in on the secrets to Middle Eastern food. "Freshness," he said, "is the most important. Attention to detail is the next most important." Although at first I thought this contention might just be a preemptive strike against customer complaints (the food does not appear at Burger King speeds), I was proved wrong by the baba ghannooj (which I love saying), the juicy falafel, and the shawarma (thinly sliced lamb grilled with spices and served on pita). One caveat: Ali closes up shop at 8 P.M. On our first visit we got there at 8:03. The only reason we didn't leave disappointed was Ali's insistence that we take with us a "sample plate" of hummus, baba ghannooj, and tabouli. The freebie fed two and made us Mazza fans for life. Hours: Monday-Saturday 11 A.M.-9 P.M. Closed Sunday.

COFFEE

Starbucks (1527 South 1500 East, 801-485-7267) is the same as every other Starbucks, except for one feature. "The thing that makes us different are the beautiful women who work here," said one of the women who works there. Buy a cup and linger on the patio at the quiet corner of 15th and 15th. Hours: Monday-Thursday 6 A.M.-8 P.M., Friday 6 A.M.-9 P.M., Saturday 6:30 A.M.-9 P.M., Sunday 7 A.M.-8 P.M.

SHOPPING

BOOKS

The King's English Bookshop (1511 South 1500 East, 801-484-9100) has a sign on the cottage-style, euonymus-covered building that reads "Dealers in Books." This should give you some indication of how serious this place is about the printed and bound. If the exterior and the name don't, co-owner Betsy Burton will. "We have the best fiction and poetry sections in the city," she said. "We also have the best children's department and the most knowledgeable staff." These are big claims, but after spending some time in The King's English, you get the feeling that if she isn't right, she ought to be. This is a bookstore the way bookstores were meant to be. It's old and cluttered, with creaking floorboards and overstuffed bookcases. This a place where you'd love to drink a cup of tea as you escape into a warm book on a cold, rainy day. That is just what some patrons do. "We had one customer who used to put a marker in the book," recalled Burton. Her staff, each member with at least an undergraduate degree, is good at answering questions but is also pleased to leave you alone to get lost in one of the store's books. The King's English hosts book signings and has had authors E. L. Doctorow, Jane Smiley, and Isabel Allende, among others. The bookstore also shares the building with the fine Fresco Italian restaurant, which means you can take a cup of coffee or tea into the store as you browse and wait for dinner. Hours: Monday-Saturday 10 A.M.-9 P.M., Sunday 11 A.M.-5 P.M.

CLOTHING

Great Garb (1510 South 1500 East, 801-486-1582) features "city-bred fashions for ski-country living." Which is to say this is a chic store filled with casual contemporary clothes for women. Hours: Monday-Saturday 10 A.M.-6:30 P.M. Closed Sunday.

GALLERIES

Artform Gallery (1519 South 1500 East, 801-466-2802) will never be confused with the Louvre, but you also can't buy frames at the famous Paris gallery. A mellow place to hang and look at Picasso knockoffs while you wait for your table at Fresco. Hours: Monday-Friday 10 A.M.-6 P.M., Saturday 10 A.M.-5 P.M.

WASATCH FRONT

7. Little Cottonwood Canyon

I fell in love with Little Cottonwood Canyon when the Cliff Lodge was half the size it is today and Springsteen's "Born in the U.S.A." was on top of the charts. As the ink on my college diploma dried, I looked west from Burlington, Vermont, and wondered ...

Then I came to my senses, bought the three-piece suits, and hurled myself at New York City with all the verve and naive optimism of a mid-1980s graduate. I hit New York and bounced. When I came to rest, the suits were hanging in an East Village thrift store, and I was standing in a kitchen apron in front of a steaming Hobart machine in the dish room at the Cliff Lodge. From atop thick black rubber mats that smelled of chicken fat and Clorox bleach, with a never-ending flow of half-eaten pork chops and globs of gelling potatoes coming at me, I saw Snowbird from its bowels. And I loved it.

With my employee pass hanging proudly around my neck, I went first-to-last tram every day for the first month. After I got the big promotion to coat-checker at the Golden Cliff restaurant, I happened to hang up the jacket of Snowbird owner Dick Bass. He stopped to talk, and I told him of my move from the East Coast. He told me that the spot I stood in then, up Little Cottonwood Canyon, was the best place in the world. I thought then, and still think, that the man was right.

Shortly after that, I ventured across the West Baldy traverse and dropped into Alta. It was afternoon, and the powder was as dry as a Bond martini, virgin as wedding-cake frosting. I devoured it.

Alta wasn't unfamiliar to me; no, this no-nonsense, old-school area reminded me of places I'd been, places that until that moment still held sway over the part of the brain reserved for legend. Alta tasted a bit like my favorite East Coast ski area, Mad River Glen, Vermont—only times ten. My powder-drunk grin must have distracted the liftie at Wildcat Chair; he didn't notice I had no ticket. Today you can do it legally, which is the greatest boon to skiers since P-Tex. By the time I dropped back through the Keyhole chute into Snowbird, I knew I had bounced into a home in the most incredible ski destination in the country.

U.S. and Canadian Free Skiing (or extreme skiing, as it used to be called) Champion Gordy Peifer came from Minnesota and had a similar epiphany. "After the first day I realized it was by far the best skiing I'd ever done," he said. "I was so jazzed, so geeked up, that people probably thought I was nuts. I was just like, 'Oh my God, this is the place!' I realized it was the best ski area in the world. Even though I've skied most of them now, my opinion hasn't changed." I know of so many great skiers who share a similar zeal that I could fill this book with their testimonials. The snow is so good, the terrain so challenging, that it forever rips you out of the stifling safety of your flatland days.

Although both Alta and Snowbird are major winter tourist destinations, the

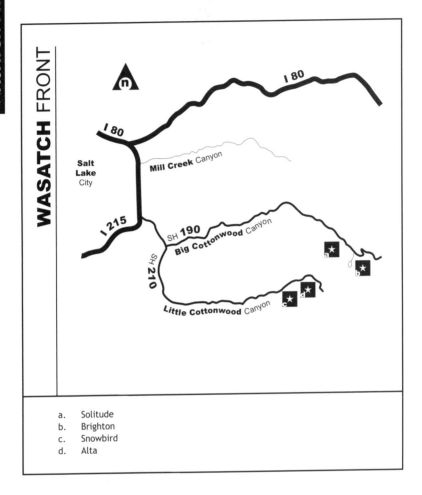

a. Solitude
b. Brighton
c. Snowbird
d. Alta

people who come to ski, ride, hike, and climb here are the kind of people you don't mind cramming in next to on the tram. These are people who would rather ski hard than look pretty. They're an adventurous breed, full of the sort of joie de vivre that great mountains inspire.

You know how every ski area has a look—a collection of brands and styles that dominate? In Aspen, the look is Jet Set and Post Card and other such high-end brands. In Vail, it's Descente and Bogner for the tourists, Napapjri for the locals. Well, in Snowbird and Alta, it's helmets. Most of the good skiers and snowboarders at both areas have taken to wearing brain buckets. Little Cottonwood is also a goggle place; sunglasses are fine for the deck but of little use when you're dropping into High Rustler or Great Scott. Backcountry gear is also de rigueur. Forget the mink but bring your skins.

Although the name is diminutive, Little Cottonwood Canyon is anything but. This U-shaped, glacially gouged canyon is the place where the serious come to play, where the best come to experience the best. In the winter, Snowbird and Alta offer the most advanced snowboarding and skiing in North America. Skied together, as these two great resorts can now be, the Snowbird-Alta area far exceeds any lower-48 destinations for steeps, consistent quality of snow, and a serious alpine experience.

But it doesn't end when the snow melts in Little Cottonwood. The climbing in this canyon is world-class. "If you meet a professional climber anywhere in the world and he tells you he lives in the States, he probably lives in Utah," said mountain diva Kristen Ulmer. Little Cottonwood is part of the reason. With its limestone buttresses and granite slabs, this canyon rocks the piton set.

The location of Little Cottonwood Canyon (the mouth is only 23 miles from Salt Lake International Airport) means you can go from the big flying bird to the 'Bird in less time than it takes to down the steaming Starbucks you bought while you waited for your luggage. The idea that such great skiing and snowboarding, as well as hiking and climbing, is only 20 minutes from a metropolitan city and an international airport has always astounded me. That's why I bristle a little when surveys in major ski mags say that the nightlife in Little Cottonwood is the worst in snow country. I'm not alone in being rankled. "That's just ridiculous," said Ulmer. "Seven miles away from Snowbird is a city of a million people where the nightlife is phenomenal. You're not just partying with skiers, but who wants to? Believe me, the party scene here is fantastic and inexpensive. It kicks Vail's ass." Yes indeed, this is a place that inspires hard-core devotion.

RESTAURANTS

Aerie Restaurant and Lounge (Cliff Lodge, Snowbird, 801-933-2160) is the best place in the state to watch the setting sun color the mountains in alpenglow. This is a fine-dining establishment where the white linen tablecloths stand in stark contrast to Snowbird owner Dick Bass's collection of dark Oriental screens. This is a place where you eat with silver forks and and the staff calls you sir. This is Tavern on the Green or Elaine's—Snowbird style. Hours: Breakfast 7 A.M.-10 A.M. daily throughout the winter. Dinner Monday-Saturday 6 P.M.-9 P.M. Closed for dinner Sunday. Sunday brunch 10 A.M.-2 P.M.

Aerie Restaurant Sushi Bar (same as Aerie Restaurant and Lounge) is a small sushi bar at the west end of the main bar. The place serves really good sushi that probably came in on the same plane you did, only it was packed in ice while you were packed in pressurized air with human cargo. People always say, "I don't know, we're a long way from an ocean." The truth is, even sushi bars in Santa Monica fly in most of their fish. The Aerie's fish is fresh, and the chefs know what they're doing. Local ski model and Snowbird poster boy Brian Beck turned me onto the sushi here. "There's no question about it," he said, "it's the best sushi in the state," he said. Even the uni is fresh. The Sushi bar opens in early December. Hours: 5 P.M.-10 P.M. nightly.

Joanie's (on the main road above the Deep Powder House, 801-742-2221) is the best place for lunch at Alta. The sign outside this funky little Alta institution reads "Serving freshies daily." And it does. This is where the locals lunch. Why? As long-time photographer and Alta denizen Lee Cohen said, "Joanie's is the coolest. It has outrageous smoothies, huge BLTs, good philly steaks; it's just the goods." From the ski hill, Joanie's is a bit of a chore to reach. First you ski to the bottom, then you grab a little rope tow, then you hoof it up several flights of stairs. It's worth it, though. Trust me on this one. Hours: 7 A.M.-7 P.M. daily. Winter only.

Keyhole Junction and Cantina (on Level A of the Cliff Lodge, 801-933-2025) features the excellent southwestern culinary talents of chef Chris Collinson. A kick-back atmosphere that's devoid of any haughtiness, the Keyhole is a place where you can fill the hole that your day on the mountain scooped out of your belly. The portions are big, and the menu far exceeds the expected. Try the goat cheese napoleon. Winter hours: Monday-Thursday 4:30 P.M.-9:30 P.M., Friday-Sunday 4:30 P.M.-10 P.M. daily. Summer and off-season hours vary. The Cantina is a private club for members only.

BEL MORGAN KERIG

Yes, the food at La Caille is as lovely and wondrous as the surroundings.

La Caille (9565 Wasatch Boulevard, 801-942-1751) provides a visit to a romantic place. As you pass beneath the ornate archway and through the pillared gates, you begin to leave Utah. Cross the low bridge between the dark ponds where proud white swans glide, and travel across an ocean of mindscape. As you climb the brick drive, under a canopy of cypress, your spirit flies to the south of France. Pass the vineyard and the paddock where emu and reindeer dwell, and you enter a magical land that's one part Gallic countryside, one part Doctor Dolittle. Beside another pond, where lilies grow and fountains bubble, sits a castle of stone wrapped in vine. Already your evening is better than you ever expected. Already you're won over. If you were served Chicken McNuggets inside, you'd still be happy. This is a magical estate of rare elegance in a no-nonsense state. But it gets better. The white-toothed hostess in a French country-style dress greets you and seats you in the dining room, where the splash and gurgle of the fountains reach your ears. You begin to wonder if the food, which is what you came for (yes, as base as it may be, you're still hungry and want some good chow for your bucks), can possibly measure up. The answer? Yes. The food here is as lovely and wondrous as the surroundings. This is a place that even a serious gourmand will be talking about for years. Hours: dinner 6 P.M.-10 P.M. nightly. Sunday brunch 10 A.M.-2 P.M. year-round.

Lone Star Taqueria (2265 East Fort Union Boulevard, 801-944-2300) is the Beehive's little bit of Baja. The fact that Lone Star is down in the traffic and stoplights of Sandy is a drag, but the food is well worth it. An old station wagon is permanently lodged in the fence surrounding this locals' favorite. The vehicle at one time had "Mexico or Bust" written across the back, but that has faded fully. The station wagon has found its home as a landmark and repository for stickers for all things cool and hip in the West. So too have "the boys" who run this hip little fish taco joint just a couple miles west (straight down Fort Union) of the base of Big Cottonwood Canyon. From the upside-down cowboy boots on the fence poles surrounding the patio to the south-of-the-border music to the sweating bottles of Corona, Dos Equis, and Tecate, Lone Star Taqueria offers the best little bit of Baja in the Wasatch. Try the pescado taco (marinated and grilled fish, with homemade jalapeño mayonnaise served on soft white corn tortillas), the shrimp tacos, or the handmade beef, chicken, or pork tamales. Takeout, including luscious buckets of margarita mix (you supply the hooch), is also available. Hours: Monday–Thursday 11 A.M.-9:30 P.M., Friday and Saturday 11 A.M.-10:30 P.M. Closed Sunday.

The Shallow Shaft (on the north side of Highway 210 in Alta, 801-742-2177) serves fine food in a rustic setting and is the best place in Little Cottonwood Canyon to take that special someone. Call early and reserve a booth by the window that looks out over Little Cottonwood and up to Alta's High Rustler. If you're lucky enough to be there on a night when it's snowing—the flakes drifting down outside match the white roses on the tables inside—and if you do get a table by the window, I recommend the following: a split of champagne, the foie gras, and the filet mignon with crabmeat and béarnaise sauce. This place is far more romantic than its name would suggest. Don't go without reservations. Hours: Dinner from 6 P.M. nightly. Winter only. During the summer, the Shallow Shaft is open Thursday through Monday, but often books private parties during these days. Call before driving up for dinner.

The Steak Pit at Snowbird Center (Level 1 of the Snowbird Center, 801-933-2260) serves high-quality, no-nonsense food from its location down in the belly of the tram building. It has top-notch food, snappy service, and an atmosphere that for some reason reminds me more of a Maine sawmill than a Utah ski resort. From the host who answered the phone with a crisp and quick East Coast cadence, to the high-backed booths of rough-hewn boards, to the family-style salad serving, the

Steak Pit is no-frills good. It gives you just what you ask for, quickly, with quality, and not an overabundance of superfluous flair. You won't form a relationship with the staff; they're all too experienced and busy for any nattering. Although the Aerie Restaurant, up the hill and on top of the Cliff Lodge, has much finer food and service, the Steak Pit is the place to come in your Ugg boots and jeans to get a feedbag on after a hard day on the hill. There's nothing on the menu that you'll struggle to pronounce, and the staff won't ever act as if they're balancing unseen balls on the tips of their upturned noses. They'll give you your food the way you like it (ask for rare and expect blood), in large portions, for a fair price. Hours: 6 P.M.-10 P.M. nightly in the winter. Summer and off-season hours vary.

COFFEEHOUSES AND CAFÉS

The Atrium Espresso Bar (on Level B of the Cliff Lodge, 801-933-2140, ext. 5700) is the spot where Cliff Lodge guests jump-start their mornings, but it's not convenient for day skiers. Hours: 6:30 A.M.-4 P.M. daily.

The 'Bird Feeder on the deck of the Snowbird Center serves up some adequate joe. Get a cup at the takeout window and sip it as you wait for your buddies. Open in the winter 8 A.M.-6 P.M. daily.

Joanie's (on the main road, 801-742-2221) sits on top of the Deep Powder House, overlooks the base of Wildcat and Collins lifts at Alta, and serves up the best joe and smoothies in the canyon. A half dozen tables and booths are clustered into this hip little café where you'll likely find Lee Cohen getting his daily dose. Hours: 7 A.M.-7 P.M. daily. Winter only.

LODGING
All of Alta's lodging properties (Alta Lodge, Alta Peruvian, Alta's Rustler Lodge, Snowpine Lodge, or Goldminer's Daughter) can be booked at the Alta Reservations Desk at 888-782-9258 or at www.alta.com. Alta is not a new, modern resort, and it sells some of the cheapest lift tickets in the country, but don't expect its lodging rates to be low. Alta is very popular with a dedicated group of perennial visitors; the rates reflect a steady and high demand for rooms.

Information on all of Snowbird's lodging properties can be accessed at 800-640-2002 or at www.snowbird.com.

Alta Lodge (801-742-3500, www.altalodge.com, 800-707-2582) is a small family-run hotel that since 1939 has offered a cozy old-school feel to guests who like to meet the people who are serving them as well as fellow vacationers. This is not the Hilton, and the staff won't cater to your every whim. This is a place to share time with people who have the same passion for the mountains that you do. Rates run from about $100 for a single bed in a dorm room during low season to $467 for a two-bedroom during high season. Lodging, full breakfast, and dinner are included in the rates.

Alta Peruvian (800-453-8488) has been providing an intimate old-world ski-lodge experience for 50 years. The service and style, as well as the ambience and atmosphere, are much the same in 2002 as they were in 1952. This is a good feature, because these people know their business. The Peruvian also has the largest heated pool in Alta. Rates include lodging, breakfast, lunch, dinner, and daily lift passes (and are quoted based on an estimated $38 lift pass). They range from about $140 a night for a dorm room (December 20, 2001, through March 31, 2002) to $237 per person for a suite with one bedroom, a sitting room (with a fireplace), a queen bed, and a hide-a-bed. A 15 percent service charge and state and local taxes are added to your tariff.

The **Cliff Lodge** (on the Bypass Road, 801-933-2222) is my favorite hotel in the world. It's not the fanciest hotel you'll ever stay in or the best at guest service. It's not the most well appointed, not the most luxurious. Yet there's something about the Cliff that connects with the type of people who come here. Perhaps it's the simplicity and grounded feeling of the massive, avalanche-proofed concrete structure. Perhaps it's the light touch of Asian design that lends a vague feel of samurai warriors. In any case, the Cliff is in sync with the no-nonsense, full-on outlook you get at Snowbird.

The Cliff Lodge is a high, narrow fortress of poured concrete and sharp angles. Within the stark concrete superstructure are Asian design elements that include owner Dick Bass's collection of Oriental rugs, one of the largest in the world. They cover the floors and hang on walls, and several drape three and four stories down the nine-story atrium that forms the central core of the Cliff.

Ten stories up, the Cliff Lodge is crowned by a rooftop swimming pool and a large Jacuzzi. This bubbling cauldron was once the best place in the world to drink an après-ski beer, but drinks are no longer served there. Still, it's the best hot tub I can think of anywhere. As the sun sets on the steep jagged mountain that seems so close you could reach out of the Jacuzzi with your steaming hand and touch it, your tired body is bubbled and boiled, while the cold air of the coming night fills your nostrils with promises of ever more tantalizing tomorrows. Keep the movie stars of Aspen's Tippler and the well-dressed hordes of Vail's Los Amigos—talk all you want about the Killington's Bear Mountain deck or Whistler's Tommy Africa's—I'll spend my money soaking in the rooftop Jacuzzi of Snowbird's Cliff Lodge.

The spa also offers the full range of massage, wraps, glows, aromatherapy, and beauty services that you'd expect to find in any world-class spa. In the solarium you can sit in silence and watch clouds drift past and snag on the craggy buttress that separates Snowbird from Alta, then drift out of the frame. It is a meditative place where you can recline on lounge chairs in a thick robe, post-steam room or massage, and allow your spirit to settle back into your body.

Rates at the Cliff Lodge vary depending on season. Summer packages start at $49 per person per night and include lodging, breakfast, a tram ride, and vouchers for discounts at Snowbird vendors. Winter rates begin at $139 per room, and during peak season (Christmas and President's Day weekend), the cheapest room starts at $209. You can pay much more as well, but there are too many packages and options at all four of Snowbird's lodging properties to begin to list them here. Pick and choose, and book your own reservations and check availability at www.snowbird.com or call 800-453-3000.

Goldminer's Daughter (801-742 2300, 800-453-4573) is located just steps from the base of Wildcat and Collins lifts. With a terrific deck and a great bar that offers the best place at Alta for an après-ski pizza, this is the place to stay if you never want to have to hoof more than a few feet for anything. The lodge has saunas, hot tubs, a game room, and an exercise room. Rates range from $84 for a bed in a dorm room during low season to $144 per person for a double room during high season.

The **Lodge at Snowbird** is not as swank as the Cliff Lodge, but it may be more comfortable. Book a one-bedroom studio with a full kitchen and a fireplace. Buy your own groceries at Salt Lake prices. Every room has a balcony that offers views of the mountain. There's also an outdoor heated pool and hot tub. Rates run from $113 a night for a studio (during low season) on up.

Snowpine (at the top of the canyon, 801-724-2000) is a cozy family-run hotel near the Albion base.

GOLF

Old Mill (6080 Wasatch Boulevard, 801-424-1302) is the newest golf course in the state. It's an eminently playable course that sits up in the bench next to the foothills of the Wasatch. For best results, play it in the morning before the wind kicks up.

MOUNTAIN BIKING

Little Cottonwood is a steep, rocky canyon, but that doesn't preclude it from having some great mountain biking. And where else will you find tram-served mountain biking? The tram is open for mountain biking seven days a week 11 A.M.-6 P.M. An all-day ticket is $18, and riders must wear a helmet and sign a liability release form. Ride ripping downhill runs through the Wasatch-Cache National Forest; then throw the bike into the big box, and in seven minutes you're on top again. Full-suspension mountain bikes are available for rental through the Snowbird Activity Center located inside Snowbird Ultimate Mountain Outfitters on the Plaza Deck, Level 3 of the Snowbird Center. For more information on mountain biking at Snowbird, call the Activity Center at 801-933-2147.

The **Albion Basin Trail** is an easy six-mile ride—easy, that is, if pedaling at 9,000 feet doesn't bother you. If you hit this ride in late June or early July, you'll be treated to some spectacular wildflowers that grow head high. Park where the pavement ends and ride a dirt road up to the Albion Basin Campground. Turn left (west) onto a doubletrack marked by a steel gate and a bike decal and head toward the base of the Sugarloaf lift. Fork right on a doubletrack that shoots down

GORDY PEIFER

Matt Smiltneek rolls through wildflowers in Alta's Albion Basin.

the east side of the canyon. Then take the next left fork and ride the Meadows trail.

PARAGLIDING

Cloud 9 Soaring Center (12665 Minuteman Drive, 801-576-6460, www.paragliders.com) is one of the West's best places to learn to paraglide or hang glide. The reason? A long grassy platform that sticks out into the valley and is aptly called Point of the Mountain. Here, steady winds blow out of the south all morning and the north all afternoon. Steve Mayer, who runs Cloud 9, teaches beginners in the morning and more advanced students and accreditation candidates in the afternoon. Cloud 9 provides all the gear, including helmet, and asks only that you wear high-topped hiking boots and come with a bottle of water (the hiking will make you thirsty).

Learning here is a true adventure. Mayer and his instructors take you step by step through flying procedures and how to set up the paraglider. Then you begin with short flights: You stand on the grassy slope, pull the paraglider into the air behind you, then run. As the kite fills with air, you leave the ground. Mayer has students progress up the hill for longer flights as skills develop. The landing area is wide and open. Although paragliding looks scary, this learning experience was not. Both the takeoffs and landings were gentle. By the fourth or fifth flight, Mayer has most students getting airborne for a 20- or 30-second flight. During this flight, Mayer uses a radio that's strapped to your chest to coach you through steering, braking, and flaring the canopy for landing. This intro course, which takes four hours and costs $65, is a perfect paragliding primer. After this class, students can judge whether paragliding is for them or not. If you want to go further, a certification course will cost you $900 and will require 8-12 lessons, depending on how well you progress and how much Mother Nature cooperates. The package includes unlimited lessons for up to six months. All equipment for the lessons is provided. Class includes ground school, canopy control, flight safety, videos, approximately 35 full flights at several sites, and radio supervision. Cloud 9 offers a number of other packages for more advanced flying as well. It also operates a store at Cloud 9 Soaring Center that sells anything wind-related (hang gliders, paragliders, paramotors, kite surfing gear, kids' kites, kite buggies, remote-control airplanes) and has a full repair shop for anything that flies. Open year-round. Store hours: Monday-Saturday 11 A.M.–6 P.M.

RELIGION/SPIRITUALITY

Our Lady of the Snows Center (on Highway 210 in Alta) must be the only avalanche-proofed Catholic Church in the country. This burly structure is formed of thick walls of poured concrete and has windows that look out over Alta and Snowbird. Catholic services are held in the center.

ROCK CLIMBING

From March through November, you'll see them in Little Cottonwood. Their parked cars line the road. They sit on tailgates in the late afternoon sun and squint up at the crags and buttresses. They are slim and lithe and browned by the Utah sun. They are an ambitious lot, always looking to climb farther skyward. They are Utah's climbers. A close-knit community of rock jocks, the faithful who gather daily in Little Cottonwood are truly the chosen, for this little slice of Zion is a paradise on earth for rock climbers. In the fine book *Rock Climbing Utah's Wasatch Range* by Stuart and Bret Ruckman (a Falcon Guide, available at Black Diamond and other climbing stores), the authors devote 166 pages to the climbing in Little Cottonwood Canyon. That's testimony to how much climbing there is here.

From the Bong Eater Buttress just above the parking lot and bus stop at the mouth of the canyon to Commitment at the top, there are hundreds of routes. Parking is something of a problem in Little Cottonwood, so carpool if you can. The routes that open first in the spring and stay dry in the fall longest are on the north side in the first mile of the canyon. Later, in the summer, as shade becomes as sought after as sun was in the winter, move up the canyon to the Gate Buttress area for cool crack climbs that are out of the hot summer sun.

Since large tracts of this canyon are privately owned—the LDS church owns a property on the lower north side of the canyon—and fragile compromises have been worked out for access, it's best to check with a local or visit Black Diamond (see entry under Sports Shops) before you go tromping up toward that granite buttress that looks so appealing from the road.

The sport-climbing wall at the 12-story Cliff Lodge, on its west wall, used to host the best sport climbers in the world in speed-climbing competitions. The wall is still there and can be climbed by appointment only by calling Snowbird Activities Center at 801-933-2147. Snowbird also has a full ropes course with a small climbing wall, a zip line, and balance lines. Run by Adventure Associates, this course also can be booked through the Snowbird Activities Center.

Rockreation (2074 East 3900 South, 801-278-7473) is an indoor rock-climbing gym located in the same complex of oddly ersatz, faux Euro buildings that also house

Black Diamond's retail shop and corporate offices. This place is a cave of poured concrete walls, color-coded, screw-in holds and bolts, and thick, brightly colored climbing ropes. Here, lithe shirtless men and lean tank-topped women scale impossibly angled routes, dangle over your head, and generally bend those laws of gravity that you thought were unassailable. With a thickly padded floor and belays running this way and that, this setting is as safe a place to learn climbing as you could want. Rockreation offers virtually every learn-to-climb option (from beginning classes to Boy Scout merit badge programs). If you're already a good climber, this is the spot to stay in shape or tune your skills. All climbers must pass a belay test and, if you're top roping or lead climbing, tests for those skills as well. Rockreation also offers free showers for climbers passing through the area who may be camping or in need of a rinse. Open year-round. Hours: Monday and Wednesday noon-11 P.M., Tuesday and Thursday 6 A.M.-11 P.M., Friday noon-9 P.M., Saturday noon-8 P.M., Sunday noon-6 P.M.

SKIING AND SNOWBOARDING

Say what you will about your Jackson Holes and Squaw Valleys, but Snowbird and Alta have better terrain, are more accessible, have better and deeper snow (500 inches a year), and have longer and more bankable seasons than just about anywhere in the world. With the addition of a chairlift in Snowbird's Mineral Basin in summer 2001, the two areas, which have always been so close that when Snowbird sneezed, Alta caught a cold, will finally ski as one. The new lift, a high-speed quad located in Mineral Basin, connects the two resorts by transporting skiers to the Sugarloaf saddle area (elevation 10,600 feet). From there skiers can drop into Alta's Albion Basin or Snowbird's Mineral Basin.

Having the two resorts combined will give skiers a chance to experience both old-school and new-school atmospheres, ride new quads and old fixed grips, and ski the best snow in the world on 4,700 acres of incredible terrain. This makes the Snowbird-Alta resort the third-largest resort in the country, behind Vail and Heavenly Valley.

There's one hitch: It's just for skiers. Alta has never allowed snowboarders, and as of press time, wasn't about to start. To keep single-plankers from dropping into Alta, the resort has a gate with a manned shack between the two areas to enforce the restriction.

The connection between the two resorts can easily be accessed by beginner-intermediate skiing from the Albion Basin side, and intermediate skiing from the Mineral Basin side. The Utah Transit Authority (UTA) will connect the resorts' base areas with an expanded bus service seven days a week. The Alta Snowbird Pass allows the combined area to offer 18 chairlifts (4 detachable quads, 1 triple chair, 2 fixed-grip triple chairs, and 11 double chairs), 1 tram, and 7 surface tows. It also has 175 acres of beginner terrain, 1,755 acres of intermediate terrain, 1,770 acres of advanced/expert terrain, 9 base lodges, 22 restaurants, 2 childcare facilities, and 2 ski schools.

Although locals have long been skiing in between the two areas (via West Baldy or the Keyhole chute), legalizing it with the two-area ski pass will forever change these areas and make them the best combined skiing experience in the world.

Each resort will continue to sell tickets good only for its resort, but each will also sell a premium Snowbird-Alta lift pass for $68 per day.

"In Europe the ski areas are connected through lifts, but in the United States I don't know of any ski resort that's like this," said professional extreme skier Kristen Ulmer. "It used to be when you talked about great skiing, you talked about Jackson, Squaw, Snowbird, Alta, and Taos. The idea of connecting two of the best ski resorts in the country makes this without question the coolest place to ski in America. In terms of terrain, accessibility, snow, and vibe, the combination of Snowbird and Alta is unbeatable. I can't think of a skier on the planet who won't want to come here."

ALTA

Alta (at the top of Little Cottonwood Canyon, 801-359-1078, www.alta.com) is a place of legend. What skier hasn't heard of this seasoned veteran of 62 winters? Who hasn't heard about the mythical and magical dumps of snow that blanket this craggy crown of Little Cottonwood Canyon? All skiers should experience Alta at least once before they hang up their boards. "Alta is a locals' mountain where even if you're there for the first time, you can feel part of the scene," said Ulmer, who's had an Alta pass for the past 15 years. "It's such a down-to-earth, granola-crunching, hardcore place that just the fact that you chose Alta makes you cool by definition."

COURTESY ALTA

Alta's powder is the stuff of legend.

Perhaps that's why Alta breeds such fierce loyalties. One is an Alta skier in the way one is a Mavericks surfer. This resort like no other sees the same visitors year after year at the same time. It's not uncommon to find families who have come to Alta every winter, in the same week, for three generations.

It's no accident that the most coveted and famous Alta souvenir is the Altaholics Anonymous T-shirt (designed and produced by longtime Alta photographer Lee Cohen and for sale in all the Alta ski shops); Alta is an addiction. And why not? People have come to Alta to score the best powder skiing in the country since 1938.

The same features that have always made Alta great are as true today as they were in ski-school founder Alf Engen's time.

ALTA SNAPSHOT

Location: Top of Little Cottonwood Canyon, 30 miles from Salt Lake International Airport
Scheduled season: mid-November to mid-April
Hours of operation: 9 A.M.-4:30 P.M.
Base elevation: 8,530 feet
Top elevation: 10,550 feet
Vertical drop: 2,020 feet
Skiable acres: 2,200
Average seasonal snowfall: 500 inches
Lifts: 13 (plus 1 detachable quad shared with Snowbird)
    4 double chairs
    1 detachable triple chair
    3 triple chairs
    5 surface tows
Uphill capacity: 11,284 skiers per hour
Runs: 45 (25 percent beginner level, 40 percent intermediate, 35 percent advanced)
Snowmaking: 50 acres
Ticket price: $38 for Alta, $68 for Snowbird-Alta combined ticket. Season pass: Alta only $895 ($795 before Labor Day), Alta and Snowbird $1,200.

The terrain is still craggy, steep, and magical. And then there's that other thing: "Dumpage! That's what it's all about here," enthused Cohen. "If you like to ski powder, Alta's the place to be."

Cohen should know; the guy has made a career out of incredible powder-to-the-chin shots in *Skiing* and *Powder* magazines. With more than 500 inches of the lightest, driest snow on earth (due to both the desert and the lake effect of Great Salt Lake to the west), Alta's powder skiing is no secret. So why wasn't it overrun long ago? Two words: slow lifts.

"For the most part, Alta hasn't jumped onto the bandwagon fast, fast, fast," said Cohen. "Alta has always been more concerned with the experience on the hill than getting a million people back up it as fast as possible. At Alta there's space to do your thing on the hill." Which means more powder for the people. You'll get far fewer vertical feet at Alta than you will at, say, Vail, but Altaholics say the quality is worth it.

"Alta is a small place, but it skis big," said Cohen, referring to Alta's misleading stat of 2,020 vertical feet. "Alta has open, straight-shot skiing all over the place." That means no run-outs or wasted turns. On runs like High Rustler, you drop in and don't stop turning until the chair. The fact that it's two chairlifts and a traverse/hike to get there means the powder stays fresh a lot longer.

Although the powder at Alta is legendary, some things have changed. "Alta used to be superfamous for old-school," said Cohen, "but it's gotten more current. You still have your old-school crowd out there, but now you have your cutting-edge jibber fashions as well."

Old school or new school, however, one fabric seems eternally associated with Alta: Gore-Tex. Functional definitely takes precedence over fashionable here. A hooded Gore-Tex shell with a powder skirt and double zippers is to an Altaholic what a Brooks Brothers suit is to a Boston banker.

One fashion statement you will not see at Alta is the snowboard. Alta is one of the few remaining resorts to continue to ban snowboarding. Whether the shared lift pass with Snowbird (which permits snowboarding) will change that remains to be seen.

THE ALTA LOOK

Equipment is the most important thing here. Mount some telemark bindings on fat skis (preferably K2's Jerry Launcher, which has Jerry Garcia-inspired graphics). Now get some Scarpa tele boots, a pair of high-cuffed Marmot gloves, and some technical but not flashy Gore-Tex, and you're good to go.

HOW TO SKI ALTA

For a long time, locals have made laps on the Wildcat and Germania chairlifts, but with the addition of a quad chairlift at Sunnyside, the Sunnyside-Sugarloaf combination may ski just as well. At Alta, the best skiing is a traverse or short hike away. It's a great place to wear a Camelback full of water.

SNOWBIRD

Snowbird (800-232-9542, www.snowbird.com), even after 30 years in this canyon, is still the new kid on the block—the new kid on steroids, that is. Snowbird is a big-mountain type of skiing environment. Although the resort has been making great strides in opening up the mountain to more family skiing and riding—family-favored ticketing (two kids under 12 ski free for each ticket-buying adult), expanded grooming, new beginner and intermediate areas, and slow-skiing zones—the place really excels in the advanced skiing department. The tram is key to what makes this such a serious-skier mountain. In just seven minutes, you're back at the top, facing down more than 3,000 vertical feet of expert terrain (choose the right route and there's almost no run-out). "The tram is it at Snowbird," said Kristen Ulmer. "Because of it you can ski for three hours and get the same amount of vertical that you get at another ski area in seven. Snowbird skiers will go ten years and ski nothing but the tram."

The terrain is the other factor that makes Snowbird legendary. From the Upper Cirque to Lower Daltons, it is steep, and for most of Snowbird's long season, it's covered with the deep, light, and dry. Those who haven't skied Snowbird for a few years and remember huge lines at the tram will want to return now because the picture has changed. Mineral Basin, the large south-facing bowl directly off the back of Hidden Peak (the tram terminus) not only offers a wide sunny bowl of benched terrain (ranging from lower-intermediate to expert) but also makes the entire mountain ski better. When Mineral Basin opens (usually an hour or so after the rest of the lifts) each day, it siphons off crowds from all the other sections of the mountain.

POWDER DAY AT THE 'BIRD

Everyone knows that a big powder dump at Snowbird is a skier's dream. It's something that will be remembered for years. The bad news is that because so many good skiers call Snowbird home, perhaps no hill in America tracks out faster on a

SNOWBIRD SNAPSHOT

Location: 29 miles from Salt Lake City International Airport
Scheduled season: mid-November to mid-May
Hours of operation: 9 A.M.-4:45 P.M.
Base elevation: 7,760 feet
Top elevation: 11,000 feet
Vertical drop: 3,240 feet
Skiable acres: 2,500+
Average seasonal snowfall: 500 inches
Lifts: 12 plus 125-person tram (2,900 vertical feet in 6 minutes)
    3 high-speed detachable quads (one shared with Alta)
    7 double chairs
    2 rope tows
Uphill capacity: 15,000 skiers per hour
Runs: 85 (25 percent beginner level, 30 percent intermediate, 45 percent advanced)
Ticket price: $56 all-day adult tram pass, $48 half-day tram; $47 adult chairs only, $40 half-day chairs only; two children 12 and under ski free with paying adult; senior discounts available. Snowbird-Alta pass is $68. Snowbird-Alta unlimited season pass is $1,200.
Address: Snowbird Ski and Summer Resort, Little Cottonwood Canyon Road, Snowbird, Utah 84092 (mailing: P.O. Box 929000, Snowbird, Utah 84092-9000)
Snowbird's central reservations: 800-453-3000
General resort information: 801-742-2222
Website: www.snowbird.com
Sister resort: Zermatt, Switzerland

powder day. Fat skis haven't helped; since they make skiing powder so much easier, now there are that many more people fighting for first tracks. Although the crud still offers great skiing, the pure untracked Utah white offers bliss.

Now the good news: Snowbird has plenty for everyone, but you must use your brain before you use the boards. Here are my suggestions for a powder day: Call the Snowbird road and snow report (801-933-2100) and make sure the road is open. Don't be fooled by the snow report. For whatever reason, Snowbird underreports (I've had some thigh-high days when the report claimed only eight inches of new snow). As soon as you know the road is open, head up. Never mind that the lifts don't open until 9 A.M.; get to the base of the canyon by 8 A.M.

Buy a tram-inclusive ticket. If you don't reach the tram early enough to beat the line, take your first two runs on the Peruvian chairlift. It will be nearly empty at this hour on a powder morning. You won't get to the peak for an extra half hour, but at least you'll be skiing while others are waiting in the tram line. Take your first tram ride and pay attention to the operator's report. Be alert for what isn't said, because the report advises what's closed, not what's open. The tram is also a great place to listen to the locals. They're easily recognizable; look for the guys with the helmets and long, fat skis. Finally, if Mineral Basin is open, drop in. Don't worry if it seems as if half the world is going there too. The two new high-speed quads can move a lot of people, and you won't find a line any longer than seven or eight minutes. From there you're on your own.

The tram is key to what makes Snowbird such a terrific mountain. In just seven minutes, you're back at the top, facing down more than 3,000 vertical feet of excellent terrain.

SNOWBIRD OUT-OF-BOUNDS

Although Snowbird has great in-area terrain, some of the best terrain is just beyond its closed ropes. The first and easiest hike, which is actually in-bounds, is West Baldy. Ski down the Chips catwalk and keep heading east on the ridge between Mineral Basin and the front side. When the trail climbs to your left (north), take off your boards and start hoofing it. Drop in anywhere off the traverse. Take it all the way into Alta if you bought a premium Alta-Snowbird ticket.

For more serious backcountry skiers (or riders), there are also lots of options for hiking out-of-bounds from Snowbird. These, however, require taking some serious precautions. First, call the Utah Avalanche Forecast Center (801-364-1581) and find out if the area and exposure you're planning are safe. Next, listen to the announcement on the tram to see if the backcountry touring gates are open. If they are, you'll need to check in with the ski patrol at the top of Gad II before touring. A short hike from Gad II are the Tri chutes and the Birthday chutes. Both of these areas are steep and offer many different exposures.

THE SNOWBIRD LOOK

Go for the subdued retro flash of new-school clothes (Orage, DNA, BFA, or Hard Corps freeride line), Smith goggles, a helmet, and long fat skis (Rossi Bandit XXX, Head Monstercross, Dynastar Bigs). Hang your helmet, with the goggles still on it, on the tips of your skis as you join the tram line. Bring breath mints for the tram and turn off your cell phone in the big box; if it rings, you will get ripped on.

First Tracks Sunrise Trams are a way to get a jump on the hordes. For $20 you meet a mountain host at 7:45 A.M. and head up on a private tram (just you and others who have ponied up a double sawbuck). This service is limited to skiers of strong intermediate or expert ability. It does not run every day and won't operate on most big-dump mornings because the ski patrol is still out on the hill doing avalanche-control work. So you probably won't get first crack at a two-foot day, but you might very well get first tracks in a foot or less. Don't expect to be skiing Great Scot or anything on the Upper Cirque; First Tracks tours generally ski Regulator Johnson or Chips. For those who like their first powder tracks unhurried and quiet, this $20 is well worth it. Those who have had the experience of a first public tram on a powder morning (picture a New York rush-hour subway filled with overly caffeinated people clutching skis and wearing slippery boots) know that it can be somewhat unnerving for the uninitiated. Snowbird is a passionate place, and never more so than on a powder morning (the locals froth).

Guided Alpine Backcountry Tours are offered from the Snowbird Activity Center on Level Three of the Snowbird Center. There are three programs: introduction to the backcountry, lift-assisted backcountry tours, and mountaineering and couloir skiing. All tours operate only when conditions permit and are tailored to meet individual conditioning and experience levels.

HELI SKIING

Wasatch Powerbird Guides (on the Bypass Road, 801-742-2800, www.heliski-wasatch.com) offers as many as 24 guests a day the chance to ski the incredible Wasatch backcountry in groups of four guests and one guide. "This is the best thing you can do when you're here," said free (extreme) skiing champion Gordy Peifer. "First you eat a killer breakfast while you're staring the chopper in the eye. Then you watch a tape and listen to a safety spiel. Then it's on. Going up with these guys is not only great skiing but it's a thrill ride. You fly up the face of Mount Superior, and the next thing you know you're on the top of a peak. It's mind-blowing." Then you ski some of the best terrain anywhere with the best guides in the lower 48. "The Powderbird guides are super-professional but low-key and fun-loving. They do it because they love to ski. There's no prima donna attitude here. It's a great op, they kick ass for sure," Peifer said. When you're done, they have cold beer or soda waiting for you. Rates range from $490 per person with preseason advance booking to $560 with standard booking during the busy season (December 15, 2001-January 18, 2002, and March 18, 2002-April 15, 2002). During the regular season (January 19, 2002-March 17, 2002), rates range from $630 per person with preseason booking to $700 per person with standard booking. Extra runs cost $60 each.

SPORTS SHOPS

Black Diamond (2092 East 3900 South, 801-278-0233) is the retail outlet that shares the same complex of buildings with Black Diamond manufacturing. Anyone who's into climbing knows Black Diamond to be a serious, high-quality brand. The retail outlet shares that feel; it's a quiet and intense place where real rock jocks shop. Hours: Monday-Friday 10 A.M.-7 P.M., Saturday 9 A.M. -7 P.M., Sunday 11 A.M.-5 P.M.

The Cotton Bottom is a beer-bar dive that's become an institution.

Deep Powder House (801-742-2400) is under Joanie's and just up the hill from the Wildcat and Collins lifts. A favorite of Alta locals, the Deep Powder House is open during the ski season from 8 A.M.-8 P.M.

Mid Gad Test Center (top of Snowbird's Mid Gad chairlift, 801-742-2222 ext. 4240) will let you test-drive any of the new stuff. If you're looking for fatties, get here early on a powder day. They go fast. Hours: 9 A.M.-3 P.M. daily.

Salty Peaks (3055 East 3300 South, 801-467-8000, www.saltypeaks.com) is *the* board shop where most Snowbird, Brighton, and Solitude riders go. Whether it's a snow, skate, snake, dirt, mountain, long, or balance board you're looking for, this is the place. If the shop's ubiquitous stickers on lift towers, boards, and bumpers are any measure of hip, then this place is the hippest. Kids could play Slug Bug with their stickers. Salty Peaks comes complete with a snowboard museum, and its Yellow Pages ad lays claim to the title "World's Finest Snowboard Specialty Shop." This is a very cool shop that does sales, rentals, and repairs. Hours: Summer Monday-Saturday 10 A.M.-8:30 P.M., Sunday noon-6:30 P.M. Winter: 9 A.M.-9 P.M. seven days a week.

SportStalker (on Levels 2 and 3 of the Snowbird Center, 801-742-2872) offers high-performance gear, demos, and rentals. Hours: 8 A.M.-9 P.M. daily.

NIGHTLIFE
BEER
Little Cottonwood is not a partier's canyon. Those as interested in après-ski as skiing will do much better in Park City than in either Little or Big Cottonwood Canyons. The twisty, narrow roads with precipitous dropoffs are not a good place to be driv-

ing after a few cold ones. In fact, some of the best watering holes are down out of the canyons along the skirts of the Wasatch (that's why I've listed the Cotton Bottom and the Hog Wallow here), but those staying up in Little Cottonwood have a few perfect spots for some celebratory suds.

Cotton Bottom (2820 East 6200 South, 801-273-9830) is a beer-bar dive that's become an institution. Tucked into a little flat-bottom nook nearly beneath Interstate 215, the Cotton Bottom attracts everyone from snowboarders to stockbrokers. With its cool old sign featuring a cotton-tailed Bugs-looking bunny, this juke joint is a must-stop for those who like their beer cold, their garlic burgers greasy and fat, and their atmosphere unscrubbed, noncorporate, and wholly unmall-like. It has a pool table where you can shoot some stick, a few TVs that play sports, and a shady patio out back. The Cotton Bottom has a roadhouse feel, with friendly enough staff to get you a beer and burger and then leave you alone. Don't expect Up With People energy or yes-sir-no-sir service, and you'll groove on the CB. Hours: Monday-Saturday 10 A.M.-1 A.M., Sunday 10 A.M.-8 P.M.

Hog Wallow Pub (3200 East Big Cottonwood Canyon Road, 801-733-5567) is a cleaned-up, expanded roadhouse that looks and feels like the Cotton Bottom in new jeans. "It used to be a biker bar," said one patron at the Hog Wallow's trough, "but now that it's been remodeled, it's more of a yuppie biker bar." As I looked out the window to where I had just parked my motorcycle beside a half dozen shiny new Harleys and one sleek BMW touring bike, I couldn't help agreeing as I laughed at myself. The man next to me in Euro leathers, who had his full-face helmet on the bar in front of him (obviously the BMW driver), leaned close and said, "Don't knock us yuppies. There hasn't been a knife fight in here since the remodel." I'm all for

The Hog Wallow's renovation is slick and the staff is fast.

authentic, but it's hard to disagree with the Beemer driver. I'll take a remodeled, cleaned-up bar over a knife fight any day.

The Hog Wallow is just that—a clean, well-ordered place that plays Neil Young and features live entertainment on Thursday, Friday, and Saturday nights. The old and new blend, just as the new hand-carved woodwork blends seamlessly with the old roof beams that still have more than 500 names that were carved into them in the 1950s. As close inspection reveals, the half-century-old carvings are not limited to initials. On the ceiling boards just over the small stage are carved a swastika and an Iron Cross. These two symbols created quite a stir a couple of years back when a woman from Salt Lake noticed them, pointed them out to the management, then became incensed when they weren't removed. At first management said, "We'll just cover it with a flower mural because we're a bunch of hippies, not Nazis." But management recanted and decided to leave the symbols in place to remind people that hatred can occur anywhere at any time. Yet you won't find hatred at the Hog Wallow. Quite the opposite. The staff is friendly and fast, and the odd mix of sub-urbanites (from the upmarket development next door), bikers, students, and yuppies gives the Hog Wallow a friendly and diverse neighborhood feel that is all too rare these days. The patio is a nice spot to spend an evening. You'll still have to go to the Cotton Bottom for a burger (there's no grill at the Hog Wallow), but the patio is a fine place to have wings, a sandwich, or some jalapeño poppers. The menu defines the term "wallow" as (1) a verb meaning "to roll the body indolently in or as if in mud, (2) to luxuriate or revel, and (3) a noun denoting that place where animals go to wallow." The Hog Wallow is aptly named. Go there, shoot some pool, mingle with people who look different but turn out to be pretty much the same as you, or listen to some good live music, and you'll see what I mean. Hours: Monday-Friday 3 P.M.-2 A.M., Saturday and Sunday 2 P.M.-2 A.M.

The Plaza Deck on the upper level of the Snowbird Center has picnic tables and a barbecue going on sunny spring afternoons. Buy a beer downstairs in General Gritts store and drink it on the deck. This is the best place to people-watch the parade that clomps through on the way to the tram.

BARS
The Aerie Lounge (Level 10, Snowbird's Cliff Lodge, 801-933-2160) is a private club where you can sip a quiet beer in refined elegance and gaze at the magnificent mountain you just skied. Unfortunately, sponsorship does not come easily here. The club will ask you to pony up for a yearly or temporary membership. Hours: Monday-Saturday 5 P.M.-11 P.M.

The Alta Peruvian Lodge Club (in the Alta Peruvian Lodge, 800-453-8488) is a private club where you can drink with a wooden Indian in a cozy little nook filled with heavy wooden tables, leather easy chairs and sofas, and a collection of stuffed and mounted creatures. When the wooden Indian starts to answer your questions, it's time to leave. A popular spot for ski instructors. Hours: Winter 4:30 P.M.-11 P.M. seven days a week.

Eagle's Nest Lounge in the Rustler Lodge at Alta (801-742-2200) was remodeled a couple of years ago, and the result is Alta's answer to Snowbird's Aerie Lounge. This slope-side spot fills daily with the guests of the posh Rustler Lodge. Eagle's Nest offers a gilded perch from which to look upon the waning golden glow on Mount Superior. The nicest upmarket place to have a drink in Alta. Hours: 3 P.M.–11 P.M. daily.

The **Sitzmark** in the Alta Lodge (801-742-3500) is the best place to get an après-ski beer in Little Cottonwood. It's also one of the hardest to find. You have to go down the stairs to the lobby of the Alta Lodge, then back up a twisting, turning stairway. Once you're there, however, it's worth running the maze. The Sitzmark is the sort of old-school loft bar where Robert Redford's *Downhill Racer* character might have broken curfew. This nook has a retro feel that instantly connects with the central cortex in every real skier's brain. "When you're there you feel you're directly in touch with the forefathers of skiing," said Gordy Peifer. "The bar is unchanged since 1940, so this is the same window that Alf Engen looked out at his tracks down High Rustler. Even the pictures on the wall bring you back to the days of wool pants and glamorous women who wore makeup to go skiing. They speak volumes about the camaraderie of skiing." The Sitzmark looks as if someone took the attic of a great ski lodge (which the Alta Lodge is) and crammed a bar into it. The ceiling is low, and the bar is down in a hole to your right as you come in. Bend down and pick up that pitcher of dark beer and take it over to the hearth. Kick back in front of the fire and watch out the window as the shadow creeps up Rustler. One caveat, though: Sitzmark is not a place where you want to be an après-ski cowboy and shoot your mouth off about how thoroughly you ripped the hill. The place is the favorite of all the rock-star skiers from Snowbird and Alta; that guy sitting next to you in the worn thermal undershirt may be Peifer or mountain madman Jeremy Nobis. Even if they're not big name skiers, the Sitzmark is the place where the locals and ski patrollers hang. Just be humble in this joint. (By the way, a "sitzmark" is exactly what it sounds like: a mark made by falling or sitting in the snow.) A private club where sponsors are easy to find. Hours: mid-November to late April 4 P.M.–10 P.M. seven days a week.

The **Tram Club** (in the Snowbird Center, 801-933-2222) is down in the heart of the Snowbird Center. From the bar you can look through thick glass panes and see the massive motor and guts of the tram. Anything you've been holding in you can let hang out here. The Tram bar gets the best of the tourists, and it's where the Snowbird restaurant workers come for a cold one after their shift. A private club. Hours: 3 P.M.-11 P.M. during the summer, and noon-midnight from Thanksgiving to the first weekend in May.

Wildflower Club (Level 3 in the Iron Blossom Lodge, 801-933-2230) is the best place at Snowbird for an après-ski wood-fired pizza, or nachos, and a beer. The lounge features a pool table, several televisions, a jukebox, and, more often than not, live music. This is the club of choice for canyon locals. A comfortable private club where sponsorships are easy to come by. Hours: Wednesday-Saturday 6 P.M.-9 P.M., Sunday 6 P.M.-9 P.M. Closed Tuesdays.

8. Big Cottonwood Canyon

D espite a recent surge in construction at Solitude ski area, Big Cottonwood is still the low-key, local's canyon of the Wasatch Front. There's a simple, quiet feel to everything here. The ski trails are uncrowded, the prices low, and the restaurants run at a far less frenetic pace than their counterparts in Little Cottonwood Canyon or Park City.

That's not to say that the recreation in Big Cottonwood is backward; in most other states, Brighton and Solitude would be touted as major world-class resorts. With an average of 500 inches of annual snowfall, varied terrain that challenges the expert but pleases the novice, and lift tickets that cost about the same as a lunch at Vail, these two little-known Utah resorts may be the best values in vertical. A decade and a half ago, I predicted that these two resorts would merge and become one of the best and biggest resorts in the country. Well, my cocksure prognostication was dead wrong; Solitude and Brighton are still separate, little-known resorts that are favored by Salt Lakers for teaching their kids to ski and ride in uncrowded, inexpensive bliss.

The one big surge toward progress has come at Solitude. Intrawest, the ski-resort behemoth that owns Whistler/Blackcomb, B.C., Copper Mountain, Colorado, and many others, has come in to build the resort village at the base of the Solitude ski area. The village has been a go-go affair of bulldozers and big timbers, and today it resembles a mini-Beaver Creek or Blackcomb. The Big Cottonwood resorts are still places where the word "potential" flavors conversations the way a lemon does weissbier. And maybe that's all it will ever be: the place with the greatest potential in Utah. Which is just fine with the people who live here, because they're enjoying it plenty today.

The mouth of the canyon is a narrow pucker of stream-cut gorge. You drive in on a twisting tongue of asphalt that climbs steeply from the valley floor. For the first seven or eight miles, there are small picnic areas tucked into the cheeks of steep

GORDY PEIFER

Alaskan heli ski guide Jim Conway trains by riding up Big Cottonwood Canyon.

rock jaws. These shady nooks are favorite summertime picnic spots for Salt Lake families looking to escape the heat of the valley.

When the mercury climbs in the summer, I too might ride out of Sugarhouse in a T-shirt, but by the time I've throttle-twisted up half the canyon, I'm yanking the leather jacket out from under the bungees. It can easily be 20 degrees cooler at the top of Big Cottonwood than it is at the bottom.

As the temperature drops, the geography improves. As you ascend Big Cottonwood, the tight rock walls of the canyon recede, and wide meadows open. Groves of aspens, known as quakies (they all quake as one), spread across the wide bowl of the Silver Fork area. Whereas the lower gorge was stream-cut, the upper canyon was gouged by glaciers. The wide-open banks and bowls the glacier left behind are as much a boon to recreationists as they were to miners. Most of the hiking and biking trails in Big Cottonwood are remnants of those logging and mining days. Back in 1850 the rich combination of good timber, silver ore, and fresh springs, led to a tent city of some 2,500 people, eight saloons, and several stores in the Silver Fork area of Big Cottonwood Canyon. More than 150 years later, Big Cottonwood has yet to reach that population again. Yet that's just what makes the place great. This is the canyon where you can experience nature at your own pace, by yourself or with a few friends. Hey, they didn't name the resort Solitude for nothing.

RESTAURANTS

Creekside (801-536-5709) is the fine-dining family restaurant in the Solitude resort village. A wide-open octagonal room with tall windows that look out to the hill, Creekside is a place where you can get a wood-fired pizza or a cold beer in a tall, chilled glass. The pastas here are inspired and served in large portions. A fine-dining experience for the whole family. Open year-round. Hours vary depending on the season.

Saint Bernard's (801-536-5709) is the most distinguished of the Solitude resort's restaurant offerings. Sit next to its large hearth and select from the best wine list in the canyon. Enjoy a fine-dining experience in a refined chalet ambience as musical standards such as "From That Moment On" keep time to the crackling fire. Saint Bernard's also serves a skier's breakfast and après-ski appetizers. A private club, Saint Bernard's has a full bar and is open daily from 7 A.M. until 10 P.M.

Silver Fork Restaurant (Star Route #1, 888-649-9551, 801-533-9977, www.silverforklodge.com) is the coolest place in the canyon for dinner. Eight years ago, owner Dan Knopp took this old stone and clapboard café (built in 1947), added a large sun deck for dining in the back, remodeled from the inside out, and created one of the best canyon restaurants in Utah. In the summer, Silver Fork is a destination dining experience for valley dwellers; in the winter, it's a hot spot for Big Cottonwood guests. That's not to say that Knopp is trying to out-gourmet anyone. "We're all about good, regular food," he said. "We stick to the same menu and work to perfect it." If you don't want a long, drawn-out discourse on proper preparation, don't ask him about the pork loin (but do order it). Knopp is a detail freak who won't offer anything unless he's convinced it's superb. It shows. Dinner at Silver Fork—whether you're savoring the views into Honeycomb Canyon from the deck during the summer or soaking up the warmth of the hearth during the winter—is the kind of down-home experience that's all too rare in today's world of cell-phone and modem communication. Face-to-face talk is as much a part of the experience here as the wide wine list and the simple and well-done menu. The T-shirts for sale in the foyer read "Silver Fork: For an atmosphere thought to be forgotten." Indeed. Hours: Monday-Thursday 8 A.M.-9:30 P.M., Friday-Sunday 8 A.M.-10 P.M.

The Yurt (801-536-5709) at Solitude is one of the coolest dining adventures you can have. Strap on the cross-country skis or snowshoes and follow a guide through moonlight-dappled evergreen sentinels. Arrive at a small, round structure that is one part tent, one part cabin. Patterned after Mongolian yurts, this is a place where you'll get more than rancid yak-butter tea. In fact, yak butter isn't even on the menu. Instead, you'll enjoy a five-course gourmet meal. This is truly a special place to come with a group or your special one. Make reservations early however—it's already booked for Valentine's Day 2002. Open seven days a week, weather and conditions permitting, winter only.

COFFEEHOUSES AND CAFÉS

The Silver Fork Lodge (Star Route #1, 888-649-9551, 801-533-9977, www.silver-forklodge.com) opens its doors early and closes them late. It not only provides supercool old-school lodging and great lunches and dinners, but it's also there for you when you need the morning jolt. There are five twirly stools at the old soda-fountain counter where you can belly up for a cup, or you can take a booth and linger over eggs and links. Serving its own blend of Salt Lake Roasting Company coffee, as well as rocket-fuel espresso, the Silver Fork is the place to stop for breakfast or joe-to-go. Hours: 8 A.M.-9:30 P.M. seven days a week.

LODGING

Most of the lodging in this canyon is in the burgeoning alpine village of Solitude resort. Located in the upper parking lot, this new village is centered around the Powderhorn building where a large Euro-style clock bongs hourly into the clear canyon air. Those familiar with the architecture at Whistler or Beaver Creek will find a similar style here. With Tyrolean accents, the scale and grandeur of the buildings are pure American mountain west.

Brighton Chalets (800-748-4824, 801-942-8824, www.brightonchalets.com) is a central reservations office that manages four affordable, clean, and well-kept lodges at the Brighton ski area. The Cottage/Studio sleeps six in two bedrooms and has one bath, a full-sized kitchen, and a wood-burning stove. Rates range from $50 per night during discount weekends to $235 per night during holidays. The Chalet is one of Brighton's funky-cool A-frame houses with a balcony, two bedrooms (sleeps six), and a wood-burning stove. It rents from $80 on discount weekends to

$395 during holidays. The Lodge sleeps 15, has three bedrooms and two baths, a large kitchen, two dining tables, pool and Ping-Pong tables, and rents from $160 during discount weekends to $790 during holidays. The Manor sleeps 19 and has five bedrooms and three baths, a large kitchen, four dining tables, a fireplace, a pool table, and a large-screen TV. It rents for $235 during discount weekends and $1,180 during holidays.

The Brighton Lodge (800-873-5512, 435-649-7940, ext. 236) is an old, two-story motel-style lodging that sits just feet from one of Brighton's chairlifts. With rates that range from $50 a night for a double-occupancy room in the summer to $110 in the winter, this old-school motel just may be the cheapest ski-in-ski-out lodge in the West.

Creekside at Solitude (800-748-4SKI, day 801-534-1400, night 801-536-5700) has 18 slope-side condos for rent. Each offers a wood-burning fireplace, TV/VCR, fully equipped kitchen, living and dining area, wet bar, private deck, and underground parking. Creekside condominium guests also have access to the rooftop hot tub. The Creekside restaurant, located on the ground level, serves up fine fare and has a nice patio where an après-ski beer or bite can be enjoyed. The condos range from $255 off-season for a one-bedroom to $660 for a three-bedroom unit during holidays.

The Inn at Solitude (800-748-4SKI, day 801-534-1400, night 801-536-5700) is a full-service, Euro-style hotel that's heavy on the *gemütlichkeit*. The heated pool is a magic place from which to watch the evening snow sift through the dark sky. Take a sauna and then enjoy a massage from the excellent staff at Big Cottonwood Sports Massage and Therapy, located on the bottom level of the hotel. The library area is another peaceful place to linger over the printed page or play a game of chess. Just to the west of the library is Saint Bernard's restaurant, a perfect place to dine well as you wind down one adventure and plot the next. The 46 rooms in this slope-side hotel are either standard, well-appointed hotel rooms or kitchenettes. New for the 2001-2002 season is an all-inclusive plan exclusively at the Inn. With your nightly rate, you receive breakfast, dinner, and a lift ticket each day. Rates range from $419 for a room during off-peak times to $595 for a kitchenette during holiday periods.

Powderhorn Lodge (800-748-4SKI, day 801-534-1400, night 801-536-5700) sits in the center of the new village and keeps time for Solitude on its large, Swiss-style clock. One-, two-, and three-bedroom condominiums are available for rates that range from $150 for a studio in the off-season to $620 for a three-bedroom unit during holidays.

The Silver Fork Lodge (Star Route #1, 888-649-9551, 801-533-9977, www.silver-forklodge.com) not only provides the canyon's most colorful dining experience and best deck but also offers a handful of great B&B-style lodging alternatives. The rooms are cozy (with homemade quilts and feather beds), rustic (no TVs or phones in the rooms), and as comfortable as grandma's house. This is a place where the floor creaks as you walk and you can almost touch the spirits of a half century of skiers and mountain folk who spun dreams and schemes between these walls. Staying here is like joining a 1950s-era ski club—you're surrounded by kindred spirits, and the staff treats you like one of them. There are five rooms with queen beds and private baths, a family suite with a queen for mom and dad and a bunk room for the kids, and one room with two twin beds. There's also a sunny family room with satellite TV, a sauna, and a workout room. Rates include breakfast. Off-season $80 a room, in-season $125 a room. The suite is $100 in slow season and $150 during peak season.

OUTDOOR RECREATION

HIKING

Big Cottonwood's glacially gouged upper canyon offers smooth, firm dirt roads and trails, many of them left over from the canyon's mining and logging days. You can hike, snowshoe, cross-country ski, or mountain bike into the quiet of the back-country while still being mere minutes from the road.

Brighton Lakes Hiking Trail winds past four different lakes—Dog Lake (which is different from the one in Mill Creek), Lake Mary, Lake Martha, and Lake Catherine— and climbs over into Little Cottonwood Canyon where you come out in Albion Basin next to Alta ski area. This is a great hike to do with a shuttle car. Drop a car at Alta, then drive up to Brighton and go point-to-point. The trailhead is on the east side of the Brighton ski resort parking lot on the service road behind the Majestic Lodge. The trail starts in the ski area, goes past the large Wasatch Mountain Club (built in 1930), then up a fairly wide and straight trail. The trail takes you through wild-flowers galore, past chillingly cold lakes (you're not supposed to swim, but every-one does), and then down into Albion Basin. It's only 3 1/4 miles but it seems much longer, and the hike is more spectacular than it sounds.

Lake Blanche is a well-maintained hiking trail through lots of superb rock for-mations to an amazing basin that contains Lakes Blanche, Florence, and Lillian. This short, steep hike (2.75 miles to climb 2,720 feet to Lake Blanche) is a gate-way to the more advanced hikes: Sundial Peak, Dromedary Peak, and Mount Superior. The Lake Blanche trailhead is at the "S" turn that is 4.5 miles up Big Cottonwood Canyon. Park in the lot marked Mill B South. Go east past the bath-rooms and head up the paved trail. Don't worry, it's not paved for long. Follow the signs for Lake Blanche.

MOUNTAIN BIKING

Solitude Resort (12000 Big Cottonwood Canyon Road, 801-534-1400, www.skisoli-tude.com) offers excellent in-area mountain biking. Whether you're using the resort's chairlifts to access the terrain or doing it the old fashioned way (pedaling up), you'll find a half dozen trails that will thrill you at this little-known moun-tain-bike playground. Single-ride chairlift tickets are $5, and all-day passes run $15. Mountain-bike rentals go for $10 an hour or $35 for a full day. Discounts are offered for multiday rentals.

GORDY PEIFER

Ashley Christensen rides the ridge at Solitude.

The **Wasatch Crest Trail** offers 28 miles of the best, most scenic, most grin-inducing alpine riding you'll find anywhere in the world. An overblown claim? Ride it and then tell me I'm wrong. It begins high up on Guardsman Pass, which runs between Big Cottonwood Canyon and Park City, and rides the crest between Mill Creek and Big Cottonwood Canyons, along the top of the Park City and Canyons ski areas, before it plunges 20-something miles all the way to Wasatch Boulevard on the east bench of the Great Salt Lake Valley. There are many ways to do this epic ride. This is my favorite: Drop a car at the bottom of Mill Creek near the Olympic Hills Shopping Center at 3800 South and Wasatch Boulevard. The Park-and-Ride lot there is a safe place to park. Drive your second car to the south on Wasatch Boulevard until you come to Big Cottonwood Canyon Road. Take a left and drive up Big Cottonwood for 13 miles until you see a sign for Guardsman Pass and Park City. Take that left (which is almost a U-turn) and drive up the Guardsman Pass road until the second time the road switchbacks to the east. Park on the side of the road here. Now ride the short downhill on the four-wheel-drive road that heads north. As the road begins to climb, find a comfortable gear and settle in. This climb is only about two miles, but it gets steeper and steeper all the way up. It will hurt less if you pace yourself. Once you're up there, however, you're in for some fun.

From the top of the climb, head west along the trail that garlands the peaks for the next half dozen miles before it drops and takes you through pine forests, across mountain meadows, and into the Mill Creek drainage. Although there are a couple of technical downhill spots, the majority of this ride is big chain ring and banked turns. After the trail dumps you out onto paved road, ride down about three miles, then turn to the right and catch the top of the Pipeline Trail for more singletrack. This trail has a precipitous drop off the left edge, but it's a gas. Take

Left Kai Larsen rides a high traverse between Solitude and Brighton ski areas. *Right* Flying high at Brighton.

it easy to avoid calamity with hikers. Take the turn for Rattlesnake Gulch and ride the steep, snakey trail back down to the road. The dirt on this section can get very silty and fine—in mid-summer it's like riding on brown baby powder—which makes a couple pitches quite tricky. Don't be too proud to walk it. Glide down the last couple of miles of paved road to your shuttle car. A couple of caveats, however: The lower portion of this ride is open to mountain bikers only on even-numbered days, and even then it can be pretty crowded between July 1 and September 1. If you go then, rein it in on the lower trail, because you will meet hikers, dogs, and other bikes. For more information on this and other trails in this area, call the Wasatch-Cache National Forest, Salt Lake Ranger District at 801-943-1794.

NORDIC SKIING
The **Nordic Skiing Center** (801-536-5774) at Solitude offers the best, high-alpine cross-country skiing experience on the Wasatch Front. Just up Big Cottonwood Canyon Road, you'll find the base of the touring center tucked into a basin at 8,700 feet. From here Nordic skiers set out on 20 kilometers of groomed trails. For a warm-up, ski diagonal stride or skate Lake Flat as it ushers you under a large cliff band that affords views in every direction. Then drop down toward the Solitude ski area base and hook through aspens and evergreens on the Cabin Loop. Crisscrossing with the ski trails are snowshoe trails that climb quickly into dense woods where you'll hear only your breathing and the shushing of the treetops in the wind. Nordic Center tickets are $10 for a full day and $7 for a half day (starting at 12:30 P.M.). Rentals and Nordic skiing workshops are available.

BRIGHTON SNAPSHOT

Location: 35 miles from Salt Lake City International Airport
Scheduled season: Early November to late April
Hours of operation: 9 A.M.-4 P.M., with night skiing 4 P.M.-9 P.M. Monday-Saturday mid-December until late April
Base elevation: 8,755 feet
Top elevation: 10,500 feet
Vertical drop: 1,745 feet
Skiable acres: 850
Average seasonal snowfall: 500 inches
Lifts: 7 plus 1 rope tow
    3 high-speed quads
    3 double chairs
    1 triple chair
    1 rope tow (at the halfpipe)
Uphill capacity: 10,100 skiers/riders per hour
Runs: 66 covering 30 miles (21 percent beginner level, 40 percent intermediate, 39 percent advanced)
Snowmaking: 200 acres
Terrain park: Yes. Lift-serviced during the day and for special night events.
Ticket price (2000-2001): $37 for full day, kids under 10 ski free.
Central reservations: 800-873-5512
General resort information: 801-532-4731
Address: Brighton Resort, Star Route #1, Brighton, Utah 84121
Website: www.skibrighton.com
Snow report: 800-873-5512, 801-532-4731

SKIING AND SNOWBOARDING IN BRIGHTON

Brighton (801-532-4731, www.skibrighton.com) was born back in 1936 when some members of the Utah Alpine Ski Club thought it might be fun to build a "skier tow" out of half-inch rope and an old elevator drum. The ensuing invention not only burned through the palms of the club members' gloves but also made Brighton the first lift-served ski resort in the state. A couple of years later, the same club decided to spare the gloves and haul skiers with an inverted T. In 1939 a second T-bar was built, and in 1946 came the first chairlift. Although these shenanigans are probably more lighthearted when viewed through the sepia tones of nostalgia, from our vantage point fifty years later, Brighton is a place that just feels as if it was founded on fun. The skiers and snowboarders (you'll find more of the latter than the former) who ply its slopes daily still share that Jones for pure and simple mountain fun.

In 1987, Boyne U.S.A., a family-owned corporation established in 1947 by Everett Kircher, bought Brighton and furthered the fun factor. Today, John Kircher, Everett's son, oversees Brighton as well as Crystal Mountain in Washington state. Anyone who has ever skied Crystal Mountain knows what fun is. Brighton has a rustic feel that doesn't take itself too seriously. Like Crystal, Brighton has tremendous terrain that the overseers don't mess with. They put up lifts and let you have at it—which is just how a mountain resort ought to be. Even the early curtain of darkness that falls over these slopes in winter doesn't stop the fun. Brighton offers the most extensive night skiing and riding in the state.

BRIGHT NIGHTS

Brighton's night skiing and riding are serviced by the Explorer triple chair, Majestic double chair, and the Crest Express. With a nocturnal uphill capacity of 1,800 people per hour, Brighton offers night riding from mid-December until early April. Pay $22 to ride 4 P.M.-9 P.M., or buy a twilight lift pass ($37) good 12:30 P.M.-9 P.M. Hardcores will want to go for a superticket, which is good 9 A.M.-9 P.M. and costs $41. (Ticket prices listed are for the 2000-2001 season.) The nighttime scene here is cool and mostly defined by snowboarders. It also provides a great alternative for visitors who arrive in town late in the afternoon and just can't wait to strap 'em on.

THE BRIGHTON LOOK

Go with snowboard wear. Special Blend or Burton gear are both good choices. Buy a cheap beanie at D.I. (Deseret Industries, the best and biggest chain of second-hand stores I can think of) and some Spy goggles. If you're a skier, go old-school with a Gerry down parka and a pair of retro-styled fatties.

SKIING AND SNOWBOARDING IN SOLITUDE

Solitude ski area (801-534-1400, www.skisolitude.com) is a place that just doesn't seem to add up. The terrain here is spectacular. From the chutes and open-bowl skiing at the 10,000-foot summit to the benched, steep terrain of the Headwall Forest or Honeycomb Canyon, you can find pockets of deep and fresh three and four days after a storm. The people here are relaxed and friendly, and the

SOLITUDE SNAPSHOT

Scheduled season: Early November through late April
Hours of operation: 9 A.M.-4 P.M.
Base elevation: 7,988 feet
Top elevation: 10,035 feet
Vertical drop: 2,047 feet
Skiable acres: 1,200
Average seasonal snowfall: 500 inches
Lifts: 7
    1 high-speed quad
    2 triple chairlifts
    4 double chairlifts
Uphill capacity: 11,200 skiers per hour
Runs: 63 trails (20 percent beginner level, 50 percent intermediate, 30 percent advanced)
Ticket price (2000-2001): $39 for adults, kids under 10 ski free.
Snow report: 801-534-1400

turnstyle lift-ticket checking system is friction-free. There's never a line for tables in the restaurants, and the sub-$40 lift ticket makes it a place where a family can still afford to ski together. So where are all the people? That's the part that has never added up for me. The lines down Middle Slope, Parachute, and Cirque offer outrageous steeps that rival Snowbird's and Alta's. The tree skiing in Honeycomb Canyon is as good as the best at The Canyons. Yet Solitude remains the province of a few visionary locals who are more into the ride than the scene. But then Solitude's logo bears the outline of a lone eagle, soaring, eyes raised as it rises above the din. Never was a totem so aptly matched.

I find it best to park at the upper lot and take the Sunrise lift to the Summit chair. Watch the board at the top to see when you're able to hike the peak. Dropping in on any of the lines you'll come to off this knife-edge hike is a thrill you won't soon forget.

THAT'S THE TICKET

Solitude is the first ski area in the country to completely do away with wickets, peel-off-stick-on punch passes, and handheld bar-code scanners. The Solitude Access Card is a thin piece of plastic about the size of a credit card. Purchase it at the ticket office, then slip it into your pocket or on an armband. When you ski up to the chairlift, a low-frequency radio signal reads the card and opens the subway-style turnstile for you. At the end of the day, drop the used card into a recycling bin so it can be used again. No paper, no sticky stuff, no wickets, and no geeky, flapping ticket. Now that is just the ticket.

THE SOLITUDE LOOK

Low-key, retro-flavored, muted-color togs are *de rigueur* here. This is not a poseur's place; it's a serious mountain that gets serious weather. Go with trusted ski-wear manufacturers that make simply styled but technical garments. Try Fila or Descente (the DNA line is perfect) and some Rossignol Bandit XXXs. Smith goggles and glasses will have you looking like a local.

SPORTS STORES

Bottom Line Snowboards (Star Route #1, 801-293-1642) is a cool little log cabin snowboard shop on the north side of the main road at about mile 12.5, just before you get to Solitude. With rentals, sales, and service, this niche and nook shop carries the original and best powder stick made: the split-tail Winterstick. Bottom Line also carries Burton equipment and Special Blend clothing. This is the hang spot on a sunny spring afternoon for all those single plankers who have been ruling the trees at Solitude and Brighton all day. First one there gets the barrel chair. Hours: Open seasonally; call for hours.

Powderhorn Adventure Center (801-536-5734) in the heart of the Solitude village is a place to rent skis, snowboards, or have repairs done on your gear. Open 8 A.M.-8 P.M. daily.

NIGHTLIFE

BEER

The Last Chance Mining Camp (801-534-1400) is an upstairs beer bar at the base of Solitude ski resort. This is where lots of kickback resort employees come to have a cold one after work or skiing. A casual, shimmy-off-the-boots-and-sit-around-in-your-stocking-feet feeling pervades. Hours: 2 P.M.-6 P.M. daily.

BARS

Molly Green's (at the top of Big Cottonwood, 801-432-4731 ext 206) is a gabled, chalet-style haunt for locals. Smells of beer, tobacco, and wet wool greet you as you step into this bastion of ski-bardom. You can drink Irish whiskey here under the watchful gaze of dusty stuffed animal heads or shoot pool with the snowboard and old-school-skier crowd that hangs here. Just a few years ago, the rift between skiers and snowboarders was purported to be as wide as the Grand Canyon, but the great gulf never was felt at Molly's. Here generations of snow sliders peacefully imbibe together. The ironic thing about the old-school skiers and the younger snowboarding crowd is that the fashions are almost identical. This is the kind of mountain bar that the famous ski bars (the Million Dollar in Jackson or the Tippler in Aspen) might have been before they were overrun by cell-phone-toting tourists. A private club, Molly Green's is open year-round. Hours: Winter Monday-Saturday 11 A.M.-11 P.M., Sunday 11 A.M.-9 P.M. Call for summer hours.

The Thirsty Squirrel (in the Powderhorn Building, 801-536-5797) used to be just like Molly Green's, but progress prodded it into the new millennium. The old Thirsty Squirrel was such a cool locals haunt that tourists and guests of the Inn at Solitude weren't comfortable in its lair. The new bar is not like that. A completely nonthreatening environment where anyone can feel at ease, the Thirsty Squirrel does have one remnant of the old days: a framed 8x10 of the famously, um, ballsy (how else to say it?) squirrel on his hind legs. A private club where membership is included in your condo rental fees but not in your Inn at Solitude tariff. Hours vary depending on the season.

9. Mill Creek Canyon

Mill Creek has always been the canyon for Salt Lakers. One of the only canyons to have thick stands of timber, Mill Creek was first home to the sawmills of the early pioneers. Years later, Mill Creek became the center for the Salt Lake chapter of the Boy Scouts of America (Salt Lake still has a strong Scout tradition). Even today, the shade and rushing waters of Mill Creek entice people out of the heat of Salt Lake and up into its midst for cook-outs and get-togethers; it's the unofficial picnic capital of Salt Lake City. Home to nine designated picnic areas with tables and barbecue pits, Mill Creek is the best spot for a drive-to canyon picnic. Vehicles pay a day-use fee of $2.25 (pedalers and pedestrians who don't park in the canyon aren't charged), bikes are allowed on trails only on odd-numbered days, and camping in Mill Creek is prohibited. Mill Creek is a refreshing place for a day hike, some good mountain biking, and some fairly challenging rock climbing. One of the best restaurants in the state is also tucked neatly away up Mill Creek.

RESTAURANT

Log Haven Restaurant (6451 East Mill Creek Canyon, 801-272-8255, www.log-haven.com) is the best canyon restaurant in Salt Lake. The food is superb, and the rare and wonderful setting is an old-world timber home in a verdant nook of a stunning canyon replete with crags, waterfalls, lush pine, and sere scrub oak. Back in 1920, L. F. Rains, a Salt Lake City businessman and member of the Metropolitan Opera Company, built this log hideaway as an anniversary gift for his wife. Over the years, it was transformed from a summer getaway to a year-round house, and as it passed from one owner to the next, each added a little something different to its structure. In 1994, Drs. Wayne and Margo Provost bought the property and completely renovated it. Now, manager Ian Campbell runs the place, and runs it well. The service is impeccable, and the staff is proud of its work. Chef David Jones was called the "city's top chef" by *Bon Appetit* magazine in 1998. The wine list is one of the best in the state, and the back patio, situated next to the sparkling waterfall that comes tumbling out of the mossy hillside, is sublime. As might be expected of an 80-year-old post-and-beam home, the interior is arranged around a roaring hearth that in the winter makes waiting for a table almost as gratifying as getting it—but only almost, for the food here is truly extraordinary. The miso-marinated *foie gras* is an incredible dish, as is the pomegranate and cinnamon braised lamb shanks. Ever wanted to try mandarin duck tacos? This is the place.

During the summer, "Culinary Concerts" are part of the restaurant's offerings. In the natural amphitheater just west and up the hill from the restaurant, guests can be entertained by some of the area's best musicians as they eat a gourmet picnic. Bring your blanket, and Log Haven will sell you the packed basket. Log Haven was also chosen by former Salt Lake City mayor Deedee Coradini for her wedding reception. My mom still talks about the place, and we last visited it more than a year ago. A truly memorable spot. Hours: Monday-Saturday dinner from 5:30 P.M.-10 P.M., Sunday from 4:30-10 P.M.

HIKING AND MOUNTAIN-BIKING TRAILS

Mill Creek has lots of good hiking trails where bikes can't readily ride, but there are no bike-only trails. Thus a biker should always plan on encountering hikers, but not vice versa.

Big Water Trail is at the top of Mill Creek Canyon. This is a nice, easy 6 1/2-mile (out and back) bike trail that may be crowded with hikers and dogs. The trail joins the Great Western Trail for a spell, then it forks left and heads for upper Mill Creek Canyon and the Wasatch Crest Trail. Stay right and keep on cranking straight through the junction with the Little Water Trail. At the Desolation Trail junction, take a left and drop down to Dog Lake. This is the spot to mow down a PowerBar or something more decadent as you hang on the banks of the pond. Most people take the same trail back, but there are several other options you can explore once you're up there. One word of caution: It's best not to go warping down the d.h. because the chances of hitting a dog or a hiker are just too great. Chill, roll easy, and be courteous so that we pedalers don't lose our privileges.

Desolation Trail is a great quickie hike that offers a panorama of the Great Salt Lake Valley (from an overlook that's just 2 miles from the trailhead) or the beginning of a 14-mile up and back to Porter Fork. This trail was originally constructed as a motorcycle trail, then throttle-twisters were prohibited when the Mount Olympus Wilderness Area was established. The trail is well graded and begins just east of Mill Creek Inn on the south side, 3.4 miles up the canyon. It climbs in shady zigzags through evergreens, then higher through scrub oak, until it comes to a great craggy overlook. Sit here on the spine and decide whether to press on or head back down. Most people head down, but going up and on will take you into a long series of trails including Dog Lake, Desolation Lake, and the Crest Trail.

Mill Creek Pipeline Trail is one of the most ridden and hiked trails in the Wasatch Range. Since the trail follows an old flume, it is graded to a gentle pitch. This singletrack garlands the south-facing slopes where plentiful sun makes it one of the first rides to open in the spring and among the last to get snowed under in the fall. Although bikers will be tempted to let it rip on this trail (the corners are bermed and the surface is mostly baby-bottom smooth), it's not a good idea. There are just too many hikers, and the drop off the side of the trail can provide a long, tumbling wake-up call. Go slow, enjoy the scenery, and live to know your grandchildren.

Bikers should park at the bottom of the canyon. Many bikers used to park at Einstein Bagel on Wasatch Boulevard to facilitate an after-ride cup or snack, but the last time I was there, the plaza manager threatened to tow our cars. There is street parking, but a Park-and-Ride lot is a safer bet. From northbound I-215, take Exit 4; from southbound I-215, take Exit 3. Ride the road up six miles and get on the Elbow Creek trailhead. The descent at the end of this ride is steep, and for some reason this is always where you will meet hikers. Go slow here and yield to those huffing and puffing their way up. For more info on the myriad other hiking and biking trails in Mill Creek, get a copy of *Hiking the Wasatch* by John Veranth (Wasatch Mountain Club) or the USGS Mount Aire, Utah, map.

ROCK CLIMBING

Mill Creek isn't noted for good climbing, but there are a couple of spots worth mentioning.

Church Fork Wall is 2.4 miles from the fee station. A limestone buttress, this shady area is right next to the Church Fork hiking trail. A lot of top-roping goes on here, or you can lead a bolted route called Bohemian Crystal on the east face.

The **Stitches Wall** is 1.5 miles from the fee station at the bottom. Park in the lot on the north side and hike up a steep slope on the north side of the road. Head for a big fin of rock that sticks out about 250 feet from the parking lot. The rock in this section tends to be sharp—hence the name—but there are a few routes (Itchy Stitches and Mr. Milkbones) that make for tricky climbing. The wall is bolted.

There are a handful of other routes on this long limestone wall. For more information on these climbs or others in the Wasatch, get a copy of *Rock Climbing Utah's Wasatch Range* by Bret and Stuart Ruckman, published by Falcon Publishing and available at area bookstores or at Black Diamond.

10. Sundance Resort

When colleges teach graduate-level courses in branding and merchandising, they should start with a case study of Sundance. Not just a resort, Sundance is also a film festival, a high-end clothing and lifestyle catalog, a cable TV channel, and an institute dedicated to furthering independent art. Never have I seen such a comprehensive and perfectly executed branding exercise. This is not to suggest that Sundance has sold out or compromised its core values for short term revenues. Quite to the contrary, every aspect of this cross-platform wonder exudes quality and integrity to a degree that is so rare as to be virtually unheard of in these days of megamergers and soulless conglomerates.

It began with the resort. Fifty-one miles south of Salt Lake City, up the north fork of the Provo River, lies a narrow-mouthed canyon that fans out into wide meadows at its upper reaches. Bordered to the west by a sharp spine of mountain called Timpanogos, this canyon was used as a summer retreat and hunting grounds by the Ute Indians. The first Europeans to settle here were the Stewart family, a clan of Scots who used the high pastures for grazing sheep. Generations of the Stewarts lived in the canyon, and in 1950 they opened Timphaven Ski Resort on the northeast-facing slopes of the canyon.

In 1969, the same year the film *Butch Cassidy and the Sundance Kid* was released, one of the film's stars, Robert Redford, bought Timphaven and much of the surrounding land from the Stewarts. He renamed the resort Sundance and from the beginning began imbuing the place with his sensibility. In Redford's case, this was a good thing. When his New York investors told him to mow down the trees and fill the canyon with hotels and condos, Redford said no. He had a vision, and it didn't involve clear-cuts or a shopping mall on a ski slope. He saw his newly acquired land as an ideal locale for environmental conservation and artistic experimentation. Exactly what and how this would manifest itself, was not immediately apparent.

After years of brainstorming and failed experiments, Redford took on the challenge of restoring artistic vitality in American film. He established the Sundance Institute and dedicated it to the support and development of emerging screenwriters and directors as well as the national and international exhibition of new, independent dramatic and documentary films. Twenty years later, Institute alumni are some of the most popular and successful filmmakers working in cinema. More than 400 filmmakers benefit annually from Sundance's programs, and at least 20,000 people attend the Sundance Film Festival (www.sundance.org). The films developed by Sundance are watched by millions, and the artists supported by the Institute have received numerous Oscars, Emmys, and International Film Festival awards. The Sundance Festival and Institute led to the establishment of the Sundance Channel (800-SUN-FILM, www.sundancechannel.com), and the great success of the resort's gestalt led to the popular Sundance catalog.

In light of all this commercial success, you'd expect to hook a left off Provo

Canyon and run into a Redford Disneyland. Some sort of Robbywood, right? Wrong. Sundance Resort is so thoughtfully designed, so architecturally harmonious, that it blends into its surroundings better than any resort you'll find. The resort center looks more like a ranch house with a bunch of outlying cabins than anyone's vision of a movie-star playground. A gurgling stream runs through the center of the small cluster of cabins, and the spiritual vortex of the place lies not within a cash register but rather in the wide confluence of two streams under the steady gaze of a bronze American Indian. Throughout the interior of the resort, every board, every beam, every piece of artwork, and every bedspread is on-theme. All of Sundance is imbued with a classy western motif that is at once relaxing and familiar, even on your first visit.

The skiing is also good, affordable, and uncrowded. What Ben and Jerry's is to ice cream, Sundance is to ski resorts: It's a quality place built with integrity and respect for the environment. The mountain biking is equally great, and the horseback riding and fly-fishing are first rate. The artists who come to Sundance impart it with a creative spirit that's magical, and much of the work done here is exceptional. Yet the real measure of Sundance is far greater than the sum of its parts. Sundance is a place of elegance without haughtiness, of grace without affectation. It's a living, breathing lesson in the power of integral synergy. For this reason, it's the best place in Utah for either a romantic getaway with someone you truly love or a sabbatical to work on the great American screenplay (which seems to have permanently replaced the great American novel).

COFFEE

The Deli Grocery (next to the Foundry Grill in the resort center) has a kick-back general-store feel and serves up passable coffee. In the summer you can take it out on the patio next to the fountain, or in the winter pull up a chair right in the little market. The Deli Annex frequently has art exhibits. Hours: 7 A.M.-10 P.M.

BARS

Owl Bar (next to the Foundry Grill) is a classically upscale rustic room arranged around a restored 1890s Victorian rosewood bar. Moved from Thermopolis, Wyoming, to Sundance in 1994, the bar is reputed to have been a hangout for Butch Cassidy and his Hole-in-the-Wall Gang. Drink where old Butch himself once bent an elbow and listen to the best jazz this side of New Orleans (or at least Salt Lake's Manhattan club). A private club, the Owl Bar is open from noon until midnight every day.

FLY-FISHERMAN

What Utah's untracked powder is to skiers, the Provo River is to fly-fishermen. There are two dams (Jordanelle and Deer Creek) within five miles of each other, which means tailwaters with consistent flow and temperature. These conditions make rich spawning and feeding grounds for trout and bountiful waters for fly-fishermen. Ninety percent of what you'll catch out here are wily German browns (there are some cutthroats and rainbows, but they're rare). The Provo, however, is not an easy river to fish. You need a lot of knowledge of the local entomology—

What Utah snow is to skiers, the Provo River is to fly-fishermen.

what works on one end of the river may not work on the other—and success here requires some skilled nymphing. For this reason, even the most accomplished fishermen will want to take a guide, at least on the first time out.

Provo River Outfitters (800-PRO-UTAH, 888-776-8824, www.utahflyfishing.com) is the top guide service in the area. Run by Dave Larsen, who grew up on the Provo River, this company is the most featured guide service on ESPN's *Fly Fishing America* and *Trout Unlimited Television*. Larsen's outfit will supply all the rods, reels, waders, flies, and vests you'll need. Trips to the Provo run daily, year-round, and generally range from about four hours to all day. If you're into fly fishing, or think you might want to try it, these are the guys. The client-to-guide ratio is never any greater than three to one, and you can either receive detailed instruction or none at all. Call for current prices. Also exceptional is Larsen's website (www.utahflyfishing.com). Want to modem out of the office for a few moments? Flyfishing.com offers vicarious sessions (Quicktime and Windows Media video clips) on the Provo River. Broadband fishermen will definitely want to check out the site.

Provo River Outfitters can also arrange exclusive lodging at a place called Boonie's Cabin. This exceptional four-bedroom cabin is deep in the woods, up the canyon from the resort. It has wide decks that loom over North Fork Creek and comes with everything you need. Picture the most perfectly decorated mountain cabin you can imagine. Picture a spot where all sounds are hushed by the soft whisper of pines in the wind and where the decor is what the Sundance catalog had in mind, and you'll get some idea of Boonie's Cabin. Available for select fly fishermen only. Rates range from $300 to $500 for the cabin rental per night.

HIKING

The Sundance Resort borders the Mount Timpanogos Wilderness Area, which was established in 1984 and spans 10,750 acres of National Forest Service land. Hikers in this area will find massive cataracts, glacial cirques, and rampant wildflowers such as Indian paintbrush, penstemon, and mountain bluebell. They won't find namby-pamby hikes: At 11,750 feet, Mount Timp is the second-highest mountain in the Wasatch Range, and the trail up it is serious but shouldn't be missed.

The hike begins at 6,861 feet at the Aspen Grove trailhead. Don't be put off because the trail begins on asphalt; it soon gives way to real hiking through aspens and high-mountain switchbacks. After about three and a half miles, you'll reach Emerald Lake. At 10,800 feet, this chilling lake forms at the foot of a glacial snow-field that lies in the shadow of Timp year-round. The hiking from here is tough but worth it. Few summits offer such a storybook setting, but be cautious. Step off one side and it's 2,000 feet straight down, off the other and you'll tumble halfway to Provo. The summit has a shelter, but it's no Hilton and not a place you'd want to move into. This 16 1/2-mile hike is rewarding so set aside the entire day. Black ice lurks on the trail in some dangerous places; this is not a trail you want to descend in the dark.

For more information on the Mount Timp and other hikes, go to www.sundanceresort.com, call 801-223-4849, or pick up a Timpanogos Cave National Forest Service map, a Uinta National Forest Service map, or the USGS Aspen Grove map.

HORSEBACK RIDING

Sundance Stables (801-223-4170) offers visitors the chance to let big beautiful animals do the hiking for you. Rides to Elk Meadows, Stewart Falls, or on the Great Western Trail are popular. All rides are on Western-style saddles and include a short instructional arena lesson. The Elk Meadows tour, which lasts about 45 minutes, will run you $35 per person and leaves at noon and 6:00 P.M. in the summer. The Stewart Falls tour takes about two hours, costs $55 per person, and departs at 10 A.M., 1 P.M., 3 P.M., and 5 P.M. The most popular choice is the Dry Lakes tour, which takes three hours, costs $75 per person, and begins at 9 A.M., 11 A.M., and 2 P.M. Overnight tours as well as combination horseback and fly-fishing adventures are also available.

LODGING

Sundance offers 96 elegant Western-style cottages. Each has a stone fireplace or woodstove, hand-crafted furnishings, Native American art, and plush down bedding. Rates run from $195 to $430 per room per night and include breakfast in the American Foundry Grill.

Just up the hill from the cottages, Sundance also offers secluded and luxurious mountain homes for $500-$1,500 a night. For details and reservations, call 800-892-1600 or go to the Lodging section of www.sundanceresort.com.

MOUNTAIN BIKING

Sundance doesn't have the huge network of mountain-bike trails available at Park City, Deer Valley, and Moab, but the trails it does have are really good. My favorite area is at the top of the Alpine Scenic Highway (State Highway 92). Park in the

Forest Service parking lot and take the Ridge Trail to the west. There's a terrific loop to be had that offers some of the best singletrack you'll ever roll down. Portions of this loop are on the Great Western Trail. There are also more than a dozen other loops and trails in this area. Call the mountain-bike center (801-223-4849) at Sundance and ask for maps and info about the Ridge Trail Complex.

You can also ride the lifts for your knobby-tire fun at Sundance. Sundance offers 25 miles of singletrack and fire-road riding from the summit of Ray's lift. Day passes, twilight passes, and season passes are available. The lift runs from the end of May through mid-October from 10 A.M. to 6:30 P.M., weather permitting. A biking day pass is $15, a half-day (starting at 2:30 P.M.) costs $12, and a twilight pass (good from 4:30 P.M. on) costs $8. Helmets are required and can be rented for $3. Bikes can be rented for about $20 for a half day and $30-$40 for a full day.

Sundance Resort is patrolled by the Sundance Mountain Bike Patrol. Van shuttles can be arranged through the mountain-bike center. There's also a Learn to Mountain Bike program at 10 A.M. and 1 P.M. daily. Reservations for bikes, helmets, clinics, and group sales may be made by calling 801-223-4TIX. Open early June through late October. Hours: 10 A.M.-6:30 P.M. daily.

RESTAURANTS

The Foundry Grill (801-223-4220) serves great food, three meals a day, offers grand views of towering Mount Timpanogos, and features hearty, down-home seasonal cooking from the restaurant's wood-burning grill, oven, and rotisserie. All dishes are seasoned and garnished with organically grown herbs and vegetables. During harvest season, items grown at Sundance Farms appear on the menu. It's not cheap—nothing at Sundance is—but that's not why you're here, right? Hours: 7:00 A.M.-10:00 P.M.

The Tree Room (801-223-4200) gets it name from the large dead tree in the center of the big dining room. The tree wasn't always dead, however, and its presence speaks volumes about Redford. When the plans were laid for the restaurant, Redford noticed that workers would have to hack down a big, old-growth pine. He didn't cotton to this idea, so they built the place around the tree, allowing it to grow right up through the roof. A year later the tree died, but what the hell, it was a brave and virtuous sentiment.

The Tree Room is hung with photographs of Redford as the Sundance Kid, Redford as Jeremiah Johnson, Redford as the Electric Horseman. By all accounts, Bob, as the locals call him, is a maverick and the menu at the Tree Room reflects that aspect. For starters, you're looking at citrus- and fennel-marinated salmon, seared Hudson Valley *foie gras* with vanilla bean-braised rhubarb and peppercress, or maybe a peekeytoe crab Napoleon with tomato confit. Yes, this menu is outrageous. The tastes coming out of that kitchen will blow your mind. You don't want to be wine-numbed for this dinner; pay attention because the food is rare and fine. The *chef de cuisine*, Jason Knibb, bears a striking resemblance to hoopster Kobe Bryant. Born in Montego Bay, Jamaica, and raised in Southern Cal, Knibb earned his stripes under the tutelage of Wolfgang Puck at Eureka in Los Angeles, David Abella at Roy's Kahana Bar and Grill on Maui, and finally at the award-winning

Joe's Restaurant in Venice Beach. He is an unlikely and exceptionally talented chef who creates dazzling food for an intimate atmosphere.

If you eat only a few meals in Utah, make one of them a Tree Room dinner. Start your night with a glass of wine in the library, then migrate to the dining room at your leisure. The light here is soft, suffused with glowing candles, and has the effect of adding a movie-star glow to the faces around your table; even your in-laws might look like matinee idols. Hours: 5 P.M.-10 P.M. nightly.

SKIING

Sundance is not a huge mountain, nor is it exceedingly steep. Yet it has great snow and fewer skiers and boarders than you'll find in any other Utah resort. I once spent a blissful, sunny powder day there with only 36 other people on the whole mountain. Here you can "8" your own tracks and not have to sprint for the sweet lines. The resort has a front and a back mountain, the latter being where the most interesting skiing lies. Bishop's Bowl, on the back mountain, offers a good, consistently steep pitch like a miniature version of Vail's Siberia Bowl. On powder days, it's worth dropping into Grizzly Bowl off the cat track on the way out of Bishop's.

Sundance was one of the late holdouts, but in 1998 it opened its lifts and slopes to snowboarders. This is a hill with plenty of the off-camber, double-fall-line, gullied nooks that can make a snowboard the tool of choice. There's also very little traversing and a popular snowboard park for jibbers.

NORDIC SKIING

Just a mile and a half beyond the Sundance downhill ski area, you'll find 24 kilometers of trails groomed for skating and classical skiing as well as 10 kilometers of separate snowshoe trails.

SUNDANCE SNAPSHOT

Location: 51 miles from Salt Lake City International Airport
Scheduled season: Thanksgiving through early April
Hours of operation: 9 A.M.-4:30 P.M.
Base elevation: 6,100 feet
Top elevation: 8,250 feet
Vertical drop: 2,150 feet
Skiable acres: 450
Average seasonal snowfall: 300 inches
Lifts: 3 chairlifts
Runs: 41 (20 percent beginner level, 40 percent intermediate, 40 percent advanced)
Snowmaking: Entire mountain
Ticket price: $27 weekdays, $32 weekends and holidays
Address: Sundance, North Fork Provo Canyon, RR3 Box A-1, Sundance, UT 84604
Resort information and reservations: 800-892-1600 or 801-225-4107
Website: www.sundanceresort.com
Snow report: 801-225-4100
Reservations: 800-892-1600
Fax: 801-226-1937

The **Sundance Nordic Center** (801-223-4170) has all the rental equipment, teaching staff, and accessories you could want. On Friday and Saturday nights, the center features twilight Nordic skiing until 9 P.M. The trails, lit by Coleman lanterns, are the stuff of long memories. Trail fees are $9 for all day and $6 after 2 P.M. Rentals range from $7 to $18 depending on equipment. Hours: Sunday-Thursday 9 A.M.-5 P.M., Friday and Saturday 9 A.M.-9 P.M.

THEATER

Set in a natural amphitheater of mountains and old-growth pines, the Sundance Theater (801-223-4110, www.sundance.org) is an outdoor venue that puts on first-rate shows in the summer. In addition to a troupe of talented locals, Sundance brings top-rate talent from New York and L.A. to work in these productions. Since 1981, the theater has staged such shows as *Gypsy, The Music Man, Carousel, A Midsummer Night's Dream, Into the Woods, Seven Brides for Seven Brothers, A Funny Thing Happened on the Way to the Forum, The Pirates of Penzance, Fiddler on the Roof,* and many more.

SUNDANCE FILM FESTIVAL

Very little of the Sundance Film Festival takes place at Sundance Resort. The fest outgrew Sundance and moved to Park City and Salt Lake City. This sprawling, colossal affair is held during the second half of January (in 2002 it will be January 10-20). For a full rundown on the fest as well as the other festivals that have ridden in on Redford's success, see the Park City section.

COURTESY SUNDANCE INSTITUTE

More than 400 filmmakers benefit annually from Sundance's programs.

SUMMIT COUNTY

11. Park City

I f being part of a state is as much about a shared state of mind as it is about tax collectors and arbitrary borders, then Park City is a place that never was—and never will be—part of the State of Utah. Park City has the feel of a Colorado town that went on a wicked bender, stumbled behind the Zion curtain, and by the time it woke up, cotton-mouthed and confused, it had hit pay dirt. Blinded by dollar signs, the Colorado party boy forgot to go home.

Even today, Park City walks and talks more like a Coloradan than a Utahan. With its mining-town roots and bawdy history, Park City is much closer to an Aspen or a Telluride than a Salt Lake or Provo. You get the sense that if it could, Park City would secede from Utah in a New York minute. In some ways, it already has. It's not uncommon to meet Park City transplants who've never set foot in Salt Lake City and are proud of it. They drive the I-215 beltway around the city on their way to the airport.

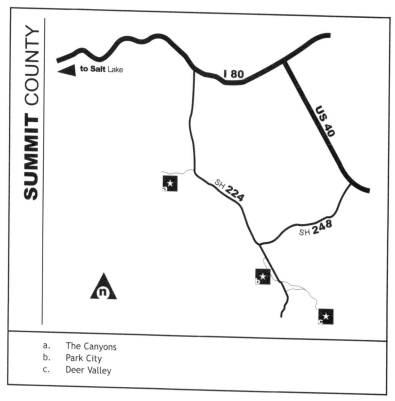

a. The Canyons
b. Park City
c. Deer Valley

Park City and Deer Valley at twilight.

"Park City is an island of sanity in a screwed-up state," said a Park City business owner who was running for local office. Although the town's initials are P.C., apparently not everyone here is concerned with political correctness: the outspoken politico's opinion is nothing new, or unique. In fact, the lines of this conflict were drawn back in the 1860s. As Brigham Young was fervently trying to turn the desert into a garden, word came of the first silver strike in what was then called Parley's Park. As all manner of rascal flooded the Wasatch in search of their scoop of pay dirt, Brother Brigham declared that mining was no mission for Mormons.

"There is no happiness in gold," said Young. And so, as Mormons watered the valley, miners drilled the mountains. As the faithful flocked to Zion, the alchemists on the hill were busy turning silver into whiskey, saloons, and houses of ill-repute. After the silver discovery in 1868, what was then known as Parley's Park City filled with hard-living, hard-drinking Irishmen, Swedes, Finns, and Scots. When miners also discovered gold, zinc, and lead, the town swelled to 10,000 residents (about its size today), and the name was shortened to Park City. At the turn of the century, it was not only one of the wealthiest towns in the West, it was also one of the wildest.

Then, in 1898, most of the town burned to the ground. A flaming stake to the heart of Sodom? Torrents of fire rained down over the damned? Nope. Unlike Sodom or Gomorrah, this town with the strong heart and pugnacious soul rebuilt itself in 18 months and kept right on charging for the next 30 years. Fortunes were made and squandered, and all sorts of hedonist hilarity ensued.

Early in the 1930s, however, the national economy pulled the rug out from under Park City's party. Plummeting mineral prices made mining superfluous, and the rails that had once carried ore to market began exporting Park City's population. The

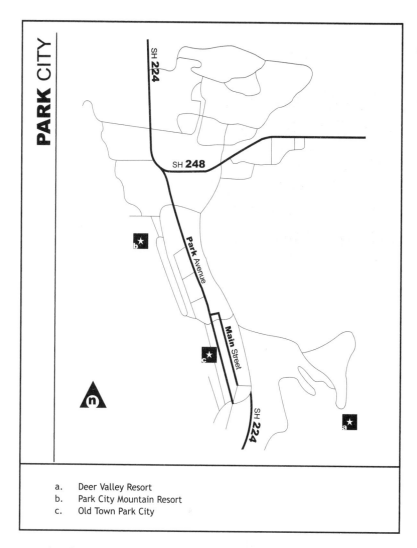

PARK CITY

SH 224

SH 248

Park Avenue

Main Street

SH 224

a. Deer Valley Resort
b. Park City Mountain Resort
c. Old Town Park City

town shut down. Mines that had once bustled with clamorous activity were suddenly silent, their timber skeletons poking from the ground like funeral pyres, and steep piles of mine tailings lay like newly dug graves under the deep Utah snow.

It wasn't long, however, before the bored and broke hangers-on found a way to turn these morbid memorials into ramps to high-flying fun. Using the timber for their launch pads and the steep tailing hills for landing zones, Park City residents soon found a new passion to fill their winter days: ski jumping. It wasn't long before Utahans were arranging winter carnivals around ski jumping and downhill slalom races.

PARK CITY VISITORS BUREAU

Park City's annual blanket of snow averages 350 inches.

Today, seventy years later, Park City is poised to host the 2002 Olympic Winter Games, the greatest winter carnival in the history of sport. And although the bordellos are long gone, Park City has remained the hedonist capital of Utah. The town has more than 100 restaurants and bars and is annually ranked among the top ski towns in the country for nightlife (in 2000, *Skiing* magazine ranked it fifth). Not bad for a town that began as a place to dig in the dirt and drink until you fell into it.

For more than this glancing blow at the history of Park City, visit the museum at 528 Main Street (435-649-6104) or the Park City Visitor Information Center at the junction of Highways 224 and 248 (435-658-4541), call the Park City Chamber and Visitors Bureau at 800-453-1360, or click to www.parkcityinfo.com. The website has just been revamped (weather to snow reports to lodging specials), and calling the Chamber and Visitors Bureau will get you answers on virtually anything you need.

Here are the best ways to get up to speed on Park City when you get there:

• Pick up a copy of the *Park Record* (published on Wednesday and Friday) or go to www.parkrecord.com.

• Tune your radio to KCPW (Park City's public radio station) at 91.9 FM.

• Pick up a copy of *This Week in Park City*, a free visitor's information guide available in most retail stores.

• Get on the free bus service, cruise town, and ask the driver questions.

• Head to Main Street and keep your ears open.

GETTING AROUND

One caveat about Park City: Parking here is tough, and most of it you'll have to pay for. The best bet is to use the transportation system, which is free. Look for the blue signs on the roadside. Buses run 6:30 A.M.-2:30 A.M.; times vary depending on route and time of year. Once you're on the buses, feel free to ask the drivers questions. They're cool, and they all seem to have been in town forever. The buses have bike and ski racks. For recorded information, call 435-615-5350. Look for Park City to develop a free, fully integrated bus system that runs from Deer Valley to Park City to The Canyons and on out to Kimball Junction during the 2001-2002 season. For road conditions, call 800-492-2400.

RESTAURANTS

There are more restaurants packed together in a small area in Park City than anywhere I can think of. The Chamber of Commerce pegs the number at 100, but it feels like more. Expect to find all manner of eateries, but one thing you won't find much of in this Wasatch resort town is lousy food. Restaurant competition is fierce in this town where owners must make their entire year's income in seven or eight months (at best). Thus, weak restaurants don't stay around long, and the new ones generally have something that makes them think they can crack the brutal market. I've included a handful of the ones I like here. For a more complete list, visit www.parkcityrestaurants.org or www.parkcityinfo.com.

350 Main Brasserie (350 Main Street, 435-649-3140) is a seriously refined restaurant with massive booths, an inspired menu, and an Upper East Side feel. The atmosphere here feels like that of a sophisticated tavern in a town known for polo. The food is slightly more adventurous—like a banker in a fuchsia tie—than you'd expect. The result is gratifying. The wine list earned *Wine Spectator*'s Award of Excellence in 2000, and the bar is a perfect place for a Stoli martini with a splash of Chambord. This place was also used as a set in the movie *Net Worth*. Hours: Winter dinner from 5:30 P.M. until 10 P.M. nightly. Summer hours vary.

Alex's Bistro (442 Main Street, 435-649-5252) is the sort of secret French restaurant that you come back to year after year. Slipping down the stairs into the lair of warm smells and gentle decor is to escape the recreate-at-full-speed pace that Park City regularly whips itself into. This is a place of succulent dishes prepared with the caring and grace attainable only by those who love their work. The Sunday brunch is a kingly affair complete with impossible to resist cakes and pastries. Hours: Winter 5:30 P.M.-10 P.M. nightly. Summer Tuesday-Saturday 5:30 P.M.-10 P.M.

Bangkok Thai on Main (605 Main Street, 435-649-8424, www.bangkokthaionmain.com) is Park City's fix for those Jonesing for peanut-sprinkled, cilantro-garnished pad Thai. The decor is predictable, and the service is fast. Dining here offers the pleasure of knowing what you're going to get, then getting it. Hours: Summer lunch noon-2 P.M., dinner 5:30 P.M.-9 P.M. daily. Winter lunch noon-2:30 P.M., dinner 4 P.M.-10 P.M. daily.

Blind Dog Grill (1781 Sidewinder Drive, 435-655-0800) is a surprisingly chic eatery that's far enough off the tourist track to attract only those in the know. The exterior of this restaurant, set in a strip mall, belies the hip, dimly lit interior. And if the ambience is a surprise, the food is an even more unexpected boon. Serving fine American fare with a nouveau flair and great sushi at the bar, the Blind Dog is fast becoming a Park City fave. The fact that part of the restaurant's marketing budget goes toward supporting Park City racer Lincoln DeWitt's efforts to go for Olympic Gold in the skeleton sled race is a testament to the business's brio. The bar here is a private club. Hours: Summer Monday-Saturday bar opens at 4 P.M., sushi bar and restaurant open at 6 P.M. Winter Monday-Saturday bar opens at 4 P.M., sushi bar and restaurant open at 5 P.M. Closing time is 1 A.M., summer and winter.

Buona Vita (427 Main Street, 435-658-0999), a favorite of locals for great Italian food at reasonable prices, was opened three years ago by Alan Galleano and Sidney Lecthar in the Memorial Building, beneath Harry O's. The exposed brick, the blond wood chairs, and the triptych of Rome give this place the feel of a simple Italian café. The attitude is also all Italian: Friends, family, and good food mix as the red wine flows. The staff has a take-it-as-it-comes attitude and won't bug out on you if your three-top grows to five and then to seven. You can just keep dragging tables together as your group expands. Need a place to meet a bunch of people with disparate agendas and get them all on the same page? Buona Vita. It's central, relaxed, and affordable. For this reason, it's my favorite dining spot during the overcrowded Sundance Film Festival week. The gnocchi bolognese will fill a hole in you like nobody's business and the handmade raviolis are superb. Hours: 5 P.M.-close nightly; closed Mondays in the summer.

Burgie's (570 Main Street, 435-649-0011) is the sort of 1950s-style burger joint that serves nostalgia on the side. Okay, it's a bit cheesy, but the burgers are good. Get off your high horse and belly up for one. This is a place where you can feel like the Fonz or Richie or Potsie as you chow down the best burger and fries in town. Healthy types will groove on the lean turkey or buffalo burgers, and non-carnivorous types will find their sandwich in the veggie burger. Hours: Summer Sunday-Thursday 11 A.M.-9 P.M., Friday and Saturday 11 A.M.-10 P.M. Winter Sunday-Thursday 11 A.M.-10 P.M., Friday and Saturday 11 A.M.-11 P.M.

Café Terigo (424 Main Street, 435-645-9555) has faux painted walls the color of the Tuscan countryside in autumn, crisp white linens, and a sunny patio that confers a refined sense of luxury as soon as you sit down. Lunching on the sun-sprinkled patio, lingering over grilled chicken and pinot grigio, and sipping a double espresso (twist of lemon, lump of raw sugar), as Park City strolls past at your feet, is a visit to the sublime. Hours: Summer Monday-Saturday 11:30 A.M.-2:30 P.M., 5:30 P.M.-10 P.M. Winter hours are the same except dinner is also served Sunday 5:30 P.M.-10 P.M.

Chez Betty (in the Copperbottom Inn on Deer Valley Drive, 435-649-8181), according to semiprofessional local restaurant connoisseur Beth Moon, is the best-kept secret in Park City. "Even a lot of locals don't know about this place," she said. Owner Jerry Garcia (no relation to the Dead one) worked for years as a sous chef at the restaurant, and then he and his brother joined forces and bought it. The decor is plain, but the service is extensive and professional. And the food? Well, when a local magazine asked the best chefs in town where they ate, all of them included Chez Betty on their lists. Hours: Thursday-Monday 6 P.M.-10 P.M., Sunday brunch 10:30 A.M.-2:30 P.M. Closed Tuesday and Wednesday.

Chimayo (368 Main Street, 435-649-6222) is an upscale southwestern cantina-style restaurant with a roaring hearth up front, large booths in the back, and big tables in the basement. The last time I went there, the hostess served us a free appetizer while we waited to be seated. A place with a creative take on southwestern food, Chimayo is very popular (for good reason), so make reservations. Hours: Winter dinner 5 P.M.-10 P.M. seven nights a week. Summer Sunday-Thursday 5:30 P.M.-9 P.M., Friday and Saturday 5:30 P.M.-9:30 P.M.

BEL MORGAN KERIG

A star of southwestern cuisine, Chimayo is one of Park City's best.

Dynamite Dom's (890 Main Street, 435-615-8457) offers new twists on old favorites like rack of lamb and seared tuna steak, a great and complete wine list as well as a full bar. In the summer, a stage is set up on a wide patio for live entertainment. A great place on a summer night. Hours: 11 A.M.-11 P.M.-ish daily.

The Eating Establishment (317 Main Street, 435-649-8284) has the best steak-and-eggs breakfast in town. This brick-walled eatery at the top end of Main Street has a simple name and a similarly simple mission: to serve good food at a fair price and a reasonable pace. It does that. For lunch try the Pickaxe burger (veggies can get an equally big garden burg), and for dinner go for a rack of baby backs and a hunk of mud pie. Hours: 8 A.M.-10 P.M. daily.

Gateway Grill (215 South Main, Kamas, 435-783-2867) is located 11 miles east of Park City in the sleepy town of Kamas. When the producers of the feature film *Net Worth* (one of whom was me) were looking for an Americana feel, they scouted all over the state and settled on Kamas. This is a place where every stool at the soda fountain in the drugstore might be filled with little girls dripping chocolate ice cream all over their Sunday dresses. The town is also the last stop before you venture out to the spectacular Uinta Mountains. Most people stop to get gas, but a few knowledgeable Park City folks drive out here just for dinner at the Gateway Grill. You'll find Park City-quality food in a down-home country atmosphere that's far from

BEL MORGAN KERIG

Left Grappa occupies a a fine spot on the top of Main Street and on the Park City must-dine list. *Right* The Irish Camel, the best hump in town. Whatever that means.

the bustle of downtown. Go for the rack of lamb, the veal picatta, or the Chilean sea bass. Bring your own wine and pay a corkage. Hours: Monday-Saturday 8 A.M.-9:30 P.M. Closed Sunday.

Grappa (151 Main Street, 435-645-0636, www.grapparestaurant.com) is considered by many to be the best restaurant in Park City. This Italian eatery has superb service and exquisite food. Even with two levels of indoor and outdoor seating, Grappa can become quite crowded, so make reservations and bring your Visa. Hours: 5:30 P.M.-10 P.M. daily.

The Happy Sumo (838 Park Avenue, 435-649-5522) isn't about the austere orderliness of a traditional sushi bar. You know, all that bowing and restraint, the kind of place where the only thing wild is the number at the bottom of the bill. The Happy Sumo isn't like that. "We're the only nouveau sushi bar in the world!" claims owner Rulen Jorgensen. Which is to say that The Happy Sumo is not without a certain amount of ebullient hyperbole. This place takes its fun and fish, but not itself, seriously. The decor is kooky. Aluminum siding is hung with framed black-and-whites of seriously large sumo wrestlers. The booth cushions are covered in sake-barrel print. There's plywood and paper lanterns. It feels like you're stepping into the set of *McHale's Navy*. The music is offbeat and loud, and you are as likely to see groups doing shots of chilled sake as savoring uni. The Happy Sumo is a fun place with the best raw fish in town. That's about all I need to know. You? Hours: Dinner 6 P.M.-10 P.M. daily. Open for lunch seasonally.

BEL MORGAN KERIG

Left Lakota offers some of the best patio dining in Park City. *Right* Mercato brings Mediterranean flair to Park City's Old Town.

Irish Camel (435 Main Street, 435-649-6645) serves only tequila and beer, so get your merlot somewhere else, L.A. boy. This is a locals hangout with killer Mexican food and stout margaritas. So what's Irish about the Camel? "Just the amount of boozing that goes on here," said Irishman and Park City resident Bob Sullivan, who's reputed to know his way around a bottle of MacCallan's. The logo proudly identifies the place as "The Best Hump on Main Street." Use your imagination. Hours: 4 P.M.-1 A.M. daily.

Lakota (751 Main Street in the Caledonian Building, 435-658-3400) is an upmarket bar and restaurant with a cherrywood bar, a young professional crowd, and a casual elegance. About a half step down from the best and fanciest restaurants in town (such as Grappa), Lakota feels more open and handles crowds well. During the summer, it has one of the best patios in town. Adjacent to the town lift, this is a terrific place to watch the nightly color display of the sinking sun. Lakota is also one of the few places to get a meal after 10 P.M. Hours: 11 A.M.-2 A.M. seven days a week.

Mercato Mediterraneo Restaurante and Caffé (corner of Main Street and Park Avenue, 435-647-0030) is owned by Eric DeBonis, a guy who definitely knows what he's doing. This Mediterranean café is done up in faux painted walls the color of butterscotch pudding, has accents of that pure Med azure, and features a chest-high stand of wildflowers on the patio. The food is superb, and the service is excellent. Hours: Summer Friday-Sunday lunch 11:30 A.M.-4 P.M., dinner 5 P.M.-10 P.M. seven days a week. Winter dinner 5 P.M.-10 P.M., seven nights a week.

Mileti's (412 Main Street, 435-649-8211) is a red-sauce Italian restaurant with a small locals bar upstairs. Socializing Dave is behind the bar upstairs (435-649-8230). This small, smoky lounge is sometimes called the Demon Lounge by locals. Say no more. Restaurant hours: 5 P.M.-10 P.M. nightly. Bar hours: 4 P.M.-1 A.M. nightly.

Morning Ray Café and Bagelry (268 Main Street, 435-649-5686) is a funky, small, wildly popular breakfast spot on the top of Main Street. This is a place where the wait will be two hours for breakfast (during the Sundance Film Festival), and people will endure it. It's that good. With the largest selection of bagels in town, espresso and cappuccino, and a full rundown of egg dishes, the Morning Ray is the hippest spot for breakfast in town. Hours: 7 A.M.-3 P.M. daily, Tuesday-Saturday 5 P.M.-10 P.M.

Mother Urban's Ratskellar (625 Main Street, underground, 435-615-7200) is not only a great jazz club, but it also serves a fine dinner menu. See the entry under Après-Ski and Nightlife, Lounges, for more details.

Mt. Air Café (1900 Park Avenue, 435-649-9868) is a straight-down-the-middle, old-school breakfast joint. Nothing fancy, nothing showy, just your basic egg-and-hash-brown type of place. That's good; many mornings you don't want any challenges or surprises, just some good solid grub. Serving breakfast, lunch, and dinner. Hours: 6 A.M.-11 P.M. daily.

Nacho Mama's (1821 Sidewinder Drive, 435-645-8226, www.NachoMamas.com) is nacho mama's and not mine either, which is fine with me because my mom don't do flautas. This is a place that serves Mexican food in an irreverent atmosphere where a cold beer is considered a side order. Hours: 5 P.M.-10 A.M. seven days a week.

Off Main Bakery and Café (1782 Prospector Avenue, 435-649-6478) is the place where locals who don't have time for Main Street go for breakfast or lunch. On the weekends, you can get only breakfast. A simple place with great food and a wide sunny patio. Hours: 8 A.M.-2 P.M. seven days a week.

Prime Steak House (804 Main Street, 435-655-9739) has the best steaks in the state. This place takes its meat seriously. "USDA prime" is the designation the government places on the top 2 percent of all beef harvested in the United States. "Select" and "choice" are other, lesser designations. As its name implies, Prime Steak House serves only prime beef. It's important to know this, because otherwise you'll get sticker shock when you see that the filet mignon is $27 and doesn't come with any sides. You wonder how it can, and does, sell out. "I make $56,000 a year, which is not a lot when you live in Park City," one ebullient patron told me, "and I never waste my money buying a steak anywhere else." Yes, it's that good. The atmosphere is that of a Chicago men's club, and the lithographs of beautiful women on the walls enhance that feeling. Could the fact that the wait staff consists of beautiful women be any coincidence? Has general manager Bryan Morgan stumbled onto some subconscious connection between beautiful women and fine steak? Ask him. I do know that Prime Steak House has patios in front and back, a fine wine list, and meat worth the hefty price of admission. Hours: Summer Thursday-Saturday 6 P.M.-10 P.M. Winter 5 P.M.-10 P.M. seven days a week.

Sage Grill (6300 North Sagewood Drive, 435-658-2267) is the place where you can get Park City food and service without the nowhere-to-park hassles and at prices that are about 25 percent less than in town. Located in a wide parking lot of a suburban shopping center like you'd find in Des Moines, the Sage has food and atmosphere that are more likely to suggest Santa Monica than Saint Paul. Hours: Summer Tuesday-Saturday 5 P.M.-10 P.M., closed Sunday and Monday. Winter 5 P.M.-10 P.M. seven days a week.

Snake Creek Grill (650 West 100 South, Heber, 435-654-2133) is located fifteen minutes out of Park City in the town of Heber. With all the excellent restaurants in Park City why would you ever leave? One reason is the Snake Creek Grill. In Heber you'll dine at a much less frenetic place; parking is not a problem. The Snake Creek Grill offers Park City service and quality with Heber prices. Go for the grilled tri-tip steak with wild mushroom sauce and crisp hash browns. Bring your own wine or drink theirs. Hours: Wednesday-Sunday 5:30 P.M.-9:30 P.M.

Wahso Asian Grill (577 Main Street, 435-615-0300) is an eatery that transports you to French-occupied Shanghai circa 1920. French Colonial influences mix with Asian elegance to create a posh atmosphere that makes you feel special just for being here. The booths that line the periphery are curtained off and provide a private, somewhat regal stage for the show-stopping entreés. This is a place that was done up right— from the Fifth Dynasty stone cat in the foyer to the gilded mirrors and chandeliers, to the delicate lillies in the centerpiece. Despite the fine elegance of Wahso, however, the vibe here is not snooty or precious; the staff has a good time and you will too. Patio seating on a high deck that overlooks Main Street is also available when weather permits. A romantic and exotic setting for amazing food, Wahso is one of Park City's finest restaurants. Hours: Winter dinner 5:30 P.M.-10 P.M. Summer dinner 5 P.M.-9 P.M.

Eat with a fifth Dynasty stone cat looking over your shoulder? Where else but Wahso.

Robert Redford's Zoom restaurant is a place for movie stars and other beautiful people to hang out.

Zoom (660 Main Street, 435-649-9108) is owned by Robert Redford's Sundance Institute and is fittingly hip, in a western, Butch-and-Sundance-meet-L.A. kind of way. With film festival black-and-white photographs on the walls, and a cowboy chic feel to the dining room and the bar area, Zoom is the sort of classy eatery you'd expect from the Sundance Kid. The patio, which is below street level and provides shelter from the wind, is the best in town. Dinner here on a summer night is as romantic as a Parisian café or as comfortable as a backyard barbecue. The food is some of the best nouveau western you'll find. You probably won't run into Bob, but at least you can enjoy some of his sanguine sensibility. Hours: lunch at 11:30 A.M., dinner at 5:30 P.M. daily.

RESTAURANTS TO GO

Mountain Express Restaurant Delivery (435-649-MENU [6368]) will deliver food from twenty-something local eateries to your home, hotel, or condo. It charges the regular price of the menu entrées plus a $3.99 service charge for orders up to $20, and 20 percent for orders over $20. The minimum order is $15. Hours: 5 P.M.-10 P.M. seven nights a week.

C O F F E E H O U S E S   A N D   C A F É S

Bad Ass Coffee of Park City (652 Park Avenue, 435-655-9811, www.parkcity-badass.com) had its logo emblazoned on an insulated, plastic coffee cup that I used to drink my coffee from (the cup reminded me of a better place and time). At the time, I lived in Los Angeles. When an especially hip barrista at a Venice Beach coffeehouse noticed the logo, she cracked up. "I can't believe they let you drink coffee *and* say 'ass' in Utah." I laughed along with her, and when I lost that cup, I returned to Bad Ass for another. Bad Ass not only sells lots of cups, T-shirts, fleece vests, turtlenecks, ski hats, and baseball caps (all imprinted with its rebel name) but also serves 100 percent pure Kona coffee in a super-cool coffee shop set in an old house across from the Kimball Arts Center near the base of Park City's Main Street. The porch is a nice place to soak up the morning sun as your central cortex sparks to life. The name comes from the "bad ass ones," who were the donkeys that hauled coffee beans up the hills of Kona, Hawaii. The attitude comes straight from the heart of iconoclastic Park City. Hours: 7 A.M.-7 P.M. daily.

Emma's Café (427 Main Street, 435-640-1298) is a wonderful little breakfast and lunch spot that has smoothies, homemade breads and pastries, sandwiches, soups, and salads. Named after co-owner Vanessa Conabee's dog, Emma's is tucked into the lower left corner of the Memorial Building, right in the middle of Park City. Vanessa and her sister Kate run the place with all the pride and zeal of new missionaries spreading the gospel of good food to the masses. Forget fishes and loaves; go for a cup of joe and one of Emma's homemade muffins. Hours: Wednesday-Monday 7:30 A.M.-5 P.M. Closed Tuesday.

Espresso Brothers (1615 Park Avenue in Cole Sport, 435-649-4806) has killer coffee and the best gossip in Park City. Want to bitch about politicians while the Maestro is making you a cup? Want to argue about sports while your Americano is growling out of the machine? Want to swap lies about how well you skied or golfed? Espresso Brothers is the place. Java junkie Bob Sullivan, a hyperkinetic whirling dervish who transplanted from Boston to sell software from his mid-mountain Deer Valley office, makes Espresso Brothers his mandatory morning stop. "What, you're gonna start your day without a trip to the Maestro and a cuppa rocket fuel?" he asks. "Not likely, chief." Drink your cup on the wide front deck of Cole Sport and wave to the worker bees as they buzz off to the hive. Hours: 6:30 A.M.-6 P.M. seven days a week.

Moguls (at the corner of the Gables Hotel in the Park City Mountain Resort Center, 435-647-0001) has that slope-side cuppa you need. Hours 8 A.M.-6 P.M. seven days a week. Closed in the summer.

For Kona coffee with a Bad Ass attitude nobody beats Bad Ass Coffee.

Park City Coffee Roaster (221 Main Street, 435-647-9097) has the best cup of coffee in town. This cool little rock-walled enclave feels like the coffee shop you'd open if you moved here. It has a cozy vibe, low ceilings, and local art on the walls. For years this place has been my hideout from the black-clad hordes at the Sundance Film Festival. Few non-locals ever find their way here. You should. Hours: Monday-Saturday 7 A.M.-6 P.M., Sunday 8 A.M.-6 P.M.

Starbucks (402 Main Street, 435-658-1832) shares a space with Cows ice cream store. The host of smells that mix and mingle in this place is mouthwatering. Hours: 7 A.M.-10 P.M. seven days a week.

LODGING

Park City has more hotels than Salt Lake has Saints. Okay, not quite that many, but it sure seems that way. Actually, the number of available beds in Park City is more like 20,000. That's a lot of beds. There is every type of lodging here, but it's hard to find much in terms of supercheap billeting.

Park City Mountain Reservations works with at least 80 percent of the properties in town. Call 800-222-PARK, www.parkcitymountainresort.com.

David Hollands R&R (888-PARK-CITY, 435-649-6175, www.parkcitylodging.com) and High Mountain Properties (435-655-8363, www.highmountainproperties.com) are property management companies that oversee lots of condo and home rentals in the Park City area. Here are a few of the many lodging options:

1904 Imperial Hotel Bed and Breakfast Inn (221 Main Street, 435-649-1904, www.1904imperial.com) is a restored 10-room B&B that's on the National Register of Historic Landmarks. Each room is done up in period decor—antiques galore and down comforters—and is named after a different local silver mine. This inn overlooks Main Street, so it's a good place for those who come to Park City as much for the scene as the skiing. Summer rates range $80-$125 double occupancy. Winter rates $140-$220 double occupancy. Add $15 per each additional person.

Chateau Après Lodge (1299 Norfolk Avenue, 800-357-3556, 435-649-9372, www.chateauapres.com) is down the hill about 150 yards from the Park City Mountain Resort. This old-school chalet-style inn is a skier's lodge for skiers. Run by the Hosenfeld family since 1963, the hotel hasn't changed much, and that's good. The place has nothing-fancy rooms, good breakfasts, and nice people—the type of people who will lend you their sleds to slide on the hill across the street. As you might expect from real-skier types, the rates here are as reasonable as you'll find anywhere in Park City. During the winter, dorm rooms rent for $28 per person. A single room in the winter goes for $85, but a four-person room will run you only $105. During the summer, you can get a single room for $45.

Old Miner's Lodge (615 Woodside Avenue, 435-645-8068, www.oldminerslodge.com) is a refurbished boardinghouse that operates now as a B&B. Built in 1889, the lodge is replete with that old prospector spirit; and each of the 12 rooms is named for a Park City turn-of-the-century personality. Old Miner's has an outdoor hot tub, a central hearth that makes a good gathering place on a winter night, and antique furnishings. The lodge is a short walk from the town chairlift as well as the restaurants and shops of Old-Town Park City. Rates range from $70 to $270 per room depending on the season, room size, holidays, and special events.

The Park City International Hostel is the best bet for cheap sleep.

Park City International Hostel (268 Main Street, 888-980-7244, 435-655-7244, www.parkcityhostel.com) can accommodate 70 guests in 16 four-person bedrooms and 1 six-person room (each room is equipped with two bunk beds, two desks, two vanities, and eight storage drawers). The hostel provides all bed and bath linens as well as pillows and blankets for $25 per person, or $90 a room per night for up to four people. Rooms can be arranged according to guests' desires. You'll find a full kitchen, a balcony, a screening room complete with DVD, surround-sound Playstation II, as well as a ski locker room. The hostel is also right upstairs from the Morning Ray Café and Club Creations. A great spot at great prices. At press time, Park City International Hostel was offering a special discount to all guests: People who bring another area's ski map that the hostel doesn't already have will get $5 off their bill. The maps are used to decorate the lobby. A cool place for adventurous travelers.

Park Station Hotel (950 Park Avenue, 435-649-0800) is a simple condo hotel at the base of Main Street with affordable rates, a hot tub, and an outdoor swimming pool. Double-room rates start at $34 per night during the summer, up to $190 per night during holiday periods.

Treasure Mountain Inn (255 Main Street, 800-344-2460, www.treasuremountaininn.com) is a cool and funky condo-hotel located at the top of Main Street across from the Wasatch Brew Pub. Consisting of three buildings with three floors each, for a total of 56 rooms, the Treasure Mountain Inn has a secluded courtyard with heated pool and Jacuzzi and offers balconies that overlook Main Street. You'll have to get in a car to go skiing, but you'll only have to walk down the stairs to be in the thick of the shopping and nightlife. Rates range from $75 per bed in off-season to $200 per bed during peak season. Studios and one-, two-, and three-bedroom units are available.

SHOPPING

Although there are many great shops in Park City, the shopkeepers must make their annual (and expensive) rent in only seven or eight months (Park City still turns into a ghost town during its shoulder seasons). This means you won't find many bargains here. The Factory Outlet Stores have opened and are thriving just off Interstate 80 at Kimball Junction; they include Brooks Brothers, Ralph Lauren, Bose, and Vans. Thus the shopping in town is becoming more specialized and boutique.

BOOKS

Dolly's (510 Main Street, 435-649-8062) is a cozy bookstore that you have to pass through a chocolate shop to enter. If you get past the enticing aromas without buying some sweets, you're a better shopper than I. Once you're in Dolly's, enjoy a living room feel (complete with snuggling cats) in a store whose offerings are well targeted at both the Park City locals and visitors. Hours: 10 A.M.-10 P.M. seven days a week.

BOOZE

Park City has two main state liquor stores and one satellite store.
- 1901 Sidewinder Drive, 435-649-7254. Hours: Monday-Saturday 10 A.M.-8 P.M. Closed Sunday and holidays.
- 524 Main Street, 435-649-3293. Hours: Monday-Saturday 11 A.M.-10 P.M. Closed Sunday and holidays.
- 2121 Park Avenue in the Radisson Inn (offering a limited selection), 435-649-5000. Hours: Monday-Saturday 7 A.M.-10 P.M.

SPORTS SHOPS

Cole Sport (1615 Park Avenue, 435-649-4806) not only buys the best ski gear and garb in Utah but also sells it with the panache and polish that only seasoned veterans of the ski world could muster. This is not a cut-rate store; it's a high-end place that, thanks to Todd Thibault and Sue Burke, sells the best cool, functional stuff to people who are serious about their recreation. Want to know how to spot the best ski shop? Count the number of Yakima and Thule racks on the cars outside. The more racks, the more serious the shop. Cole Sport has a big parking lot teeming with roof racks. In the summer, Cole is also the best place to buy or rent a mountain bike. Kip and Co. will style you with the best full or front suspension bikes you'll find in town. Several scenes in the movie *Net Worth* were filmed around the bikes in the back of Cole Sport. Cole has five stores in the Park City area and is open 8 A.M.-9 P.M. daily, year-round. In the summer Cole Sport has group mountain-bike rides leaving its main store at 6 P.M. Monday nights.

Jans Mountain Outfitters (1600 Park Avenue, 435-649-4949, www.jans.com) In the winter Jans is a high-end ski shop. In the summer Jans is a great place to get your fly-fishing gear and info. In the summer Jans has group mountain-bike rides leaving the shop on Tuesday nights at 6 P.M. Hours: Summer 9 A.M.-7 P.M. daily. Winter 8 A.M.-9 P.M. daily.

Milo Sport (1351 Kearns Boulevard, 435-658-1616) is a skate and snowboard shop located off the beaten track on Kearns Boulevard. This place is hip enough to have pro snowboarder Noah Brandon working there. Hours: Summer Monday-Friday 11 A.M.-7 P.M., Saturday 11 A.M.-6 P.M., Sunday 11 A.M.-5 P.M. Winter 8 A.M.-8 P.M. seven days a week.

Nordic Equipment and Outdoor Gear (1612 Ute Boulevard, 435-655-7225, www.nordicequipment.com) sells a wide selection of cross-country skis, snowshoes, and road bikes. Hours: Monday-Friday 10 A.M.-6 P.M., Saturday 10 P.M.-5 P.M. Closed Sunday.

White Pine Touring Center (435-649-8710) is the best shop in town for hiking and backcountry skiing. You can also rent or buy a full suspension Ellsworth bike here. In the summer White Pine has night rides leaving the shop at 6 P.M. Thursdays. Hours: Winter 9 A.M.-9 P.M. daily. Summer 9 A.M.-7 P.M. daily.

OUTDOOR RECREATION
BALLOONING
Care to see Park City from the air? There are several balloon operators in town who will take you up on early morning scenic flights. Be sure to ask for the trip that includes ceremonial champagne at the landing field.

Park City Balloon Adventures (800-396-UPUP, 435-645-UPUP, www.pcballoonadventures.com) has fully insured, professional FAA-licensed pilots and offers daily flights year-round, weather permitting.

FRISBEE
Ultimate Frisbee (435-647-0791) games are held every summer Sunday at 5 P.M. at the Ecker Hill Middle School.

GOLF
Homestead Golf Course (700 North Homestead Drive, Midway, 800-327-7220, 435-654-1102) is an 18-hole course with two completely different nines. The front nine is open, and the back nine is narrow. This course still feels a bit like the pasture it used to be, but the views are spectacular at sunset. Rates: Monday-Thursday $45 with a cart, Friday-Sunday $55 with a cart during peak season.

Park City Municipal Golf Course (Park Avenue, 435-615-5800) is an 18-hole course that runs up into the Wasatch. It's also one of the nicest muni courses you'll ever play. All the tees are well kept and grass, and the greens provide roller-coaster undulations that (in my case) lead to inevitable three-putts. The par-five finishing hole, with its island green, is one of the toughest birdie holes you'll ever find. The newly opened driving range provides a good place to warm up, or return to after you've hacked the course to pieces. Pro-shop hours change with the season. Rates: May-September, $37 or $51 with a cart for 18 holes. Before May and after September, $29 or $43 with a cart for 18 holes.

Wasatch Mountain State Park Golf Course (1281 Warm Springs Road, Midway; 435-654-0532) was built in 1962 and has two 18-hole courses. The mountain course is not only exceedingly challenging but also an adventure in nature. It's not unusual to see deer, wild turkey, and even moose on this loop. Rates: $33 with a cart for 18 holes on weekends.

HIKING
Park City is all about hiking. There are miles and miles of trails here, but don't expect to find the kind of solitude that you'd find in Big Cottonwood or Mill Creek canyons. The trail system here is so well organized that you will have company. Pick up the free Park City Trail Map at Cole Sport or any bike or sport shop in town. The best shop for all things hiking is White Pine Touring.

MOUNTAIN BIKING
After Moab, Park City has the second-best mountain biking in the state. Which is rather like saying that except for Waimea, your surf break is the best in the Pacific. In short, the riding here rules. Not only did the old miners leave many old roads crisscrossing these hills like an elaborate latticework, but Park City and Deer Valley resorts have also been building their own interconnected networks of trails for the past decade. The result is a knobby-tire playground. Before you go grinding up any of the climbs, however, pick up the free Park City Trail Map available in any local bike shop. The map shows the mountain-bike routes, ski lifts, and the topo lines so that you can see where the steep climbs are. Free group rides are offered by Cole Sport (Monday night), Jans Mountain Outfitters (Tuesday), and White Pine Touring (Thursday). All depart at 6 P.M.

Spiro to Lower Tour des Suds is a good solid uphill grunt on shady, switchbacking singletrack. Park at Cole Sport at the corner of Park Avenue and Deer Valley Drive. Ride toward the mountain resort on the pavement and take your first right, then take the next right and the first left. The trailhead is very well marked and begins with a little-ring climb. Grind through beautiful singletrack of aspens and evergreens, across the Park City Mountain Resort ski trails, and up to an old mine. Keep grinding up the double track until you get to the snow hut. This is the top of the climb. From here you have many options. Watch for orange or green plastic signs that point the way. I like to head down a bit and look for a tricky little right-hand turn. This puts you onto a traversing singletrack that takes you over into the lower Tour des Suds area. Any trail you choose in this area will drop you down into Old-Town Park City. I recommend ending your ride with a stop at Wasatch Brew Pub at the top of Main Street for a little liquid refreshment.

Sweeney Switchbacks is steep and twisty climb through aspens and evergreens offers a good hour-and-a-half loop for a proficient rider. Park at the Park City Mountain Resort parking lots and head south (and uphill) on Lowell Avenue. When the road switchbacks, go straight and through the gate. Now look for the trailhead sign and the orange trail markers. Taking this loop in a clockwise direction is easier than the other way, but both can be done.

Tour des Suds is a classic Park City ride that begins on Daly Canyon Road, just up from the top of Main Street. There's a good parking lot behind Wasatch Brew Pub, but you'll have to pay to park there. You'll ride up the pavement for a while, then go through a gate where the trail turns to dirt. Crank up here until the water tank. Go around it counterclockwise and into the switchback. Pass the fork to the right and keep climbing the double track. There will be all sorts of opportunities for exploring on this section of the trail. Have at it. Don't worry; this is a popular trail so you will have company. Wrong turns don't turn out to be wrong; every road eventually leads back down. And you *do* have that map, right?

SCUBA DIVING

Yes, you read that right. Scuba diving. Nineteen miles to the east of Park City lies the little town of Midway. Driving into this town will make you feel you've driven into the label for Swiss Miss hot chocolate. Following the example of the original Swiss settlers, Midway is all edelweiss and gingerbread architecture. Drive up the road to where a 55-foot crater pokes out of the ground. The effect is even more surreal when you walk in the side tunnel of the crater to where the scuba tanks, flippers, and masks hang. There's something vaguely James Bondish about the whole thing and you're feeling just a little tweaked as you sign the waiver and don the flippers. A diving deck extends into the middle of the water-filled crater. Light flows in through the hole at the top of the cone where lava once spewed out.

Then you drop into the water. The temperature of a warm bath you've soaked in for twenty minutes, the crater water comes from a thermal hot spring somewhere under the cone. Dive down, swim around; this is a unique experience. Bubbles float up, but they're not from some center-of-the-earth belch, they're coming from the divers who've been down at the crater's floor, 65 feet beneath you. Snorkel over and watch them ascend from the deep darkness. What a weird trip. And irresistible too. Dive masters Dan and Kathy Howlett teach scuba diving in the crater and can even get you certified in two days. This is a cool, eerie place that's more than worth the ten bucks admission.

After about 40 minutes, they're supposed to ask you to leave, but no one seems to pay much attention to this rule. After 40 minutes of poking around at the crater walls and diving down to the submerged platforms, you're ready to leave anyway.

A dip in the crater costs $10 on weekdays and $15 on weekends. Snorkeling equipment can be rented for $5. A one-hour scuba-diving introduction with equipment included is $75 on weekdays, $100 on weekends. Certified divers can explore the warm waters of the crater for a maximum of 35 minutes at a depth of 55 feet for $20 on weekdays and $25 on weekends. Rental scuba equipment is $15 and is available on-site. Five-session public-certification courses are also offered. Hours for Homestead Crater are 10 A.M.–8 P.M. year-round. Call 800-327-7220 for information and to reserve dive times.

And if you really get into cave diving, contact the National Speleological Society at 256-852-1300 or visit www.caves.org. It's not in Park City, but I thought it was cool enough to put in anyway.

SKIING AND SNOWBOARDING

The Park City resort is a sprawling mountain of 3,100 vertical feet with more nooks, crannies, and secret stashes than a pack rat's antebellum mansion. This ski area has pedigree, poise, and the kind of polish that fifty years of operation will give a place. Boasting more Olympians per capita than any ski resort in North America, Park City is home to the U.S. Ski and Snowboard teams and will host the snowboarding and giant slalom events during the 2002 Olympics.

Park City has always been a place to watch the best strut their stuff—the freestyle team running their mogul course on the lower mountain, the racers ripping the gates during one of the resort's many world-class competitions, the snowboarders boosting out of the superpipe—but it is also a playground for all manner of skiers and riders.

Experts should head for McConkey's (named for free-skier Shane McConkey's dad, Madman McConkey) and Jupiter lifts. Tucked way out behind the hordes are 750 acres of wide-open, steep bowl riding in Jupiter, Scott's, Blueslip, McConkey's, Homelite, and Puma bowls. Out here the best skiing is had by hoofing. Hike Pinyon Ridge off McConkey's lift to Jupiter Peak and drop in at any time. If you're a skier that likes rock drops into powder, this is your nook. From the Jupiter lift, you can shop for your lines, whether in the main bowl, out in Scott's, or off the peak.

Intermediates will want to stay on the well-groomed and maintained King Con area (serviced by a high-speed quad), while beginners have the First Time and Three Kings lifts.

The New and Reigning King of Snowboarding

A lot of locals raised eyebrows when the 2002 Olympic snowboarding competitions were awarded to an area that, at the time, didn't even allow snowboarding. Park City got up to speed so fast, however, that any grumbling from the jibber crowd (snowboarders and new-school skiers) has long since turned to rabid enthusiasm.

Park City now has the best park and pipe riding in the state. It has two terrain parks, one for beginners and another for advanced skiers and riders. The Superpark, located on the Sitka Trail, has huge tabletops, quarter pipes, hips, a

PARK CITY SNAPSHOT

Location: 36 miles east of Salt Lake City International Airport
Scheduled season: November 10 to mid-April
Hours of operation: 9 A.M.-4 P.M. daily
Night skiing/riding: 4:00 P.M.-9:00 P.M. (opening late December)
Base elevation: 6,900 feet
Top elevation: 10,000 feet
Vertical drop: 3,100 feet
Skiable acres: 3,300
Average seasonal snowfall: 350 inches
Lifts: 14
    4 high-speed six-passenger chairs
    1 high-speed quad
    5 triple chairs
    4 double chairs
Uphill capacity: 27,200 guests per hour
Runs: 100 trails (18 beginner level, 44 intermediate, 38 expert)
Snowmaking: 500 acres (top to bottom)
Ticket price: There are so many deals, sliding rates, and packages that you may pay anywhere from the high fifties to the mid-sixties for a ticket here.
General resort information: www.parkcityresort.com
Website: www.parkcitymountainresort.com
Snow report: 800-222-PARK, www.parkcitymountainresort.com
Sister resort: Courcheval, France

long spine, lots of rollers, and a high rail. It also offers The Bowl, a snow rider's version of skating a massive pool. The more mellow park is off the Pick 'n' Shovel lift. It has all the same type of hits that its big Superpark brother has, just smaller. The New Eagle Superpipe is where the Olympic halfpipe competitions will be held. Located off the New Eagle triple chair, this is a serious pipe for serious riders.

For more information on weather or lift ticket rates, call 1-800-222-PARK or visit www.parkcitymountainresort.com.

The Three-Area Passport
Park City, The Canyons, and Deer Valley offer a pass that is good at all three areas if you purchase it in advance and in conjunction with lodging. Although rates may vary, this is a good deal. Since the three resorts ski so differently, having the flexibility to choose where you want to go is the way to get the most out of your visit. Call 800-453-1360 or visit www.parkcityinfo.com for more information.

TAKE THE CHAIR
Park City also offers lift-served mountain biking, hiking, and scenic chairlift rides on a limited basis from Memorial Day to June 8, after which operations expand to seven days a week 10 A.M.-6 P.M. Tickets are $8.50 per single ride or $16 for an all-day pass.

THE UTAH INTERCONNECT ADVENTURE TOUR

Want powder without the heli? Longing to taste the flavors of five of the top resorts in Utah without popping for five lift tickets? How about doing it in one day with no driving? That's just what the **Utah Interconnect Adventure Tour** *(801-534-1907, www.skiutah.com) offers. Since Deer Valley, Park City, The Canyons, Solitude, Brighton, Snowbird, and Alta are all so close you can ski off the top of one into the lap of another, this guided back-country tour is able to bring advanced skiers to as many as five resorts in one day. From Park City Mountain Resort, you ski off the backside and down into Solitude. Then it's over to Brighton and out the south side to Alta. Go back into Mineral Basin and come up the chair into Snowbird. Finish your day on the sunny Snowbird Center deck, and then take a shuttle (provided in the tour) back to Park City. If this circumnavigation doesn't tickle your fancy, you can also do it the other way: Start at Snowbird, ski through Alta, then Brighton, and then over to Solitude Mountain Resort.*

The tour takes about eight hours and gives you time for a few runs in each resort. The $150 per person fee includes guide service, lunch, lift tickets, ski school lift-line privileges, an avalanche beacon, and transportation back to your point of origin. This is not only a good deal and the best way to sample Utah's resorts, but it's also a "what-if" look at the possible future of a European-style Utah megaresort (which could be accomplished with a few chairlifts and a lot of bargaining). Tours leave at 8:30 A.M. Reservations are recommended and can be made Monday-Friday, 8 A.M.-5 P.M. at 801-534-1907.

TRAMPOLINE

In the summer, Park City sets up the Legacy Launcher Trampoline at the Resort Center (near the base of the Pay Day lift). This trampoline has a bungee harness that allows you to bounce higher more safely, because it also prevents you from flying off the tramp. Six bucks buys you all the bouncing you'll need. Hours: 10 A.M.-10 P.M. seven days a week.

MASSAGE

I don't know how anyone could visit snow country for just two weeks a year, ski and party his or her brains out, and not get at least one massage. I'm sore just thinking about it. Luckily, Park City is home to a small army of licensed massage therapists. Call either **Massage Express** (1200 Little Kate Road, 435-645-8144) or **Massage Professionals** (435-649-1233) for an LMT who will come to your hotel, home, or condo. Expect to pay $80 to $100 by the time you tip.

Silver Mountain Sports Club and Spa (2080 Gold Dust Lane, 435-647-0500) offers massage therapy as well as a full-service sports club (including racquetball and swimming). Salon and spa hours: Monday-Saturday 8 A.M.-6 P.M. (open later in the winter). Sports club hours: Monday-Friday 5 A.M.-10 P.M., Saturday and Sunday 7 A.M.-9 P.M.

MOVIES AND THEATER

Park City Film Series (1255 Park Avenue in the Jim Santy Auditorium in the Park City Library building, www.parkcityfilmseries.com) shows independent, rare, and eclectic films (such as Ed Harris's *Pollock*) on Friday and Saturday nights at 8 P.M. The venue isn't plush, but the films are the best you'll see in Park City.

Sundance Film Festival (801-328-3456, www.sundance.org) is a massive film festival that takes over the town for ten days in January (the 10th through the 20th in 2002) and is hosted by a dozen venues in and around Park City and Salt Lake City. Although it's a good place to see indie films before anyone else does, Sundance is much more than a place and time to see movies. For a full rundown, see page 178.

THEATER

The Eccles Center (The George S. and Dolores Doré Eccles Center for the Performing Arts, 1750 Kearns Boulevard, 435-655-3114) is a huge state-of-the-art theater complex that seats 1,269 and is where the Sundance Film Festival stages its world premieres.

Egyptian Theater (328 Main Street, 435-649-9371, www.egyptiantheater.org) is an old vaudeville theater located at the top of Main Street. Fresh from a complete overhaul, the Egyptian is a beautifully restored venue where you'll see local and touring companies stage national-caliber drama. The Egyptian is also one of the premier venues for the Sundance Film Festival. Call for show times and reservations.

APRÈS-SKI AND NIGHTLIFE

Unlike at Aspen or Telluride, where the trails come right down into town, Park City's trails end a half mile away from the best bars on Main Street. Not to worry, however; the Resort Center has a few that'll provide liquid salve for sore legs.

Baja Cantina (in the Resort Center, 435-649-BAJA, www.bajaparkcity.com) is one of a few obvious choices for après-ski at the resort. This wild little Mexican eatery has a great patio that pushes into the plaza. From here you can throw back a margarita, power down a huge burrito, and watch the passing parade. In the winter, grab a high stool in the greenhouse area and watch as Park City's ski crowd swirls at your feet. This is more of a visitors place than a locals hang. Hours: Sunday-Thursday 11:30 A.M.-10 P.M., Friday and Saturday 11:30 A.M.-10:30 P.M.

Moose's Pub and Grill (at the Resort Center, 435-649-8600), directly across from the ticket windows, is where everyone comes for a cold one after skiing or mountain biking. The wide patio on the upper deck of the resort is the perfect place to

FILM FESTIVALS

SUNDANCE

It's *de rigueur* for Park City locals to pooh-pooh the **Sundance Film Festival** (801-328-3456, www.sundance.org), and who can blame them? Let's face it, any event that sees thousands of city folk flood a mountain town in the middle of winter is sure to provide more than its share of mockable behavior. But in truth, the annual Sundance Film Festival is by far the coolest, most interesting, most fun, and most unlikely annual event ever to hit Utah. Not only that, Sundance has also played a major role in the hipification of this once-staid state.

Every year, in the second half of January, 25,000 people descend on Park City for ten days of film watching, deal making, and slope-side schmoozing. As the halogen halos of *Entertainment Tonight* and *Wild On E!* and dozens of other TV crews prowl the streets, the Sundance Film Festival screens some of the best indie films (*Go, Memento, Lock, Stock and Two Smoking Barrels, Hedwig and the Angry Inch, Dogtown and Z Boys, Enigma, Sexy Beast, Caveman's Valentine, Series 7, Girlfight, Dark Days, You Can Count on Me, Three Seasons, American Movie, Slam, Central Station, Smoke Signals, Sex, Lies, and Videotape, and Hoop Dreams*), throws some of the best parties, and attracts some of the most interesting people to town.

When Robert Redford set out, some twenty years ago, to create the Sundance Institute to showcase independent film, he probably never dreamed its Sundance Film Festival would become the premier international showcase for indies and contribute more than $30 million to the Utah tourism industry. Yet that's what this annual event has done. Sundance has also become the preeminent North American supermarket for studios to acquire new films and talent. What the NFL draft is to football players, the Sundance Film Festival is to indie filmmakers. It's that big.

In fact, some locals think it's too big. Not so the town of Park City; in May 2001, the Sundance Institute and Park City agreed to enter a multiyear deal that will maintain Park City as the Sundance Film Festival headquarters, at least through 2005 and, with a renewal option, possibly through 2008.

Every year the town and festival organizers work to make it better, and every year they succeed. Whereas just a few years ago it was impossible to get tickets to anything, now it's possible to see almost any film you want. If you know how.

First-time visitors to Sundance expect to drive up and be at the festival (as if they were going to a trade show at the Las Vegas Hilton), but it's not like that. Spread across a dozen theaters from Park City to Salt Lake City to Sundance to Ogden, the festival is an amorphous beast that's well worth the trouble of wrestling into submission.

(continued on page 180)

slosh back some suds as the sun sinks in the western sky. The picnic tables out front are the best place to sit, but if the weather isn't cooperating, the moose-themed decor indoors will make up for it. This is a fun-inspired, no-attitude type of place that also attracts more visitors than locals. A good place for burgers, chicken, or an infamous moose dog. Hours: Winter 8 A.M.-8 P.M. daily. Summer 11:30 A.M.-5 P.M. daily.

BARS

In keeping with its history, Park City is still a rowdy place to go out and tie one on. The tight confines of Main Street make barhopping a matter of only a few drunken steps. Whether you're partaking or spectating, the nightly Main Street slalom is an event to behold.

Beer

Wasatch Brew Pub (250 Main Street, 435-649-0900) brews its own beer and always has at least 10 fresh varieties on tap. This is a place where the fish and chips are English-pub good and there are lots of sports on the numerous satellite TVs. The pub also sells lots of memorabilia with its great motto: "We drink our share and sell the rest." You gotta love guys like that. Hours: 11 A.M.-11 P.M. daily.

Dives

Although you won't find the same (low) level dives in Park City that you'd find in Salt Lake (where the rents are a fraction of those on Park City's Main Street), there are several great, low-key bars where you can belly up in jeans and your snow-shoveling boots. These places are just dark enough that you won't worry about what you look like, and just friendly enough to keep you thinking you're lookin' good.

No Name Saloon (447 Main Street, 435-649-6667) used to be called the Alamo, which was fitting because it felt like a place where you'd go for your last drink. With the No Name shingle hanging from the Victorian facade, this bar has elevated itself to the quasi-

BEL MORGAN KERIG

A bar this good doesn't need a name.

(continued from page 178)

If you're looking to attend the films, discussions, and the official parties, you'll need to buy a package. Ranging from $200 to $3,000 (less for locals), packages usually sell out (mostly to film industry insiders) before December. All package buyers get discounts on ski lift tickets at Deer Valley, Park City, and The Canyons. To buy a package, call 801-328-3456 or go to www.sundance.org. Note that you're buying sight unseen; a package you order will include a certain number of films but you won't know what the films are going to be. After you buy a package, you're sent the film guide. Then you go to the site (www.sundance.org) and select the films you want to see. Films show from 8 A.M. until midnight for ten days in January (in 2002, the dates are January 10-20). Tickets cost $8, $10 for premieres, and $15 for panel discussions.

Whether you plan ahead or wing it, the most important tool is the *Official Film Guide*. To get it before the festival, either call the Institute or email them a note (festivalinfo@sundance.org) asking to be put on the mailing list. Once the festival begins, you can pick up a guide at the headquarters and hospitality suite at the Shadow Ridge Hotel and Conference Center (50 Shadow Ridge Road, Park City, 801-328-3456, 435-645-8688, or www.sundance.org) or at any of the 12 theaters that host the films. Use the guide as a planning tool, or if you're going to call and order tickets, use the worksheet in the back to speed your order.

If you don't buy a package or tickets well in advance, you'll still be able to see films; you'll just have to work harder. A limited number of tickets are released at 8 A.M. the day of the show. These are released at Park City's Gateway Center Box Office, but the less popular place to buy them is at the Trolley Square Box Office in Salt Lake City (700 East 500 South on the second level of the mall). Although you'll have to wait in line to buy them, this is one of the best ways to get tickets to films.

Another way is to arrive at the venue that's playing your desired film a little more than an hour before the slated showtime. You'll wait in line to get a number. Once you have the number, go get a coffee or have lunch to kill an hour. When you come back, staffers line you up according to your number. As showtime approaches, they'll start selling tickets (that were held for sponsors or press) in the order of the numbers given out earlier in the day. This approach once was an exercise in frustration, but these days it works most of the time. The big difference is the massive Eccles Theater where all the premieres are shown. This state-of-the-art, 1,297-seat facility has taken the pressure off the other venues and made it possible for you to see 90 percent of the films you choose, even if you don't buy a package.

The final way to get a ticket (this has worked for me more than any other) is just to show up at the theater and offer to buy extra tickets from people going in. This works best at early morning shows. It also works better if

(continued on page 182)

The Phat Tire Saloon is a place for locals and guests alike to cool their engines with a cold tap beer.

mythic status of the artist formerly known as Prince. Like the diminutive rocker, this place doesn't need a hook. No elaborate Madison Avenue branding going on here. Why? Because the No Name has the goods. It's a great old joint filled with ancient memorabilia, a classic bar, and an old shuffleboard game that miraculously gets much easier to play as your bar tab grows. Hours: 10:30 A.M.-2 A.M. seven days a week.

O'Shucks (427 Main Street, 435-645-3999) is a basement bar where you can throw your peanut shells on the floor and throw back cold ones to your heart's content. A super-kickback locals bar, O'Shucks jams to a rock-steady beat that's perfect for full-on ski bums or anyone who wants to leave all that work-stress b.s. way behind. Tuesday is locals night. Hours: 10 A.M.-1 A.M. seven days a week.

Phat Tire Saloon (438 Main Street, 435-658-2699, www.phattiresaloon.com) is a basement bar down the stairs from Main Street. In this dimly lit place, you can let it all hang out. Consisting of one room with pool and foosball tables, a main room with a long bar, and a third band room where small concerts are held, the Phat Tire is gaining a reputation as Park City's biker bar, but that's not quite right. "I happen to ride a Harley and have a lot of fun with it," said owner Casey Kalm, "but the Phat Tire is for everyone." A former professional ice hockey player (he was the enforcer on a Vancouver team and also a London squad), Kalm takes great pride in running a safe business. "If a lady wants to come down here alone, she'll be very safe and greeted cordially," he said. "It's all about fun, partying, and having a good time. But we make sure it's a clean, safe environment for everyone." With live music on Wednesday, Friday, and Saturday nights, the Phat Tire is a place to see such underground talent as the L.A. Guns, Faster Pussycat, and the Bullet

(continued from page 180)
you're alone. This tactic, however, probably won't get you into premieres or films with a lot of buzz or a big star in them. *Go* turned away hundreds of people from the Eccles, and the *Enigma* premiere looked like a rock concert.

It's generally much easier to get into the Salt Lake City venues than the theaters in Park City. It's also very easy to get into the films shown in Ogden, although not many films are screened there.

RELATED EVENTS

Live Theater at the Festival (www.sundance.org, in the Elks Building at 550 Main Street, Park City) is a new offering that provides terrific entertainment for cinema-weary festival-goers. The Sundance Institute annually presents live theater productions that have been developed at its Theater Lab. Held in the same space as the Music Café (upstairs in the Elks Building at 550 Main Street, Park City), the live theater presentations are edgy, daring, and first-rate. Tickets are $10 at the door.

The Screenplay Coffeehouse (Prospector Square, 2200 Sidewinder Drive) is a place where espresso and sandwiches are served and the Writers Guild of America has scripts for most of the films showing at the festival. This is a terrific place to spend time between films. I especially like being able to read the script of the movie I just saw or am about to see. The WGA also schedules Q&A sessions with screenwriters in the coffeehouse throughout the festival. Unlike so many of the other festival features, the Screenplay Coffeehouse is open to anyone, whether you have a badge or not.

Sundance Digital Center is a testament to the transition that the whole film world is making to digital. Bytes and bits will forever change the way films are made, distributed, and watched. To see and play with the toys and tools that are shaping this transformation, check out the Digital Center in the Main Street mall in Park City (333 Main Street). There you'll find cutting-edge equipment from companies such as Sony, Dolby, Avid, and Panavision as well as computer monitors where you can watch the Sundance Online Film Festival. If it's dialogues and presentations on digital cinema you're interested in, you'll want to want to stop in at the Prospector Square Lodging and Conference Center (2200 Sidewinder Drive, Park City). There you'll find industry experts who'll address questions and give talks on issues affecting digital technology and filmmaking. Both venues of the Sundance Digital Center are open to the general public.

The Sundance Music Café (www.sundance.org, in the Elks Building at 550 Main Street, Park City) is another new addition to the festival lineup.
(continued on page 184)

Boys. Kalm also reincarnated an annual motorcycle ride called Hog Holiday on July 14 and other throttle-twisting fun such as an annual motorcycle show and bikini wash. Hours 11 A.M.-1 A.M. seven days a week.

Taverns

J. B. Mulligan's Club and Pub (804 Main Street, 435-658-0717) is the only good Irish bar remaining in Park City, which is a bit sad considering all the Irish who dug and drank in this area. This is a great pub with Guinness and good food (which to many of us is a redundant statement), sports on the TVs, and a congenial atmosphere that the Irish old-timers would have approved of. A rustic room with wide-slatted floors and a large wraparound bar, Mulligan's is probably the only place where you can mow down fish and chips, tap your feet to an Irish band, and wash it down with a Bushmills. Try one of the sardonically inspired Irish car bombs. Hours: Summer Monday–Thursday 6 P.M.-1 A.M., Friday–Sunday 1 P.M.-1 A.M. Winter 2 P.M.-1 A.M. seven days a week.

Lounges

Thanks to the transplants and tourists that Park City draws, the town is able to support the kind of upscale, refined lounges (serving martinis and fine wines) that you don't find east of L.A. and San Francisco or west of Manhattan. Here are a couple of my favorites. Both are private clubs where the usual membership issues exist, but they aren't much of a problem.

Mother Urban's Ratskellar (625 Main Street, underground, 435-615-7200) sits at the junction of "old" and "new" Main streets, which is fitting because this new bar is bringing back the old jazz sounds amid antique Park City memorabilia. Owner Michael Kaplan brings Utah's best jazz talent down the spiral staircase and into his basement club. Although the decor is rustic, this is no dive, and those cats jamming on the stage in the corner are no hodads. This is a hip little hole with leather couches, chilled martini glasses, and the kind of riffs that are all too rare this side of New Orleans. Hours: 5 P.M.-1 A.M. seven days a week.

Renee's Bar and Café (136 Heber Avenue, 435-615-8357) is the new favorite for the kind of longtime locals who have a good job, a sophisticated palate, and have progressed past the swill-your-face-off nights of their 20s. This no-smoking, martini and wine bar serves an all-vegetarian menu and has live acoustic shows on a small stage beneath 1930s-style framed Euro posters. Sit at the elliptical bar and savor excellent wines without having to buy the whole bottle. The staff here is exceedingly friendly and will let you taste-test a wine before ordering a glass. Renee's is a relaxed, classy place where you can drink wine without being able to pronounce it. A welcome addition to Park City, Renee's offers a terrific change from the closeted, stuffy private-club feel of so many other clubs of its ilk. Hours: noon-1 A.M. seven days a week.

(continued from page 182)
Sponsored by ASCAP, the Music Café is open to all Film Festival badge holders (anyone who's purchased any package), and presentations are held in a
long room upstairs in the old Elks building. In this cozy setting, you can watch
top talent play minisets in the middle of the day for free. Sprawl on a bean-
bag and watch the likes of Jill Sobule, Corey Harris, Amy Correira, or Otis
Taylor. For some reason, these miniconcerts aren't crowded, and they're a
terrific way to spend time between movies.

The Sundance Online Film Festival (www.sundance.org) offers a forum for
works produced for distribution on the Internet. Although it's new and thin
compared with its real-world counterpart, the online fest has some cool and
funny shorts that are best viewed at DSL or cable modem speeds. If you're in
Park City during the festival, you can check into the virtual fest on the monitors in the Digital Center in the Main Street mall in Park City (333 Main Street).

MORE TIPS
Dining during Sundance is a show unto itself. Park City's restaurants are
where the schmoozing goes on full-blast. Every night large tables are packed
by people in black (locals actually call them PIBs). Film industry agents and
producers book the best tables in the best eateries—Grappa, Mercato, Wahso,
The Riverhorse—a year in advance. Getting a table in any of the town's top
restaurants is difficult but worth the hassle, if only to witness a full-on
Hollywood schmooze-a-thon.

Parking? Don't even think about it. This is the biggest hassle of the festival, and
when it snows, it becomes a nightmare. Next to Park City's espresso sellers, the
tow-truck drivers are the busiest people in town during the festival. Park on the
outskirts of Park City and take the free shuttle buses into town. If you're staying in town, just walk. Sundance also has its own free shuttle system.

Partying? The official parties are fine and fun, although they're only for
package holders, press, and sponsors. The best bashes, however, are thrown
by movie industry companies such as Miramax or Fox Searchlight. These are
often mobbed, star-studded affairs that are more fun to try to get into than
they are once you're in, but that's just my opinion. My favorite is always the
Directors Guild of America party that's usually held at Cisero's. DGA organizers not only have free booze and food but also always book top musical talent. A couple of years ago they had Dishwalla play to a crowd of about 50.

Star-spotting is a Main Street sport in Park City. You will see stars during
these two weeks, but you likely will be disappointed. They all tend to be
(continued on page 186)

A no-smoking, martini and wine bar, Park City's Renee's has an elliptical bar, a Euro feel, and live acoustic music.

NIGHTCLUBS

All of Park City's nightclubs are private clubs, which means you have to be a member or be sponsored by a member to get in. The Park City clubs, however, are more lenient about membership than their Salt Lake City neighbors. Although it's easy to find a sponsor in any of the clubs I've mentioned here, my advice is just throw down the five bucks and get yourself temporary memberships at a couple of the following clubs. Split the cost with your friends.

Cisero's Nightclub (306 Main Street, 435-649-6800, www.ciseros.com) is a cornerstone of the Park City nightlife. A basement bar with pool tables, a dance floor, and stage, Cisero's packs them in almost every night (except Sunday). A cool, old-school establishment bar with brass rails and burnished wood, Cisero's is a private club that often has cover charges for bands. Every year, the Director's Guild of America throws a party at Cisero's during the Sundance Film Festival. A couple of years ago, I caught Dishwalla at this fete and was much impressed. If you're going out on the town in Park City, you'll end up at Cisero's sooner or later. Hours: Monday-Saturday 5 P.M.-1 A.M. Closed Sundays.

Club Creation (268 Main Street, 435-615-7588) is the best underground techno and electronica club in the state. In addition to its house deejays, Club Creation brings in great electronica talent from all over the world. This is a place where you can dance and dance and dance in the building where Mrs. Field once baked her cookies. There are also cool little nooks for chilling out and zoning on the hypnotic, sneakers-in-the-dryer beat. Staying open until four or five in the morning, Club Creation has captured the true vibe of the techno/electronica scene. Club

(continued from page 184)
shorter, more prone to the ill effects of the mountain environment, and generally less beautiful than they were in the movies. My advice is not to bother with star-spotting; just remember them as they are in the flicks.

As for meeting festival people and getting invited to parties, the best bet is to go skiing at Deer Valley. Look for large posses of black-clad skiers. Ski single and ride the chair with them. This tactic worked well for former world freestyle champion Frank Beddor. Somehow Beddor, who skis in a lemon-yellow Bogner one-piece, cornered the right producer on the lift and pitched the project he was hoping to produce. When the film exec expressed interest, Beddor whipped the script out of his Bogner. Fast forward a couple of years and there was Beddor finally bringing the script to the screen. *There's Something About Mary*, starring Cameron Diaz, Ben Stiller, and Matt Dillon, grossed enough worldwide to buy a Third World country. Beddor, however, still wears the lemon-yellow Bogner.

THE OTHER FESTIVALS

Sundance has become so big and popular that it has reaped the most sincere form of flattery: guerrilla marketing. During those two weeks in January, Park City hosts not only the Sundance Film Festival but also the No Dance, Slamdance, and X Dance film festivals.

NoDance Film and Multimedia Festival (310-937-6363, www.nodance.com) is focused on alternative digital film with an emphasis on converging technologies. No Dance is in its fifth year and claims it was the world's first DVD-projected film festival. No Dance screenings are held on Main Street (venue was under negotiation at press time) and are free to the public. Competition films are eligible for the Grand Jury and Audience Awards, and No Dance also awards the Golden Orbs award for the most creative guerrilla-marketing campaign on the mountain. No Dance hosts industry panels, networking events, and desktop-technology demonstrations. During the 2000 program in Park City, No Dance had four short films acquired by Atomfilms.com, and one picked up by Mediatrip.com. No Dance also offers the only walk-on participant forum for filmmakers.

Slamdance (323-466-1786, www.slamdance.com) was the first to jump on the guerrilla-marketing bandwagon. Many film festivals have cropped up across the country (Austin, L.A., Chicago, New York, Maui, Nantucket, and on and on), but back in 1995, Slamdance was the first one with the audacity to do it right in Park City, in the midst of the Sundance festival.

Directors Dan Mirvish (*Omaha: The Movie*), Shane Kuhn (*Redneck*), and Jon Fitzgerald (*Self-Portrait*) all had made films that were rejected by Sundance. So they decided to bring their films to Park City, hire a venue, and screen them concurrently with the official Sundance films. They called their stunt "Slamdance '95—Anarchy in Utah: The First Annual Guerrilla International Film Festival." Their hope was to steal a tiny bit of the exposure that Sundance drew and shine it on their films. They put out a call, and other films showed up on their doorstep. The intrepid trio arrived in Park City with a dozen films and a cool concept built on the soul of independent film: anarchy. They slapped stickers and posters on every wall, phone booth, trash can, and mailbox in town.

By the end of the week, the Slamdancers had capacity crowds at their venue and crowded, low-budget parties that everyone was invited to. Even though Sundance founder Robert Redford wasn't thrilled by the parasitic action, he admitted that it was good for independent film.

The Slamdancers have put on their film festival every year since. In 2001, Slamdance gave away $70,000 in cash and prizes, had several films picked up for distribution, and had almost all its films invited to other festivals. Slamdance films have been nominated for Spirit Awards and even an Oscar. The Slamdancers get 1,000 entries for their screenwriting competition, and their website has become a full-service indie film locale. Festival organizers expect to screen about 60 films in 2002, and they're even talking about launching a finishing fund and distribution service.

Festival passes are $350 and include all events. Individual tickets are $6 and available at the venue box office, which at press time was scheduled to be at the Park City Silver Mine. Yes, that's right, in a real silver mine. Now that's underground.

The X Dance Film Festival (www.x-dance.com) is the Sundance of action (extreme) sports. X Dance provides a hip space in Harry O's on Main Street in Park City where you can check out the best of the new adrenaline sports flicks. Launched during the 2001 Sundance Film Festival, X Dance screened 22 of the world's best action sports films. Admission was free and shows were packed. The festival also includes panels on action sports filmmaking with industry veterans and extreme sports stars such as skier Scot Schmidt. In 2001, X Dance's award ceremony and closing party was the wildest bash of the festival. Featuring world-famous deejay Paul Oakenfold, who filled the house at Harry O's, the party was webcast live on Warner Brothers Online; it drew nearly a million hits.

For the 2002 festival (January 12-15, 2002), X Dance festival organizers Brian Wimmer, Kevin Kerslake, Eric Barrett, Ann Wycoff, and Mark Wheadon have enlisted top athletes and icons from the skiing and snowboarding worlds and plan to bring them together with A-list deejays and live bands. Their parties combine pyrotechnics, fire dancers, world-class musical talent, and fur-clad go-go girls. These X Dancers throw a mean bash. **U**

Creation serves alcohol until 1 A.M., then juice and water for the rest of the night. Open Thursday-Saturday. Call for hours. Closed Sundays.

Harry O's (427 Main Street, 435-647-9494, concert hot line 435-615-7561) was born when Park City's Kenny Griswold bought the Memorial Building, which used to house the defunct Z Club, and decided to open one of the state's biggest nightclubs. His friends thought he was nuts. It's a classy joint, with deco accents in the sprawling U-shaped balcony, but many thought that a room that needs 500 people in it before you feel you're not alone was just too big for Park City. Griswold grinned and then introduced his partner, Doug Illman, who was running the most popular bar/nightclub in California's Manhattan Beach. Illman stepped in and proved all the doubters wrong. Today Harry O's has the biggest dance floor in the state and is consistently the wildest, most fun bar this side of Vegas. On Thursday, Friday, and Saturday nights, there'll be 1,000 people inside and another 100 waiting in line. It's not uncommon to meet people who've driven from Ogden or Orem to party at Harry O's. With one of the best stages in the state, Harry O's regularly hosts major national talent such as Primus, The Cult, Sammy Hagar, Third Eye Blind, and Sugar Ray. Pool tables take up space on the dance floor when it's not going off. During the Sundance Film Festival, Harry O's hosts the biggest, wildest parties, including the notoriously wild bash, Lapdance. Hours: 8 P.M.-2 A.M. seven days a week.

12. The Canyons

The Canyons Resort (4000 The Canyons Resort Drive, 435-649-5400, www.thecanyons.
com) is one of a trio of ski areas that together more closely resemble a small dys-
functional family than the three distinct entities the press kits would have you
believe. The *patris dominis* of the clan is Park City, the well-behaved golden child is
Deer Valley, and the hard-charging five-year-old is The Canyons. The Canyons was
always the little brother with the huge potential, but now that struggling sibling has
come into his own like the skinny, acne-challenged sophomore who suddenly becomes
captain of the football team. Today, The Canyons is Utah's biggest resort and the fifth-
largest resort in the country.

   The clientele covers a broad spectrum that speaks to The Canyon's past as well
as its future. First and foremost, there are lots of young skiers and snowboarders
who discovered the terrain here back when it was Wolf Mountain, the only resort
in Summit County to allow snowboarding. The young energy that came to this hill
then has stayed loyal despite Park City's Olympic-ringed marriage with snowboarding. Many teens also take advantage of a special free pass for honor-roll students, or, for the less accomplished, a deeply discounted student pass.

   Then there are the more mature locals who knew The Canyons in its previous
incarnation as Park West ski area. They grew accustomed to the absence of lift
queues and the preponderance of great powder lines. They too stuck with the
place through its intermediate tenure as Wolf Mountain. And then there are the
moms and dads who've discovered that The Canyons is Utah's best family resort.
Located a mere 26 miles of interstate driving from the Salt Lake City International,
The Canyons is the most airport-accessible (less time for kids to go nuts in the car)
of all Utah's resorts. There's also a self-contained, safe feeling to The Canyons
Resort Village that allows for a lot of unfettered wandering for kids and worry-free
vacations for parents.

   Day-trippers park at the base of the mountain and take the Cabriolet people-
mover lift up to the resort village. Although I had my doubts about this idea, I was
sold the first time I rode in the open-air, stand-up gondola as it whisked me to the
village. Since then I've found that the five minutes in the Cabriolet is a welcome
transition time to unhook the fetters of the work-a-day world and leave it behind,
in the parking lot, where it belongs.

   The mountain itself is a series of interconnected peaks, valleys, ravines, and
meadows. Although the skiing or riding here is as much about exploration as exhil-
aration, The Canyons is not the resort where you'll find wild nightlife. The restaurants are great but few, and the watering-hole options are good but limited. If
you're looking for Mr. Goodbar, you'll be better served in Old-Town Park City.
While Old Town is close enough (six miles) for you to make the trip for dinner or
drinks, once you're at The Canyons you probably won't want to leave.

   The Canyons is a new and special place where you feel you're still in on a discovery—not fifty years too late. This year-round resort has kept true to its strong

The Canyons offers the kind of seclusion that families enjoy, as well as proximity to Park City's nightlife (above), which is just a cab ride away.

local following while becoming a world-class destination. It's a resort filled with newly cut trails and state-of-the-art lifts that glide you to lines you can make your own. You can have a sublime ski day, swim in the pool, sip a cocktail on the deck as the sun goes down, dine on big-city fare in western elegance, and most important, retreat to your suite feeling that you're more than a digitally encoded swipe of credit-card plastic. You'll feel you're part of the program—and isn't that what we all want?

RESTAURANTS

The Cabin (4000 The Canyons Resort Drive, in the Grand Summit Lodge, 435-615-8060) isn't about cheap eats, but it is about an eclectic western-inspired menu. Although guests of the Grand Summit make up most of the clientele here, knowledgeable locals have begun finding it too. This excellent eatery offers a surprisingly hassle-free alternative to Park City's Old Town. Instead of driving into Park City, jockeying for a place to park, feeding the meter, and then fighting the hordes, savvy locals have taken to driving to Grand Summit, pulling up to the valet, and handing him the keys. Then they go inside and have one of the best dining experiences in the Park City area. Ask the waiter to call the valet as you're finishing your dessert and your car will be ready, warm, and waiting when you leave. A truly luxurious way to spend a night. Open for lunch and dinner daily. Hours: 11:30 A.M.-3 P.M. for lunch and 6 P.M.-10 P.M. for dinner.

Lookout Cabin (at the top of the Lookout and Raptor chairlifts, 435-615-3406), perched at the top of the Lookout (the strange, sideways one) and Golden Eagle chairlifts, offers sit-down dining around a wide hearth or on a large deck that has the best views at the resort. "Ski hard early, eat late, and have a cold one on the Lookout deck," advises Canyons season-pass holder Bob Sullivan. I heartily concur. This is the best bet for lunch at The Canyons. Go for the Caesar salad with grilled steak. Open 11 A.M.-4 P.M. daily. Closed during the summer.

Red Pine (at the top of the Flight of the Canyons Gondola, 435-615-2888) is a beautiful lodge that sits in a high mountain meadow (8,000 feet) and is surrounded by the peaks of Ninety-nine 90, Tombstone, and Square Top. Sit in the beach chairs and dine on pizzas, grilled entrées, soups, a salad bar, or a New York-style deli. Reach Red Pine by riding the gondola. Open year-round. Hours: 9 A.M.-4 P.M. daily.

Smokies Smokehouse (in the base village, 435-615-2891) is a good place to have a low-key, nothing-fancy dinner. Families groove on the kickback atmosphere where they can dine on barbecue, burgers, or Cajun entrées. Slather on the barbecue sauce and bring on the bibs and a draft beer for Dad. Open daily. Hours: 10:30 A.M.-10 P.M.

Sun Lodge (under the Snow Canyon chairlift, 435-615-2890) features Mexican and Asian food in a sunny, sheltered location at the base of the south wall of Condor Mountain. From here, look longingly at Square Top, which you should never ski (unless you have a death wish). Hours: 9 A.M.-4 P.M. daily.

The **Viking Yurt** (www.parkcityyurts.com, 435-615-YURT) is a dining experience you won't soon forget. You and 27 other folks take a snowcat-pulled sleigh ride up the mountain to Red Pine Lodge. Don't worry about the cold; they'll drape you with thick blankets if it's a chilly night. Once at Red Pine, you put on cross-country skis or snowshoes and follow the guide down an easy cat track (by the bottom of Saddleback lift) until you see golden light glowing from the yurt. A tentlike cylindrical structure with a conical roof first used by the Mongol people of central Asia, the yurt of today bears little resemblance to its yak-skin forebears. The Viking Yurt has wooden floors, propane heat, and is to the Mongol yurts what an Audi A6 Quattro is to a covered wagon. Inside the yurt, long wooden tables are laid with glowing candles and oversized mugs. Norwegian hospitality envelops you as you sit down to a six-course Scandinavian meal that includes the Euro touch of a cheese, fruit, and nut course. Also open for lunch. Reservations only.

COFFEEHOUSES AND CAFÉS

At the heart of The Canyons resort village lies a collection of takeout eateries and shops that create a fun, carnival atmosphere around a circular skating rink. But you don't care much about that, do you? You just want your cuppa, and who can blame you? Okay, then, here they are:

The **Café in the Grand Summit Lodge** (4000 The Canyons Resort Drive, 435-649-5400) offers espresso and pastries daily 7 A.M.-4 P.M., summer 7 A.M.-7 P.M.

Montana Pub and Café (435-658-2445, 4000 The Canyons Resort Drive Sundial Court, Suite 8) fires up a mean cup. Get your espresso here and sip it on your way up the hill in the Flight of the Canyons Gondola. Hours vary according to season.

LODGING

The Beaver Creek-style resort village is still not complete, but the two properties that are—the Grand Summit Lodge and the Sundial Lodge—boast a level of luxury that's matched only by their perfect proximity to the Flight of the Canyons Gondola.

The **Grand Summit** (4000 The Canyons Resort Drive 888-CANYONS, www.thecanyons. com) is a 360-room luxury hotel with well-appointed suites, posh rooms, and all the amenities you'd expect of a world-class hotel. Pick up your boards at the ski check, walk down a dozen steps, and you're at the Flight of the Canyons Gondola. That's slope-side. After skiing, try the heated pool. Wade into the warm water inside, then swim out into the open air. Stroke through the steam and on over to the waterfall. Let it cascade over you for maximum escape. Now hop out and slide into one of the simmering Jacuzzis. What's next? A massage perhaps? Swim back inside and book it. The treatment rooms are right across the hall. Open year-round. Rates range from $274-$616 per room per night depending on the room and the season.

Sundial Lodge (4000 The Canyons Resort Drive, 888-CANYONS, www.thecanyons.com) offers condominium-style accommodations and has a rooftop hot tub and pool. Rates: $206-$467 per room per night.

SKIING

There's nothing about skiing or riding The Canyons that's obvious. This is a place that tucks its treasures among its many folds and pleats. Yet the best skiing for my money is at the top. Which means that after you've ridden the Cabriolet to the resort village, your mission is to get to the high peaks as fast as possible. The straight line is the eight-passenger Flight of the Canyons Gondola. This will take you to the Red Pine mid-mountain lodge. From there, the ski area fans out in every direction, and the crowds do too.

If the Flight of the Canyons is crowded, start your day on the chairs. Cut through the line that's waiting at the gondola and hike up the short snow-covered hill in front of you. Now click in and glide down to the Golden Eagle Chairlift. From here you can drop down to the Snow Canyon Express or Condor lifts and work the northern nooks. Since I prefer the Tombstone, Ninety-nine 90, and Peak 5 lifts, I usually opt to traverse over to Red Pine, which is at the top of the Flight of the Canyons Gondola.

From Red Pine, skate over the bridge to your left, then use the easy trail as a warm-up on your way to the Tombstone Express (a high-speed detachable quad). At the top of this lift, go to your left and take your first right to get to either the Ninety-nine 90 or Peak 5 chairlifts. There are so many good lines off these lifts that you can spend your whole day there.

My favorite line is under the Ninety-nine 90 lift. Most people go to either the north or south side of this lift, but right beneath it is a spine that offers the best

The Grand Summit offers luxurious rooms and perfect proximity to the flight of the Canyons Gondola.

fall-line, steep skiing on the hill. After hooking around to either side off the lift, you'll drop through evergreens, then across a traverse into aspens, and on down a real heart-in-the-throat chute. When you hit the basin at the bottom of this steep section, go straight into the aspens on the south side of the lift. These trees are tight, but the lines between them are excellent and little skied.

The best thing about skiing The Canyons, however, is the variety. You'll find whatever you want here—whether it's vertiginous lines or baby's-bottom-smooth grooming. The variety also allows families to go up the gondola together, split while each person skis his or her type of terrain, then easily meet for lunch. If Park City is the Aspen of Utah, then The Canyons is the Vail of Zion.

HIKE FOR THE GOODS

Every time you ride either the Peak 5 or Ninety-nine 90 chairlift, you'll be tempted by this massive headwall that looms up just to the west of the top of the Ninety-nine 90 lift. After a half dozen in-area runs, I'm usually ready to go get it. When ski patrol deems it safe, they'll open a gate at the top of the Ninety-nine 90 chairlift. If you have the necessary avalanche beacon, shovel, and knowledge of how to use them, you'll want to hike this headwall. Get off the chair, unclip, and start hiking. At the top of the first rise, clip your board back on, ride down to the base of the ridge hike, then start hoofing it again. After twenty minutes of hiking, you'll find yourself staring at terrain that is heli-skiing good. Which is to say it's a steep fall line on north- and east-facing fields of untracked snow.

You'll also be tempted by the wide, open face of Square Top. Although it looks like the most perfect powder line you could imagine, and it's only a ten-minute hike up the ridge, this is one temptation you must resist. Anyone who has hiked or mountain biked to this area in the summer has seen the sheer vertical slab of

Courtesy The Canyons

THE CANYONS SNAPSHOT

Location: 26 miles from Salt Lake City International Airport
Scheduled season: November to April
Hours of operation: Weekdays 9 A.M.-4 P.M., weekends: 8:30 A.M.-4 P.M.
Base elevation: 6,800 feet
Summit elevation: 9,990 feet
Vertical rise: 3,190 feet
Skiable acres: 3,625
Average seasonal snowfall: 355 inches
Lifts: 15
    1 eight-passenger high-speed gondola
    5 high-speed quads chairlifts
    4 quad chairlifts
    1 triple chairlift
    1 double fixed-grip chairlift
    2 surface lifts
    1 eight-passenger high-speed Cabriolet
Uphill capacity: 25,700 riders per hour
Total trails: 134 (14 percent beginner level, 44 percent intermediate, 42 percent expert)
Snowmaking: 150 acres
Ticket price: $59
Reservations resort information: 888-CANYONS
Website: www.thecanyons.com
Address: 4000 The Canyons Resort Drive, Park City, Utah 84098
Snow report: (435) 615-3456

rock that forms the face of Square Top. So smooth is the face of this buttress that it's a wonder any snow ever sticks to it. Generally it does, until a skier or snowboarder drops in on it. Then it slides, right down to the rock. This area has already taken lives; don't let it take yours.

BARS

Doc's (Level 3 of the Grand Summit Lodge, 888-CANYONS) is a Western-themed, slope-side bar. Whether you skied to the bottom or took the Flight of the Canyons down, you'll find yourself staring Doc's in the face. Don't fight it. When the weather is inhospitable, Doc's is the opposite, but when the weather is fine, Doc's, with its elevated deck that catches the receding afternoon rays, is pure luxury. Hours vary depending on season.

The **Lobby Bar in the Grand Summit** (4000 The Canyons Resort Drive, 888-CANYONS) serves drinks, coffee, tea and a light menu in a posh, western atmosphere. Hours vary depending on season.

Smokies Smokehouse (in the base village, 435-615-2891) is a remnant from the old Wolf Mountain days, which in this case is a good thing. Smokies has a great west-facing deck where you can drink a cold one in the sun after skiing. Hours: 10:30 A.M.-10 P.M.

13. Deer Valley

The homepage on Deer Valley's website reads "No snowboards, please." The fact that D.V. prohibits the single-plank set tells you one thing about the place, but a more important clue is contained within the word "Please." Right there, in that one word, you've got Deer Valley.

If the resort were a socialite, it would make Emily Post look like a rugby queen. If Deer Valley were a hockey player, it would win the Lady Bing Trophy (for outstanding sportsmanship). If Deer Valley were a pie, it would be lemon meringue. A drink? Sloe gin fizz.

Simply put, Deer Valley is the nicest, most polite ski resort you'll ever meet. This place invented guest service and reigns as the undisputed champion of the people-pleasing world. Drive up to the skier drop-off and watch the guys in the green Deer Valley uniforms jump out to take the skis off the rack of your car. Chiclet-toothed hosts line your walk to the ticket window. The lady behind the counter thanks you for coming, and the lift attendant brushes errant snowflakes off your chairlift before you sit down. In ski circles, Deer Valley's service is the stuff of legend, and its trail grooming is not far behind. At Deer Valley, they don't mow the trails; they tailor them. Can corduroy be fashioned of silk? At Deer Valley it can be.

But then that's the rep, right? Deer Valley is the posh place with the happy employees in Smurf suits. This is true, but there's more; Deer Valley has its secrets. The first is shady, lying between the swaths of flawless white, and it is this: Deer Valley has the best tree skiing in the Wasatch.

Yeah, but the mountain is flat, you say. Wrong again. This country-club resort has such precipitous runs they'll scare the polo player off your Ralph Lauren horse. Believe it. Deer Valley also has the kind of bump runs that got it selected as host of the freestyle moguls event for the 2002 Winter Olympic Games. And there's yet another dirty secret about Deer Valley. This one becomes known only after the last flakes have melted and the hard-cores have traded boards for bikes. This secret lies in the unlikely world of knobbies and endos, pedals and spokes. Incongruously, Deer Valley (and neighboring Park City) has the second-best network of mountain-biking trails in a state often called the Mecca of mountain biking. It's not better than Moab, but it's close.

Sure, Deer Valley is still the ski area where Stein Eriksen sets the Bogner standard, and the cafeteria lunches rival the fine-dining fare of most resort restaurants, but Deer Valley is also a place for serious underground fun that benefits from the direct contrast with the full-on foo foo.

RESTAURANTS

The opulence of Deer Valley is complemented by lots of chic eateries. The Olive Barrel on Royal Street and Sai-Sommet at the Deer Valley Club are spectacular. McHenry's offers a great alternative for families, and the Goldener Hirsch has a refined sense of Euro style that is hard to resist, but I was most charmed by one of Deer Valley's newest restaurants.

Bistro Toujours (7815 Royal Street East, 435-940-2200) has a slick press kit that describes this new French bistro's fare as *"la cuisine de maitre,"* which translates as the "cooking of the master." This is a bold statement; these guys either have the goods or more than their share of chutzpah. Tucked into the first floor of the tremendously upscale Chateaux at Silver Lake, Bistro Toujours has all the trappings—the white linen, the beautiful woodwork, the staff in black and white—of the finest establishments.

Yet, the test is how a place makes you feel. It doesn't matter how good the food or wine is, if the staff is snotty, humorless, or in the business of trying to make you feel inferior (ever had a waiter scoff at a slight mispronunciation?), then you'd just as soon tell them where they can put their gold-plated crumbers.

So it was with trepidation that I entered the place that claimed "the cooking of the master." It began well: The maître d' was polite and happy to see us, and our waiter, a wide-eyed cherubic man, was bursting to tell us about all the specials. We chose the *degustation* menu, a seven-course sampler that began with bourbon and red-onion cappuccino as well as a more standard array of appetizers, salads, and entrées. Then Randall F. Corcoran, the sommelier (wine steward to you and me) stepped to the table. He was nattily attired in a sharp tuxedo, wore small glasses, and carried a high-voltage enthusiasm. Uh-oh, I thought, here comes Mr. Pronunciation. Wrong. He was unassuming, knowledgeable, and obviously passionate about his profession. I asked him to match each of our courses with a wine of his choosing. After both our waiter and sommelier went out of their way to praise their executive chef, Bryan Moscatello, I consulted the press kit. After learning his chops at Aspen's Little Nell Hotel, Moscatello brought "an unpretentious classic cooking style to the Bistro Toujours."

Indeed he did. Every course was unique and strongly flavored. The presentation was artful, and although the portions were small, I couldn't have eaten another morsel of food this rich and piquant. The wines Corcoran chose complemented each course with unexpected and nontraditional (a pinot noir with roasted sea bass) precision. Over the next three hours of our meal, all the ingredients came together. The Bistro Toujours offers the best connoisseur's dining experience in Utah. The one caveat, of course, is price. This is not your every-Thursday-night regular spot but rather one for special occasions. From soup to cheese platter to dessert, with all the wines and a 20 percent tip, our tally came to $250 for two people.

Buvez is the private-club, full-service bar that's attached to the restaurant. It specializes in martinis and cognacs. Bistro Toujours also serves breakfast and lunch during the winter. Dinner hours: 5 P.M.-10 P.M. seven nights a week. Summer hours: Sunday-Thursday 5 P.M.-9 P.M., Friday and Saturday 5 P.M.-10 P.M.

COFFEEHOUSES AND CAFÉS

Pick up a to-go cup from the cart on the stairway of the Deer Valley base lodge, or get one from Ralph the Maestro at Espresso Brothers in the Silver Lake Lodge at mid-mountain. As for hip coffeehouses, you're going to have to go a mile down the hill to Park City (see Park City section).

LODGING

Deer Valley has many upscale lodging properties—from condos to houses to hotels—but no inexpensive places to stay. Most properties can be accessed by calling 888-754-8477 or visiting www.deervalley.com.

OUTDOOR RECREATION

HIKING

If you like hiking amid beautiful aspens and evergreens while staying close to civilization, this place is for you. Although D.V. has become a mountain-bike haven, many trails are for hiking only. Choose from a half dozen trails that take you to the top of the Sterling lift, then, save your knees, and take a free chairlift ride down. Pick up your free map at the base or at the Silver Lake Lodge. Here are a few hiking-only trails:

Flagstaff Mountain Connector is the half-mile trail that connects Bald Mountain to Flagstaff Mountain. Once you get there, you'll find many options. One of the best ways to return is via the Ontario Canyon trail.

Silver Lake Trail is a two-mile trek that encircles the top half of Bald Mountain and offers great mountain views in all directions.

MOUNTAIN BIKING

Deer Valley's 50 miles of incredible mountain-biking trails are the reason the resort annually ranks in the top ten mountain-bike destinations (according to *Mountain Bike Action* magazine) and plays host to a major NORBA (National Off-Road Bicycling Association) mountain-bike race every June. As you roll on up to Deer Valley, you'll be astonished to find tattooed, rad-looking guys blasting down the hill on fully suspended two-wheeled rockets. The reason? Lift-served mountain biking. Deer Valley runs the Sterling lift from 9 A.M. until 5 P.M. beginning in mid-June and continuing through Labor Day; Wednesdays through Sundays and holidays (conditions permitting). After Labor Day, lift-served mountain biking is offered only on weekends through September (conditions permitting). Bikes and helmet rentals, repairs, and riding instruction are available at the base. All of Deer Valley's trails are well marked and rated. Here are a few downhill runs:

Aspen Slalom is a two-mile, tight singletrack through aspens that you drop into from the Summer Road.

The **Fire Swamp** is the state championship downhill course. On this one-and-a-half-mile funhouse ride, anything can happen. Deer Valley resort management recommends you wear pads for this one. That's probably not bad advice.

Homeward Bound is three miles of steeper, faster downhilling that will take about 15 minutes to descend. From the top of Sterling, go toward the reflector shields, then wind around to the Homeward Bound ski run.

The **Naildriver Downhill** is three miles of sharp switchbacks and big views. Take Sunset west from the top of the Sterling chair and drop in to your right. Be careful of slower riders on this one.

Tour des Suds can be ridden from the top of Main Street in Park City (see page 173), or as a six-mile cross-country/downhill from Deer Valley, around Flagstaff Mountain and down to Daly Canyon. Give way to uphill riders; they're working, and you just rode the chair.

Twist and Shout is a tough 1.7-mile, steep, serpentine singletrack through the trees. Access it off the top of Naildriver.

SKIING

Deer Valley doesn't have the big vertical of a Snowbird or an Alta, but it does have the best grooming, the best tree skiing, and some unexpected steeps across a wide expanse of eminently skiable mountain. Oh, yeah, and it also has Olympic-caliber mogul, aerial, and slalom hills.

The mountain has a lower base lodge as well as an upper one. You can drive to both. I usually opt for the upper, Silver Lake Lodge, as that's where the best skiing is. There is more parking at the lower lodge, however, and the resort is seamless in getting you from your car up the lifts and skiing.

Although much of Deer Valley consists of wide thoroughfares of groomed runs, the islands of dark woods next to many runs are perfectly spaced, properly sloped, and virtually unpeopled. "While all the tourists are hanging out on Birdseye," said Deer Valley weekday skier Bob Sullivan, "those of us who know where to go are ripping freshies all day in the trees." Two days after a storm, you (and Sully) will still be getting the fresh in the woods at Deer Valley while at Snowbird or Alta, the tree lines are tracked by noon.

The Black Forest Trees, just west of Stein's Way, offer some of the best, most accessible tree skiing you'll find. This is double-fall-line, north-facing, evergreen-protected, steep terrain. Accessed from either Sultan, Sterling, or Wasatch chairlifts, Black Forest gives experts serious challenge while their less accomplished pals can ply the groomer (Perseverance) only a few feet away. The aspens of Triangle Trees, between Tycoon and Reward (enter off lower Reward), are also hard to beat on a powder day.

Here's another gem: Deer Valley, the king of the groomers, now has steeps. For the past few years, locals on big fat sticks with helmets and serious-looking goggles have been quietly slipping out to the Daly Chutes for some of the most un-skied steeps in the state. Get off the top of the Empire Express chair and go south, down the ridge and into the trees through the gate. Traverse out past the Anchor Trees to the last chute before the rope line. This is Chute 4, and it's hairball steep. It has only ten turns, but each one is a must-make.

Another reason to go to D.V. is its easy to access the goods. "On powder days I get on the Wasatch chair at 9 A.M. and am skiing thigh-deep freshies in Triangle Trees at 9:08," said Sullivan. "Since the lifts are always empty, I'm legless by 11 A.M."

Courtesy Deer Valley Resort

Most Deer Valley skiers tend to stay on the groomed trails, which leaves a lot of powder for the locals ... and you.

The efforts of Deer Valley's cadre of snowcats between storms are renowned, but there's more to this hill than grooming. Ask yourself why a resort known for grooming would be selected for the biggest mogul competition in the world. Because it has the best, consistently steep mogul field in the state, that's why. Lying between Big Stick and Know You Don't, the champion mogul course has the kind of elevator-drop bumps that are all but impossible to ski at slow speeds. Which means that very few Deer Valley skiers ever try them. These moguls start out as machine-made bumps (as do most World Cup courses nowadays), then are skied by members of the U.S. freestyle team and a handful of bumping locals until they're the stuff of legend. The word in ski circles is that Colorado's Winter Park has the best bumps in the country. Well, I know this: A run down Outhouse will never scare the heck out of you as will a warp-factor foray down D.V.'s champion mogul course.

The Deer Valley Look
Locals here wear Schoffel or Fire and Ice togs and Oakley goggles and ski on Volant Ti Chubbs. Slip your sunglasses into your jacket for proper lounging on the beach.

A New Backdoor
Deer Valley recently opened the Jordanelle Express Gondola, which comes up from the Heber side of the area. This entrée to the mountain is virtually empty most days and provides a quiet prelude to any ski day. Access it off Highway 40, near the Jordanelle Dam.

DEER VALLEY SNAPSHOT

Location: 39 miles from Salt Lake City International Airport
Scheduled season: Early December until mid-April (December 8, 2001-April 7, 2002)
Hours of operation: 9 A.M.-4 P.M. daily
Top elevation: Empire Canyon summit, 9,570 feet
Vertical drop: 3,000 feet
Skiable acres: 1,750
Average seasonal snowfall: 350 inches
Lifts: 19
> 1 high-speed four-passenger gondola
> 6 high-speed quad lifts
> 3 fixed-grip quad lifts
> 7 triple chairs
> 2 double chairs

Uphill capacity: 39,700 skiers per hour
Runs: 88 (15 percent beginner level, 50 percent intermediate, 35 percent expert)
Snowmaking: 500 acres
Ticket price: $65 during regular season, $67 peak season.
Address: P.O. Box 1525, Park City UT 84060; 2250 Deer Valley Drive, South Park City UT 84060
Central reservations: 800-558-3337
General resort information: 800-424-3337
Website: www.deervalley.com
Snow report: 800-424-DEER (435-649-2000)

Deer Valley Out-of-Bounds?

I'm unsure of the legality, but many Deer Valley locals make their last run down Daly Canyon. They ski to the base of the Northside lift, use a cell phone to call a taxi that will pick them up at the end of the run (435-649-TAXI), and depart the area just to the north of the lift. They drop into the woods and ski down through the aspen trees. When they hit the cat road, they ski down it to the right. When the snowfield opens on the left, drop in and ski a dozen nice steep turns down toward an old abandoned mine. Next there's a short section of old mining road to be hiked up until it levels. Drop through the woods to the left to enjoy three tree shots and a meadow before you arrive at Daly Avenue.

Sports Shops

Cole Sport (7620 Royal Street East, first floor of the Royal Plaza Building, 435-649-4601) has Kip and Todd and Carolyn and Jackie, who will do you right for retail, rentals, repairs. Winter hours: 8 A.M.-7 P.M. Closed in the summer.

BARS

The best place to enjoy a beer or a drink is Deer Valley's outdoor "beach." Formed of reclining lounge chairs outside the Silver Lake Lodge, "the beach" is a place where you can let the sun kiss your face or have it air-kissed by a thousand Los

Angelenos. This is *the* place in Deer Valley to see and be seen. During the Sundance Film Festival, the beach is where you'll see a few movie stars, dozens of agents, and a zillion producers. Look for a tall guy in a yellow Bogner suit. That will be *There's Something About Mary* producer Frank Beddor. He'll likely be with his short, energetic pal Paul Rosenberg, who produced *Go*. During ten days in February, Deer Valley plays host to Beddor, Rosenberg (both former members of the U.S. freestyle ski team), and large groups of cell-phone-toting celluloid heroes. Whether it's during Sundance or on any sunny day, the thing to do is buy a beer inside and take it back to your chair on the Beach. Rumor has it that a martini bar may be opened on the beach soon.

Goldener Hirsch (7570 Royal Street East, 435-649-7770) is a full-on Euro bar that serves the best tall Spatens in chilled glasses. Open 11:30 A.M.-11 P.M. daily.

Stein Eriksen Lodge (7700 Stein Way, 435-649-3700) is the classic Deer Valley spot for après-ski. It has a full bar with the best coffee drinks around and a great beer and wine-by-the-glass selection, but the coolest thing here is checking out Stein's gold medals in the display case. A seriously upscale lodge with a classic Euro feel, this is the place where you're most likely to run into the ski legend himself. "Stein still skis nearly every day, and he comes in here probably four times a week," said assistant food and beverage manager Chris Miller. "He doesn't mind if you go over and talk to him; he's one of the most personable guys you'll ever meet." If a real live ski celeb isn't enough to entice you into Stein's, consider the great decks where you can watch the sun dip from the sky. A wonderful place with real history, Stein's is a posh spot you must check out at least once. Hours: 10:30 A.M.-midnight daily.

NORTHERN UTAH

14. Snow Basin

The **Snow Basin Winter Resort** (P.O. Box 460, 3925 East Snow Basin Road, Huntsville, Utah 84317, 888-437-5488) is a mountain you may not have heard of, but one that's not to be missed. If I were limited to one word to fill you in on Snow Basin, that word would be "go." If you gave me two, I'd say "go now." This is an amazing place. From the spectacular 9,570-foot Mount Ogden that rises over the resort to unsurpassed views of the Great Salt Lake, the scenic beauty is magnificent, and the skiing is world-class.

Have you ever met someone who is so perfectly beautiful, charming, and talented that you instantly start composing your "I knew them when" stories? Have you known someone who was so surely fated to become a star that you knew you

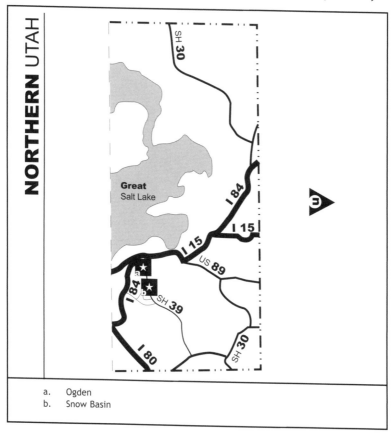

a. Ogden
b. Snow Basin

David Crim

State-of-the-art Snow Basin, near Ogden, is so empty it's surreal.

were going to lose touch with them? It's a strange, bittersweet feeling. You connect, see the promise, and get ready to release the person to fame. If you have ever had this feeling, you'll know why I'm telling you to go to Snow Basin now.

I started hearing about this rising star in the 1980s. Back then I lived in Vail, Colorado, and Pete Siebert, the man who "discovered" Vail, had just made news by leaving his world-famous star behind and moving to a little-known resort in Ogden, Utah. The word was that Pete had tired of the traffic in Vail and decided to go hermit in Utah, but the scuttlebutt was wrong. Pete was on to something.

At the time, Snow Basin was a local skier's powder stash. The winding road that led to the day-use area made Salt Lake City more than an hour away, on dry roads. But the roads were almost never dry; it snows an average of 33 feet a season at Snow Basin. There were other challenges: The lifts were old, there was no lodging, and the cafeteria facility was ramshackle. So it stayed a small local-skier's powder paradise.

After trying in vain to secure enough land to build a proper base village, Siebert decided to sell the place. He called Sun Valley owner Earl Holden, who summarily turned him down. "Pete, one ski area is enough," Holden told Siebert. "I'm not even going to come look at it."

Anyone who has ever met Pete Siebert knows how he feels about the word "no." Holden came to Snow Basin and soon thereafter bought the place. What followed was an uphill battle of Sisyphean proportions. In the end, Holden did a land swap with the U.S. Forest Service and secured land for a base village. Instrumental in this process was the hairy downhill course that college racers had been taking their licks on for years. Out of all the possible schusses in the state, this one stood the best chance of hosting Olympic downhill and super-g courses.

And so it was that enough land was secured for a base lodge, Salt Lake City

SNOW BASIN VITAL STATS

Where: 40 miles from downtown Salt Lake City.
What: 2,940 vertical feet, 3,200 acres, nine lifts.
Prices: $43 adult, $25 for children 7-12, 6 years and under ski free. (2000-2001 season prices. 2001-2002 prices not available at press time.) Phone: 888-437-5488
Web: www.snowbasin.com
Season: November until mid-April.
Local lore: In December 2000 a local pilot flew his small single-engine prop plane too close to the face of Mount Ogden. He crashed into the face and was killed instantly. The plane is still there.

was awarded the 2002 Olympics, and Snow Basin had a date for a debutante ball in front of an estimated viewing audience of some two billion people.

Fast forward through $100 million in development that included a new mountain road that cuts the trip from Salt Lake from 53 miles to 40 (drive time 40 minutes), a vast snow-making system that covers virtually the entire hill, state-of-the-art avalanche control, two eight-passenger gondolas, four triple chairs, a minitram, and a high-speed quad chairlift. The result? Snowbasin is a star who's all dressed up for a party.

The effect of all this development is completely surreal. Picture state-of-the-art lifts, massive yellow pine lodges, 3,000 vertical feet of untracked powder (some of it consistently steep from top to bottom), tremendous views (the Great Salt Lake off one side, Pineview Reservoir off the other)—and all of a hundred skiers on the hill. As I was riding the new Strawberry Express gondola, I didn't see another person. Not a soul. When I reached the top, I saw about a dozen in one place—all waiting for a patrolman to drop the rope into the Demoisy Peak area. I got there just as he did. I followed what turned out to be a Teton Gravity Research film crew up the short hike to the top of Demoisy Peak.

The chute straight down from the peak was steeper perhaps than anything in-bounds at Snowbird. After the TGR honchos straight-ran the thing, I made slow turns through the foot-plus of powder. Though I whooped with delight, there was absolutely no one around to hear me. If a nut screams on the mountain and there's no one to hear it, did he ever scream at all?

Metaphysical questions notwithstanding, Snow Basin is a place you simply must visit, whether it's to ski the 2,770 vertical feet of the Bernhard Russi-designed Olympic downhill and super-g courses (women's and men's), to form your own "I knew it when" story, or just to have a great day. Snowboarding is allowed at Snow Basin, and although the area doesn't have a terrain park, its natural gullies and ravines more than make up for it.

A few caveats must be offered, however. The first is the elevation: With a base elevation of 6,400 feet and a summit of 9,400 feet, Snow Basin is low. In some places this might mean less snow, but here it seems to mean that the copious snow is a bit heavier than you'd find at Alta, Snowbird, Brighton, or Solitude. Thus far, this drawback is more than compensated for by the lack of skiers and riders.

Another heads up: If there are any races in progress, the entire north side of the mountain (the John Paul area) may be closed. This will eliminate most of the best expert terrain on the mountain. And believe me, this expert terrain is something you don't want to miss. Experts, call before you go. The intermediate terrain, on the other hand, is well groomed, covered with machine-made snow, and as bankable as any terrain in the state.

RESTAURANT AND BAR

Shooting Star Saloon (7345 East 200 South Huntsville, 801-745-2002) is the only place to go after a day of skiing or riding at Snow Basin. This 122-year-old joint is the oldest continually serving bar in Utah. Proprietor Heidi Posnien, a Berlin-born buxom and brazen woman of indeterminate age, will not be fazed by you or anyone else who walks through the ancient and battered door. Heidi has seen and heard it all, from a visit from Charles Kuralt to the Hell's Angels, and still manages to smile. One reason may be her take-no-crap demeanor.

"God grant me the serenity to accept the things I cannot change," reads one of her signs, "the courage to change the things I can, and the wisdom to hide the bodies of the people I had to kill because they pissed me off."

The Shooting Star serves beer and burgers. Period. Although it's a heart attack in a bun, the Shooting Star's signature burger (two beef patties, cheese, onion and peppers, and Polish knockwurst) is a must-have, and you needn't take my word for it. In 1991, USA Today called the Shooting Star burgers the "best in the West."

Burgers come with potato chips, and Heidi and Co. will tell you in no uncertain terms that you will get your food the way they make it and no other way. If Burger King has a polar opposite, the Shooting Star is it. Never mind feng-shuied, nonsmoking joints where you can get your ahi on a bed of arugula. The Shooting Star will serve you meat and brew in a shotgun shack building that's been shaded by a century's worth of cigar smoke.

Despite the hard-ass facade, however, the Shooting Star brims with a real-folk kindness that's hard to find in so many more polite environs. Just ask to read the guest books, and you'll see what I mean. The decor has not been designed; it's just sort of collected. From the one-dollar bills pinned to the ceiling (write your name on one and Heidi will tack it up there for you) to the mounted and stuffed Saint Bernard on the wall, this is a place where real people come to eat, drink, and smoke. You'll find tourists from France at the bar next to ranchers from Eden (just down the road). Après-ski crowds mix with farmers, and the weekends draw lots of motorcyclists. No one under 21 allowed, ever. Hours: Monday-Saturday noon until Heidi feels like closing, Sunday after church (about 2 P.M.) until Heidi gets tired of you.

CENTRAL UTAH

15. Brian Head

With a base lodge at 9,600 feet, Brian Head is Utah's highest ski resort. It won't challenge any of the northern Utah areas for expert skiing (even Deer Valley has more steeps than Brian Head), but it's the best place to learn to snowboard with your kids. This is not just my opinion but a fact supported by painstaking, research missions that took me from the chairlifts to the Jacuzzis of this resort. Everywhere I went, I found young fathers who had taken up snowboarding right alongside their kids.

Why? Well, the terrain is tame, the snow is drier than anywhere in the state (which means no ice), and the slopes are empty (except for the parents flailing around as their kids whoosh past them). The secluded atmosphere here also guarantees that your CEO won't ever see you behaving like a rebellious teen.

The skiing and snowboarding here are easy but good. There are six lifts—five triple chairs and one double—500 skiable/ridable acres, 53 runs, and an average annual snowfall of 425 inches. The base is always deep, and even days after a storm there's lots of untracked. The cross-country skiing is also good and beautiful as it winds through the dark green cedars and deep red of the southern Utah rock.

The mountain biking and hiking are good in their short summer season. Because of the lift-served terrain and well-bermed tracks, downhill mountain bikers will have a ball here. The fly-fishing is also reputed to be awesome.

Just down the road is a scenic wonder that's off the main national park loop: Cedar Breaks. A huge multihued, 2,500-foot natural amphitheater carved out of the cedar forest, Cedar Breaks is worth a good long look or a hike into its midst. In winter you can ski some pretty steep and unique lines (through red rock goblinlike formations called "hoo doos") down through Falls Breaks, which is just down the road from Cedar Breaks and shares the same spectacular characteristics.

LODGING

The **Cedar Breaks Lodge** (223 Hunter Ridge Road, 888 AT CEDAR, www.cedarbreakslodge.com) is the only three-star hotel in this part of central Utah. A three-story modern structure with large rooms (many that include fireplaces) is not exactly homey or unique, but the rooms are comfortable and well appointed with microwaves and refrigerators. The spa at this place, however, is terrific and a big surprise up here at 9,600 feet. A pool, several hot tubs, a steam room, and a sauna look out over a high alpine meadow. Soaking in the sauna takes on a privileged air when you're watching snow fly sideways outside. Nonparents beware. If you are someone who gets easily flustered by splashing kids, you'll want to avoid the après-ski hours. Brian Head's popularity as a family spot means kids, and to a kid, a pool is just a party begging to happen.

The Cedar Breaks Lodge is owned by the Sedona Resort Management Company,

CENTRAL UTAH

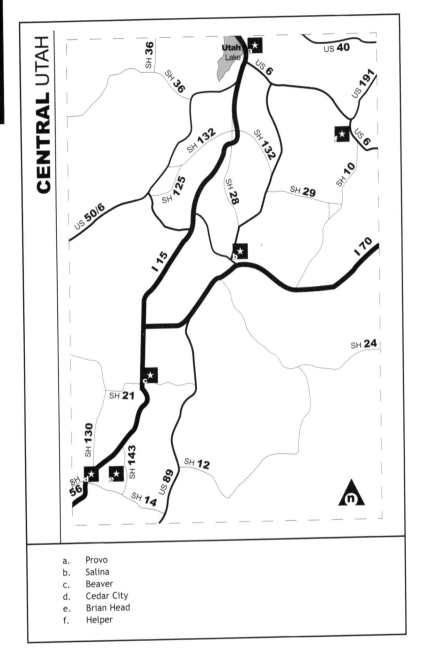

a. Provo
b. Salina
c. Beaver
d. Cedar City
e. Brian Head
f. Helper

Courtesy Brian Head

Cedar Breaks National Monument is off the national park tourist trap loop.

which also owns the Enchantment Resort in Sedona, Arizona. This may explain the professional and luxurious full-service day spa. With amenities such as aromatherapy, pedicure, manicures, and facials, as well as Swedish, shiatsu, and deep-tissue massage, this spa is truly a mother's little helper.

The Pinnacle Breaks Bar and Grill at Cedar Breaks Lodge is a private club, which always means there's a full bar. Guests get memberships with their rooms, and there always seem to be plenty of willing sponsors for nonhotel guests. The food in the Pinnacle Breaks is quite good, even if the service is kickback and in no rush.

Inner Harmony (800-214-0174, www.innerharmonyyoga.com) is a yoga retreat and wellness center in the summer and cross-country bed-and-breakfast inn in the winter. Located far out in the woods at an elevation of 9,300 feet, it's not a place where you're going to be hassled by phone solicitors or pesky neighbors wanting to borrow the lawn-seed spreader. This remoteness is why Inner Harmony has become so popular for yoga and meditation retreats. It provides the yoga mats, blocks, belts, and blankets that any mind-body could ask for.

On the Anusara Yoga and Hiking Retreat, Inner Harmony offers a "a truly profound experience of Anusara yoga, meditation, pranayama, and hiking." Anusara yoga master John Friend guides guests on "a body, mind, spirit journey that will forever enrich your soul." Another yoga retreat offers an introduction to Tantra, which incorporates "all the tools of yoga including asana, pranayama, as well as a nearly endless variety of profound meditation, contemplation, and energetic techniques." These retreats are offered in the summer, when the scenery at this mountaintop retreat is spectacular.

In the winter, Inner Harmony becomes a bed and breakfast for skiers (www.brianheadnordic.com) and offers guests a snowmobile or snowcat ride into the lodge,

GORDY PEIFER

The cedars and the stone; Jim Conway rides Brian Head.

then miles of groomed and backcountry cross-country ski trails. This place gets more than 350 inches of snow every year, so you're bound to find ample cover and plenty of fresh powder to play in. Whether you're cross-country skiing or snowshoeing, Inner Harmony provides an unparalleled escape into nature. It also offers guided group or solo backcountry tours, lodging, food, Jacuzzis, and sauna.

16. Beaver, Helper, and Salina

Beaver

Beaver was settled in 1856 by Mormon pioneers, who named it for the plentiful little tree-gnawing creatures that lived in the area. Beaver was also the birthplace of the inventor of television, Philo T. Farnsworth, and the much-mythologized outlaw Butch Cassidy. History or no, however, you probably won't spend much time in Beaver. You'll probably do what I always do: pull off the highway, gas up (at 200 miles south of Salt Lake City, this is where my motorcycle runs out of gas), loop through town, and stop and eat. For more information on Beaver, visit www.beaverutah.net.

RESTAURANTS

As for eating in Beaver, you have two choices.

Arshel's Cafe (711 North Main Street, 435-438-2977) has but one color permeating its frilled and grandmotherly interior: rose. The tables are rose, the flowers on them as well, the woodwork, the menu, the ruffle on the curtains—all rose. It's such a sweet place that the air seems rose. The best bet is rose-colored food: pan-fried rainbow trout. Strains of Neil Diamond float out of the kitchen, and the waitress, a perky and efficient young woman, sang along in an elegant and soft voice as she served the trout. It was big and good, with all the trimmings, even a salad in a rose-colored bowl. Hours: Summer 7 A.M.-10 P.M. Winter 7 A.M.-9 P.M. Open seven days a week.

El Bambi Café (935 North Main Street, 435-438-2983) is the place for anyone wanting a real greasy spoon serving up real road food. The sign, which features Bambi in a fetchin' pose, is great Americana kitsch. Inside, this is a full-on old-school grease and grub, which, in my book anyway, is not a slam. The best thing about El Bambi is the hours: it's always open (except Christmas Day and New Year's Eve). Twenty-four hours a day you can get a hunk of pie and a cup of joe. The one downside of El Bambi is that it also serves as a Greyhound bus stop. Which means that if you happen to be there when the big rig pulls in, you'll be inundated with bathroom-goers and all sorts of colorful characters. Open 24 hours a day, every day.

Helper

Highway 6 from Green River north to Price and on up to American Fork is a lonely and despicable, rutted two-laner filled with annoyingly short passing zones and speed traps galore. There is, however, a road stop that makes the stretch bearable, or at least breaks it in two. The stop is Helper, which most people know only as a place where they got a speeding ticket. Helper is just east of Highway 6 between Price and Soldier Summit. It's a sleepy old mining town, nearly closed down but trying for a comeback.

RESTAURANTS

Balance Rock Eatery and Pub (148 South Main, 435-472-0403) is like a Lyle Lovett song ("If I had a pony I'd ride it on my boat") that makes no sense. Yet like a Lovett lyric, it is precisely the way it doesn't make sense, the way it hints that it might be logical in the fourth dimension, that makes this place special. It has plastic statues of spilled food and plates of half-twirled spaghetti. You can quaff a beer, shoot some pool, and shop for curios and antiques all at the same time. This is a place where the smell of fries mingles with a high, grandmotherly boof of mothballs off the ancient quilts. Get a quarter-pound burger for $2.95 or a World War II helmet for $25. You can't help but grin. The food's good too. Hours: Monday-Thursday 9:30 A.M.-8 P.M., Friday and Saturday 8:30 A.M.-10 P.M., Sunday 8:30 A.M.-8 P.M. Open year-round.

Salina

Salina is known for two things: proximity to I-70, and world-famous Mom's Café.

RESTAURANTS

Mom's Café (10 East Main Street, Salina, 435-529-3921). So your first question is: "Who's Mom?" Right? Well, you won't have to wait long for an answer. When you walk in the door of Mom's, you'll see Carolyn Jensen, seated at her wide, cluttered desk in the middle of the restaurant. With half-glasses perched on the end of her nose, Mom Jensen is the latest in a long succession of Moms who've run the café since 1878. That's a lot of Moms. "It's so old that we don't have people around anymore who know anything about how it began," said Mom. This is a place that delivers the same picture you hold in your mind. Yep there are the chrome stools at the Formica counter. Yep, there are the shiny metal napkin holders and those big cold-looking metal boxes that held the milk at your elementary school. Homemade pies and the simple good food that you haven't had since you moved out of your own Mom's house? Check. Mom's even has liver and onions. Yes, Mom's is everything you'd hope Mom's Café would be, right down to the teal-green waitress uniforms with the pink bands at the sleeve and throat. Hours: Summer 7 A.M.-10 P.M., daily. Winter 7 A.M.-9 P.M. daily.

SOUTHERN UTAH

17. Highway 12 Loop

n 1996, President Bill Clinton declared 1.7 million acres of the Grand Staircase-Escalante a national monument. This decree had many ranchers and miners in Southern Utah up in arms. They damn sure didn't want Uncle Sam telling them what they could or couldn't do with the land that surrounded towns like Escalante and Boulder. Although the Bush administration is currently working to reverse the protective effects of the monument designation (coal mining is one of the proposed uses), at present the Grand Staircase-Escalante is the largest national monument in the country. Named for the explorer priest who was looking for an overland route from Santa Fe, New Mexico, to Alta, California, this little-known, barely developed, yet huge expanse of beautiful and diverse country should be seen and experienced now, rather than later. Since this area is managed by the Bureau of Land Management (it's the only national monument that is), dogs are still allowed to run without a leash, and there is a more low-key feeling than you'll find in most national or state parks.

Whether it's for hiking, mountain biking, horseback riding, or just taking in the scenery, this area is my top pick for off-the-beaten-track touring and recreating. Few among the hordes who visit Bryce and Zion national parks to the south ever venture up into the Grand Staircase-Escalante area. This leaves the roads uncrowded and the towns unmarred by fast-food joints, chain hotels, and T-shirt shops. In fact, it wasn't the scenery but rather a squiggly line on a map that first drew me to Escalante. For throttle-twisters, snaky blue lines on a road map are as exciting as zeros behind a dollar sign are to an accountant.

Traveling by bike changes the emphasis of the whole experience. As soon as you get in a car, you're thinking of arriving at your destination. The drive is to be tolerated, smoothed over by CDs, radio, and books on tape. It's the opposite on a bike. Motorcyclists yearn for the ride, the wind and the sun on their leathery skin and jackets. They accept the destination, not the drive, as a necessary evil.

The first time I drove through Escalante on a cruiser I turned around at Panguitch and drove Highway 12 all the way back to Torrey, then did it again. The road is that good. The scenery is a stunning mix of slickrock that looks as if it's underwater, alpine tundra, and piñon and juniper forest. The tiny towns on the route are simple and honest places where life is slow and the weather is more important than CNN or the NASDAQ.

When it's traveled west to east, Highway 12 begins seven miles south of Panguitch and runs in a 120-mile semicircle through Garfield County (home of three national parks, three state parks, a national recreation area, and the new national monument) and Wayne County. It begins in the red rock formations of Dixie National Forest's Red Canyon, continues eastward through the northern section of Bryce Canyon National Park, through Grand Staircase-Escalante National

SOUTHERN UTAH

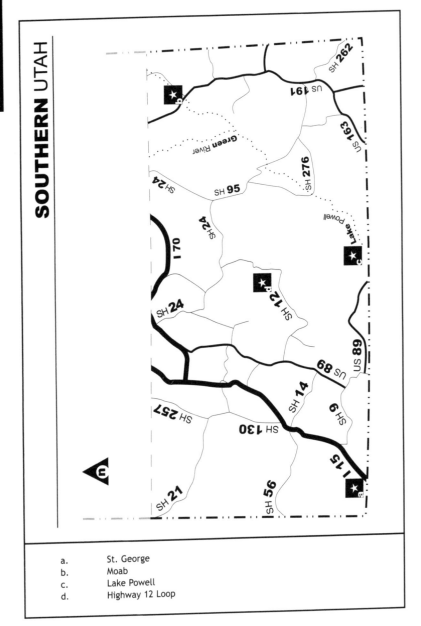

a. St. George
b. Moab
c. Lake Powell
d. Highway 12 Loop

GORDY PEIFER

Southern Utah is filled with the kind of incredible terrain that can make all of us a little bit crazy. Here Kris Baughman goes big in the backcountry.

Monument, through Anasazi Indian Village State Park, and over Boulder Mountain, and then turns northward to end at the gateway to Capitol Reef National Park. This route may be the best motorcycle road in the country, but it's wonderful whether you're on a Harley or in a Hyundai.

Panguitch

For three seasons of the year, not much happens in this sleepy little town, but in the summer, Panguitch becomes a place where everyone seems to stop for gas and directions and to get out and stretch the legs. If you happen to hit the town around coffee break or dinnertime, however, I'd advise taking a few extra minutes.

RESTAURANTS

Cowboy's Smokehouse (95 North Main Street, 435-676-8030) has a long wall filled with business cards from all over the world, but that's not what you care about. What you care about is meat. And by "meat" I mean barbecue. This place takes its BBQ seriously. The owner regularly takes off with a long trailer hitched behind his truck in search of the best mesquite he can find. "This is not baked Utah barbecue," he will tell you with a sneer. "This is real barbecue." Which means a mesquite wood fire in an old barrel-shaped smoker that takes hours to turn meat into savory magic. Cowboy's serves up its smoked meat dry; you sauce it up with their secret blend. How secret is it? "I've worked here six years and still don't know what's in it," said one waiter.

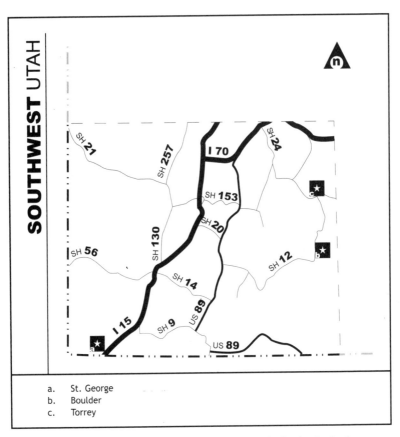

SOUTHWEST UTAH

SH 21

SH 257

I 70

SH 24

SH 153

SH 130

SH 20

SH 56

SH 12

SH 14

I 15

SH 9

US 89

US 89

a. St. George
b. Boulder
c. Torrey

If the best damn barbecue in the state is not enough, Cowboy's also has country entertainment six nights a week in the summer. Don't look for napkins here, however, because all you get is paper towels—one roll per table. Beer is served. Hours: Monday-Saturday 11:30 A.M.-9:30 P.M., with extended hours in July and August. Closed Sunday.

COFFEEHOUSES AND CAFÉS

Buffalo Java (47 North Main Street, 435-676-8900) is a great coffee and bagel store with a hip little gift shop attached to it. The coffee comes from the Salt Lake Roasting Company, and the bagels taste as good as New York roundies, but that conclusion might be the result of desert-hunger sauce. Hours: 7:30 A.M.-6 P.M. Memorial Day through October 1. Open later (8 or 9 P.M.) June to September. Closed in the winter.

Escalante

Escalante is a one-street town that's in the process of changing from a ranchers' center to a tourist town. A few new cafés and outfitters are springing up, but it's too soon to gauge their merit. There is, however, one classic lunch spot that'll fuel you with plenty of low-grade coffee, grease, and carbs for the road ahead.

COFFEEHOUSES AND CAFÉS

The Golden Loop Café (39 West Main Street, 435-826-4433) is just the sort of old-school greasy spoon that road-trip memories are made of. From the sepia-tone photographs of famous outlaws (complete with faded, handwritten captions) to that welcoming smell of burning coffee, this is a place that's perfect for taking a load off and chewing the fat. Is the food good? Good enough. The service? Affable as you'll find. Hours: 7 A.M.-9 P.M. seven days a week.

Somewhere Out There

COFFEEHOUSES AND CAFÉS

The Kiva Koffeehouse (at mile marker 73.86 on Highway 12, 435-826-4550) is a little gem that's built into a bluff all by itself on the road between Escalante and Boulder. It's also as beautiful a café as you'll find anywhere. From the inspired log-and-glass kiva architecture to the eclectic menu to the first-rate espresso drinks, this place offers a perfect respite from the road. As you sit on the patio of the Kiva, looking over the ruggedly beautiful folds of the Escalante, you can read about the Kiva's creator—87-year-old Bradshaw Bowman. He is described as an artist, mentor, and inventor. The Kiva is run by his daughter and granddaughters, which may explain the warm and harmonious atmosphere. Open May-October, Wednesday-Sunday, hours vary. Closed Monday and Tuesday.

Boulder

Seated on a high plateau adjacent to the Grand Staircase-Escalante National Monument, Boulder got its name from the black lava boulders that dot the landscape here. Living there, amid the bowling balls of black rock, is the strangest enclave of eccentrics in southern Utah. "There's no one in Boulder you'd consider normal," said Boulder's resident geologist and guide Keith Watts. "If you do find someone, they're living with someone who's definitely abnormal, which makes them suspect."

For me, such a remark is high praise for a place and reason enough to put down the kickstand and have a look around. Settled as a small LDS ranching community high on the hill, today's Boulder is in the middle of a shift toward "evolved tourism." Unlike the famous national parks that lie to its south, Boulder is not a bus-tour type of place. "People are drawn here because this country nourishes them spiritually," said innkeeper Gwendolyn Zeta. "We want to make that available to people and at the same time work toward preserving it."

Thus far, the people of Boulder have been able to walk that fine line. Boulder is a place where adventurous travelers come to experience the solace of the high desert and proximity of a stunning expanse of national park, national monument, state park, and Bureau of Land Management acreage that is unequaled in the lower 48. But it's the attitude here you'll find that really makes it special. There is a certain reverence for the land common to all the people of Boulder. Whether it is the hula-hooping Buddhist who owns the eclectic gourmet restaurant, the surf-dog rancher, or the llama wrangler, they all hold respectful yet playful spiritual underpinnings that gave Boulder such a good feel I almost didn't want to write about it. Yes, even guidebook writers occasionally want to slam the door shut behind them.

RESTAURANTS

Hell's Backbone Grill (20 North Highway 12, 435-335-7464, hellsbackbone-grill@color-country.net) is run by two women, Jen Castle and Blake Campbell, who were told that their planned venture would never work. Blake, a devoted student of Tibetan Buddhism (Tibetan prayer flags hang over the sun-dappled deck), has tried to mold the business in keeping with the right livelihood tenets of Buddhism's eightfold path. By all accounts, she not only has lived up to her spiritual ambitions but also has created what may be the best menu in the state. Featuring organically grown vegetables from the on-site garden and locally raised natural meats, the Hell's Backbone menu has multiple inspirations—cowboy, Mormon, and Pueblo Indian, among others. If that sounds both wacky and wonderful, it is.

Although the vegetarian entrées were outstanding, and the red trout was delicious, I had what I believe was the best filet mignon I've ever eaten. Rubbed with Hell's Backbone's blend of spices, the meat was seared on the outside and perfectly rare on the inside (hard to get in a restaurant these days). After dinner we shook everything loose with the fur-covered hula hoops that Jen and Blake use to keep everyone smiling. They worked as well as the food. The one drawback to the Hell's Backbone: It doesn't have a wine license, and this food cries out for a glass. Still, it is the best unexpected meal in the state. Open March 15-November 15. Hours: breakfast 7:30 A.M.-10:30 A.M., takeout lunch, dinner 6 P.M.-9:30 P.M. seven days a week.

LODGING

Boulder Mountain Lodge (at the junction of Highway 12 and the Burr Trail, 800-556-3446, www.boulder-utah.com) has a lot to live up to because its brochure touts it as "the most beautiful inn on the most beautiful road." I can offer nothing but enthusiastic agreement. From the moment you walk into the office, you're greeted by a sense of oasis. Manager Gwendolyn Zeta has created a small gallery of distinguished southwestern art here. At this lodge, you won't hear the incessant babble of television or the pesky chirp of cell phones; the place is sans TV, and cell phones don't work here. This peaceful quietude is enhanced by the simple elegance of the 18 rooms—many of which open out onto decks that overlook the wild bird sanctuary of Schoolhouse Lake.

Quiet-phobes need not worry, because the birds in the lake offer a nonstop chorus from dawn to dusk. The Boulder Mountain Lodge is a perfect place to regroup and recharge, either from life's frenzied pace or from the adventures had with Boulder's top-notch, colorful outfitters. Or, as my wife put it, "This is where the

Tibetan monks come on their vacation, so you know it's got to be relaxing." Rates vary depending on season, but start at $59 for a single and go up to $149 for a two-room suite.

Boulder Mountain Ranch (435-335-7480, www.boulderutah.com/bmr) offers five rooms and three cabins. See entry under Activities section.

ACTIVITIES AND OUTFITTERS

Boulder Mountain Ranch (435-335-7480, www.boulderutah.com/bmr,) is owned and run by Surfer Bob and his wife Sioux Cochran. Remember the weathered and charismatic officer Robert Duvall played in *Apocalypse Now?* Remember "Charlie don't surf"? Surfer Bob Cochran should have played that role. He revels in running this sprawling ranch, but his surf trips to Scorpion Bay really give him juice. His long-boards lie in wait in the rafters, just over the horses in the barn. His laconic wit and wry smile will keep you grinning long after you've left Boulder. The guest ranch has taken on the personalities of Bob, his spirited wife Sioux, and their three sons: Ry, Cru, and Dawz. If you're looking for a dude ranch where you can ride nose-to-tail in long lines, look elsewhere. The horses here are spirited, and if you've got the chops, you're free to gallop through miles and miles of canyon, slickrock, or high alpine terrain. Beware, however, because at the BMR if you say you can ride and you fall off, you're buying Bob a bottle of whiskey. House rules. If you're not at that level yet, they'll gladly give you instruction (and you won't have to buy any booze). If you're not into riding but would still like to chill on a beautiful and secluded working ranch, the BMR's five rooms in the ranch house and three cabins will also work well for you. Rates vary depending on season and which type of lodging you chose. Open year-round, but the ranch may shut down for periods when there's a swell in Baja.

Boulder Outdoor Survival School (800-335-7404, P.O. Box 1590, Boulder, Colorado 80306, http://boss-inc.com) has its office in Boulder, Colorado, but the survival school itself is in Boulder, Utah. Doppelgänger confusion notwithstanding, BOSS is the boss of adventure schools; for what could be more adventurous than survival at its most basic level? This total-immersion program is neither a "hoods in the woods" project nor a military boot camp. Instead, BOSS was founded in 1968 as a school geared toward adults who wanted to learn traditional survival skills and be put to a serious test. "We're not for everyone," said BOSS president Josh Bernstein (a native New Yorker who was first a student, then an instructor, and now runs the whole show), "but for the right person at the right time, it's an unbelievable experience."

That experience can be a corporate retreat, a weeklong field course, or the school's signature 28-day course. The latter is designed to teach students to build a fire without matches (remember that sequence in *Castaway?* BOSS consulted on it), find water in the desert, navigate by compass and the stars, tell the difference between edible and nonedible plants, and hunt and trap for food. If that sounds taxing, it is. BOSS supplements students' caloric intake as they master their survival skills, but only up to a total of 1,500 calories a day. That's why it's common for

GORDY PEIFER

Dave Steiner rides under the big southern Utah sky.

students to lose weight during the course, some as much as 20 pounds. "By strengthening our participants' connections with the natural world and furthering their knowledge and skill, BOSS tries to teach more than just wilderness survival," said Bernstein. "We hope to teach lifelong confidence and competence." Open April-October. Rates vary depending on course chosen.

Earth Tours (435-691-1241 fall–spring, 307-733-4261 summer) is run by geologist Keith Watts. An incredibly enthusiastic man with an out-of-control penchant for maps, Watts can take you on van tours (his van is more like a four-wheel-drive classroom) or hikes into the Escalante and Capitol Reef country. Watts is a font of information and earth knowledge, and his zeal is matched only by his energy. Take a trip out the Burr Trail Road to the Water Pocket Fold and you'll learn more than most geology students. Even if you spend only a half day with this Ph.D., it's worth it to know what you're hiking on and through and how it all came to be. Running tours in the spring and fall. All trips are customized to your needs, so rates vary.

Escalante Canyon Outfitters (888-326-4453,www.ecohike.com) will rent you all the gear you need for multiday hikes into the Escalante Canyons, pack it onto horses for you, and provide you with good food and guides who are passionate about the area. From Anasazi petroglyphs to amazing narrows cut by the Escalante River, you'll see incredible sights as guides take you on a low-impact multiday trip geared toward intermediate to advanced hikers. Itineraries and prices vary with the season.

Red Rock 'n Llamas (877-9llamas, www.redrocknllamas.com) offers a way to hike deep into the wilderness without having to carry your home on your back. That's because sure-footed llamas will carry all your stuff for you. Run by the able Bevin McCabe, Red Rock 'n Llamas is based in the secluded and beautiful outback of Deer Creek. Just show up with five days' worth of clothes, and Bevin will supply the rest. At press time, she was also setting up lodging on her spectacular property in Deer Creek. Open March-October. A four-day trip costs about $700, all-inclusive.

Torrey

Torrey sits on the high plateau in an area known as Robber's Roost. Back in the 1800s, the imposing and confusing terrain of Robber's Roost made the area a perfect hideout for cattle rustlers and bank robbers. The most famous of these outlaws were Butch Cassidy, the Sundance Kid, and the Hole-in-the-Wall Gang.

Today, it's still the geography that gives this town cachet among knowledgeable travelers. Sitting on the western edge of Capitol Reef National Park and at the beginning of Scenic Highway 12, Torrey has become a gateway and stopping place for tourists. Don't expect a tourist town, however. Except for the chain hotels that have sprung up on the eastern edge of town, Torrey still feels rustic and quietly charming.

RESTAURANTS

Café Diablo (599 West Main Street, 435-425-3070, www.cafediablo.com) has not only the best food in Torrey, but some of the best you'll find in the state. The simple little building on the edge of town—with its terra cotta tiled floor, and suburban-style patio—belies the amazingly ornamental culinary feats that are performed within. This is a truly superb place to eat a wonderful meal. And the other good news? Café Diablo has a full liquor license, including a wide array of fine wines and tequilas. If you order margaritas, opt for the more expensive tequila. Open April 1-October 15. Hours: 5 P.M.-10 P.M. seven days a week.

Capitol Reef Inn and Café (360 West Main Street, 435-425-3271) is a motel and restaurant with a down-home casual air that serves surprisingly good grub. The fare is neither fancy nor as refined as the Café Diablo across the street, but it is healthy and reasonably priced (the rainbow trout is a great bet). The rooms in the motel are basic but clean and inexpensive at about $40. They'll also make you a takeout meal that you can tote to your campsite. Beer and wine are served. Open Easter to Halloween. Hours: 7 A.M.-9 P.M. seven days a week.

BOOKS AND COFFEE

Robber's Roost Books and Beverages (185 West Main Street, 435-425-3265) is an unlikely place to find here in the middle of the high desert. The bookstore-café combo offers a kickback, quiet place to read or sip espresso. A sign on the register prohibits "polyphasia," which is a fancy way of saying "no multitasking." This is a place to relax and be single-minded. The book selection reflects a sophisticated, western taste (from cowboy poets to Larry McMurtry). Robber's Roost also serves as headquarters for Entrada, a nonprofit group dedicated to both conservation and promoting the arts. Entrada holds writing seminars and workshops at Robber's Roost. The patio out back is hushed by the soothing sounds of a small stream, and slightly off to the west, under a canopy of cottonwoods, is a large and cozy hammock that's perfect for reading or catching an afternoon nap. A special place. Open Easter to Halloween. Hours: Monday-Thursday 9 A.M.–8 P.M., Friday-Saturday 9 A.M.–9 P.M., Sunday 10 A.M.–6 P.M.

LODGING

Capitol Reef Inn and Café (360 West Main Street, 435-425-3271) is a family-run motel with inexpensive rooms. See the entry in the Restaurants section for more details.

The Chuckwagon Lodge (12 West Main Street, 435-425-3335, www.austins-chuckwagonmotel.com) sits behind an old general store with a wide porch where you can sit and watch the world go by at a very slow pace. The lodge has a relatively new motel in the back, guest cabins out front, and four small and inexpensive rooms above the general store. I prefer the latter. These rooms remind me of summer camp. The lodge has a good outdoor pool and Jacuzzi, and the newer motel rooms offer DirecTV satellite service. So if you've been out of touch too long or just need to catch that playoff game, this is the place. There are also a few new guest cabins that are great for a family or a group. Room rates range from about $49 to $120 and vary with the season. Open March–November.

The Lodge at Red River Ranch (2900 West Highway 24, 800-20-LODGE or 435-425-3322, www.redriverranch.com) is technically in Teasdale, but it's close enough to talk about in the same breath. Only a half dozen miles west of Torrey, this place is on a completely different level from every other lodging alternative in southern Utah. The rustic log construction is complemented with such perfectly elegant antique western furnishings that you're not sure whether you're in a hotel or on a movie set. This lodge is nothing short of stunning. From the picturesque setting under the red rock cliffs on the Fremont River (the lodge has five miles of private fishing rights), to the three-story great room that's decorated with an Indian rug that probably cost more than the entire structure of most inns, to the 15 guest rooms (each with its own bathroom, fireplace, and balcony), the Lodge at Red River simply blows away every other inn for grandeur and classic western elegance. Picture a place where Teddy Roosevelt might have stayed, hunted, and fly-fished. Now picture a lodge built in that old-school, masculine, western-White House style that's less than a decade old, and you'll get a sense of this place. Hunting and fishing guides are available, and the lodge possesses a year-round permit for upland game-bird hunting (pheasant, chukar partridge, and quail). In the fall, guide service is available for elk hunting, and in the winter, it's duck. Rooms run $95–$120 a night, which is a quite good value for what you get here. Open mid-April–late October.

Muley Twist Inn B&B (800-530-1038 or 435-425-3640, www.go-utah.com/
muleytwist) is also in Teasdale, but it's close enough to Torrey to paint it with the
same brush. Muley Twist is run by Eric and Penny Kinsman, a charming couple of
former bicycle racers from Aspen, Colorado. Named for a great hiking trail in
nearby Capitol Reef National Park, the new bed and breakfast sits on 30 acres of
land, in a grove of piñon pine that backs up to an imposing dome of white Navajo
sandstone. Its 7,000 foot elevation means it stays cool here well into the heart of
the summer. With a porch that overlooks the beautiful Fremont River Valley and
the red rock cliffs of Thousand Lakes Mountain, this is a house that, according to
Eric, was "built around a porch." The B&B has five well-appointed rooms, is
wheelchair-accessible, and has lots of cool bicycles hanging around. The breakfasts are great (check out Eric's baked Italian eggs with marinara sauce). Open
April-October. Rates run $79-$99 a night, breakfast included.

Sky Ridge B&B (on Highway 24 at the east end of Torrey beyond the intersection
with Highway 12, 435-425-3222, www.bbiu.org/skyridge) is one of the most
thoughtfully designed and decorated B&Bs you'll find. Perhaps that's because
Karen Kesler, one of the two owners, was formerly the director of the Mendocino
Art Center. The ebullient former Californian designed the inn and hand-painted
nearly everything inside it, from the faux-finish walls to the handmade furniture.
As the name suggests, Sky Ridge perches high atop a ridge and provides hundred-
mile views in every direction. Sunsets taken in from the front porch are a tonic.
Each of the six rooms is different and special; the best is the Sagebrush Room,
which offers a private Jacuzzi tub on a secluded deck that overlooks Sky Ridge's
60 acres and Capitol Reef National Park. Karen and her animated partner, Sally
Elliot, host a daily happy hour that features smoked trout, iced herbal tea, and
incredibly good homemade sangria (Karen's secret: use brandy instead of sugar).
Open year-round. Rates range about $100-$160 per night, breakfast included.

18. St. George

Back around the same time that an angry bunch of rebels were turning Boston Harbor into the biggest cup of tea in history, Fathers Dominguez and Escalante were tromping through what is now southwestern Utah. The padres didn't see much future for the spectacularly scenic area (postcards weren't invented yet), so they kept right on going until they reached the Pacific. Their route, which led from Santa Fe, New Mexico, to Monterey, California, became known as the Old Spanish Trail, and for nearly 70 years, all of southern Utah existed as merely another trailside attraction—if that.

Suddenly several events changed that. The United States won the Mexican-American War in 1848, which garnered huge chunks of land for the burgeoning Union. With the war in the West won, and things heating up back home, Brigham Young brought his pioneers west and into the Great Salt Lake Valley. As if keeping the pioneers alive, turning the desert into a garden, and balancing a delicate relationship with the Yutak Indians (their original name, but due to a typo in a Spanish document, they became known as the Ute Indians) weren't enough, Young would soon have more to worry about.

On April 12, 1861, at 4:30 in the morning, Confederate soldiers under General Pierre Beauregard fired 50 cannons at Fort Sumter in Charleston, South Carolina, igniting the American Civil War. For Brigham Young and his people, the war meant that supplies from the South (especially cotton) would be discontinued. So in May 1861, Brigham Young stood on a ridge of the Rio Virgin Valley and looked over a desolate valley near present-day St. George. His followers must have wondered when he surveyed lava fields and rock moonscapes and said, "There will be built between those volcanic ridges a city with spires, towers, and homes with many inhabitants."

Soon thereafter he dispatched 309 families into the region with instructions to plant cotton and other Dixie crops (which is why this region is still known as Utah's Dixie). By all accounts, those families struggled mightily in their new settlement, yet they still held such regard for their prophetic leader that they named the place Brigham Young. In 1862, however, they incorporated it for a man named George who was something of a Johnny Appleseed—except with potatoes. One of the earliest pioneers to make the trek from Illinois to Salt Lake City, George had the foresight to plant potatoes all along the trail. George's spuds saved many starving pioneers as they journeyed toward Zion; for this they considered him a saint. Hence the town's name: St. George.

Fast-forward through a century, during which not much happened in sleepy St. George. In the second half of the twentieth century, however, visiting pretty places became a popular pastime for people from all over the world. So St. George, with its proximity to so much natural beauty, began to draw tourists by the busload. They came through St. George on their way to Zion, Bryce Canyon, and Grand Canyon National Parks; Cedar Breaks and Pipe Springs National Monuments; and Snow Canyon State Park.

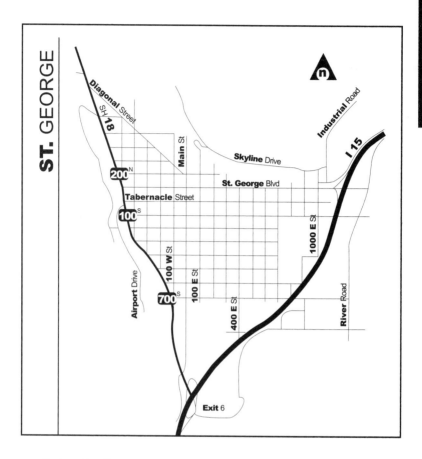

The hot, dry climate also became desirable to those with respiratory problems and aching joints. Early Chamber of Commerce efforts included the slogan "Where the summer sun spends the winter." Local hoteliers offered free rooms on any day the sun didn't shine. Word has it they didn't have to give away many. Thus arrived the retirees and the golf courses. Soon St. George found its niche as a destination for those with the fresh gold watch in their pocket. In 1994, it was even ranked among the top five retirement destinations by *Retirement Places Rated*.

Several nationwide trends brought more growth to St. George. First came the growth of golf. Once a sport for the retired and idle rich, it suddenly became a sport of the middle class. At the same time that suburbanites were finding week-end salvation on putting greens, many others were looking for greener spiritual pastures and gave birth to the so-called New Age spiritual movement. As this was happening, the nation became self-conscious about its flabby spare tire, and the fitness boom was born. All this boded well for St. George. The most recent shift has been the advent of "modem cowboys," who can make their living anywhere they choose. Many have chosen places ripe with recreation and relatively inexpensive costs of living, such as St. George. All these trends spelled expansion for St. George.

Today St. George has nine golf courses—all good and some spectacular enough to turn into video games—and a new consciousness is springing up like desert roses. Not only are there more young and young-minded people moving in, but there's also an earth-based spirituality burgeoning here in small pockets. What began as "New Age" has been transformed into a spiritual stew of Native American, Eastern, and earth-based healing practices. "I think there's a momentum building in St. George," said multifaceted artist Daniel Pettigrew, who owns Xetava Gardens café and bookstore. "I think this will be a Mecca of healing and healers. People who want to tap into a higher spiritual life will continue to be interested in St. George. This place used to feel like a retirement community, but now there are more and more people who are interested in things like drumming circles. There are little sparks here and there, but there isn't a roaring fire here yet. Still, I think St. George could become the next Sedona, only better."

The red rock canyons and the beautiful high desert of St. George have also become a Mecca for hikers. Large destination spas such as the Red Mountain Adventure Spa have quietly opened their doors and grown into successful and integral parts of the community. And in this once noncaffeinated hamlet, you can even find a good cup of coffee in several places.

Good restaurants have opened amid the chains (now that St. George has passed the 100,000 mark in population, the chain stores and their ilk see enough of a market to move in), and a mall of outlet stores that are lousy to look at but offer good bargains now draws many to St. George. Growth, especially fast growth, can be sloppy and ruinous. Although the inevitable effects of growth are being felt in St. George, there seems to be a concurrent trend toward preserving the essence and the natural beauty of St. George even as it's made more accessible.

The town itself is a strange mix of Winnebago and bus tourists, ranchers, college students (from Dixie), New Agers, and large Mormon families. Out near the highway, St. George has the same suburban sprawl of any other town situated by an interstate, but as you drive up St. George Boulevard, you begin to see and feel more of the old town with its wide streets and rivulets of water running down the sidewalk irrigation ditches.

Outside of the town center, St. George is ringed with new development. Some of it is cheesy and cookie-cutter; some of it is revolutionary in its respect for the environment. The best example of the latter is the Kayenta residential community. Built with harmonious designs of low-lying adobe red rock homes that blend seamlessly into the landscape, Kayenta is the embodiment of a philosophy that reveres the energy of the high, wild desert. "There's definitely a strong healing energy here," said Pettigrew. "Call it a vortex or just the power of the desert, but it's something you can feel here."

Whatever you call "it" and the rest of this burgeoning town in the southwestern corner of the state, St. George is gaining a vibrant, physical, and spiritual momentum that's turning it into an increasingly fun and varied place to visit and live. You still won't find much in the way of alcohol-related relaxation in this Dixie town (you can get a drink or wine with your meal in several places, but don't expect wild nightclubs or big ole' bar rails to belly up to). The locals who want a wild night drive down Interstate 15 and across the border to Mesquite (less than an hour down the road) or Las Vegas (about two hours away).

The city's official website is www.cityofstgeorge.com, but it wouldn't work when I tried it; instead it sent me directly to www.sgcity.org. Other websites where you can learn more about St. George are www.southernutahdiversity.com, a site for open-minded people who want to celebrate diversity in this not-so-diverse area, and www.utah.com., the official travel site of the State of Utah.

RESTAURANTS

Ancestor Square (2 West St. George Boulevard) is a little enclave of restaurants, shops, and galleries set in a historic area in the middle of town. Here you'll find an oasis of good food in this barren land of fast-food outlets. Characterized by a unique, non-chain-store mentality, these businesses provide a good atmosphere for sitting on a patio and feeling the pulse of the new St. George. Here are the top spots within this cluster.

Irmita's (515 South Bluff Street, 435-652-0161) has the best Mexican food in St. George. Offering a full bar, it also serves up a mean margarita. Hours: Monday lunch 11 A.M.-3:30 P.M., Tuesday-Saturday 11 A.M.-8 P.M.

J.J. Hunan Asian Cuisine (downstairs from the Painted Pony, 435-628-7219, jjhunan.com) is a boldly decorated Asian restaurant that serves a variety of Chinese, Japanese, and other Asian dishes. Hours: Monday-Saturday 11:30 A.M.-9:45 P.M., Sunday noon-9 P.M.

Painted Pony (second floor of the Tower Building, 435-634-1700) is one of the best restaurants in town. From the modern desert motif to the upscale southwestern menu—everything from New Zealand lamb chops to Utah trout—to the full bar and wine list, this place is a must-visit for anyone with a discerning palate. Hours: Monday-Saturday 11:30 A.M.-10 P.M. Closed Sunday.

Painted Pony Express Café (in the middle of the Square) is a little espresso bar where musicians sometimes play. Set next to the old jail, this is a place where you can sip coffee on the sun-dappled patio and reflect on how much better you have it than the poor suckers who were locked up in that dollhouse-sized jail. Hours: Monday-Saturday 9 A.M.-9:30 P.M.

Panama Grill (in the back of the Square, 435-673-7671) is a new Mexican restaurant with the best margaritas in St. George. Hours: Monday-Saturday 11 A.M.-9 P.M.

The Pasta Factory (in the front of the Square, 435-674-3753) offers as extensive an array of pastas and sauces as you'll find anywhere. It also has a terrific patio out front. Hours: Monday-Saturday 11 A.M.-10 P.M.

Scaldoni's Grill (929 West Sunset Boulevard in Phoenix Plaza, 435-674-1300, www.scaldonis.com) serves an eclectic menu of seafood, steak, and Italian food in a cute little American-Italian atmosphere. With a full bar and a wine list, Scaldoni's has single-handedly saved St. George cuisine. Hours: Monday-Saturday 11 A.M.-10 P.M. Closed Sunday.

COFFEEHOUSES AND CAFÉS

The Bean Scene (511 East St. George Boulevard, 435-628-0735) is a cozy little nook where you can get a cup in a comfortable, homey atmosphere. There's also a drive-through for joe-on-the-go, and the place offers lots of free samples of the goodies beneath the glass counter. Hours: Monday-Saturday 6 A.M.-6 P.M., Sunday 8 A.M.-noon.

Bear Paw Coffee Company (75 North Main Street, 435-634-0126) serves good espresso and cappuccino, but it really shines in the breakfast department. Featuring the best breakfast, both for quality and value, in town, the Bear Paw is where mountain bikers chow down next to a retired couple playing backgammon on magnetic boards. The decor is somewhere between elderly quaint and 1970s style—deep carpet, hanging ferns, and white wicker chairs. Not coffeehouse chic by any stretch, but the fare is first-rate, and the people you'll meet here are exceedingly nice. Hours: open Monday-Saturday 7 A.M.-3 P.M. 365 days a year.

Jazzy Java (285 North Bluff Street, 435-656-0823) is the only coffee roaster in southern Utah. With framed black-and-white glossies of musicians from Jim Morrison to Elton John and of icons from Jimmy Dean to the Tin Woodsman, Jazzy Java isn't East Village hip, but it's as good as you'll get in St. George (and you won't get mugged outside the door). Hours: Monday-Friday 6 A.M.-6 P.M., Saturday 7 A.M.-4 P.M., Sunday 8 A.M.-1 P.M.

Xetava Gardens (815 Coyote Gulch Court, Ivins, 435-656-0165) is seven miles west of St. George in Ivins, near the red rock cliffs of Snow Canyon. It's a place that's hard to get a handle on: You remember it and want to tell other people about it, yet when you begin speaking, your words come up way short. Perhaps that's because Xetava (pronounced "Zay-taw-va") embodies so much more than its heavy hand-carved doors and eight-sided hogan-shaped structure actually holds. Owned and operated by Daniel Pettigrew, a local artist, Xetava Gardens is one part coffee shop, one part earth-centered book and card store, one part desert garden and arboretum, and one part spiritual hub of a thoughtful, low-impact, and upscale desert community called Kayenta. Pettigrew is effusive when asked about Xetava, and if he has his way, the little hub will not only teach pottery and other arts but also spread desert wisdom and a spiritual reverence for the land. "Xetava is an island within an oasis surrounded by a sea of overdevelopment," he said. Pettigrew, like many people you'll find in these parts, grew up Mormon but broadened his views to include other forms of spirituality. "When I created this business, I was looking to balance out the Mormon influence with earth-based spirituality." By all accounts, he has succeeded, and he has drawn to him others like himself. To this cool place where wind chimes tinkle and the tableau of desert sky and mountains is etched into the rock come like-minded people from all parts of the world. "Before, there was no place for the birds to land. Now the flock is gathering."

In addition to his day-to-day business, Pettigrew organizes two festivals a year: the Mother Earth Festival on Easter weekend, and the Harvest Moon Festival on the first weekend in October.

Though Xetava is in flux and hard to pinpoint, there exists a quiet calm within its kiva-style structure that's worth the drive out there. Oh, yeah, the coffee and smoothies are good too. Hours: Tuesday-Friday 9 A.M.-5 P.M., Saturday and Sunday 10 A.M.-5 P.M.

SHOPPING

Gaia (73 North Main Street, 435-674-5005) was more of a head shop when owner Isha Nadir took it over. The energetic proprietor was eager to steer hard drug users into higher and non-self-destructive realms. "I thought I could help the people on meth and get them into crystal healing," she said, "but it was too big of a job. So I got rid of all the head-shop stuff." Now Nadir's boutique is a sweet little gift shop, slanted toward alternative, earth-based religions. It's a place where you can buy a silk kimono, velvet hippie hats, gem stones, crystals, or a golden Buddha. Hours: Monday-Saturday 10 A.M.-6 P.M.

Jolley's Ranch Wear (1 North Main Street, 435-673-3280) is the kind of non-touristy western-wear place where rodeo cowboys and real ride-the-range ropers get their Tony Lamas, Carhartts, and Stetsons. Hip rodeo queens can find their red Ropers, and cowboy mamas can find Wrangler denim diaper covers for their little buckaroos. With duds like these, it's hard to imagine that even cowgirls get the blues (with apologies to Tom Robbins). Hours: Monday-Saturday 9 A.M.-6 P.M.

Roland Lee Guitar Gallery (35 North Main Street, 435-688-9500) is a place that hangs its guitars on the wall like fine art. That's to be expected, since owner Roland Lee is one of the most prolific and well known painters in southern Utah (his Zion collection is superb). Lee's watercolors also adorn the walls but to a lesser extent than the six-string art. The gallery also holds weekly guitar concerts in the large airy recital hall above the store. The musical styles range from bluegrass to calypso, and the performers include internationally renowned musical talent. Shows start at 7:30 P.M. Tickets are $5. Gallery hours: 10 A.M.-6 P.M.

RECREATION
BIKING

St. George is a sweet place to ride your road or mountain bike. Many of the roads in and around the city have bike lanes, a paved bike path takes riders up Snow Canyon, and the Green Valley Mountain Bike Trail offers all the BMX-style rollers, berms, and whoop-dees you could want. Ride Dixie Drive out of downtown and along the Santa Clara River, and take a left on Sunbrook Road and go past the golf

GORDY PEIFER

J. C. Young and Dave Steiner take in the view from the Virgin River Rim near Zion.

course. Take a dirt road through The Gap and then hang on for a killer ride. The trail ends in Bloomington. Take Bloomington Drive and then the Virgin River Recreational Trail back.

Bike Shops

The Red Rock Bicycle Company (190 South Main Street, 435-674-3185) has a huge porch out front where you can fiddle with your bike, swap lies about how strong you were going up that climb, or just lounge. This full-service bicycle center is located in an old house on a shady corner of St. George. It stocks a full range of equipment and offers weekly mountain-bike club rides at 6:30 P.M. on Thursdays. Hours: Monday-Friday 9 A.M.-6 P.M., Saturday 9 A.M.-5 P.M.

GOLF

St. George may be the best value golf destination in the country. This is not hyperbole. The courses are incredibly scenic, mostly uncrowded, and extremely affordable. Lodging is inexpensive, and some hotels offer golf discounts to their guests (ask before you check in). The weather in St. George is sunny most of the time and does get hot in June, July, and August. Those who haven't experienced this kind of heat, however, may be surprised at how comfortable the 90s and even low 100s can feel with a steady, dry desert wind blowing over you.

Bloomington Country Club (3174 Bloomington Drive, 435-673-2029) is a solid 18-hole track and one of the few country clubs in the southern part of the state. Fees vary; call for details.

Coral Canyon (1925 North Canyon Greens Drive in Washington, 435-688-1700, www.coralcanyongolf.com) is a little north of St. George, on the way to Springdale and Zion, but the 20-minute drive is well worth it. This new course is almost as captivating as Entrada but has a different, more serious feel. It's a tough course, with not as many stunt holes as Entrada, and for serious players. Greens fees vary depending on season: October-May $78, June-September $55. The sunset rates are the best deal. After 2 P.M. play for $35 October-May and $25 June-September. Greens fees include carts.

Dixie Red Hills (1250 North 645 West, 435-634-5852) was the first course to be developed by the City of St. George in the 1960s. It's a nine-hole, fairly shady course and not the place where championship players will want to tee it up, but it is a great and popular venue, set in incredibly diverse scenery, for the recreational player. Fees: October-May 18 holes $27 plus $5.50 per person for a cart, June-September 18 holes $18 and up plus $5.50 per person for a cart. After 3 P.M. $20 including cart.

Entrada at Snow Canyon (2511 West Entrada Trail, 435-674-7500) is the most spectacular golf course I have ever played. The bright green fairways stand out against the red rock in a way that has you questioning the reality of the setting. Then you come to water holes where cataracts flow down out of seemingly arid plateaus and you wonder again. When you get to the back nine, where the narrow holes are surrounded by otherworldly black lava flows, you know you've left the ordinary so far behind that you wonder if you can get back. It's no wonder this course has been turned into a computer game. I played on a Sunday morning and had the course all to myself. As if the hot wind that blows across this course, the lava, and the forget-about-it rough weren't enough of a challenge, course designer Johnny Miller also throws you a 600-yard, dogleg-right par five over a canyon. Leave the $5 balls in the bag and play the x-ed-outs. The toughest and most beautiful course in the state. Don't miss this one. Utah residents pay $45, non-Utah residents pay $50. Fee includes course and range balls.

St. George Golf Club (2190 South 1400 East, 435-634-5854) is a course where you are watching out for either the "desert rough" (which makes any shot off the fairway a bunker shot) or the water. The double green for both the 9th and 18th holes and the course is another beautiful experience in this desert where strips of green grass somehow grow. Fees: October-May 18 holes $27 plus $11 for a cart, June-September 18 holes $18 plus $11 for a cart. After 3 P.M. $20 including cart.

Southgate (1975 Tonaquint Drive, 435-628-0000) is a course where big-hitters might as well leave the driver in the trunk (unless you can whack it with pinpoint accuracy). You wouldn't think of a desert course as a place where you'll probably get more splashes than birdies, but you just might. The front nine goes back and forth across the Santa Clara River, and the back nine climbs up along Tonaquint Mountain and has the kind of sloping greens where there's no shame in a three-putt. Fees: October-May 18 holes $27 plus $11 per person for a cart, June-September 18 holes $18 plus $11 per person for a cart. After 3 P.M. $20 including cart.

Sunbrook Golf Club (2366 West Sunbrook Drive, 435-634-5866) is another serious players' course. *Golf Digest* picked it as the No.1 publicly owned golf course in the state, and it's the only course in southwestern Utah that offers 27 holes. The three nines—the Point Nine, the Woodbridge Nine, and the Black Rock Nine— are all distinctly different and named after their signature holes. This is another course where the volcanic activity may cause your score to erupt into realms you didn't want to explore. Fees: October-May 18 holes $42.50 plus $11 per person for cart, June-September 18 holes $23 plus $11 for cart. After 3 P.M. it's $25.00 including a cart.

MIND-BODY WORK

Nancy Furst (435-634-0514) is a crystal and gemstone healer—a Native American card reader and spiritualist who practices in her home in Kayenta. Furst guides people into an altered state that "opens the door for deep change." Although sessions differ and are tailored to fit the needs of each client, here is a typical visit: You meet Nancy in her clean and airy home office, then sit down and talk for a while until you're comfortable. Next she asks you to pick out your favorite stones from her wide collection. Then she uses three decks of cards (like tarot but of Native American origin) and has you pick several. Then, based on the information she has gained, she tailors the treatment to fit you. It might involve singing, drumming, or smudging, but it will always involve the laying of stones upon your body. This is meant to help you balance your chakras (energy centers). The effect is deeply relaxing and tends to bring clarity. Call for appointment.

Red Mountain Resort: The Adventure Spa (435-673-4905, 800-407-3002, www. redmountainspa.com) offers a full-on spa and health care experience in an amazingly beautiful red-rock desert setting. Did you ever dream of going to a place where they cook healthy meals for you, take you on adventures, and teach you how to change your life for the better? Did you ever dream of a place that's one part summer camp for adults, one part self-help retreat, one part nutritional seminar? Did you ever dream of a place where you could go for a week and shave the spare tire (or saddlebags) and learn how to keep it off? Red Mountain Adventure Spa is all that and more.

Red Mountain began its existence 21 years ago as a fat farm. Here, the chubby and waistline-challenged came to be deprived of calories and hiked until their tummies tightened. After the spa went through several manifestations and differing takes on fitness, the Pivotal Group, a Phoenix, Arizona, company, bought the spa in the late 1990s and brought aboard Debra Evans, a veteran of twenty-some years in the spa business. Evans, a self-confessed former hippie and granola-muncher, had different ideas about what a spa should be. "The part that so many other spas forget is the spiritual and emotional component of this kind of work," she said. "Red Mountain looks to give guests every opportunity to explore, challenge, and celebrate their spirits."

With 200 employees and 200 guests at peak capacity, Red Mountain is a resort and spa that is long on guest services and opportunities for recreation and instruction. Whether you're an ultra-athlete or a just-off-the-couch potato, Red Mountain offers you the same fitness assessment and training guidance that professional athletes get. In the METAbeat assessment system, guests are fitted with a mouthpiece and tube through which they breathe during the test, and a heart-rate monitor. As they walk on a treadmill, a computer measures the amount of gases inhaled and exhaled as well as the effect of increased workload on the heart rate. The result is an individualized metabolic profile that tells guests the amount of fat and calories burned at each level of exercise. "The METAbeat takes all the guesswork out of how hard a guest should be exercising for the best effects," said Brad Crump, D.C., a licensed chiropractor and health services director at Red Mountain.

That's just the beginning of the experience you can have at Red Mountain. If you're into exercise and weight loss, Red Mountain has dozens of daily activities that guests can participate in. From hiking (the most popular and offered several times a day in three levels) to rock climbing to tai chi to yoga to cardio kick boxing, guests can tailor a complete fitness program to their desires.

In addition to all the physical activities, Red Mountain offers cooking classes, nutrition lectures, orienteering workshops, pottery classes, animal-tracking classes, and a wide range of mind-body awareness instruction. Of course, Red Mountain has every spa service known to man, but those cost extra.

When it's time to eat, guests need not worry about blowing the diet. Meals are served in a large dining hall (breakfast and lunch are cafeteria-style and dinner is served restaurant-style), and all the food is healthy and diverse but not bland. Unlike the previous fat-farm operators, Red Mountain permits guests to eat as much as they like. "We're definitely not the food police," said Evans.

Nonetheless, the healthy bent of the offerings encourages healthy and moderate eating (every entrée and snack has a card next to it listing the amount of calories, fat, etc.), and after a few days you find yourself naturally gearing your diet to sensible amounts. "The experience that our guests get at Red Mountain is very positive," said Evans, "but the real value is what they take home."

Open year-round. Rates include most activities, all meals, and lodging. They vary depending on whether you select a private room or a four-to-a-room option, as well as how long you stay. The least expensive option is about $1,000 for seven nights in a quad room. The most expensive is four nights in a king-single room for about $1,275. For more information, call or visit the slick and functional website.

Zion and Springdale

Zion National Park is an awesome place. With massive red sandstone buttresses that reach from the floor of the Virgin River up thousands of feet, the park has a sacred and spiritual feel—if you're not surrounded by other gawkers. This place deserves serenity and time to walk in the canyons unfettered by the multitudes. Unfortunately, that kind of solitude is hard to come by unless you go in April, early May, or November. During the summer months, I wouldn't bother. The heat is overwhelming, and that's when most of the 3 million annual visitors descend upon it. To deal with these hordes, Zion has implemented a very efficient shuttle system (only those staying at the in-the-park Zion Lodge are allowed to drive their vehicles in the park). Although this system does a good job of preserving the park and concentrating visitation in a small area where it can be controlled, it also serves to turn a summer visit into more of a Disneyland experience than you might prefer. Despite the summertime army of tourists (mostly of bus-tour and Winnebago ilk) there have sprung up some relatively cool haunts where you can get a cold beer or a hot coffee.

RESTAURANTS AND BARS

Merlin's 101 (no phone) just off Highway 9 between Virgin and Rockville, is the oldest bar in Washington County, and it looks the part. Opened in 1942 by the descendants of the infamous John D. Lee, Merlin's made a brief appearance in *The Electric Horseman* (Jane Fonda ran in the bar and did a short scene). In 1979, Willie Nelson also played at Merlin's. Today people can't help but wonder at the Formica bar top. At some point in the distant past, it was dark brown. Now, on the customer side of the bar, all the brown has been worn off. It boggles the mind to wonder how many elbows it would take to wear the paint out of brown Formica. For this kind of contemplation, you certainly need a beer. Martie, the grandmotherly moll behind the bar, will serve you one. Open year-round. Hours: Whenever Martie gets there until she gets tired.

SPRINGDALE

Springdale is at the main entrance to the park. This town has a main strip of stores and restaurants on the way to the park. In the summer it can be bumper-to-bumper, but at other times of the year it becomes quiet and charming.

Bit and Spur Mexican Restaurant and Saloon (1212 Zion Park Boulevard, 435-772-3498) is the place where all the rock jocks and guides in the area tend to congregate. The sweet potato tamales are perfect (but sell out early), and the crawfish cakes in chorizo sausage gravy are three-alarm. Good thing there's plenty of beer or booze to be had here. Pool shooters smack their balls around on the small table, and cigarette smokers can burn on the front porch. Sports fans can catch a game on the tube here too. A local's place that attracts good folks from all over. Hours vary depending on the season. Call to be sure.

Sol Foods (95 Zion Park Boulevard, 435-772-0277) is run by Max and Julie Gregoric, a cool Alta couple who traded the snow for the sun. They're still honing their business, but Sol Foods offers great deli lunches, salad bar, ethnic and gourmet foods, cold beer, and a shady patio by the river on which to consume it all. The Gregorics will also cater your picnic or make box lunches for your group. Hours vary depending on the season. Summer 8 A.M.-9 P.M. seven days a week, but they change drastically for the winter. Call to be sure.

Zion Pizza and Noodle (868 Zion Park Boulevard, 435-772-3815, www.zionpizzanoodle.com) has a lame name, but it's in a cool old building and it serves great pies and platters of pasta. The beer, southern Utah's largest selection of microbrewed drafts, attracts a young crowd, and you're as likely to find dreadlocks here as Doc Martens. Good calzones. Hours vary depending on the season. Call to be sure.

19. Lake Powell

The imposing Glen Canyon Dam—710 feet high, 1,560 feet wide, and 300 feet thick—was completed in 1964. The dam's main purpose was to provide water storage and hydroelectricity. The benefit to the 2.6 million people who annually visit Lake Powell—the reservoir formed by the damming of the Colorado River and named for Civil War veteran John Wesley Powell—has been the creation of a recreational area like no other. Seventeen years after the construction of the dam, Lake Powell, which starts in northern Arizona and extends into southern Utah, finally filled up.

Today, for all of its 186-mile length and 1,960 miles of shoreline, Lake Powell is a surreal study in contrasts. Glassy lake water laps against desert red rock, and although your mind tells you this combination shouldn't exist, there it is. Great

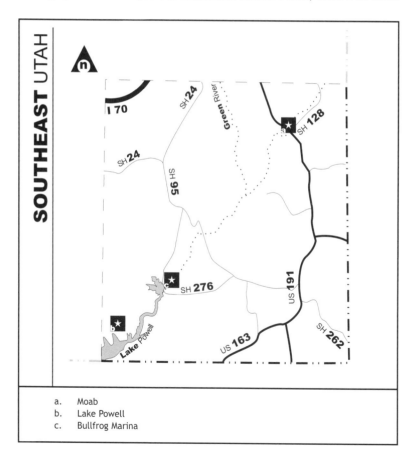

a. Moab
b. Lake Powell
c. Bullfrog Marina

cathedrals of rock rise out of the wake of a ski boat, desert paintbrush drinks in the spray off a slalom ski, and you're left gaping, fascinated by the incongruous beauty of it all.

This is a place to reconfigure notions of what should and shouldn't be. Open your mind as you pull out of Bullfrog or Wahweap marina in your houseboat. Although you'll have to work nowadays to find coves and canyons where the sounds of jet skis and speed craft aren't heard, Lake Powell is still an incredible destination.

The best way to experience Powell is with a group. It has long been a favorite spot for end-of-season employee parties for resort folk from Colorado, Wyoming, and Utah. Rent a houseboat (rates range $1,100-$3,100 for three days and $1,900-$6,000 for a week) and split the cost among a group; rent a ski boat too (about $310 a day) and maybe a couple of jet skis. Kayaks, water skis, wakeboards, and just about any other water toy or tool you can think of are also available for rent. Then set sail for a secluded corner of this massive and convoluted body of water.

Bullfrog Marina on the north side (in Utah) is 298 miles from Salt Lake City and 480 miles from Denver, Colorado. On the south side, Wahweap Marina in Arizona is 267 miles from Las Vegas, 280 from Phoenix, 388 from Albuquerque, and 540 from Los Angeles. Charter flights are available through Frog Air (American Aviation at 801-537-1537) from Salt Lake City to Bullfrog, Halls Crossing, and Page (Arizona).

The lake's marinas and service facilities are managed by Aramark, a concessionaire for the National Forest Service. For more information or to make reservations, call 800-528-6154, or click to www.visitlakepowell.com.

The National Park Service (NPS) also charges fees for using the park and lake. Entry is $3 for an individual and $10 per vehicle (1-7 days) or $20 for more than 7 days. Boats cost $10 for a week and $20 for an annual pass. Additional boats are $4.

Hiking and camping abound in the area surrounding the lake, but because so many people use Lake Powell, new Forest Service regulations require the use of portable toilets when camping more than 200 yards from NPS toilet facilities at Lone Rock Beach, Upper and Lower Bullfrog, Stanton Creek, Farley Canyon, and designated camps on the Colorado River between Glen Canyon Dam and Lee's Ferry. As distasteful as people find it, disposal of human and pet excrement is an issue at Powell. Many rules and regulations govern this problem. Check into them (www.lakepowell.com) before going, and for the greater good, obey them while you're there.

Page, Arizona, is close to the southern end of the lake. There you can stock up on food and fuel or stay in one of the many motels. For more information, contact the Page Chamber of Commerce at 520-645-2741, or visit www.page-lakepowell.com.

20. Moab

A bumper sticker popular among a small group of mountain bikers who rode in Moab during the mid- and late 1980s read "New York, Paris, London, Moab." Back then, the sticker had a comic irony because most people had never heard of Moab. Today that same sticker is sold—and I'm sure sells far better than it used to—but the irony is gone. Anyone who thinks that Moab is still this unknown little hamlet in the southeastern Utah desert need only sit in the corner of Rim Cyclery or the Jailhouse Café and listen to how many different languages are being spoken by the patrons (and sometimes the staff).

Although Moab is now known around the world as a mountain-bike Mecca and major-league tourist attraction, it is a tough place to "get." Like an onion that's grown through heat and drought, through thaws and blizzards, through loving care and utter neglect, Moab has so many layers that are so varied—so tough, tender, ugly, beautiful, sweet, and vile—that it's a wonder it can all be contained in one skin. The fact that the town is growing at an astounding rate is fascinating and—to the people who live here—disconcerting. Moab is a nutty place filled with out-laws and grandmas, mountain bikers and desert hikers, Winnebago drivers and school bus dwellers, rock climbers and rock collectors, chain hotels and no-tell motels, range-hardened cowboys and spa-softened celebrities, movie makers and peyote takers, beermeisters and Mormon bishops—you name it, they're in Moab. But then Moab has always been a colorful place.

A couple thousand years ago, as the Fremont people were hunting antelope and buffalo around what would one day become Moab, on the other side of the globe, the Old Testament was being written. In it was told the tale of Lot, who although he had fled Sodom and Gomorrah, left with some nasty notions of proper parenting. Shortly after returning from the twin cities of temptation, Lot slept with both his daughters. Talk about out of the frying pan and into the fire.

The first child born of this incestuous and cursed union was named Moab, which meant "of my father." As Moab grew up, he was not very popular, so as soon as he could, he left his father's kingdom and started his own. Although he might have started with a clean slate, ego got the better of the boy, and he named it after himself. This was not a good idea: Curses rained down on him, his place, and his people. "And Moab shall be destroyed from being a people, because he hath magnified himself against the Lord," reads Jeremiah 48:42.

And it came to pass that the land Moab settled, which he also called Moab, became a vile little place fit only for pariahs. And according to the Old Testament, God wasn't having it. "O ye that dwell in Moab," spoke the prophet Jeremiah, "leave the cities, and dwell in the rock and be like the dove that maketh her nest in the sides of the hole's mouth."

I'm not exactly sure what Jeremiah had in mind—doves and holes and all—but it seems certain that things weren't looking good for Moab: "There shall be lamentation generally upon all the housetops of Moab and the streets thereof: for

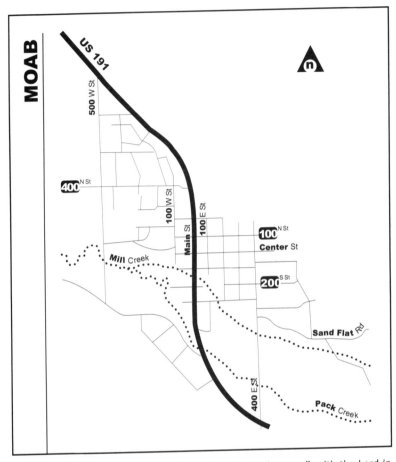

MOAB

US 191

500 W St

400 N St

100 W St

Main St

100 E St

100 N St

Center St

200 S St

Mill Creek

Sand Flat Rd

400 E St

Pack Creek

I have broken Moab like a vessel wherein there's no pleasure," saith the Lord in Jeremiah 38:48.

So it was a strange, perhaps even sadistic impulse that led Mormon postmaster William Pierce, reputed to have been a Bible scholar, to rename Spanish Valley after that broken place: Moab. Since that fateful day in 1881, conflict and turmoil have been Moab's constant companions.

After the dinosaurs left their bones, and the Anasazi and Fremont people left their cliff art (petroglyphs and pictographs), there came the Utes, the Spanish, and in 1885 a party of 43 Mormon men led by Alfred Billings. Billings and his boys from Manti set up shop in the Elk Mountain Mission in Spanish Valley and began a hesitant but stable relationship with the Ute Indians. Many accounts of early Mormon settlement in Utah tell of trade relations between the pioneers and the indigenous people and a peaceful coexistence. Yet the fragile cords of relationship were soon to be strained, and worse, in Moab.

There is debate among historians as to what happened next. Some say the Utes were so enamored with their new neighbors, and so eager to help them with their stated goal of starting families, that they offered the 43 married men some of their Ute women as wives. When an abashed Billings declined the generous offer, the Utes were deeply offended and killed a handful of Billings's men. Other accounts leave out the offered-wives part and say that one day the Utes simply had had enough of their encroaching neighbors. Whatever the cause, the effect is agreed upon. Some of Billings's men were massacred, and he assembled the rest and retreated to Manti. Their departure may have pleased the Utes, but there would be more who would come and have a go in the abandoned fort of the Elk Mountain Mission. The next wave included cattle rustlers William Granstaff (better known at the time as "Nigger Bill" and for whom "Negro Bill" canyon is now named) and his Canadian companion "Frenchie." After these two had their run-in with the Utes, they also left. There followed a succession of harder and harder men and the gradual settlement and conquest of the place.

By the late 1880s and 1890s, Moab had become an outlaw town frequented by the likes of now-legendary Butch Cassidy and the Sundance Kid as well as cattle ranchers and rustlers, saloon keepers, women of ill-repute, sheep farmers, more Mormon pioneers (with their women this time), and all manner of misfits and miscreants. At the turn of the century, Moab was the wildest and meanest town in the West; gunfights were a nightly occurrence.

When in 1896 Utah became one of the first states in the country to give women the right to vote, and the Mormon voting bloc formed a majority in Moab, the battle over the bottle was added to the frontier town's conflicts. For the next thirty years, Moab was at war; the people fought over souls, land, cattle, religion, and demon alcohol. When prohibition became the law of the land, Moab and its many outlaw canyons became a bastion for bootleggers.

In 1929, Herbert Hoover signed a proclamation declaring the Arches region a national monument. This incensed the local ranchers, who didn't want to lose their grazing rights (much as President Clinton would tweak the residents living just to the south and west when, seventy years later, when he declared Grand Staircase-Escalante a national monument). The depression was hard on Moab, and World Wars I and II weren't much better. The nadir for Moab may have come during World War II when it briefly hosted a Japanese internment camp. Apparently the camp was the worst of the worst.

After the war, things started looking up for Moab. Renowned film director John Ford, tired of using Monument Valley for the backdrops in his films, had a new star by the name of John Wayne and wanted a fresh canvas on which to paint his picture. He found Moab and shot *Wagon Master* and *Rio Grande* there. Although having the handsome hotshots from Hollywood in its backyard buoyed the town's spirits, it did little for its coffers.

That situation changed in 1952 when Charlie Steen discovered uranium in Moab. Steen set off an explosion of growth that poured money and people into Moab in unprecedented amounts. The country's first independently operated uranium mill soon set up shop, and Steen and others of his ilk became fabulously rich overnight. The U.S. government was the only legal buyer for Moab's uranium, and for a while it paid top dollar. Then, when it had stockpiled enough, Uncle Sam zipped his purse and stopped buying. The boom lasted a decade; Charlie Steen sold his uranium mill in 1962. Despite a run on potash, a chemical fertilizer that could be extracted from the salt beds surrounding Moab, the town fell into another economic hole. It struggled on with potash production, a dribbling of mining, and some tourism. Proposals were floated throughout the 1970s and 1980s to make Moab a nuclear dump site or even to build a toxic-waste incinerator there. Luckily, these proposals never came to fruition.

In 1971, Arches National Monument was upgraded to a 525-acre National Park, and tourism jumped. Still, the hard-bitten ranchers and ex-miners couldn't see any long-term viable solution to their economic woes. Then, in the early 1980s, boom times hit Moab again. This time the call came not from the ticking of a Geiger counter but from the clicking of chain rings; the mountain bike rolled in and changed Moab.

Rob and Bill Groff, two former uranium workers, were the first to get on the roll. They converted an old motorcycle track on a slickrock bluff above town into a mountain-bike trail. Within a couple of years, the Slickrock Trail became a mountain-bike Mecca, and the Groffs opened a shop called Rim Cyclery. The gearheads came in droves at the same time that the baby boomers were hitting the road in their RVs to see America. The two movements had Moab in their crosshairs.

Since the mid-1980s, massive growth has come to Moab. Even in the late 1980s, it was big news when Rim Cyclery began operating an espresso cart outside its front door so that the shaved-leg set could get their dose of high-test bean juice. Today the number of espresso machines per capita rivals that of Seattle.

As tourism has grown beyond most Moabites' wildest dreams, however, something has also been lost. The sentiment heard most in Moab is "it's not what it used to be." This lament comes not only from recent transplants who want to shut the door behind them but from lifelong residents as well. The theme colors many a coffee-shop or barstool conversation, most of the politics, and half the stories in the newspapers.

I hereby agree—Moab is not what it used to be. Then again, neither am I, and neither are you. I have friends who were beautiful and brilliant when they were young and filled with promise. They have turned into brilliant and beautiful adults who are complicated and fascinating and without that annoying sophomoric self-centeredness that can be such an embarrassment in retrospect. Along the way they have lost some of their promise, have made choices that have taken them down one road and forever given up another, but that's what makes them interesting. So too Moab.

It's had a troubled, colorful, and rich history. Today it is a popular and commercially successful tourist destination. Yet the place is also filled with curmudgeons and outlaws who play host with great reluctance. Many people in Moab care deeply about the land, more deeply than they do about money. That's not all bad.

Although today's Moab is definitely on the map and on the grid, anyone who tells you not to go to Moab because it's ruined is dead wrong. The place is still beautiful, still blessed with magic formations of desert and rock and sky wherever you look. Although the center of Moab is not the sleepy town it was only two decades ago, not all of that growth is evil. Moab is a more friendly, more hospitable place than it's ever been, and you don't want to miss it. The official Visitors Information Center, which is larger than some town high schools in Utah, is at the corner of Main and Center Streets in the middle of town. It has a wide selection of free and for-sale printed material as well as staffers who are pumped about their jobs and about showing you your way into Moab.

Another great way to get clued in on Moab is to pick up a copy of *The Zephyr* newspaper (435-259-7773, or check it out at www.canyoncountryzephyr.com). This self-described "funky little biweekly" reports on local issues with an environmental bent and some good, thoughtful writing. The slogan over the masthead reads "All the news that causes fits." This paper is such an intelligent gadfly, it so raises consciousness of the issues, that it should be required reading for anyone rolling into town in a Jeep, an RV, or with a pair of knobby-tired bikes on the roof. For an on-line look into Moab, go to www.moabutah.com or www.moab-utah.com, or www.moabhappenings.com.

RESTAURANTS

Center Café (60 North 100 West, 435-259-4295) holds memories for me that will never fade. In 1993, I accompanied my friend and screenwriting mentor Ken Friedman onto the set of Walter Hill's *Geronimo*, which was shooting outside Moab. The set was a full-blown western fort, and on hand was an army of extras. Gene Hackman was baking on his horse in the hot sun as the assistant director tried valiantly to get the extras and horses back on their marks for another take. Finally, I got a chance to talk to director Walter Hill. I wanted to ask him about directing, about Hackman's character arc, about how one breathed new life into the legend of Geronimo; Walter wanted to talk only about dinner. "You're not going to believe the restaurant," he said. "It's nothing you'd believe exists here in Utah." Later that evening, Walter took Ken and me to the Center Café. He relished every sip of the wine, luxuriated in the fine food. He was, after all, in the desert, working, and had not expected fine dining. It was a meal I will always remember. Walter was expansive, the staff bought him a bottle of champagne, and the food was tremendous. As I returned to the Center Café eight years later, I wondered if it could live up to the rose-colored lens of memory. It did. The atmosphere is fine, and the food is the best (and probably most expensive) in Moab. You can picture the cast and crew of a Hollywood movie flocking to it. It has that sort of upscale vibe. Yet the Center Café still feels like Moab, albeit a dressed-up, civilized Moab. Hours: 5:30 P.M.-10 P.M. seven nights a week.

EklectiCafé (352 North Main Street, 435-259-6896). See entry in the Coffeehouses and Cafés section.

Jailhouse Café (101 North Main Street, 435-259-3900) has this slogan on its postcards: "Good enough for a last meal." That would be great if your gunfight was

The Jailhouse Café has the best breakfast in Moab.

slated for high noon, but if you died at night, you'd go to hell hungry. That's because the Jailhouse Café only serves breakfast. That's fine, because it's the best breakfast in town. This small brick and adobe-walled café in the center of town is the undisputed king of the egg-and-coffee trade. "It's cool inside" reads the slogan on the T-shirts worn by the friendly and fast wait staff. With two-feet-thick adobe walls enclosing this former jail and courthouse, it is indeed cool inside. You don't have to dine indoors; the Jailhouse has a wide, shady patio that extends out to the north and doubles the size of this popular but small eatery. It serves great griddle cakes, coffee, and quite possibly the best southwestern eggs Benedict in the world. Hours: Monday-Friday 7 A.M.-noon., Saturday and Sunday 7 A.M.-1 P.M.

The Moab Diner (189 South Main, 435-259-4006) is the way diners ought to be. If Barry Levinson were going to shoot his seminal guy film in the West, it would have to be in the Moab Diner. It's just like a 1950s diner, because it is a 1950s diner. Nothing has changed. The biscuits and gravy will stay with you through a White Rim ride, and the breakfast burritos will still be sending salvos after a Gold Bar Rim ride. Lunches bring on the kokopelli chicken sandwich (a grilled chicken breast with Spanish seasonings, melted Swiss cheese, tomato slices, and a slab of green chili) or big and killer burgers. For dinner, go with the Santa Fe platter. Banana splits for dessert. Hours: 6 A.M.-10 P.M. seven days a week.

Pasta Jay's (4 South Main Street, 435-259-2900) is owned by the same folks that own Pasta Jay's on Pearl Street in Boulder, Colorado. The Moab café takes the same approach. It's not fancy, and there's nothing on the menu that you'll have trouble pronouncing. Quite to the contrary, this place has the down-home Italian-American fare (lots of red sauce, red-and-white checkered tablecloths, those fat little parmesan and chili pepper shakers) that you crave on mile 28 of your 30-mile Porcupine Rim ride. Sit on the patio on a warm summer night and load up the carbs for the following day's White Rim odyssey or just for a sound sleep with a full belly. Hours: 11:30 A.M.-10 P.M. seven days a week.

COFFEEHOUSES AND CAFÉS

EklectiCafé (352 North Main Street, 435-259-6896) is a warmly welcoming, cottage-style café with a coffee cup out front big enough to bathe in, a warren of flowering vines and towering shrubs, and a porch that's shaded from the sometimes sweltering sun of Moab. The air here is redolent of rich coffee (from inside) and honeysuckle (from outside). The Eklectic, as locals call it, is owned by once Salt Laker, then New Yorker, now full-time Moabite Julie Fox. Happy in her current life, Fox smilingly serves up "healthy food for carnivores, omnivores, and herbivores." That means the vegetarian soups and entrées are great, but so is the meat. Right alongside the lentil soup, Fox sells curios and antiques—an unlikely mix that somehow works at EklectiCafé. A great place for coffee, breakfast, lunch, or an afternoon pastry. Hours: Monday-Saturday 7 A.M.-3 P.M., Sunday 7 A.M.-1 P.M.

Lisa Fox, owner of the EklectiCafé (formerly Eclectica), smilingly serves up "healthy food for carnivores, omnivores, and herbivores."

Mondo Café (59 South Main Street, McStiff's Plaza #6, 435-259-5551) is a good place to get a simple cup of joe, a great pair of eggs, or a postride panini. There's plenty of parking out front, and it sits next door to Eddie McStiff's brew pub, just in case you want to ratchet up from bean juice to beer. Hours: 6:30 A.M.-6 P.M. seven days a week.

Slickrock Café (5 North Main Street, 435-259-8004) is a touristy little café that serves good food and fine espresso drinks and sells a lot of T-shirts and hats, but the best part is the Internet service upstairs. This is the place to check your emails. The first five minutes will cost you $2, with each additional minute running 35 cents, or just pay $12 for an hour, $9 for a half hour. A way to run the office from the heart of Moab? Now that's progress. Hours: 7 A.M.-10 P.M. seven days a week.

LODGING

The Gonzo Inn (100 West 200 South, 800-GO-GONZO, 435-259-2515, www.gonzoinn.com) is a hip and fun hotel with a sense of style and humor. Although the sign on

Main Street depicted a portly and desperate-looking lizard in a gaudy Hawaiian shirt, the artificial plant inside one of the rooms was a seven-foot pot plant, and the interior motif was reminiscent of so much Ralph Steadman (who did the cover art for *Fear and Loathing in Las Vegas*), the woman at the front desk told us that the Gonzo Inn had nothing whatsoever to do with the founder of gonzo journalism and patron saint of pill-popping reportage and overindulgence, Hunter Thompson. I think she thought I was looking to tattle on her for something. She needn't have worried; I'm a Thompson fan. Now in its fourth year, the Gonzo Inn is a hotel that dares to be different from—and better than—the other hotels in town. The decor, textures, and design elements are bold and daring: deco sofas with a desert motif, modern and chic Italian-design lamps with big clunky industrial-sized nuts on the pull chains, plush and private balconies with old 1950s metal chairs. Throughout the hotel are

The Gonzo Inn is a hip and fun hotel with a sense of style and humor

colors so rich and varied you can almost taste them (in the way your mouth begins to taste the flavors of the Jelly Bellies when you pass them in the market). This hotel is first-class with a hint of the rascal at every turn. Witness the mural that depicts the "Arch Pilot" (who flew his plane under one of the arches in Arches National Park) as you go up the stairs to your room. Yet this is not one of those places where you have to sacrifice function for hip. The amenities are well thought out here. The Gonzo Inn has a bike wash and repair area, secured bike storage, and the best touch: an on-site espresso bar. You'll find an outdoor swimming pool and indoor meeting rooms. Suites come with wet bars, kitchenettes, fireplaces, VCRs, and jetted tubs. Rates range from $119 to $299 per night.

Hotel Off Center (96 East Center Street, 435-259-4244) is the thrift-store version of the Gonzo Inn. That's not such a bad thing. If you prefer thrift shops to department stores, Goodwill to the Gap, you'll groove on the Off Center. The place was created by a movie and commercial set designer and prop master who used only vintage, thrift-store, and garage-sale furniture. Each room has a theme—1970s, 1950s, the Vineyard room—but don't expect cleaned-up, year-2001 replica furniture; everything is so authentic to the period that you'll feel as if you entered a time warp, or a movie set. Even the handmade robes in the rooms match the period. Check into the 1950s room, don the robe, and feel like Ward Cleaver (find your own pipe to smoke). The set designer, Tim Knouff, is often away on location, so his mom, Irene, runs the front desk and just may be the friendliest innkeeper in Moab. "Come see us and we'll have a party," she said.

The rooms share common bathrooms, a kitchen, and a dining area of retro diner booths by the front window. Irene wouldn't dream of parting you from either your pet or your prized possession: your bike. Both are allowed in the rooms. At $49 for a couple, $39 for a single, and $12 for each brave soul who opts for the dorm room, this may be the best value in town. Stay here and spend the money you save at the Center Café. Open year-round, but call ahead in the winter.

Los Vados Canyon House (801-971-3325, www.losvados.com) is the best getaway destination in the state. Los Vados is about 15 miles out of Moab. Though a four-wheel drive is not necessary, you will need a sturdy vehicle with adequate ground clearance to get down the road that leads to Los Vados. You'll go through several miles of stream crossings and a cattle ranch and eventually come to a small, unassuming metal-roofed house. High red rock cliffs bookend the house. It sits in a narrow valley of sage and piñon where a serpentine stream runs year-round through a dense green gauntlet of cottonwoods. Step up onto the front porch of the house, pull open the sliding corrugated aluminum door, and enter an airy, magical home where you won't be sure where the outside ends and the inside begins. Designed by San Francisco architect Patrick Christopher and artist-designer Jim Bischoff, the house is the type you'd find in coffee-table picture books or in *Architectural Digest*.

Everything about the layout of the home is oriented to the gurgling creek. Between the two small bedrooms in the back, farthest from the creek, is a long thin bathroom that can be divided with more sliding doors. There are two toilets, a deep Japanese tub, and a shower tiled in desert tones. The two small bedrooms, both done up in subdued safari motif, side the house. A spacious kitchen with a long sliding window faces a deck and swimming pool to the north. Here, guests can sit on low stools on the deck and talk across the kitchen counter to the chef. A dozen galvanized-steel gas lamps stand in a row on a window ledge next to the kitchen table. Although there's plenty of electricity available, the gas lamps provide a warmer glow at night when you're sitting on the chaises by the new grove of apple trees. The middle room of the house is a cozy den of canvas couches, high bookcases filled with the sort of summer reading material you'd expect to find at a summer house in the Hamptons, and an iron-grated hearth. The front porch, which is really more of a room than a porch, can be opened on three sides—sliding aluminum doors on two sides and thick canvas awnings such as might be used on an African safari on the other—to offer an open-air dining and sitting area around the other side of the house's central hearth. The decks drift westward and drop down to a lower platform that sits just feet from the gurgling stream. In this high desert landscape, the effect of the stream, which can be heard from all corners of the house, is incongruous and eminently soothing.

The house is owned by Bill Ferguson, a Salt Lake City-based documentary and feature film maker. You need not be shy around him about gushing over the beautiful surroundings; even after owning the house for two years, he still can't contain himself. "You will not find another house like this, in a setting like this, anywhere in the world," he said as he sipped wine on the creekside deck. He was right.

The Los Vados house sits on 40 acres of Ferguson's land, which is surrounded on all sides by either state or federal land. From the front deck of the house, you can look up and see petroglyphs made a thousand years ago. It's an amazing sight, but don't get too excited. Save that for the tenth and fifteenth and fiftieth petroglyphs you see, because the walls of this canyon are covered with them: depictions of hunters and hunted; of mothers and babes; of strange men with T-shaped heads; of other humanoid figures in close-pressed groups of five that look like European sevens; of antlers that coil like DNA from antelope heads and reach toward the sky; and of strange wavelike ceilings floating above flocks of antelopes. What is now Mill Creek must have been quite the stomping grounds for the Anasazi.

Hike from the Los Vados house and find the granary, then hike farther up the steep cliff walls and find deep caves with petroglyphs at the entrance where ceremonies may have been held. The fact that all these petroglyphs and relics are in your backyard and not off some paved scenic-vista parking lot makes them all the more special.

The house is solar-powered with a back-up generator, has a cell phone (on its own tower) that "works 80 percent of the time," a TV/VCR on which you can watch movies but not television, and is stocked with everything you need in the way of linens, utensils, condiments, and appliances. You bring your own food and overshop, because once you're in this oasis on the high Colorado Plateau, you won't want to leave, and you won't be calling Domino's. Los Vados is truly a place where you can retreat and not be found by the world. Perfect for one couple or two, and at rates of $200-$245 a night (there is a three-night minimum), the Los Vados is the best, most reasonably priced getaway you could ask for. Renting year-round by appointment. Call Ferguson or make reservations online at www.losvados.com.

SHOPPING
BOOKS
Back of Beyond Books (83 North Main Street, 800-700-2859, 435-259-5154) is an excellent bookstore right on Main Street that's well stocked with outdoor guides, natural history, and Native American books. The store's manager and buyer, Jose Knighton, is a fountain of information on all things Moab. So much so that in 1994, after he "got tired of people asking him for a brief history of Moab," he sat down and wrote one. His *Coyote's History of Moab* is written with an environmental bent and employs a bandito motif throughout. It's a good read, costs only six bucks, and at sixty pages is a quick way to absorb a working knowledge of Moab. Knighton also wrote *Canyon Country's La Sal Mountains Hiking and Nature Handbook*, which despite its clunky title is a good guide to the best hikes in the area. The bookstore Knighton has run for a dozen years is a quiet, cool place, where you can duck out of the relentless recreating going on in Moab and savor a slice of the printed page. It's something of a sanctuary in this outlaw town, because as Knighton explains it, "The front door of a bookstore is the greatest human filter on earth; there are just some people who I know will never walk into a bookstore." A superb place to read and refresh. Hours: 9 A.M.-10 P.M., seven days a week.

GALLERIES

Tom Till Gallery (61 North Main Street, 888-479-9808, 435-259-9808, www.tomtill.com) is owned by one of the nation's most published photographers. Till is a man who knows this land and how to take a beautiful photograph; every one of his shots reflect his reverence for the natural beauty of the desert southwest. The gallery sells all the books that have featured his (and other great photographers') work. Hours: 9 A.M.-10 P.M. seven days a week.

METAPHYSICS

Soul Food (59 South Main Street #5, 435-259-5395) is southern Utah's largest metaphysical store. Although Moab is more rough-and-tumble than crystals-and-patchouli, there is a powerful underground of earth-based spirituality that's growing by the day here. Tap into all that energy at Soul Food. Call for hours.

MOVIE THEATERS

Moab can, and does, wear you down. There's so much to see and do during the day, and enough to do at night to keep you out late blowing the foam off a few, that sometimes you need to bow out of the whole scene for a while. Two hours is about the right amount of time. Fortunately for all of us who like to escape to a dark room and watch someone else's dreams projected on a thirty-foot screen, Moab has a movie theater.

Slickrock Cinemas 3 (580 Kane Creek Road, 435-259-4441) is nothing you wouldn't find in your hometown, but it's a nice clean theater that shows first-run films.

MOAB'S MOVIE LOCATIONS

Serious cinema buffs might also be interested in tracking down the locations where so many feature films have been shot in and around Moab. If this sounds appealing, go to the Moab Information Center (435-259-8825) at the corner of Center and Main Streets and ask for the Moab Area Movie Locations Auto Tour. In it you'll find directions and descriptions to the locations used in the shooting of *Wagon Master, Rio Grande, Taza, Son of Cochise, Warlock, Ten Who Dared, The Comancheros, Cheyenne Autumn, The Greatest Story Ever Told, Rio Conchos, Blue, Against a Crooked Sky, Space Hunter, Choke Canyon, Sundown, Indiana Jones and the Last Crusade, Thelma and Louise, Slaughter of the Innocents, Lightning Jack, Geronimo,* and *City Slickers 2.* You can also visit the Moab to Monument Valley Film Commission at 40 North 100 East (435-259-6388) to learn more about making movies in Moab.

RECREATION
BEST BIKE RIDES

Entire books have been written on the best rides in Moab. There are also lots of maps, which offer different variations, and then there are guide services that all have their own secret singletracks (usually named for one of their guides who crashed there). At least 50 rides are great and worth discussion, but I don't have room here to do it. My advice is to go talk to the folks at any of the bike shops I've listed and ask what trails are riding well. The few rides I've recommended here are don't-miss ones. Start your visit with these and work up to the farther-afield tracks.

Gemini Bridges is a fun and fairly easy downhill ride that involves the kind of long shuttle and car drop-off procedures that make riding this one with a group a better experience than riding it with only one friend. Drive out of town on Highway 191. Go 11 miles and leave your shuttle car in the dirt parking lot to your left. Then go farther north a bit and turn left onto Highway 313. Go another 12 miles until you come to the Gemini Bridges trailhead. This ride is mostly four-wheel-drive road, but it does offer a lot of little spurs around the Gemini Bridges area where you can test yourself and see some amazing rock formations. Bring your camera on this ride. You're gonna want it.

Onion Creek is an out-of-town ride that offers a zillion creek crossings and a red and white canyon that looks as if it should be in a national park somewhere, but it's just a mostly deserted road in the middle of nowhere and thus has a private feel. This ride doesn't have any singletrack, but it's loose enough to be technical on the climbs and descents. The creek crossings also require certain special skills, but by the end of the ride, you'll be whipping through them fast enough to send a head-high wall of water from your back tire. To get there, drive out of town to the north and turn east on Highway 128. Go 20 miles, take a right on the road where the sign reads Fisher Valley Ranch, and park in the parking area.

Tip: Throw a bottle of chain lube in your saddlebag or jersey. All the creek crossings will take the grease off your chain and make it creak and scream at you for forgetting the lube.

Porcupine Rim (up Sand Flats Road) is another on my too-popular-but-must-be-ridden list. Although you can drop a car at the top of Sand Flats Road and shorten your climb to about four miles, riding it all the way from town is the big-dog way to do this one. One caveat: Don't ride from town in the middle of the day when all the car-shuttlers are driving up the dirt road; the dust will leave your glasses and sweaty face looking like a powdered doughnut. Do this ride very early in the morning. If you're going to drive it, do it in a beater car, a rental, or a good solid high-clearance truck, because the washboards are nasty. Four-wheelers with high clearance will be able to drive another two miles past where regular passenger cars have left their oil-pan and transmission-case scars on the rocks. After the climb up the road and past the water tank, the road ascends in ledges to one of the best views in this corner of the state (that's saying a lot). John Wayne's ghost must still be riding this canyon with Geronimo and the Marlboro Man. It's all post-card. The singletrack down is long and gets pretty hairy near the end (another place where pedaling is prudent only for the most proficient—there's no shame in walking this stretch). Ride Highway 128 along the Colorado River back to town (or pile into your shuttle car).

Tip: The first time you ride it, don't rage too hard on the singletrack. There are a lot of sharp little sandy corners that will take you out on the top part, and the bottom section is vertigo incarnate.

Slickrock Trail is the most famous trail in Moab and maybe the world. Yeah, it got all the press a dozen years ago. Yeah, it is too popular and at times can feel more like a skateboard park for bikes than a bike ride. And yeah, most Moab initiates won't go near it anymore, and it even seems to be worth bragging about how long it's been since they rode Slickrock. Riding Slickrock has become to bikers what skiing Corbett's Couloir at Jackson Hole is to skiers or golfing at Augusta National is to duffers; you just have to do it. Despite everything, Slickrock is still the most amazing terrain you'll ever ride. If you go very early in the morning, before the crowds, you won't be sorry.

The trail begins 3 1/2 miles up Sand Flats Road, which is uphill from Moab. Conditioned riders use this as a nice warm-up to Slick Rock. The trail itself is about 12 miles and can be done in a little over an hour by an expert, but two hours is a comfortable pace. If you're looking for a place to put your head down and churn out the miles, or race the clock, this is not your spot anyway. On Slickrock, every crank of the pedal offers something different. It's all berms and banks and whoop-de-dos and barely makable climbs and I-can't-believe-I-rode-that sections. The feature that makes this ride so wonderful is the Navajo sandstone, which contrary to the trail name is not slick at all. It's as abrasive and grippy as coarse sandpaper. The folds and forms of this sandstone provide an incredible maze of twisting, turning, diving, and rising rock trail that will leave you feeling you're rolling over the surface of the earth's brain. It's also amazing to watch this mass of rock change color as the day goes by.

Tips: Keep going; stopping just makes the trail look tougher. Keep your eyes ahead and not on your front tire. That thing that you don't think you can make is probably much more makeable than you'd ever believe. Don't be afraid to walk tricky sections; Slickrock will make you pay for your endos in nasty road rash, or worse.

Following are a few of the many books that explore the

Megan Brown rides the Slickrock Trail.

area's bike trails in detail. These books are available at most of the bike shops I've listed (with the exception of Bridgers's book, which I found only at his shop), at Back of Beyond Books on Main Street, or online at www.offroadpub.com.

• *Above and Beyond Slickrock*, by Todd Campbell (University of Utah Press, 1999) is a thorough guidebook and the favorite of the guys at Chile Pepper Bike Shop.

• *Canyon Country Slickrock Hiking and Biking*, by F. A. Barnes (Canyon Country Series, Arch Hunter Books, 1990).

• *Mountain Bike America—Moab*, by Lee Bridgers (Outside America Guides, Beachway Press, 2000), a local bike shop owner and guide (see Moab Bike Boutique listing under bike shops), is more colorful and opinionated than any of the other guides. Bridgers doesn't sugarcoat anything and isn't afraid to go over the top in his descriptions. When considering his descriptions, it's best to go to his shop, chat with him a few minutes, then consider the source. Inflammatory opinions notwithstanding, his maps and detailed descriptions are great. I also like his two-page spread that shows all the ride profiles at a glance.

• *Mountain Biking Moab*, by David Crowell (Falcon Publishing, 1997) is a solid guide to the 42 most popular rides. It's clearly written and fits into a jersey pocket.

• *Moab, Utah: A Travelguide to Slickrock Bike Trail and Mountain Biking Adventures*, by Bob Ward (Mountain Air Books, 1995).

Many maps of the area are available as well. The best is a trio of maps produced by a company called Latitude 40. They are made of durable, tear-resistant plastic that won't soak up your sweat or tear when you cram them in a jersey pocket. The three maps—"Slickrock Bike Trail," "Moab East Mountain Biking and Recreation," and "Moab West Mountain Biking and Recreation"—will give you all the squiggly lines, mileage, and topo beta you need. Get them at the Visitors Center, any of the local bike shops, or Back of Beyond Books on Main Street, or buy them online at www.offroadpub.com.

I also like the Cheap Is Real maps that you'll find in most of the bike shops. Each consists of one piece of folded paper, printed on one side, and the maps are by the ride. They are not waterproof or tearproof, but they have solid info written by riders who ride and have fun with it. And, of course, they're cheap.

Numerous guide services in Moab will take you on guided mountain-bike adventures. Here are a few:

• Dreamride (435-259-6419, www.dreamride.com) is another business owned by the irascible Lee Bridgers. Dreamride offers single-day tours, and the best thing about touring with this group is the great full-suspension Ellsworth bikes.

• Kaibab Adventure Outfitters (435-259-7423, www.kaibabtours.com).

• Nichols Expeditions (800-648-8488) is owned by the same folks who own Poison Spider Bicycles.

• Pro Guide (435-259-9775, www.rideproguide.com) is the outfit that operates through Poison Spider Bicycles. Single-day trips only.

• Rim Tours (1233 South U.S. Highway 191, 800-626-7335, 435-259-5223, www.rimtours.com).

• Western Spirit Cycling (478 Mill Creek Drive, 800-845-2453, 435-259-8732, www.westernspirit.com).

Bike Shops

Chile Pepper Bike Shop (702 South Main Street, 888-677-4688, 435-259-4688, www.chilebikes.com) may be the most friendly bike shop in town. I know it has the best combination of businesses I can think of: a bike shop and an espresso bar. There's nothing better than combining addictions (to bikes and the bean) under one roof. Chill out on the big blue couch, slurp an espresso, and check out the Wall of Shame photos. The Chile Pepper also has a good rental fleet of front- and full-suspension bikes (Santa Cruz, Schwinn, and Cannondale) and will also let you demo a sweet, handmade Moots titanium. Hours: 8 A.M.-6 P.M. seven days a week.

Moab Bike Boutique (59 East Center Street, 435-259-6419) is the lair of the much maligned but colorful Lee Bridgers. Bridgers's book *Mountain Bike America—Moab* pissed off the whole town. He showed me all the clippings and told me of the threatening phone calls. Over a guidebook? I wondered aloud. He seemed a nice enough guy, a bit of a crank but quite passionate about bikes and biking (a quality I trust implicitly). He does have that mean-streak demeanor that's common in small bike shops, ski shops, vintage record stores, and restaurants whose chefs went to fancy cooking schools, but I'm used to that shtick. For whatever reason, I've often found the best mechanics and cooks dwell inside prickly shells. Still, I wondered how a guide to mountain biking could rankle so many. I had to buy it to find out.

Lee and Marie-Jose Bridgers sit outside their Moab Bike Boutique shop.

GORDY PEIFER

Megan Brown and Dave Steiner ride the Amasa Back trail.

Eighteen bucks and only a few pages later, I had my answer. In short order, Bridgers manages to slam Bible toters, white people, black people, the Utes, the Navajos, middle-aged women, blond schoolboys, and of course (the group that everyone in Utah seems to maintain a year-round open season on) the Mormons. It's in the back of his book where Bridgers really opens a can of whoop-ass on the local eateries, lodges, events, and other bike shops. One local merchant told me that Bridgers seemed to have been vying for the "Biggest Jerk in Town" award and won. (From one guidebook writer to another: "Were you trying to get yourself run out of town, Lee?") Are his opinions funny or mean? You be the judge. I will tell you that Bridgers is a colorful, cantankerous character who runs a small, high-end shop with great bikes and one-on-one attention. Remember the *Seinfeld* "Soup Nazi" episode? The guy behind the ladle is like Bridgers at his best (or worst), but if you like your bikes the way Kramer liked his soup, head for Moab Bike Boutique. Call for hours.

Poison Spider Bicycles (497 North Main Street, 435-259-7882, www.poison-spiderbicycles.com) was the second bike store to open in town, and it's still one of the best. Unlike some of the smaller shops, Poison Spider has a slick, well-merchandised, and air-conditioned store. The help is good and friendly, and the atmosphere is the most nonthreatening in town. You can feel comfortable here if you don't know a chain ring from a ladder rung. The store also has an impressive array of its own gear. From megalarge coffee cups to CD holders to Frisbees, Poison Spider sells all sorts of cool gear adorned with its hip logo. The Poison Spider bike jersey, with its fat black-widow spider on it, is the coolest souvenir in town. Poison Spider has a large rental fleet and rates of $32 for a single day of front suspension (Trek 8000 or a Gary Fisher) and $25 per day after that; and $38 for one day of full suspension (Gary Fisher, Rocky Mountain, or Trek Fuel 90) and $33 per day after that. They also rent high-end (Intense or Titus) full-suspension downhill bikes for $50 a day. Hours: Sunday-Thursday 8 A.M.-6 P.M., Friday and Saturday 8 A.M.-8 P.M.

Rim Cyclery (94 West 100 North, 435-259-5333, www.rimcyclery.com) is the best bike shop in town. It was also the first. Owned by local legends Robin and Bill Groff, Rim is and has been the hub from which all bike things spin. If you want the soup-to-nuts setup, this is the place. Experienced riders who know Moab well and just want a tube or some special attention may do better at any of the half dozen other shops, but for rentals, for the quick beta download on riding here, or for one-stop Moab bike shopping, Rim is the place. The rental fleet consists completely of full-suspension bikes that are good quality, well maintained, and plentiful. Rent a bike, and Rim will supply you with a helmet, pump, patch kit, water bottle, info, and advice. A regular full-suspension bike (Specialized Rockhopper) runs $32 a day for the first two days and $26 a day from the third day on. Premium full-suspension bikes (GT I-Drive 2.0 or a Merlin Echo titanium soft-tail) rent for $40 a day for the first two days and $34 a day from the third day on. Hours: Monday-Thursday 9 A.M.-6 P.M., Friday and Saturday 8 A.M.-6 P.M.

RIVER RUNNING
Moab is awash with river running, white water, and even jet-boating options. When your legs tire from riding, or you get sick of that grit between your teeth, take a float on the Colorado River. Here are a couple of guide services:

• Adrift Adventures (378 North Main Street, 800-874-4483, 435-259-8594, www.adrift.net).
• Tex's Riverways (691 North 500 West, 435-259-5101, www.texsriverways.com).

ROCK CLIMBING
Wall Street is to Moab climbers what Slickrock is to Moab bikers. One of the best sport-climbing areas in the state, Wall Street (or Potash Road as it's known on the maps) has more than 300 routes up a 500-foot Navajo sandstone cliff that was carved by the Colorado River, which flows just across the road from all the climbing. Not only is this vertical gauntlet striped with perfectly formed cracks, but it's also south-facing, which means plenty of sun; you'll find lithe climbers plying its walls from February until late November. Unless you go in December or January, don't expect to have the place to yourself. This level of rock climbing is rare and attracts climbers from all over the world. Just as Slickrock is an incredible place to ride but only the beginning, the Wall Street area is just the most accessible, first place in Moab to climb. The other climbing in and around Moab is tougher to locate, however. For that I recommend visiting Brian Jonas at Pagan Mountaineering (see below) or buying one of the following guidebooks:

• *Desert Rock: Wall Street to the San Rafael Swell*, by Eric Bjornstad (Chockstone Press, 1998).
• *Rock Climbing Utah*, by Stewart M. Green (Falcon Publishing, 1998).

NIGHTLIFE

BEER

The idea that tiny Moab has not one but two breweries is a testament to (A) the desert heat; (B) a serious need for liquefied preride carbo loading; (C) a serious need to swallow suds after a day spent in a Winnebago; or (D) Moabites' historical proclivity (dating back to the time of Lot) to do everything in excess. The answer, of course, is (E)—all of the above.

Yet for me, the issue is not quantity but quality. I contend that the beer in both of these places is not only as good as but better than any you're drinking at home. (If you happen to live in Ireland, that land of Guinness, nectar of the gods, I hereby and feebly retract my contention.) Try a blind taste-test and see if you don't come to the same conclusion. Anyway, the point is, the beer brewed at both of these Moab breweries is great. Try it.

Eddie McStiff's (57 South Main Street, 435-259-BEER) was opened back in 1991 on Saint Patrick's Day (March 17). It was the first brewery in town, and I for one was vocal in predicting it would never survive. I'm sure glad I was wrong. Not only did the brewery make it, but now the entire plaza is named McStiff's Plaza. The name, by the way, comes from a combination of the original three owners' names (Eddie Snyder, Michael McTigue, and Steve Patterson, who was called "Stiff" because neighborhood kids couldn't pronounce "Steve" during his childhood in Beirut). Today McStiff's is a Moab institution. It serves everything from pizza to pasta to steak to Mexican food. There are always 12 local-brewed beers on tap; the most interesting is the Raspberry Wheat, which goes down like Koolaid with bubbles and a kick. McStiff's holds both tavern and restaurant liquor licenses, which means in the tavern part (which is just the bar), you must be 21 and you can't drink hard liquor. In the restaurant, you can buy beer or booze, as long as you eat. The patio is restful and flower-draped. Thursday is open-mike night. Hours: 11:30 A.M.-1 A.M. seven days a week.

The Moab Brewery (686 South Main Street, 435-259-6333) is on the south side of town, but that doesn't mean it's downhill in terms of variety or quality from its midtown neighbor Eddie McStiff's. The best brew and the best slogan belong to Dead Horse Ale, which is named for Dead Horse Point. Kudos to the marketing hack who attached the tag line "You can't beat a Dead Horse." Clever slogans notwithstanding, my fave is still the Black Raven Oatmeal Stout. The Moab Brewery also serves fine if predictable lunch and dinner, and has sports on television, pool tables, and a nice patio. A fun and friendly atmosphere pervades. Hours: 11 A.M.-10 P.M. seven days a week.

BARS

Outlaw Saloon (44 West 200 North, 435-259-2654) attracts tourists, but they're definitely in the minority. Also, not many women frequent the place (a 15-to-1 ratio isn't uncommon). It has three pool tables, a stage in the back, and animal skins on the wall. When you ask bartender Brendan Moore what kind of entertainment the place has, he'll tell you it's "good." When you press, he'll tell you the entertainment is the bartender. It's the kind of place where Brendan knows everyone's name and calls the patrons "a bunch of old drunks." The Outlaw holds pool tournaments and has "just enough fights to keep it interesting." Don't worry, though—"they usually take it outside," Moore said. Serving corn dogs, pizzas, and other "total bar food," it's the kind of place I rather like (but I don't tell my mom, as she still worries). Tavern license. Hours: 11 A.M.-1 A.M. seven days a week.

The Rio Restaurant and Cantina (2 South 100 West, 435-259-6666) has the best mix of locals and young, mountain-bike type tourists. The Rio serves the kind of southwestern food you crave after a long day's ride (in short, enough grams of fat and carbs to reload you completely). It also features live bands (Stonefed or Insatiable are the best) on Friday and Saturday nights. There are three TVs, including one large screen for sports. The outside patio is soothing on a cool summer night. Membership for this private club is only $12 ($5 for a temporary), but you won't have a problem getting a sponsor here. Hours: 11 A.M.-1 A.M. seven days a week.

World Famous Woody's Tavern (221 South Main, 435-259-9323) is the only bar on Main Street and possibly the only such joint where you'll find writer Edward Abbey's name carved into the bar. Bartender April Williamson describes Woody's as "a working-man's bar." There's nothing fancy here. It's the kind of place that if John Wayne didn't drink it, no one makes it. Except Woody's does—it's that sort of joint, if you know what I mean. It has four pool tables, two foosball tables, five TVs, and several dart boards, so you won't get bored as you throw back a few. Woody's gets a good mix of mountain bikers, climbers, boaters, and tourists. The food is typical bar fare: burgers, tacos, nachos, and the like. There's live entertainment on weekends, but don't expect country. "We're a working-man's bar, and we play working-man's music," said April, "and that means rock 'n' roll." Private club. Hours: 2 P.M.-1:30 A.M. seven nights a week.

SUGGESTED READING

The Chuting Gallery: A Guide to Steep Skiing in the Wasatch Mountains, by Andrew McLean. Park City, Utah: Paw Prints Press, 1998.

Coyote's History of Moab, by José Knighton. Moab, Utah: Arch Hunter Books, 1994.

Desert Solitaire, by Edward Abbey. Ballantine Books, 1991.

Hiking the Wasatch, by John Vernath. University of Utah Press, 1999.

The Historical Guide to Utah Ghost Towns, by Stephen L. Carr. Western Epics, 1972.

The Insider's Guide to Salt Lake City, by Kate Duffy and Brian Larsen. Helena, Mont.: Insider's Publishing Inc., 2000.

Mountain Bike America—Moab, by Lee Bridgers. Gilford, Conn.: Beachway Press, 2000.

Mountain Biking Moab, by David Crowell. Helena, Mont.: Falcon Publishing, 1997.

Mountain Biking Utah, by Gregg Bromka. Helena, Mont.: Falcon Publishing, 1999.

The Outlaw Trail: A History of Butch Cassidy and His Wild Bunch, by Charles Kelly. Lincoln, Nebr.: Bison Books and University of Nebraska Press, 1996.

Rock Climbing Utah's Wasatch Range, by Bret Ruckman and Stuart Ruckman. Helena, Mont.: Chockstone Press, 1998.

Running After Antelope, by Scott Carrier. Counterpoint Press, 2001.

City Smart: Salt Lake City, by Margaret Sandberg Godfrey. Santa Fe, N.M.: City Smart Guidebook, Avalon Travel Publishing, 1999.

Utah Handbook, by Bill Weir and W. C. McRae. Emeryville, Calif.: Moon Handbooks and Avalon Travel Publishing, 1997.

Utah: Off the Beaten Path, 3rd ed., by Michael Rutter. Gilford, Conn.: Globe Pequot Press, 2001.

Utah Place-Names, by John W. Van Cott and Kimball T. Harper. Salt Lake City: University of Utah Press, 1991.

Wild Utah, by Bill Cunningham and Polly Burke. Helena, Mont.: Falcon Publishing, 1998.

INDEX

References to maps are printed in boldface type. Numbers in italics refer to photographs.

ABOUT THE AUTHOR

Boston-born Bill Kerig started his Utah research in 1984 as a ski bum/dishwasher at Snowbird. He then spent a decade skiing on the Pro Mogul Tour and writing for *Skiing* magazine. Kerig is the author of *The Snowboarder's Total Guide to Life* (Villard, 1997) and his work has also appeared in *Men's Health*, *Fast Company*, and *Bicycling* magazines. He wrote and produced the Utah-based feature film *Net Worth* and was a producer for CBS at the 1998 Winter Olympics in Nagano, Japan. He was also an ESPN Winter X Games commentator, a host for Private Lessons ski tips on The Weather Channel, and the co-host of the Fox Sports show "Playing in Style." Most recently, he was president of an Internet company. Kerig is currently a contributing editor for *Skiing* and *Digital IQ* magazines and lives in Salt Lake City.